Using
Technology
in the Classroom

FOURTH EDITION

Using Technology in the Classroom

Gary G. Bitter

Arizona State University

Melissa E. Pierson

Arizona State University

Allyn and Bacon

Boston ■ London ■ Toronto ■ Sydney ■ Tokyo ■ Singapore

Vice President: *Sean W. Wakely*
Senior Editor: *Virginia Lanigan*
Editorial Assistant: *Bridget Keane*
Marketing Manager: *Ellen Mann Dolberg/Brad Parkins*
Editorial-Production Service: *Omegatype Typography, Inc.*
Manufacturing Buyer: *Suzanne Lareau*
Cover Administrator: *Jenny Hart*
Composition and Prepress Buyer: *Linda Cox*

Between the time Website information is gathered and then published, it is not unusual
for some sites to have closed. Also, the transcription of URLs can result in unintended
typographical errors. The publisher would appreciate notification where these occur so
that they may be corrected in subsequent editions.

Library of Congress Cataloging-in-Publication Data

Bitter, Gary G.
       Using technology in the classroom / Gary G.
   Bitter, Melissa E. Pierson. — 4th ed.
          p.   cm.
   Includes bibliographical references.
   ISBN 0-205-28769-7
       1. Computer-assisted instruction.
   2. Microcomputers. I. Pierson, Melissa.   II. Title.
   LB1028.5.B47   1999
   371.33'4–dc21   98-30037
                                             CIP

Printed in the United States of America

10   9   8   7   6   5   4   3   2   1   03   02   01   00   99   98

CONTENTS

12   Organizing with Technology   200

PREFACE

Using Technology in the Classroom was written to help classroom teachers, laypersons, and school personnel understand the role of computers in education. Based on experiences with children, adults, and schools, an attempt is made to explain clearly the most important information about computers and their applications in the educational environment. Technical jargon has been avoided as much as possible. The book may be read from cover to cover for a total perspective, or topics of special interest may be selected as needed.

The book has been especially designed for undergraduate and graduate technology-based education courses. It is intended for the introductory undergraduate or graduate education student who needs an overview of the role and use of technology in education. Specific education examples and applications at all levels are provided throughout the book. Learner activities have been designed for students to further explore specific educational understanding or applications.

The introductory chapter gives an overview of technological literacy and its effect on education. The chapter includes the Technology Foundation standards and profiles for all students developed by the International Society for Technology in Education (ISTE). The National Educational Technology (NETS) Profiles can be used to judge the technological proficiency of students at grades 2, 5, 8, and 12. Included is an overview of microcomputer applications in society as a whole and the microcomputer's potential contributions to the school and home. The chapter concludes with a brief historical discussion of early computing devices, leading to an overview of hardware components.

Chapter 2 summarizes some of the current research on the effects of technology on teaching and learning. Results from the "Apple Classrooms of Tomorrow" project are used to highlight expected changes that may come with an infusion of technology into the classroom, and other related research findings round out the picture.

Electronic communication is expected to play a major role in education in the near future. Chapter 3 introduces the basic concepts of electronic mail, focusing on e-mail procedures, etiquette, and educational applications. Listservs are introduced and their relevance for education is detailed.

Chapter 4 continues the discussion of online applications in education, defining the structure of the Internet. Strategies and tips are given for finding the kind of information that you want, and security issues dealing with students exploring the online world are presented.

Educational software is one of the first ways teachers new to technology attempt to include computers in their teaching. Chapter 5 presents an index of the unique features of each educational software application area, including drill and practice, instructional games, integrated learning systems, problem solving, reference, simulations, tools, and tutorials. The chapter includes descriptions of each category, along with tips for practical classroom integration and illustrative classroom vignettes.

Chapter 6 provides information that can help in the continuing search for good software. A detailed evaluation instrument is included. Selection and review criteria are presented to help you make well-informed buying decisions. In addition, a demonstration version of ASCD's *Only the Best* CD-ROM is included free with every copy of this text.

Only the Best provides a searchable database of reviews of hundreds of commercially-available K–12 educational software programs.

The resources available on the World Wide Web hold much promise for educators at all levels. Chapter 7 highlights a selection of excellent web resources, presented according to a helpful organizing framework. The framework includes "Planting" new resources, "Harvesting" those sites that have useful information, and encouraging collaboration with "Cultivating" websites. The chapter concludes with a brief overview of distance learning concepts.

Continuing with the discussion of Web resources begun in Chapter 7, Chapter 8 focuses on creating original web-based instruction and information. Helpful considerations are suggested for planning an effective website, and specific instructions are given for creating a web page by using either the HTML language or an HTML editor.

Chapters 9 and 10 present a series of lesson plans to help you implement a technology-integrated curriculum. Lesson plans for five curriculum areas are given in Chapter 9: language arts, social science, mathematics, science, and special education. Chapter 10 introduces a number of courseware packages currently available on the market. It is our hope that you will use these lesson plans as a springboard for your own creativity to develop lesson plans that meet the unique needs of your students.

Chapters 11, 12, and 13 help teachers understand the practical issues in using technological tools to manage teaching and learning. Chapter 11 suggests ways to use basic software applications to perform the myriad of daily administrative tasks a teacher must do, such as keeping records and producing materials. Chapter 12 gives ideas for using technology to create multimedia products and present them to others. This chapter is aimed at both teachers and learners, reflecting the blurring of the control roles in new educational philosophy. Finally, Chapter 13 aims to supply very practical procedures for keeping the technologically oriented class organized. Specific emphasis is given for using computers both in computer lab settings and in classroom settings.

The last two chapters deal with timely issues facing the educational field as technology brings us into the new century. Chapter 14 discusses the new and ever-changing ethical and equity issues, which must be faced as technology allows us easy access to protected intellectual material and software. The mere presence of computers in some classrooms and not in others heightens the already prevalent equity and cultural disparities. Chapter 15 faces educators toward the future, with a look at newly emerging technology and what these advancements might mean for students of the future.

Finally, the appendixes provide supplemental information on the names and addresses of software manufacturers, using Logo in the classroom, and basic operating procedures for word processing, spreadsheet, and database software.

We would like to express our appreciation to the persons and organizations that have contributed in some way to this publication. Specifically, we thank the pre-service teachers of Arizona State University for challenging us to create an always-changing course on technology integration. We are also grateful to Ann Gavin, media specialist, and the students of Kyrene de la Sierra elementary school in Phoenix, Arizona, for allowing us to take pictures of them hard at work. Finally, thanks to those who reviewed this manuscript: Bonnie Beach, Ohio University; and Michael Blocher, Arizona State University.

We hope you'll find ways to make your computer part of your teaching and your students' learning in meaningful and authentic ways. The possibilities technology presents are endless and can only create continued excitement for the processes of learning.

Using Technology in the Classroom

1 Getting Started with Technology

FOCUS QUESTIONS

1. How have societal trends during the Information Age been influenced by technological advances?
2. In what ways can basic technology standards and profiles be used to plan for technology integration at all levels of education?
3. What terminology is necessary for successful operation of current computer hardware components?

Introduction

The growth of the use and application of technology in the world continues to increase. In a few years, we have seen the use of technology permeate our lives. In the early eighties, a student assignment was to list all the ways technology plays a role in our lives, but now the question becomes an attempt to list ways in which technology does not play a role in our lives. Daily announcements on technology breakthroughs are common and limitless. No end appears in sight. One method of predicting the future is based on Moore's Law, which seems to successfully predict future computing power.

In 1965, Gordon Moore was preparing a speech and made a memorable observation. When he started to graph data about the growth in memory chip performance, he realized there was a striking trend. Each new chip contained roughly twice as much capacity as its predecessor, and each chip was released within 18 to 24 months of the previous chip. If this trend continued, he reasoned, computing power would rise exponentially over relatively brief periods of time. Moore's observation, now known as Moore's Law, described a trend that has continued and is still remarkably accurate. It is the basis for many planners' performance forecasts. In 25 years, as Moore's Law predicted, the number of transistors on a chip has increased more than 2,300 times, from 2,300 on the 4004 in 1971 to 5.5 million on the Pentium Pro processor. Intel's cofounder predicted transistor density on microprocessors would double every two years. This prediction, so far, has proven amazingly accurate. If it continues, Intel processors should contain between 50 to 100 million transistors by the turn of the century and execute 2 billion instructions per second (<www.intel.com>).

Website <www.intel.com> has a graph of Moore's Law and related information. Predictions such as Moore's Law imply that technology will continue to impact our lives as well as the role of technology in education.

Literacy

During the 1980s, society grappled with the issue of defining literacy. The definition of literacy as a process developed cognitively and organizationally through verbal and visual thinking was expanded to include oral literacy (listening and speaking), textual literacy (reading and writing), visual literacy (producing, creating, composing, and understanding images), and computer literacy. The capabilities that a literate person possessed and demonstrated were elevated due to the widening chasm between skilled and unskilled laborers in the workplace. An X or a personal signature once was the measure of literacy. Now the ability to read and write at a sixth-grade level is required; to read a ballot, a driver's license test, or the IRS tax forms are three experiences used to determine literacy. Reading, writing, thinking, and formulating opinions and the ability to continue one's learning are essential literacy skills needed for all Information Age participants. Illiteracy is at the root of industrial accidents, prison costs, and public assistance. Nearly 50 percent of adult illiterates are under the age of 50 and are key to the rate of unemployment and poor job performance. Eighty-five percent of today's workforce will still be active in the year 2000. Estimates of economic losses stemming from illiteracy range from $20 to $225 billion and affect the United States' ability to compete in the global marketplace.

Parallel to the expansion of oral and written literacy concepts, the notion of computer literacy now includes measures of graphic and visual literacy. Expanded definitions suggest that students acquire basic computer skills between fourth and sixth grade. The ability to create, compose, communicate, and conduct critical analyses using the microcomputer with other interfacing technologies is a rising expectation as people examine the nature and trends of the Information Age.

Trends of the Information Age

The formative years of the Information Age, 1956 and 1957, were marked by the launching of Sputnik and the increased numbers of white-collar workers in relationship to blue-collar workers. The Sputnik launch marked the beginnings of satellite community applications, other opportunities to develop global perspectives, and the space industry. The number and capability of workers are indicative of a change in the nature of the kind of commodity being produced. As we moved from the Industrial Age into the Information Age, more workers became involved in the creation, management, and transfer of information than in the manufacturing aspect of products. An economy built on information rather than goods and services began to emerge. Knowledge (cognition) and knowing how to learn (meta cognition) increased in global importance, significance, and value.

Three significant trends with implications for education earmark the Information Age: a shift in demographics, an acceleration of technology, and an ever-expanding base of available data through which to search, sift, sort, and select. It is estimated the amount of information in the world doubles every 900 days. Therefore, by the time a first-grader progresses through the traditional public educational system and is preparing for high school graduation, the information base will have quadrupled.

The shift in demographics is startling, somewhat frightening, and potentially overwhelming. The number of children in nontraditional familial structures, children with special educational, developmental, and social needs, and children engulfed in poverty continues to rise. Most of these children have never lived in a noncomputerized society.

Great portions of their leisure time are spent viewing television and playing electronic interactive adventure games within imagined, fanciful environments. Due to the rising number of children raised by single parents with limited income potential due to court-established child support and only one adult fully contributing to the household account, the opportunity to have sophisticated, later-model microcomputers and other technological peripherals and devices will be lessened, which means schools will become even more responsible for providing access to (including economic access) and the opportunity to learn and use technology. These children present new, formidable challenges to educators.

The acceleration of technology increases the pace of change. Within the Agrarian Society, the pace of change was established by the seasons; each season had specific activities, events, and purposes. The yearly calendar and the almanac were used to mark time. Time orientation moved to the present within the Industrial Age. The 40-hour workweek and time clocks were used to measure productivity and profit. In the Information Age, the orientation has become the future. Satellite communications now allow information to travel across time, space, and distance as the information float collapses.

Racing Toward the Twenty-First Century: The Third Millennium

The year 2000 has become for many people a destination: the journey's end. It is a dichotomy; depending on your perspective, either a time of apocalypse or a Golden Age for humanity. Either way, it is being viewed as a time to close the door on the past and begin anew. Organizations involved in formal planning processes use the year 2000 as one criterion for achievement. "By the year 2000 . . ." is a common phrase as people establish goals, set time lines, and identify benchmarks to meet objectives. The advent of the Third Millennium is similar to the arrival of Halley's comet. People are already planning where and how they will spend New Year's Eve to welcome in the twenty-first century. Accomplishments are serving as foundation blocks in the twilight of the twentieth century to create still another time orientation: infinity. The acceleration of technology has allowed the communication and application of information, especially within the fields of science and mathematics, to be rapidly disseminated. Scientists are able to share knowledge and to build cooperative projects wherein information explodes as problems are addressed, breakthroughs are made, and ills are conquered. Electronic information networks shuttle data and discoveries that have increased life expectancy, designed artificial organ implants, formulated chemicals that alter the genetic makeup of plants and vegetables, and manage domino organ-transplant operations.

Within the Biotechnology Age, the valued resources will be mind and life. The mind as a resource of value demands that people not only be literate, but competent, critical, and creative thinkers. People must become independent, lifelong learners, constantly updating their skills, knowledge, and experiences. The ability to fully participate in a technologically rich society will require people to scan entire landscapes of information; to select that which is pertinent, meaningful, and applicable to the task and their thinking; to construct problems and simulations that test hypotheses; to analyze and to integrate information; to evaluate results; and to compose and communicate their thoughts and opinions to form new knowledge.

What Is of Such Intrinsic Value?

Knowing that information will quadruple within a student's traditional school experience has teachers asking what skills, concepts, and information will students need as participants within such a society. What knowledge is of such intrinsic value that each child from every culture must have and share it within the "global village"? What skills will teachers need? What responsibility must teachers share? What will be the role of the teacher? How will educators effect responsiveness in such an expansive, ever-changing environment?

Imagine receiving a one-way ticket to a far-off land to which you must travel. You are limited in the amount of goods and provisions you may take with you. However, you will have communication access to the information, people, culture, and events you leave behind. What would you take with you into your future to use for your survival and prosperity? What would you want safely deposited for future electronic access? Many educators believe the traditional, basic 3 R's will no longer be the end products students possess, but will become means to create the qualities of independence, integrity, image, and invention within each student. The development of students as thinkers, problem solvers, and creators requires teachers to create and invent scenarios and projects in which students work with ideas, symbols, and abstractions. Student work will require them to do something with the information they access and acquire.

How Is This Affecting Education and Educators?

The publication of *A Nation at Risk* (1983) served as a harbinger of the educational reform movement. Arguments still rage as to the depth and degree of restructuring needed to bring about the levels of educational equity and excellence desired. Much of the reform movement's impetus is being fueled by corporate, industry, and business interests. The shrinking of the U.S. middle class due to the change in demographics and family structures and the emergence of a global economy determined by "information haves" and "information have-nots" are creating a situation in which, for America to continue to lead, compete, or cooperate within a global marketplace, the outlook must change. We must move from an oil-powered and man-powered labor force to a brain-powered force that creates, invents, maintains, and dominates the technology-driven industry and society. In some ways, the end of the twentieth century is reminiscent of its beginning. Today's students are also ethnically diverse and impoverished, with tenuous familial roots as were the immigrants to the United States at the turn of the twentieth century. Literacy was an issue then and is an issue now. Education was seen to be the means to achievement and success. It was also seen to be the handmaiden of industry. Today, industry and education are becoming fast allies as they realize that they are now in the same business.

The educational system is regarded as the force that, when functioning properly, promotes literacy or, when failing, causes illiteracy, regardless of policies and practices. Many U.S. corporations have undergone a transformation to respond to the changes in the world marketplace and have installed state-of-the art equipment, robotics, and technology to make the workplace more efficient, economical, and safe. They have retooled the workplace and are presently retraining their workers. With the installation of new technology, the training of employees needs to be at a compatible level. There are very few places within the workplace now for the unskilled and the high school dropout. Many of those jobs are now exported to Third World nations where the labor laws are few and the costs are minimal. Business has accepted the double financial burden of both retooling and retraining. However, the enormous retraining costs cannot be incurred indefinitely solely by industry. Education must share the responsibility of developing technologically literate people, not only to help people maintain a standard of living, but also to help people create a balanced lifestyle.

Fear of the unknown, of trying something new, has caused some educators to avoid or ignore the microcomputer's presence in society, let alone the classroom. Steve Jobs, cofounder of Apple Computer, has suggested that people can be classified in two categories: b.c. or a.c. (before computers or after computers). Since the inception of the microcomputer in 1977, a "generation" (one 12-year cycle) of students has progressed through the school system. The knowledge and experiences with computers that they produced and gained depended on the visions and financial priorities of their teachers, administrators, and state and community leadership. In many cases, they left high school less prepared than their parents for the demands of the workplace and the decisions of the lifestyle they dream of enjoying.

Business and government interests are forming new coalitions for the purposes of raising the educational expectations and standards for determining proficiency and competency. Professional organizations for educators have issued position statements regarding the availability and use of computers in the classroom. One of the most prominent groups that has developed technology foundations, standards, and profiles is the International Society for Technology in Education (ISTE). These are the recommended foundations in technology standards for teachers.

ISTE-Recommended Foundations in Technology for All Teachers

The ISTE Foundation Standards for teachers reflect professional studies in education that provide fundamental concepts and skills for applying information technology in educational settings. All candidates seeking initial certification or endorsements in teacher preparation programs should have opportunities to meet the educational technology foundations standards.

Basic Computer/Technology Operations and Concepts. Candidates will use computer systems to run software; to access, generate and manipulate data; and to publish results. They will also evaluate performance of hardware and software components of computer systems and apply basic troubleshooting strategies as needed.

1. Operate a multimedia computer system with related peripheral devices to successfully install and use a variety of software packages.
2. Use terminology related to computers and technology appropriately in written and oral communications.
3. Describe and implement basic troubleshooting techniques for multimedia computer systems with related peripheral devices.
4. Use imaging devices such as scanners, digital cameras, and/or video cameras with computer systems and software.
5. Demonstrate knowledge of uses of computers and technology in business, industry, and society.

Personal and Professional Use of Technology.   Candidates will apply tools for enhancing their own professional growth and productivity. They will use technology in communicating, collaborating, conducting research, and solving problems. In addition, they will plan and participate in activities that encourage lifelong learning and will promote equitable, ethical, and legal use of computer/technology resources.

1. Use productivity tools for word processing, database management, and spreadsheet applications.
2. Apply productivity tools for creating multimedia presentations.
3. Use computer-based technologies including telecommunications to access information and enhance personal and professional productivity.
4. Use computers to support problem solving, data collection, information management, communications, presentations, and decision making.
5. Demonstrate awareness of resources for adaptive assistive devices for student with special needs.
6. Demonstrate knowledge of equity, ethics, legal, and human issues concerning use of computers and technology.
7. Identify computer and related technology resources for facilitating lifelong learning and emerging roles of the learner and the educator.
8. Observe demonstrations or uses of broadcast instruction, audio/video conferencing, and other distant learning applications.

Application of Technology in Instruction.   Candidates will apply computers and related technologies to support instruction in their grade level and subject areas. They must plan and deliver instructional units that integrate a variety of software, applications, and learning tools. Lessons developed must reflect effective grouping and assessment strategies for diverse populations.

1. Explore, evaluate, and use computer/technology resources including applications, tools, educational software, and associated documentation.
2. Describe current instructional principles, research, and appropriate assessment practices as related to the use of computers and technology resources in the curriculum.

3. Design, deliver, and assess student learning activities that integrate computers/technology for a variety of student group strategies and for diverse student populations.
4. Design student learning activities that foster equitable, ethical, and legal use of technology by students.
5. Practice responsible, ethical, and legal use of technology, information, and software resources.

Teacher education should emphasize these foundations in technology courses, integrated technology-content methods courses and real classroom experiences.

The National Educational Technology Standards (NETS) Project is designed to develop technology performance standards for PreK–12 students, establish specific applications of technology through the curriculum, provide standards for support of technology in schools and address student assessment and evaluation of technology use to improve learning (Bitter et al., 1997).

The following are recommended standards and profiles for students in grades K–12.*

ISTE Technology Foundation Standards for All Students

The technology foundation standards for students are divided into six broad categories. Standards within each category are to be introduced, reinforced, and mastered by students. These categories provide a framework for linking performance indicators found within the Profiles for Technology Literate Students to the standards. Teachers can use these standards and profiles as guidelines for planning technology-based activities in which students achieve success in learning, communication, and life skills.

Technology Foundation Standards for Students

1. Basic operations and concepts
   - Students demonstrate a sound understanding of the nature and operation of technology systems.
   - Students are proficient in the use of technology.
2. Social, ethical, and human issues
   - Students understand the ethical, cultural, and societal issues related to technology.
   - Students practice responsible use of technology systems, information, and software.
   - Students develop positive attitudes toward technology uses that support lifelong learning, collaboration, personal pursuits, and productivity.

---

*All NETS material reprinted with permission from National Educational Technology Standards for Students (June, 1998), published by the International Society for Techology in Education (ISTE), NETS Project. The full document is available from ISTE, 1-800-336-5191, and at the following Web address: <http://cnets.iste.org>

3. Technology productivity tools
   - Students use technology tools to enhance learning, increase productivity, and promote creativity.
   - Students use productivity tools to collaborate in constructing technology-enhanced models, preparing publications, and producing other creative works.
4. Technology communications tools
   - Students use telecommunications to collaborate, publish, and interact with peers, experts, and other audiences.
   - Students use a variety of media and formats to communicate information and ideas effectively to multiple audiences.
5. Technology research tools
   - Students use technology to locate, evaluate, and collect information from a variety of sources.
   - Students use technology tools to process data and report results.
   - Students evaluate and select new information resources and technological innovations based on the appropriateness to specific tasks.
6. Technology problem-solving and decision-making tools
   - Students use technology resources for solving problems and making informed decisions.
   - Students employ technology in the development of strategies for solving problems in the real world.

NETS Profiles of Technology-Literate *K–12 Students*

A major component of the ISTE standards project for students grades K–12 is the creation of general profiles of technology-literate students at key developmental points in their pre-college education. These profiles provide rather broad descriptors of technology competencies that students should have developed by the time that they exit the target grades.

These profiles reflect the underlying assumptions that all students should have the opportunity to develop technology skills that support learning, personal productivity, ethical and responsible behaviors, decision making, and daily life. They prepare students to be lifelong learners and make informed decisions about the role of technology in their lives.

These profiles are indicators of achievement at certain points in K–12 education. Technology skills are to be developed by coordinated activities that support learning throughout a child's education. They must be introduced, reinforced, and finally mastered and integrated into an individual's personal learning and social framework.

The profiles reflect the following basic principles and assumptions:

1. Students acquire steadily increasing skills and knowledge related to the use of technology for enhancing personal and collaborative abilities.
2. Students acquire steadily increasing ability to make quality decisions related to managing their own learning.

3. Students acquire steadily increasing skills to work in collaboration with others, with hardware and software and information resources, and to some problems with the support technology tools.
4. Students become responsible citizens and users of technology and information.
5. Students have access to current technology resources, including telecommunications and multimedia enhancements.
6. Students acquire skills that prepare them to learn new software and hardware technology to adapt to the complex technology environments that emerge in their lifetime.

Profiles for Technology-Literate Students
Grades PreK–12

Numbers in parentheses listed after each performance indicator in the following profiles refer to the standards category to which the performance is linked. The categories are:

1. Basic operations and concepts
2. Social, ethical, and human issues
3. Technology productivity tools
4. Technology communications tools
5. Technology research tools
6. Technology problem-solving and decision-making tools

GRADES PREK–2

Performance Indicators. All students should have opportunities to demonstrate the following performances. Prior to completion of Grade 2 students will:

1. Use input devices (e.g., mouse, keyboard, remote control) and output devices (e.g., monitor, printer) to successfully operate computers, VCRs, audiotapes, and other technologies. (1)
2. Use a variety of media and technology resources for directed and independent learning activities. (1, 3)
3. Communicate about technology using developmentally appropriate and accurate terminology. (1)
4. Use developmentally appropriate multimedia resources (e.g., interactive books, educational software, elementary multimedia encyclopedias) to support learning. (1)
5. Work cooperatively and collaboratively with peers, family members, and others when using technology in the classroom. (2)

6. Demonstrate positive social and ethical behaviors when using technology. (2)
7. Practice responsible use of technology systems and software. (2)
8. Create developmentally appropriate multimedia products with support from teachers, family members, or student partners. (3)
9. Use technology resources (e.g., puzzles, logical thinking programs, writing tools, digital cameras, drawing tools) for problem solving, communication, and illustration of thoughts, ideas, and stories. (3, 4, 5, 6)
10. Gather information and communicate with others using telecommunications, with support from teachers, family members, or student partners. (4)

GRADES 3–5

Performance Indicators.   All students should have opportunities to demonstrate the following performances. Prior to completion of Grade 5 students will:

1. Use keyboards and other common input and output devices (including adaptive devices when necessary) efficiently and effectively. (1)
2. Discuss common uses of technology in daily life and the advantages and disadvantages those uses provide. (1, 2)
3. Discuss basic issues related to responsible use of technology and information and describe personal consequences of inappropriate use. (2)
4. Use general purpose productivity tools and peripherals to support personal productivity, remediate skill deficits, and facilitate learning throughout the curriculum. (3)
5. Use technology tools (e.g., multimedia authoring, presentation, Web tools, digital cameras, scanners) for individual and collaborative writing, communication, and publishing activities to create knowledge products for audiences inside and outside the classroom. (3, 4)
6. Use telecommunications efficiently and effectively to access remote information, communicate with others in support of direct and independent learning, and pursue personal interests. (4)
7. Use telecommunications and online resources (e.g., e-mail, online discussions, Web environments) to participate in collaborative problem-solving activities for the purpose of developing solutions or products for audiences inside and outside the classroom. (4, 5)
8. Use technology resources (e.g., calculators, data collection probes, videos, educational software) for problem-solving, self-directed learning, and extended learning activities. (5, 6)
9. Determine when technology is useful and select the appropriate tool(s) and technology resources to address a variety of tasks and problems. (5, 6)
10. Evaluate the accuracy, relevance, appropriateness, comprehensiveness, and bias of electronic information sources. (6)

GRADES 6–8

Performance Indicators.   All students should have opportunities to demonstrate the following performances. Prior to completion of Grade 8 students will:

1. Apply strategies for identifying and solving routine hardware and software problems that occur during everyday use. (1)
2. Demonstrate knowledge of current changes in information technologies and the effect those changes have on the workplace and society. (2)
3. Exhibit legal and ethical behaviors when using information and technology, and discuss consequences of misuse. (2)
4. Use content-specific tools, software, and simulations (e.g., environmental probes, graphing calculators, exploratory environments, Web tools) to support learning and research. (3, 5)
5. Apply productivity/multimedia tools and peripherals to support personal productivity, group collaboration, and learning throughout the curriculum. (3, 6)
6. Design, develop, publish, and present products (e.g., Web pages, videotapes) using technology resources that demonstrate and communicate curriculum concepts to audiences inside and outside the classroom. (4, 5, 6)
7. Collaborate with peers, experts, and others using telecommunications and collaborative tools to investigate curriculum-related problems, issues, and information, and to develop solutions or products for audiences inside and outside the classroom. (4, 5)
8. Select and use appropriate tools and technology resources to accomplish a variety of tasks and solve problems. (5, 6)
9. Demonstrate an understanding of concepts underlying hardware, software, and connectivity, and of practical applications to learning and problem solving. (1, 6)
10. Research and evaluate the accuracy, relevance, appropriateness, comprehensiveness, and bias of electronic information sources concerning real-world problems. (2, 5, 6)

GRADES 9–12

Performance Indicators.   All students should have opportunities to demonstrate the following performances. Prior to completion of Grade 12 students will:

1. Identify capabilities and limitations of contemporary and emerging technology resources and assess the potential of these systems and services to address personal, lifelong learning, and workplace needs. (2)
2. Make informed choices among technology systems, resources, and services. (1,2)
3. Analyze advantages and disadvantages of widespread use and reliance of technology in the workplace and in society as a whole. (2)

4. Demonstrate and advocate for legal and ethical behaviors among peers, family, and community regarding the use of technology and information. (2)

5. Use technology tools and resources for managing and communicating personal/ professional information (e.g., finances, schedules, addresses, purchases, correspondence). (3, 4)

6. Evaluate technology-based options, including distance and distributed education, for lifelong learning. (5)

7. Routinely and efficiently use online information resources to meet needs for collaboration, research, publications, communications, and productivity. (4, 5, 6)

8. Select and apply technology tools for research, information analysis, problemsolving, and decision-making in content learning. (4, 5)

9. Investigate and apply expert systems, intelligent agents, and simulations in realworld situations. (3, 5, 6)

10. Collaborate with peers, experts, and others to contribute to a content-related knowledge base by using technology to compile, synthesize, produce, and disseminate information, models, and other creative works. (4, 5, 6)

This NETS project is ongoing and will continue to be updated as technology continues to change, which causes basic skills to change.

Now is the time for schools and educators to be retooled and retrained. For some time, education may face the same double financial burden that business has been shouldering: tools and training. Financial constraints have spurred educational systems to set priorities and develop strategies that encourage the acquisition of new technological skills and information. Some school systems are finding that some of the ideas of the 1960s and 1970s, such as open-space classrooms, peer tutoring, modular scheduling, and individualized instruction, are now more likely to succeed because instructional strategies such as cooperative learning and state-of-the-art technology can meet the logistical, managerial, and instructional needs of large numbers of students, sources, and faculty. Outside funding, business alliances and partnerships, and foundation grants are being promoted as sound investments in the development of a cooperative, interdependent system of human enterprise based on Francis Bacon's premise: knowledge is power.

Computer Usage in Society

In today's business world, computers have become standard equipment. The most familiar application of computers in business is data processing. Businesses are faced with an extensive number of accounting and bookkeeping procedures that must be performed routinely, quickly, and accurately. The computer's ability to perform mathematical calculations with lightning speed and virtual infallibility accounts for its immediate and widespread acceptance in the world of business.

Computers control the ability to expedite and reduce the plethora of paperwork necessary to keep a business running. Computers perform inventory, record keeping, billing, payroll, and a seemingly infinite number of other functions. Word processing technology has changed the nature of secretarial work and freed many secretaries to perform other tasks, which has resulted in many positions being upgraded to administrative assistantships.

Another attractive feature of computers is that they can be programmed to make accurate predictions that help managers make sound decisions. The computer can consider a wide variety of contingencies and predict what conditions will arise in the event of such contingencies. Such predictions may save businesses vast amounts of money by anticipating adverse conditions and, in many cases, can increase businesses' profits by forecasting favorable conditions.

Not only is the computer an invaluable tool in the business office, but it is also a vital part of industry. The use of robotic technology in manufacturing is one example. Robots perform work that is boring, repetitive, difficult, or dangerous for human workers to do; indeed, they can function around the clock without tiring or requiring breaks.

Another application of robots is quality control. First, a robot is programmed with information about a product of acceptable quality. Then it can perform routine tests to determine if the items being manufactured meet acceptable standards. The robot is capable of checking minute details that may not be visible to the human eye.

Computers are used widely in the field of engineering. Computer-aided design (CAD) refers to the use of computers in designing and testing new products. The computer can speculate about various design ideas to determine which will work and which will not. It can simulate conditions for testing new products to determine their feasibility. In the past, design and research was an expensive and time-consuming process because engineers relied on actual physical models of designs to perform such tests. CAD helps eliminate costly mistakes in research and development.

The business world is not the only place where computers are found. Computer technology makes work faster and more efficient on the farm, where computers help farmers evaluate climatic conditions, control inventory, feed and care for livestock, and keep up with many accounting and bookkeeping procedures. Although computers may seem out of place among chickens and silos, they are helping to make agriculture more productive and cost-effective.

Another facet of society where computers have become an integral part is the arts. In music, for example, electronic and digital sound synthesizers are producing a popular sound often referred to as "New Age." Computers are being used in music composition, and they are also useful in designing and choreographing marching band performances.

An exciting development of computers in the arts has resulted from increasingly sophisticated computer graphics technology. Stunning visual displays can be created by computers with graphics capabilities. Animation created by human artists is time-consuming and astronomically expensive, but computers can create equally striking effects in a fraction of the time required for an artist to produce similar effects. Computers with graphics capabilities allow textile artists and weavers to design fabrics and then interface their looms with computers to execute their computer-created designs.

Computers expedite the complicated process of filmmaking in other ways as well. They are useful in film editing, calculating the number of frames of film per scene, and controlling property inventory. The applications of computers to the entertainment industry are numerous and many are applicable to multimedia and hypermedia concepts.

Among the largest users of computers are federal, state, and local governments. Governmental agencies collect vast amounts of data that must be processed and stored in various ways. Consider, for example, the amount of data generated by a national census. Computers expedite the process of handling these data so that they can be used for research and allocation of funds and grants that improve the quality of the lives of many citizens.

The annual task of assessing and collecting taxes is one more job that has been simplified by the use of computers. Computers record vast amounts of information submitted by taxpayers and employers, calculate and verify tax returns, and generate refund checks.

Governments also use computers for processes such as license renewal and vote tabulations. Using computers to tabulate election results has made for much faster and more accurate reports of election results. Computers are used to predict election results even while votes are still being cast and tabulated.

Yet, perhaps the fastest growing area of computer application in our society is occurring in our own homes. Declining costs of owning and operating personal computer systems have put computer power in the hands of the average person. A popular use of personal computers is computer games, which are fun, challenging, entertaining, and often educational. They provide an enjoyable and nonthreatening means of interacting with the computer system. Advances in computer graphics constantly heighten the appeal of these games.

Personal computer users perform accounting and record-keeping functions on their systems, much as large corporations do. Personal computers can also monitor checking accounts, maintain household inventory, generate budgets, store important records, and perform many other tasks that keep a household running smoothly.

Another application of the home computer is education. Educational software enables parents to participate in, enrich, reinforce, and supplement the education of their children. The computer is a versatile tutor; it can help to teach reading skills to a small child or sophisticated, graduate-level university courses to a well-educated adult. It can be a useful tool in learning many subjects included in conventional academic curricula.

For example, in mathematics, students can use numerical and symbolic computation and scientific visualization. In the Mathematica program, students begin with interactive calculations, quickly create publication-quality two- and three-dimensional graphics, apply hundreds of built-in functions to problems, and use them as building blocks to extend the system and develop Mathematica programs. Mathematica notebooks are ideal for documenting work and creating technical reports and presentations that mix text, active formulas, and graphics. Mathematica notebooks are transferable among more than 20 different platforms (see Figures 1-1, 1-2, and 1-3).

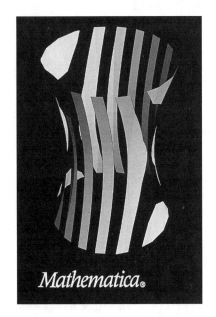

FIGURE 1-1 Modeling in mathematics using Mathematica. (*Courtesy of Wolfram Research*)

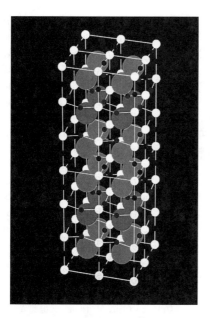

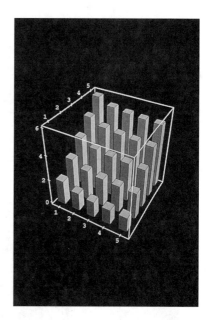

FIGURE 1-2 Mathematica showing a crystal structure of a high-temperature superconductor. (*Courtesy of Wolfram Research*)

FIGURE 1-3 Mathematica lets users display data or functions in specialized formats, such as bar charts, pie charts, or log–log plots. (*Courtesy of Wolfram Research*)

Personal computers keep their users aware and informed in an information-rich society. The personal computer user can gain access to nationwide databases that provide the latest information about current news, issues, sports updates, and leisure interests. Many online services provide newspapers stock reports, weather information, shopping and travel services, reference encyclopedias, and movie and TV reviews. Bulletin boards and electronic mail are also available.

A Brief History of Computers

A logical first step in becoming computer literate is to appreciate the origins of computers. Computers are the result of a long history of mathematical explorations and innovations. They have their earliest roots in primitive systems of counting that relied on fingers and toes or stones to enumerate objects.

Eventually, these primitive systems gave way to mechanical devices aimed at making complex calculations quickly and accurately. One of the earliest of such devices was Babbage's Analytic Engine. Charles Babbage was a nineteenth-century mathematician who designed the Difference Engine. He saw a need for such a device because, in an era of increasing use of mathematics, people were making large numbers of errors in building logarithm tables.

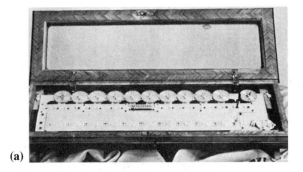

(a)

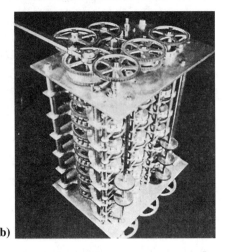

(b)

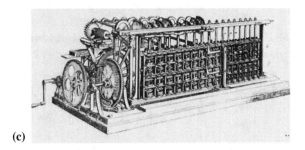

(c)

FIGURE 1-4   (a) Pascal's mechanical calculator.
(b) Charles Babbage's Difference Engine. (c) Scheutz's
Printing Calculating Machine. (*Courtesy New York
Public Library*)

Babbage sought to eliminate the repetitive and time-consuming creation of these tables.

The Difference Engine was the first result of his efforts. It was a combination of rods, gears, and ratchets that jammed constantly and made the Difference Engine impractical to use. Undaunted, Babbage set to work on a more ambitious project: the Analytic Engine. A forerunner of the computer, Babbage's device had an input section that read data from holes punched in cards. It also had provisions for printing results. More importantly, Babbage provided a "control" unit for operating the computer, a "mill" unit for performing calculations, and a "store" unit for holding up to 1,000 fifty-digit numbers.

The Analytic Engine was, in many ways, analogous to computers of today in that it could store, execute, and change instructions. The machine was doomed to failure, however, because it was a victim of its times. The state of technology in Babbage's day was such that the 50,000 parts necessary to manufacture a single Analytic Engine could not be produced (see Figure 1-4).

Fortunately for us, Babbage had an excellent assistant in his efforts. Ada Augusta Byron worked closely with Babbage in his research. Formally titled Lady Lovelace, Ada Augusta Byron was the only daughter of the poet Lord Byron (George Gordon) and his wife Annabelle. Following in her mother's footsteps, Byron was an accomplished mathematician.

Upon meeting Babbage, Byron took an immediate interest in his work. For many years, Byron kept meticulous records of Babbage's work so that we are able to retrace his efforts today. Personal correspondence between the two indicates that Byron was much more than a passive observer of Babbage's work. In fact, she sometimes suggested alternative hypotheses and methods to Babbage as well as encouraging him to persevere when his efforts seemed to be fruitless.

In recognition of her contributions to the development of computer technology, Byron was honored by having a computer programming language, ADA, named for her.

Although designed in 1847, Babbage's Engine No. 2 was not built until 1891. His calculator delivers more precise answers because it can extend an answer to 31 digits. Modern-day calculators are faster due to their electronic design. Babbage's calculator is operated by turning a crank or handle. To get an answer carried out to 31 digits, the operator must turn the handle 27,000 times!

The next influential invention was the census machine of Herman Hollerith. In the late nineteenth century, census taking had become a major task; tabulation of such a vast amount of data was slow and problematical. In an effort to find a faster way to compile raw statistical data, the Census Bureau sponsored a contest. Herman Hollerith's device was chosen as the most effective and practical.

Hollerith had designed a device that read data from punched cards and kept track of the count. The keypunch system of data processing was popular for many years, although recently it has succumbed to faster and less cumbersome methods (see Figure 1-5). Hollerith was so successful, in fact, that he left the Census Bureau in 1896 to form International Business Machines Corporation (IBM), a recognized leader in the field of data-processing technology even today.

Then, in 1939, the first digital-computing device was constructed by John V. Atanasoff. As the cost of producing electronic components decreased, a group of Harvard scientists headed by Howard Aiken and working in conjunction with IBM developed the Mark I. This computer is considered to be the forerunner of the first generation of computers.

The First Generation of Computers

Developed in 1944, the Mark I was primarily electromechanical; that is, it was made up of mechanical switches that opened and closed by electrical current. It was 51 feet long, 8 feet high, and contained 1 million components and over 500 miles of electric wire. It was capable of adding three 8-digit numbers per second. The Mark I was noisy, slow, and cumbersome compared to computers in use today.

At approximately the same time, Grace Hopper and others were beginning to develop the computer languages that were necessary to program these new electronic computers.

Hopper was responsible for the development of the first compiler in 1952. Five

(a)

(b)

FIGURE 1-5 (a) Mechanical keypunch machine. (b) Card tabulating machine. (*Courtesy of the New York Public Library*)

years later, in 1957, Hopper designed the first English-language compiler, which was a major breakthrough in the human–computer interface. She is also considered to be the "grandmother" of the programming language COBOL (Common Business-Oriented Language).

The next major development in computer technology culminated in the Electronic Numerical Integrator And Computer (ENIAC). Designed by John W. Mauchly and J. Prespert Eckert, Jr., ENIAC was intended to be used by the military. It was programmed by means of switches and connections. ENIAC was more than one thousand times faster than the Mark I, performing 5,000 calculations per second. Weighing 60,000 pounds and containing nearly 2,000 vacuum tubes, ENIAC required tremendous amounts of electricity and gave off large amounts of heat (see Figure 1-6).

The most significant feature of ENIAC was that it introduced vacuum-tube technology, and no longer were calculations and operations performed by moving mechanical parts. This gesture allowed for greatly increased speed of performance.

The next computer was developed by Mauchly, Eckert, and others and was called the Electronic Discrete Variable Automatic Computer (EDVAC). It was smaller and more powerful than its predecessors. It also had two other important features: it used the binary numbering system and it could store internally instructions in numeric form. Today, all data and programs are stored in binary form. This method of storing instructions inside the computer is far more efficient than paper-tape storage used with earlier devices.

Another member of the first generation of computers was the Electronic Delayed Storage Automatic Computer (EDSAC) built at Cambridge University in England. This computer introduced the concept of stored programs. Before this, computers often had to be used for specific applications. Their memories were incapable of storing more than one program at a time. EDSAC helped eliminate time-consuming and costly rewiring procedures.

At this point, computers were built primarily for scientific applications. In 1946, however, Mauchly and Eckert formed a corporation to build computers for commercial use; in 1951, the UNIVAC (Universal Automatic Computer) was the first electronic computer used by large business firms. This launched the major growth of computers into the business field.

(a)

(b)

FIGURE 1-6   (a) The Electronic Numerical Integrator And Computer (ENIAC), designed by John W. Mauchly and J. Prespert Eckert, Jr. (b) The ENIAC contained nearly 2,000 vacuum tubes.

As computer technology expanded from military and scientific applications into the world of business, it became necessary to develop a programming language particularly suited to business applications. Thus, the COBOL language was developed by Jean Sammet and others in 1959. Working with her colleagues at IBM, Sammet also participated in the development of another language, FORMAC (Formula Manipulation Compiler), which was the first programming language used on a practical basis to solve mathematical problems.

The first generation of computers, which thrived from 1951 until 1959, is characterized by vacuum-tube technology. Although they were amazing devices in their time, they were large, were expensive to operate, and required almost constant maintenance to function properly. The next generation of computers attempted to resolve some of these problems.

The Second Generation of Computers

The second generation of computers extended from 1959 until 1964 and was characterized by transistor technology. The transistor was developed in 1947 by John Bardeen at Bell Laboratories in New Jersey. Bardeen studied substances that permitted a limited flow of electricity through semiconductors. Transistors that used semiconductor material could perform the work of vacuum tubes, and took up much less space.

Because transistors were smaller, the distance between operating parts was reduced and speed of performance was increased significantly. Transistors were also much cooler than vacuum tubes, reducing the need for expensive air conditioning in areas where computers were housed (see Figure 1-7).

Transistors did present several problems, though. They were relatively expensive because each transistor and its related parts had to be inserted individually into holes in a plastic board. Also, wires had to be fastened by floating boards in a pool of molten solder. The number of parts required for even the simplest transistors was staggering. Even though the distance between individual parts was reduced, it was still great enough to limit the speed of computer operations. The next generation of computers helped to alleviate some of these problems.

FIGURE 1-7 Electronic panel containing transistors. Invention of the transistor made possible a decrease in the size and an increase in the power of computers.

The Third Generation of Computers

The development of integrated circuits in 1963 spawned the third generation of computers, lasting from 1964 until 1975. Integrated circuits developed from a need to mass produce in a few simple production steps.

The production process begins when tubes of silicon are sliced into wafer-thin disks that are chemically pure and cannot hold electrical charge. Then a preconceived design is etched onto the surface of the wafer with the use of light rays. Once the entire surface of the wafer has been processed, the wafer is placed in an acid bath to eliminate all unexposed areas. To enable the wafer to carry an electrical impulse, slight traces of impurities must be added in a specified pattern. Finally, a fine diamond saw slices through the wafer and divides it into dozens of blocks, like postage stamps in a large sheet. Each tiny piece is now a chip. After discarding unusable chips, the manufacturer encases the wafer and connects it to the outside of the case with gold wires. This is the integrated circuit—a sandwich of carefully treated silicon that now forms the transistor, a device that acts as an electrical switch (see Figure 1-8).

The integrated circuit continued the trend toward miniaturization that has resulted in the popularity of the microcomputer and the personal computer system. Because the chips are tiny, the pathways through which electrical current must pass are short. Therefore, the number of calculations that can be performed each second is increased tremendously. Also the chip is manufactured in such a way that its performance is virtually guaranteed for a practically unlimited life span.

Integrated-circuit technology spawned a generation of computers that had greater storage capacity and tremendously increased speeds of performance. Also during this period,

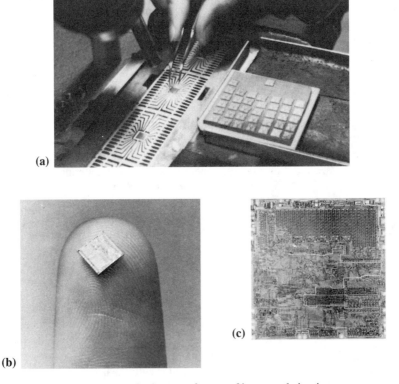

(a)

(b)

(c)

FIGURE 1-8   (a) One step in the manufacture of integrated circuits. (*Courtesy Texas Instruments*) (b) The integrated circuit led to smaller computers. (*Courtesy Texas Instruments*) (c) Magnified view of an integrated circuit. (*Courtesy Hewlett-Packard*)

many accessory devices were developed and marketed, such as magnetic-tape drives and disk drives. Popular programming languages were developed and refined, many of which are still in use today. Time-sharing was introduced as a way of maximizing the efficiency of systems that performed calculations at incredible speeds.

Third-generation computers were not aimed at specific applications such as business or scientific use. Rather, they were designed as general-purpose computers. They represented a giant leap forward in the data-processing field. Not only were speed and reliability enhanced, but power consumption was decreased markedly. Computers became smaller and less expensive, putting computer power into the hands of a greater number of users than ever before. Computer technology began to accelerate.

The Fourth Generation of Computers

Engineers were not satisfied with the degree of miniaturization that resulted from the integrated circuit. Also, the integrated circuits of the third generation were designed primarily with chips having only one function. For example, a chip might perform calculations or amplify weak currents in a television or radio. As engineers learned how to manufacture chips more easily, they conceived the idea of grouping an assortment of functions on a single chip, creating a microelectronic "system" capable of performing various tasks required for a single job. This technology became known as large-scale integration (LSI). Thus, the fourth generation of computers was born in the mid-1970s.

LSI has many applications other than large-scale computers. One such application is the pocket calculator so common today. This calculator has a single "block" that contains 6,000 transistors capable of adding, subtracting, dividing, and multiplying. Another device made possible by LSI technology is the digital watch. It contains 2,000 transistors on a single chip. Today's video games also rely on LSI technology.

Still another innovation of LSI technology is the computer-on-a-chip. Its manufacturers compress nearly all the subsystems of a computer into 1/20 square inch. Over 15,000 transistors combine to form a brain that stores, processes, and retrieves data with a capacity that rivals room-sized computers of a decade earlier.

LSI technology is responsible for the popularity of the microcomputer. These "little giants" fit easily on a desktop and put computer power in the hands of an increased number of people (see Figures 1-9, 1-10 and 1-11). Declining prices of powerful computer systems have encouraged development of the electronics field in general. LSI turned computer technology into big business (see Table 1-1).

Another benefit of LSI technology is the production of computers that are easier to maintain and upgrade. The early computers required almost constant attention by highly

FIGURE 1-9 Original Apple I. (*Courtesy Apple Computer, Inc.*)

FIGURE 1-10   Apple I board. (*Courtesy of Apple Computer, Inc.*)

FIGURE 1-11   Steve Job's garage, where the original Apple computer was produced. (*Courtesy of Apple Computer, Inc.*)

trained computer technicians. Microcomputers, on the other hand, are relatively easy to own and maintain. This is one reason why so many people, adults and children alike, are exploring the many advantages of computers without needing to have a thorough knowledge of electronics.

Computer technology continues to advance at a tremendous rate. Today, we are living with fourth-generation computers, but already new developments are surfacing that give us some idea of what future generations of computers will be like (see Figure 1-12).

Future Generations of Computers

A hint of tomorrow's computer capability can be found in very large-scale integrated (VLSI) circuitry, a concept that was essentially a refinement of LSI technology. VLSI circuitry further increased the speed at which computers were able to function.

Multiprocessing, the simultaneous running of several programs by one computer, is being developed further in fifth-generation computers. Multiprocessing makes computerized data processing even more cost-effective.

TABLE 1-1   Decreasing Cost of Computer Operations

Generations	Technology	Cost per 100,000 Computations	
First	Vacuum tubes		$1.25
Second	Transistors		0.25
Third	Integrated circuits		0.10
Fourth	LSI	Less than	0.01

FIGURE 1-12 Supercomputer Cray X-MP/48. (*Courtesy of Cray Research, a Silicon Graphics Company*)

Today, the microcomputer has become an important interactive tool for teaching and learning. Multimedia peripherals, CD-ROM (compact disc read-only memory), and DVD (digital versatile disc) can be interfaced with the microcomputer and the World Wide Web, which greatly expanded its utilization. Microcomputers with their multimedia capabilities are continually being integrated into the classroom curriculum. Using microcomputers and the World Wide Web, educators are creating new learning environments. Within these environments, teachers become facilitators and students become constructors of knowledge. Together, teachers and students become "knowledge navigators," a term coined by John Sculley, past CEO of Apple Computers.

Certainly, the trend of miniaturization witnessed throughout the past several generations of computers will also continue in the next generations, concentrating greater amounts of computer capacity in ever smaller spaces (Moore's Law). Not only are computers becoming smaller, but their prices are lower. Advanced manufacturing technology will lead to much more affordable computer systems within the near future. An excellent source of information for classroom ideas and hardware information is *The Journey Inside Newsletter* located at <www.intel.com/intel/educate>. This is a joint publication of the Intel Corporation and the International Society for Technology in Education.

Analog and Digital Computers

Computers fall into two categories, depending on the system by which they operate, *analog* and *digital*. *Analog computers* represent numbers internally by measuring quantities and then converting electrical energy into impulses that run mechanical devices. They perform work that is tiring, boring, or dangerous for human workers. Examples of instruments with analog readouts include a mercury thermometer, older-style radios with dials, televisions, a conventional typewriter, spring-wound wristwatches, and an odometer.

In contrast, *digital computers* convert information in the form of numbers, letters, and special characters into digital form. The digital system is binary; that is, it depends on the system of numeration that includes only 0 and 1. Information is converted into electrical impulses during which a switch is either off (0) or on (1). The digital computer accepts input, converts input into electrical impulses, processes and manipulates data and information, and produces output.

Whether analog or digital, computers depend entirely on the humans who design, build, program, operate, and maintain them. Used properly, the computer is a tool that can help humans accomplish the work necessary to participate in an increasingly complex society.

Analog-to-Digital Conversion.   Modern science labs in industry, research, and universities now use microcomputers for the collection of scientific data. At the heart of scientific applications of computer power are hardware components that allow analog measurements (such as temperature, pressure, and movement) to be converted to the digital form (or signal) understood by computers. Most microprocessors deal with 8-bit or 16-bit binary numbers, called bytes, most ranging from 0 to 255. Therefore, the analog-to-digital converter accepts physical measurements (input), which are processed by a transducer and support circuits; a computer program collects the measurements and they are converted to digital form. The computer displays the results of the calculations based on the measurements.

Researchers have developed hardware and software of this particular type, but it is not useful for all applications. Other special interfaces have been designed and are available.

Almost daily, newspapers and news broadcasts report new advances in computer technology. It is vital that people become technologically literate with computers and their capabilities because computers are becoming standard appliances in homes, and play an integral part in businesses and industrial occupations. Used widely, computers can and do enhance the quality of our lives.

The Language of Computers

There are a number of terms that are basic to an understanding of computer operations. One term is software. Software, also called computer programs, refers to the commands that instruct the computer to perform tasks in a specific logical sequence. People who write these instructions are called *computer programmers.*

There are two types of software. *Systems software* instructs the computer to carry out its basic operations. *Language interpreters,* which allow a person to program in various computer languages, are examples of systems software. The second type, *applications software,* instructs the computer to carry out specific tasks, such as writing payroll checks.

Software may originate from one of several sources. Large computer installations usually hire computer programmers on a full-time basis to write software to meet the installation's particular needs. Smaller computer users may purchase prepackaged programs from commercial software developers. Many personal computer users learn computer languages that enable them to write software for use on their own systems, allowing them to tailor software to their own individual needs.

In contrast to software, *computer hardware* is the physical machinery that makes up the computer system. Hardware is the equipment that you see when you visit a computer room or computer retail store. Computer hardware is sophisticated electronic equipment that must be handled and used appropriately and safely, and maintained properly in order for the computer system to operate with optimal efficiency.

The heart of the computer system is the *central processing unit* (CPU). The CPU controls all the computer's functions since it is made up of circuitry that interprets and carries out instructions written into software. The CPU also retrieves software instructions before decoding and executing them. The components of the CPU are the *arithmetic/logic unit* (ALU), the *memory,* and the *control unit* (see Figures 1-13 and 1-14).

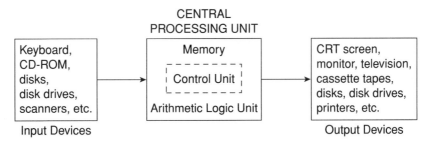

CENTRAL
PROCESSING UNIT

| Keyboard, CD-ROM, disks, disk drives, scanners, etc. | Memory
 Control Unit
 Arithmetic Logic Unit | CRT screen, monitor, television, cassette tapes, disks, disk drives, printers, etc. |

Input Devices   Output Devices

FIGURE 1-13   The central processing unit (CPU).

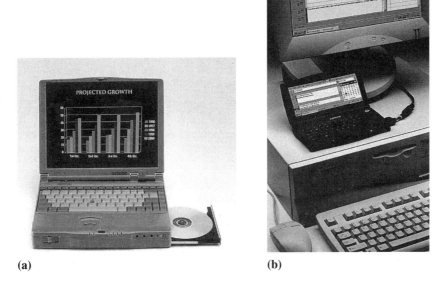

(a)   **(b)**

FIGURE 1-14   (a) Toshiba notebook computer. (*Courtesy of Toshiba*) (b) Compaq's PC Companion. (*Courtesy of Compaq*)

The ALU is that part of the CPU capable of performing mathematical calculations required for many data-processing applications. The ALU performs these calculations with greater speed and accuracy than humans do. Imagine, for example, how the mathematical capabilities of the computer's ALU have revolutionized the work of the Internal Revenue Service in calculating tax returns.

The *memory* of the CPU is made up of integrated circuitry where information can be stored. Software instructions are retained in memory that is directly accessible to the CPU.

When the computer requires these instructions for operations, the CPU retrieves them from memory, decodes them, and then carries them out.

The *control unit* of the CPU controls the flow of the computer's operations, including data transfer, acceptance of input, functioning of the ALU, and other related functions. The control unit is a vital part of the operation of the computer system.

Primary Components of a Microcomputer

Microcomputers are big business primarily because they put computer power in the hands of individual users. They are being used to maintain household budgets and accounts; provide hours of challenging entertainment, and supplement and enrich learning; edit textual material; and expedite the business procedures of owners of large and small businesses. The list of microcomputer applications seems limitless, indeed.

What is this powerful "little giant" that is making daily life simpler and more enjoyable? The microcomputer is made up of several hardware devices that function similarly to very large computer systems (see Figure 1-15).

The Keyboard/CPU

The brain of the microcomputer system resides in the CPU. Through the keyboard, instructions and data are entered into the computer system. The microcomputer keyboard is similar to a standard typewriter keyboard. It is made up of keys that represent letters of the alphabet and numbers, as well as special symbols such as @, $, %, and *. In addition to these familiar characters, the microcomputer keyboard usually includes special function keys that instruct the computer to perform specific tasks. The microcomputer keyboard is simple and comfortable to use (see Figures 1-16 and 1-17).

In some microcomputer systems, the keyboard is included in the same housing as the CPU. As in larger systems, the CPU is made up of the control unit, the ALU, and memory. The size of a microcomputer system's memory is vital to the speed and efficiency with which the system will operate. Some of the most impressive advances in microcomputers

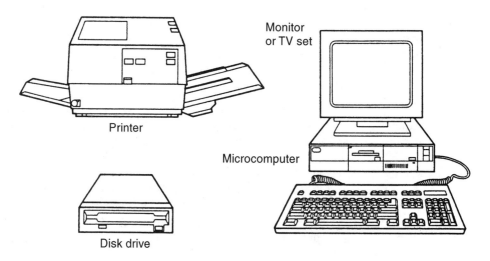

Printer

Monitor or TV set

Microcomputer

Disk drive

FIGURE 1-15   Primary components of a microcomputer system.

FIGURE 1-16 Wireless keyboard. (*Courtesy of Interlink Electronics*)

FIGURE 1-17 PC touchpad offering precise cursor pointing via a fingertip, gloved hand, or common stylus. (*Courtesy of Interlink Electronics*)

during the last several years have been substantial increases in memory and, thus, in speed.

Microcomputer Memory

The advent of the microcomputer age began with silicon chip technology. The technical properties of silicon chips will be discussed later, but it is important to note here that the silicon chip has brought about the miniaturization of electronic equipment. Consequently, a greater amount of memory capacity can be included in the CPU than was previously possible. This has significantly increased the power of microcomputer systems.

The typical microcomputer system includes *boards* onto which chips with memory capability have been fastened. At the time of purchase, a microcomputer will possess a certain amount of memory capacity; this amount can be increased according to the user's needs by inserting additional components. Memory components have become more affordable to the average microcomputer owner. Adding memory to a microcomputer is a simple process that most users can perform themselves (see Figure 1-18).

To determine the memory size of a microcomputer system, it is necessary to understand several quantitative terms that apply to computer capability. A digital computer operates using a binary system of 0's and 1's. A *bi*nary digi*t* is called a *bit,* and is the smallest unit of digital information. A *byte* is the number of bits necessary to store one character of text. A byte is usually 8 or 16 bits. These bits represent combinations of 0's and 1's, according to the binary system.

Computer memory capacity is generally measured in *kilobytes* (K) or *megabytes* (M). In the binary system, a kilo refers to 1,024, or 2 raised to the tenth power. The amount of memory capacity required to store 1,024 bytes of information is referred to as 1K.

In microcomputers that have *hard* or *fixed* disk memory, which enables them to store far greater amounts of data, memory is usually measured in *megabytes*. A megabyte is approximately 1 million bytes of information.

A major advantage of microcomputer systems is that extra memory space can be added simply and quickly as the needs of the user expand. Extra memory space allows the system

FIGURE 1-18 Motherboard of an IBM Personal Computer. Computer chips inserted on board contain RAM (random-access memory) and ROM (read-only memory). *(Courtesy of IBM)*

to operate with greater speed and efficiency. More complex programs with lengthier instructions can be stored and run on a system to which extra memory space has been added.

There are two major types of semiconductor memory: *random-access memory* (RAM) and *read-only memory* (ROM). RAM is designed to store new data and programs. Data and program instructions are entered into the memory of the central processing unit and then accessed, or retrieved from memory, in random fashion. RAM is not permanent memory. For example, if the computer system loses power during operation, the information stored in RAM is lost forever. This requires that the lost information be reloaded into memory.

To maintain program instructions and data in the assigned RAM locations, the system must "refresh" its memory. The system does this by supplying small amounts of electricity to memory locations at the rapid speed of several hundreds or even thousands of times per second.

In contrast to RAM, ROM (read-only memory) is comprised of computer chips that have had program instructions manufactured into them permanently. Information stored on ROM chips cannot be lost in the event of a power failure. ROM chips contain programs that are used repeatedly for various applications; programs that control the video terminal and programs that control the mechanical operations of devices such as disk drives are two examples of programs stored on ROM chips.

ROM can be built into computers at the time they are manufactured, or it can be purchased in modules to be inserted into special receptacles built into a computer. Some ROM chips contain programs that make the task of programming easier or more enjoyable. For instance, some ROM chips include a shape table, much like a dictionary, that holds a set of shapes already done so that the programmer can reuse these shapes numerous times without having to recreate them for each use. The primary difference between RAM and ROM is that RAM is programmed by the user and ROM is programmed by the manufacturer. There is one variation of ROM, however, that cuts across the distinctions between RAM and ROM. This variation is *erasable programmable memory* (EPROM) or *programmable read-only memory* (PROM). EPROM chips come with program instructions stored on the chips by the manufacturer. If the purchaser wishes to alter these program instructions, it is possible to erase them and then store new instructions on the chips.

Memory Storage Devices

Another essential part of computer hardware is the memory storage device. Storage devices retain data and instructions outside of the computer's central processing unit so that information is not lost when the computer is turned off. This allows the data and instructions stored to be used repeatedly or kept for future reference. Several popular storage devices are available for use with microcomputer systems.

The most popular storage device in use for computers in general is the *magnetic disk drive.* The disk drive reads and records information stored on *magnetic disks.* These *hard disks* look very much like the plastic 45-rpm disks (but much smaller) used to record music and are stored inside the computer so that the user does not have to handle them (see Figure 1-19). Each disk has two recording surfaces: top and bottom. On the recording surfaces are concentric circles moving outward from the center of the disk to its edge. Inside the disk drive are mounted several *read/write heads* that record and retrieve information on magnetic disks.

Information stored on magnetic disks is relatively safe from loss. Loss of stored material may result from writing too much information onto a disk. Disks may also be erased by a computer-controlled device called a *bulk eraser.* Accidental loss of information stored on magnetic disks is unusual, though, and this factor adds to the popularity of magnetic disk storage.

Although the *floppy disk* functions similarly to the hard disk, it is different because it is flexible rather than rigid. Floppy disks (or diskettes) come in a variety of sizes. Early microcomputers used disks that were 5¼ inches in diameter. One or both surfaces were used for recording. Presently, the most popular disk has a diameter of 3½ inches, and it is enclosed within a hard plastic container. Despite its smaller size, it can hold many times more information than a 5¼-inch diskette. Many other types of memory devices exist, including CD-ROMs with read/write capabilities, DVD-ROM, various types of data cards, and the use of network capabilities (see Figures 1-20 to 1-24).

As we have already seen, ROM chips are another way of retaining program instructions externally to the computer system. The instructions on ROM chips are manufactured into the chips and are, therefore, permanently stored there. Hence, ROM chips are safe from loss of information.

Magnetic tapes remain a common method of storage in large computer systems. Back-up storage for computer systems and networks is usually on magnetic tape. Magnetic tape provides an inexpensive and convenient means of storing great quantities of data that are not needed on a day-to-day basis.

Scanners are another method of entering information into the computer. *Text scanners* can "read" textual information printed on a page from a magazine or book, from a

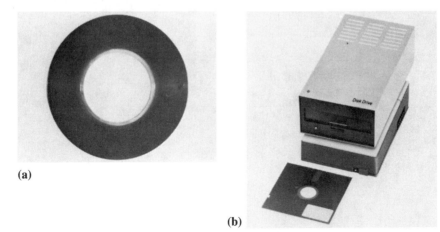

(a)

(b)

FIGURE 1-19 (a) Hard disk. (b) 5¼-inch diskette with disk drive.

FIGURE 1-20   Portable CD-ROM drive with built in speakers. (*Courtesy of Panasonic*)

FIGURE 1-21   32X CD ROM drive. (*Courtesy Samsung Electronics America, Inc.*)

FIGURE 1-22   *(left)* 100-disk CD changer. *(right)* 50-disk CD changer. (*Courtesy of Panasonic*)

FIGURE 1-23   Compact disk recorder. (*Courtesy of Panasonic*)

FIGURE 1-24 DVD-ROM drive. (*Courtesy of Samsung Electronics America, Inc.*)

FIGURE 1-25 Page scanner. (*Courtesy of Plustek*)

dot-matrix printer, or from laser printer or a typewritten page. Some scanners can also read cursive writing. *Image scanners* "read" black-and-white and color images. These scanners convert the analog information to digital information. Some scanners also convert text to speech.

A scanner may be configured as a flatbed, operating similar to a copy machine in which the user lifts the lid and places the material to be scanned flat on the bed of the scanner. Scanners may also be sheet-fed, hand-held, or attached to a printer (see Figure 1-25).

Still other methods of inputting information are *optical character readers* (OCRs), *optical mark readers* (OMRs), and bar-code readers. For example, OCRs "read" the characters on the bottom of personal checks as well as all mail sent to a post office. Some uses of OMRs are to score objective tests where the answers have been blacked in, to control the inventory of library books, and to monitor classroom attendance.

Display Devices

For the computer to work efficiently with the humans who use it, it must include some means of communicating. Display devices enable humans to see what instructions are being given to the computer; to respond to erroneous information; to enter data and verify data for correctness; and to see the output, or final product, of the computer's operation. Several hardware devices for display are available.

Microcomputer systems rely on a variety of *video screens* for display purposes. Many computers can be adapted for use with ordinary television screens, the most common video screen in our society. Video games that plug into the family television set are popular examples. As computer graphics technology advances, the visual displays on video screens are becoming more sophisticated (see Figures 1-26 and 1-27).

Other terms for video screens are *monitors* or *cathode-ray tubes* (CRTs). CRTs rely on the same cathode-ray tube technology that television is based on, but are designed strictly for use with computers. Images are generated on the screen when a series of points are lighted to create a pattern of images. Simple CRTs display characters in green or white on a black background; more complex monitors can generate characters in a range of colors. Liquid-crystal projection panels and displays (LCDs) are often used to project for

FIGURE 1-26   SVGA monitors. (*Courtesy of SMILE International, Inc.*)

FIGURE 1-27   Flat panel multimedia monitor. (*Courtesy of Samsung Electronics America, Inc.*)

presentations and classroom lessons (see Figure 1-28).

The next generation of displays for television and computers is HDTV (high-definition television). This display provides much clearer displays. The advent of HDTV will mean the demise of one of the last vacuum tubes—the television picture tube.

Printing Devices

Once the computer has completed its data-processing function, it is necessary to generate some human-readable, permanent copy of the resulting output. A record of computer transactions printed onto paper is referred to as hard copy. Hard copies are often necessary for filing purposes or for reporting the results of data processing to many departments within an organization.

The printer usually cannot be used as an input device; it functions as an output device. Data are read from the computer, processed according to instructions, and the results written out by the printer. Printers operate within a wide range of speeds from very slow to extremely fast, from 10 characters per second to many thousands of characters per second.

Several factors determine the rate at which a printer operates. The type of printer is one factor. Some printers print material one character at a time, a relatively slow method of printing. A faster method is to set up a line of text at a time and then print the entire line. Another enhancement is to print in two directions, from left to right and then from right to left. This saves the time spent in returning to the left margin of the page to print each subsequent line.

One method of printing is *thermal printing,* which generates characters on heat-sensitive paper. These printers have the advantage of functioning very quietly, whereas other printers may cause a distracting level of noise in their immediate vicinity. However, thermal printing usually does not produce high-quality copies and requires the purchase of special paper.

(a)   (b)

FIGURE 1-28   (a) LCD projector. (b) LCD panel. (*Courtesy of Sharp Electronics Corp.*)

Another method of printing is *impact printing*. In impact printing, characters are formed when the printing element, the part that includes the pattern or mold for characters, strikes or contacts the paper. This process is quite similar to the process of a typewriter key striking a ribbon against a sheet of typing paper to produce the image of a character.

A common type of impact printer is the *dot-matrix printer.* The writing head of the dot-matrix printer is made up of wires that represent each letter, number, or symbol. Because each character is printed by a combination of separate wires, the resulting copy generally has a dotty appearance that may be unacceptable when high-quality copies are required. Dot-matrix printers that print a high density of dots per inch produce the best quality copies.

A higher-quality impact printer is the daisy wheel printer. These include print wheels that have letters, numbers, and other characters molded on them. The print wheel is rotated until the desired character is in the striking position on impact. Daisy wheel printers are usually more expensive and somewhat slower than dot-matrix printers, but they produce copy comparable to that produced by sophisticated typewriters.

Inexpensive dot-matrix printers with near-letter-quality printing have helped to blur the distinctions between dot-matrix and letter-quality printers. These near-letter-quality or correspondence-quality printers have become a common choice for schools, homes, and businesses because they serve a dual role: letter quality and graphics printing. Pictures, graphs, maps, charts, and various typefaces can be printed out on paper, as can professionally typed documents.

Special graphics plotters are also available; they allow the user to print detailed drawings and blueprints on paper. Some models include color capabilities to make the output even more attractive (see Figure 1-29).

The most popular type of printer is the *laser printer.* Based on laser technology, this printer employs some design concepts that have been used in photocopying machines. The

FIGURE 1-29   Color printer. (*Courtesy of Fargo Electronics, Inc.*)

FIGURE 1-30   Laser printer. (*Courtesy of Mita*)

laser printer is much quieter than other types of printers. It also has much more flexible and sophisticated printing capabilities than a basic printer such as the dot-matrix printer. Laser printers are capable of printing copy of nearly *typeset* quality. However, the laser printer is more expensive than most other printers (see Figure 1-30).

Using Your Microcomputer

Now that you have a moderate vocabulary of computer terminology and can recognize the function of various kinds of computer hardware, you are probably eager to try working with the microcomputer. Microcomputers have an amazing amount of capability and using the technology correctly will help to unleash its potential power.

The microcomputer is user-oriented. It is said to be "user-friendly"; that is, using a microcomputer does not require an extensive background in computer science or an orientation toward electronics. Many owners of microcomputers begin slowly and find themselves learning more with continued use and experimentation.

There is, of course, a significant difference between *operating* a microcomputer and *programming* one. Operating the computer refers to the process of controlling the functions of the system, selecting software, and manipulating the equipment to cause it to perform given tasks. Programming, on the other hand, refers to the process of writing instructions that tell the computer how to perform its operations. Programming requires a more extensive knowledge of the computer and of computer languages than does merely operating the computer.

Often microcomputer users begin by learning to operate their systems using prepackaged software. Software publishing is a fast-growing industry with newer and better software available all the time. This software can perform many types of applications so that the microcomputer user need not know how to program the computer in order to use it.

Educational programs are available for use in homes and schools. More educational institutions are installing microcomputers in their classrooms for a number of reasons. Not only does the computer execute programs that cover topics that teachers may not be familiar with, but it can also present those topics in interesting and colorful ways. In addition, the computer is a patient teacher, offering feedback, reinforcement, repetition, flexibility, and remediation whenever appropriate.

Educational software is available to teach mathematics, spelling, reading, grammar, and practically any other subject typically covered in traditional curricula. Whether students use such programs at home or in the classroom, they are learning several important lessons simultaneously. Not only are students tutored and drilled in academic subject areas, but they are also given an opportunity to become familiar and comfortable with microcomputer systems. This is important for children who will live in an increasingly computerized world.

Along with educational software, programs that help the microcomputer user manage personal business are also popular. Some programs are written to keep track of household accounts and budgets. Others help the user to determine whether a hypothetical purchase is a wise investment or not. Still others store records of financial transactions for future reference and help the homeowner with physical tasks such as turning lights on or off, setting clocks accurately, and monitoring locked doors for security.

Software is available that maintains household inventories, computes income taxes, and analyzes the stock exchange. Many microcomputer users find that computerizing their personal business makes such chores easier and faster to accomplish, and the results more accurate.

Perhaps the single most popular type of prepackaged software is software that entertains the user. These programs usually involve games of strategy, skill, or chance and are very popular. Some computer games can be played either with other people or with the computer itself as competitor. The computer keeps track of the score as well as recording each player's moves.

Many computer games can be adjusted for players at different ability levels and may be enjoyed by players of all ages. Games that include graphics are visually exciting to play. Computer games are currently the fastest selling type of prepackaged software on the personal computer market.

The variety and availability of prepackaged software for use on microcomputer systems makes operating a personal computer simple and enjoyable for the novice. Of course, the new microcomputer owner should follow instruction manuals and materials carefully in setting up the system properly. Most microcomputer retailers are happy to assist the novice in setting up and learning to operate a microcomputer system. Many personal computer owners find that once they have become familiar with the operations of their systems, they want to learn more about computers and about programming languages so that they can write software suitable for their own needs.

Programming Your Microcomputer

A novice computer programmer can begin to learn by using programs published in computer-oriented periodicals or available on the World Wide Web (WWW). While keying in the program instructions (or code, as it is called by programmers), the user can begin to learn about the structure of computer programs. Programs may be written specifically for use on a system other than the one the user owns, and changes may be necessary.

FIGURE 1-31   On-screen interaction to object-oriented computing. (*Courtesy of FTG Data Systems*)

In the beginning, adapting such programs may be largely a trial-and-error endeavor. As in all new experiences, though, the user can learn as much from failures as from successes. The range of possibilities of writing and adapting microcomputer software is limited only by the user's imagination. Writing and altering programs also has the advantage of making the user's involvement with the microcomputer system more active and creative so that eventually the user becomes more computer literate.

Some microcomputer users will wish to study programming languages in a more structured way. A number of books are available on the subject of computer programming. As personal computers become more popular, numerous courses are being offered by universities, community colleges, and technical schools. Any of these will provide an adequate background to the user who wishes to program. Many communities now have clubs and organizations of personal computer hobbyists where the novice can interact with others having similar experiences and problems with their computers.

Microcomputer users who learn to write their own software will need to purchase hardware devices for storing and printing program instructions (see Figure 1-31).

Besides needing to store the programs they write, microcomputer users will also want to generate hard copies of their software for their own use and so that they may share their software with other personal computer users. To do this, they must purchase a printing device. Computer retailers are trained to assess the user's needs and to recommend appropriate hardware.

The Personal Computer and the WWW

The fastest growing use of personal computers in the home and in schools is as a communication tool. Schools and homes are connecting at a very rapid pace to the Internet (see Figures 1-32 and 1-33). Electronic mail and the World Wide Web provide many opportunities in education. Later chapters will detail these uses and applications.

Summary

Because computers are pervasive in our society, there is a great need for people, young and old, to become aware of computers and to be computer literate. Computer awareness refers to the ability to recognize computers and work comfortably with them. Computer literacy, often referred to as technology literacy, refers to a fundamental understanding of computer operations and terms, applications of computers in society, and uses and limitations of technology.

FIGURE 1-32 Modem PC card. (*Courtesy of TDK Systems*)

Basic foundations, standards and profiles are essential for all students. Technology literacy is a given in our society.

One reasonable place to begin with computer and technology literacy is to gain an understanding of the history of the machines themselves. Although many primitive mathematical devices contributed to the development of computer technology, the first generation of computers was considered to have begun with the introduction of vacuum-tube technology. The second generation of computers incorporated transistor technology in an attempt to resolve some of the problems presented by vacuum tubes. The third generation of computers was based on integrated-circuit technology, which was enhanced in the large-scale integrated (LSI) circuits of the fourth generation of computers.

We can speculate about the future generations of computers based on the trends that are currently emerging. Very large-scale integration (VLSI) technology has continued the trend toward miniaturization, making computer systems smaller, more powerful, and more affordable. As this occurs, computers will gain even more popularity. The logical

FIGURE 1-33 Intranet media server. (*Courtesy of Mitsubishi*)

consequence of this trend will be an increased need for computer literacy for people of all ages and occupations.

Computers are a vital part of our society today. The personal computer industry with the advent of electronic mail and the WWW is booming, indicating that a great number of people are discovering the benefits of computing and technology. This will require that technology users acquire a greater degree of technological literacy.

Software refers to the written instructions that tell a computer how to operate. Hardware refers to the electronic equipment that carries out the software instructions. The central processing unit, the brains of the computer system, is made up of the arithmetic/logic unit, the control unit, and memory. Other hardware devices include storage devices such as magnetic disk drives and display devices such as the video screen, input devices such as keyboards, and output devices such as thermal printers, impact printers, and laser printers.

Microcomputers are said to be user-oriented because their operation does not require an extensive knowledge of computers. They are designed to be used by the average person. Many personal computer users choose to learn more about computers and about programming languages. This enables them to tailor software to their own individual needs and to become more actively involved with their computer systems.

LEARNER ACTIVITIES

1. Visit the Intel website and review the graph of Moore's Law and relevant data on present-day technology capabilities. Does his model still hold true? Justify your answer.

2. Interview a local businessperson and write a report about how his or her company uses microcomputers.

3. List at least five major advantages of using microcomputers in business, in school, and in the home.

4. Determine the technology teacher foundations required in your state. How do they compare to the ISTE requirements?

5. Research the contributions of women (other than those discussed in this chapter) to the development of computers.

6. Design a sequence of lessons for one ISTE Technology Foundation standard for students.

7. Develop a portfolio assessment plan for one of the Technology Literate student profiles.

8. Select one of the performance indicators and provide student activities to determine a students understanding of the content listed.

9. Outline the need for computer literacy education in the public schools. At what age should students be introduced to computers?

10. Design a lesson plan that introduces one major application of computers in our society.

11. Research and prepare a report on how extensively computers are used in your local school district for administrative functions and curriculum enhancement.

12. Research and prepare a report on the extent to which the International Society for Technology in Education (ISTE) teacher foundation standards regarding computers have been implemented in college and university teacher preparation programs.

13. Research and prepare a report on how computers are used in the musical and/or visual arts. In what ways are computers being used in the composition of music? How are computers used in teaching piano keyboarding skills? How are textile artists and weavers using computers to design their handwoven pieces?

14. Visit a retail store that sells primarily electronic equipment. Observe and prepare a report on how the use of the computer-on-a-chip has influenced the size and capability of electronic "gadgets."

15. Outline a plan for implementing the NETS K–12 student profiles into education in the United States. Include factors of cost, availability, and education implications.

16. Visit a local computer retail store and prepare a list of microcomputer hardware currently on the market.

17. Write a brief report on the different devices used with microcomputers. Discuss how these devices could enhance the use of the computer in the curriculum.

18. Research current developments in microcomputer memory technology. Identify major trends.

19. Write a brief report that discusses the similarities and differences of various printers. Include in your report a discussion of the variety of applications for each type of printer.

20. Design a lesson plan to demonstrate the flow of information into and out of the computer: INPUT—PROCESSING—OUTPUT.

21. Prepare a report including a time line of the evolution of the microcomputer.

22. List the most common analog devices.

23. Prepare a set of transparencies to present a brief lesson on the components of a microcomputer.

24. Describe the difference between the Dvorak and Qwerty keyboards.

25. Prepare a list of common input and output methods for computers.

BIBLIOGRAPHY

Bitter, G. G. (1991). Vision: Technologically enriched school of tomorrow (TEST) communicator. *Journal of the California Association for the Gifted, 21*(1), 20–21.

Bitter, G. G. (1992). *Macmillan encyclopedia of computers.* New York: Macmillan.

Bitter, G. G., Thomas, L., Knezek, D. G., Friske, J., Taylor, H., Wiebe, J., & Kelly, M. G. (1997). National educational technology standards: Developing new learning environments for today's 1998 classrooms. *Bulletin of the National Association of Secondary Principals, 81*(592), 52–58.

Brady, M. L. (1991). Keeping current with technology. *Mathematics Teacher, 84,* 92–96.

Bush, G. (1991). *America 2000–source book.* Washington, D.C.: U.S. Department of Education.

Carter, C. N., Childress, N. A., Mullican, S. L., & Sheubrooks, L. D. (1996). Computers in the classroom of the future. *TECHNOS, 5*(2), 28–32.

Chung, J. (1991). Collaborative learning systems: The design of instructional environments for the emerging new school. *Educational Technology, 31*(12), 15–22.

Clements, D. H. (1991). Enhancement of creativity in computer environments. *American Educational Research Journal, 28,* 173–187.

Collins, A. (1991). The role of technology in restructuring schools. *Phi Delta Kappan, 73,* 28–36.

Collins, A., Hawkins, J., & Frederickson, J. R. (1991). *Three different views of students: The role of technology in assessing student performance.* New York: Center for Children and Technology, Bank Street College of Education.

David, J. L. (1991). Restructuring and technology: Partners in change. *Phi Delta Kappan, 73,* 37–40.

Flagg, B. N. (1990). *Formative Evaluation for Educational Technologies.* Hillsdale, NJ: Lawrence Erlbaum.

Fulton, K. (1997). *Learning in a digital age: Insights into the issues.* Santa Monica, CA: Milken Exchange on Educational Technology.

Integrating technology into teaching. (1997 November). Alexandria, VA. *Educational Leadership, 55*(3), Association for Supervision and Curriculum Development.

Johnson, D. L., & Maddux, C. D., (Eds.). (1997). *Using technology in the classroom.* New York: The Haworth Press.

Kinnaman, D. E. (1990). What's the research telling us? *Classroom Computer Learning, 10*(6), 31–39.

McCarthy, R. (1990). The hardware dilemma. *Electronic Learning, 9*(5), 20–24.

Nation at risk, a. (1983). National Commission on Excellence in Education. U.S. Department of Education.

National educational technology standards. (1998 June). Eugene, OR: International Society for Technology in Education.

Papert, S. (1980). *Mindstorms: Children, computers, and powerful ideas.* New York: Basic Books.

Solomon, C. (1986). *Computer environments for children.* Cambridge, MA: The MIT Press.

Sutton, R. E. (1991). Equity and computers in the schools: A decade of research. *Review of Educational Research, 61*(4), 475–503.

Taylor, R. (1980). *The computer in the school: Tutor, tool, tutee.* New York: Teachers College Press.

Tomas Rivera Center. (1986). *The new information technology and the education of Hispanics.* Claremont, CA: Author.

U.S. Congress, Office of Technology Assessment. (1988). *Power on! New tools for teaching and learning,* OTA-SET-379. Washington, DC: U.S. Government Printing Office.

Vockell, E. L. (1990). Instruction principles behind computer use. *The Computing Teacher, 18*(1), 10–15.

WEBSITES

Intel Corporation: <www.intel.com>
International Society for Technology in Education: <www.iste.org>
The Journey Inside Newsletter: <www.intel.com/intel/educate>
National Educational Technology Standards for Students: <http://cnets.iste.org>
NCATE Technology Report: <www.ncate.org>
Technology Based Learning and Research: <tblr.ed.asu.edu>

2 What Have We Learned from Research?

FOCUS QUESTIONS

1. How do classroom teaching and learning behaviors alter as a result of introducing computers to the curriculum?
2. Does computer use lead to academic gains in all subject areas?
3. What are reasonable effects to expect from integrating technology in typical classrooms?

In 1996, the United States Department of Education issued a report entitled *Getting America's Students Ready for the 21st Century*. The Secretary of Education at the time, Richard Riley, urged the nation's national and local leaders to initiate change that would prepare our nation's younger generations for success in the twenty-first century. This report was written to support the Technology Literacy Challenge put forth by President Bill Clinton. The four goals central to this challenge provide some direction for future efforts:

1. All teachers in the nation will have the training and support they need to help students learn using computers and the information superhighway.
2. All teachers and students will have modern multimedia computers in their classrooms.
3. Every classroom will be connected to the information superhighway.
4. Effective software and online learning resources will be an integral part of every school's curriculum (U.S. Department of Education, 1996).

Although common sense and experience tells educators that even the greatest of technological expenditures will not magically whisk away America's social injustices, computer innovations are being given a place in classrooms across the country in increasing numbers. Every teacher must be prepared for the substantial changes technology could imply for the teaching and learning processes in classrooms at all levels. Unfortunately, as the technology wave crashes into traditional educational practices, teachers are infrequently being made aware of the latest research findings. In order to integrate technology into the lives of students in a way that makes the most educational sense, teachers need to

FIGURE 2-1   Students work together to complete a task using a computer.

be able to weigh the evidence. Do computers make students smarter? How do actual classroom teaching and learning behaviors alter as a result of introducing computers to the curriculum? Is this technological revolution really good for our children, or is this just education's attempt to just stay up with the times?

This chapter is intended to give a practical overview of current research on technology's effect on teaching and learning. Any expected change in classrooms as a result of technology hinges on teachers' perceptions and understandings of the potential benefits and barriers. Becoming aware of some current research findings will hopefully serve to begin an ongoing, informed dialogue among teachers so that the benefit of technology can be fully enjoyed by America's students. The chapter will first look at a unique study that exemplifies the vision of technology without boundaries and review what effects this environment has on students and teachers. Next, research findings in more typical classrooms will be examined. Finally, some caveats will be proposed to guide future discussions of technology's place in America's classrooms (see Figure 2-1).

Apple Classrooms of Tomorrow

It is common to hear educational advocates lament the fact that schools do not have enough money to purchase state-of-the-art resources required to ready students for a competitive future in the international marketplace. Imagine, if you will, schools that *do* have the money and the resources beyond their greatest expectations. Picture an educational utopia created specifically for the exploration of technology's use in the classroom. Envision the best education possible for students learning under the most ideal conditions with a generous amount of support, and the vision will likely resemble what is still a dream for most schools but is, in fact, a reality for the Apple Classrooms of Tomorrow (ACOT) project.

ACOT is a long-term research project, sponsored by Apple Computer, that began in 1985 to investigate what would happen to the processes of teaching and learning if participants had regular, convenient access to technology (David, 1995). Computers were not found in abundance in most classrooms at the time. The plan involved giving every teacher and every student from test classrooms across the country two computers each, one to use at school and one to bring home. The intent was to create model, technology-rich learning environments where teachers and students could use computers on a routine, authentic basis. Computers were meant to be used in the most appropriate ways to enhance learning, as just one of a number of learning tools. The partnerships between Apple and the schools were mutually beneficial. The computer company supplied the hardware, software, and support necessary to maintain the systems, and the schools contributed what they could, a real-world proving ground with participants who were ready to take some risks and provide ongoing, always-changing data. During the study, outside researchers joined the inside participants in uncovering the range of effects that this routine use of technology had on the classrooms.

Findings

In terms of general learning behaviors, students and teachers made broad and varied gains, some that were expected by project planners and some that were pleasant surprises (Apple Classrooms of Tomorrow, 1995). With any experiment, initial assumptions do not frequently remain unrevised for the duration of the venture, and that was surely the case with the ACOT project. Project planners had optimistically hoped that the mere influx of this abundant amount of technology would bring about substantial changes in the dynamics of the classrooms, but the noticeable changes in teacher and student activities have occurred slowly over the first 10 years of the project.

Changes in Teachers

Changes in teaching practices did not take place instantaneously (Ringstaff, Sandholtz, & Dwyer, 1995). What ACOT researchers found, and what other futurists have postulated as well, is that new technology is typically slotted into a place determined by old teaching habits. Teachers and students initially followed the traditional classroom patterns with which they were familiar (O'Neil, 1995). With support devices built into the program, such as communication channels and training, teachers worked to establish fundamental changes in classroom practice. Gradually, over years of participating in the study, teachers began making noticeable alterations in the dynamics of the learning environments, based on the new thinking the technology sparked. Teachers were finding out that one person, whether it be themselves or a student, could not always be the expert on every facet of a new technology medium. Between the teacher and a room full of students, however, *someone* might be. Recognizing the potential for student involvement in the teaching of peers was a difficult shift for many teachers who had grown accustomed to the traditional teacher–student relationship structure. When teachers were able to move past that pervasive teacher-centered view of education, students and teachers, as communities of learners, were able to benefit from the range of individual areas of expertise represented by the entire group.

Physical Space.　In addition to holding on to traditional teaching methods, the ACOT teachers retained, at first, other conventional ideas about teaching, such as how to physically arrange the classroom (Stuebing, Celsi, & Cousineau, 1995). Teachers began the study with certain convictions that students needed their own desks and teachers needed to see, at a glance, each of the computer screens in the class. These ideas regarding something that on the surface seems trivial are actually indications of a developmental stage of technology integration. As teachers allowed themselves to change with the potential technology presented, letting the learning in the room be focused on the children instead of on a central curriculum, they opened up to considering some new flexible arrangements for their classrooms. Classrooms gradually shifted to allow space for presentations and work of variably sized groups, for increased communication, even around the somewhat cumbersome computer screens, and for flexibility in using the technology for multiple activities. These changes were brought about because of the addition of technology into the physical space of the classrooms, but the changes reflect a much larger transformation in the concepts of teaching and learning.

Collegial Relationships.   As teachers ventured through this learning process, they discovered new facets of relationships they shared with each other (Ringstaff et al., 1995). In a traditional school, teachers are fairly autonomous; once the classroom door closes, the majority of their time is spent with their students. Contact with other adults happens only during breaks or after school. Because of the special circumstances involved with the introduction of this large amount of technology, teachers in the ACOT schools began new patterns of collegial interaction. At the beginning, teachers communicated with each other primarily to commiserate on their unfamiliar experiences and to support each other. As the teachers grew accustomed to having and using the technology, they used their relationships with other teachers for broader purposes. Teachers supplied each other with support on using the hardware and software, passed along instructional ideas and strategies, and ultimately collaborated with team members to develop innovative new teaching methods and curricula. Technology proved to be a phenomenon that inspired collegiality in more than one way. It was the topic of conversation and also the medium through which much of the communication was made possible (see Figure 2-2).

FIGURE 2-2   Students challenge themselves to explore new and creative projects.

Stages of Integration.   Every teacher who participated in the ACOT project was a volunteer, but in no way did every one of the brave participants bring with them experience with technology. Throughout the years of the study, teachers first struggled to incorporate the computer-filled rooms into their established teaching styles, and then watched as, sometimes without even meaning it to happen, the technology incited dramatic changes in their own roles and those of their students. Researchers were able to identify five distinct stages through which teachers new to technology progressed in their pursuit of technology integration (Sandholtz, Ringstaff, & Dwyer, 1997). The stages of entry, adoption, adaptation, appropriation, and invention were arrived at developmentally, after different amounts of time for each individual.

The *entry* stage was one of frequently painful growth. Experienced classroom teachers ran headlong into the very basic challenges that generally plague rookie teachers. In many ways, though, these teachers *were* rookies, standing in front of unfamiliar classrooms filled with unfamiliar machines. Hardware had to be physically set up and plugged in. Students had to be taught the basic operating procedures for the computers. Everyone involved was required learn to live with very different classrooms than those in which they were used to teaching and learning. Teachers had to contend with students experimenting with new cheating techniques, such as copying assignments from someone else's disk; technical problems, which they often had to attempt to solve themselves or risk losing much valuable class time; and the annoyances of surroundings not built specifically for computers, which made the efficient use of the computers a challenge. At this initial stage, teachers found themselves reacting to the small issues and overlooking the larger issues involved with integrating the computers into effective instructional agendas.

Teachers transitioned into the *adoption* stage as they began to take more of a proactive stance toward meeting the challenges presented by the computers. They began teaching students how to use the hardware and software. They developed strategies for dealing with cheating. They initiated policies for making classrooms more livable, such as limiting the time the noisy printers could be running. In general, they were learning from their mistakes and beginning to settle into some tolerable patterns of classroom life, which often meant accepting a level of movement and activity in the classroom that they might not have earlier found acceptable.

In the *adaptation* stage, teachers finally began making the technology work for them. The traditional lecture format perpetuated in classes throughout the study, but productive measurable learning was taking place. Teachers were able to get past issues of teaching the technology and get back to teaching content, using technology as the tool. Teachers also reported that administrative duties, such as record keeping and test creation, were easier and less time-consuming.

As inexperienced as many teachers are when they begin attempting to find a place for technology in their teaching, ACOT researchers found that most teachers eventually do gain the confidence needed to let the new machines become a natural part of life in their classrooms. This happened during the *appropriation* stage. Teachers were able to move past simply accommodating computers and squeezing them into the traditional daily routine and began to personally accept the new teaching possibilities technology offers.

Ultimately, the teachers arrived at the *invention* stage, when they were not only ready, but were eager to break out of typical, teacher-controlled classroom routines. At this stage, teachers communicated with each other a great deal, sharing ideas and innovations, and even bringing together groups of students for authentic, project-based activities. Working with and learning from other teachers and students characterized this changed philosophy of education where technology became the medium for inquiry, collaboration, and constant reflection on what was being accomplished and what was yet attainable.

Changes in Students

As the studies in the ACOT classrooms continued, it became clear that the roles of the students, along with those of the teachers, were indeed changing. When compared with students in traditional classrooms, students participating in the ACOT program were more apt to work together, which made school more interesting, and, consequently, improved students' attitudes about themselves and their learning. Rather than merely fulfilling what was asked of them in assignments, these students surpassed original goals, challenging themselves to explore new and creative projects and often choosing to work during their free time (Sandholtz, Ringstaff, & Dwyer, 1995b). Teachers, in fact, had trouble at times getting students to move on to other projects. Students did not, as was feared at the outset, become solo workers in front of their personal computer screens, but developed and demonstrated the ability to use social interaction to enhance their learning by sharing knowledge and explaining processes as they were undertaken (see Figure 2-3).

Along with those for whom computers facilitated a richer learning experience, teachers also encountered those students who became just as bored with technology as they did with traditional teaching. This was the case when the technology was not used as just one of a selection of classroom tools, but was focused on in an artificial manner. Students worked best when technology was not the topic itself but was integrated into the entire curriculum.

High school students, who had unlimited access to technology during their entire high school career, matured into self-starting problem solvers and self-assured collaborators (Tierney et al., 1995). They were able to verbalize the role computers played in their growth as students, and they saw how the unique abilities they had gained during those four years had empowered them to future success.

FIGURE 2-3   A student creates a story using a word processor.

ACOT Results

Although the ACOT project is merely one research endeavor, with potentially biased commercial beginnings, it provides educators with some long-term goals at which to aim. The lessons learned imply that changes such as those that took place in this case require some specific conditions to be met.

1. Teachers must be ready to make some changes in their teaching beliefs and methodologies in order to give innovations a chance.
2. Technology by itself cannot be expected to revolutionize education, but rather should be seen as one of a collection of tools that might spark and facilitate innovative thinking.
3. An environment of support and sharing will encourage teachers to take risks.
4. Any changes initiated by the introduction of technology to classrooms must be expected to occur over time and with a great deal of dedication and effort (Sandholtz et al., 1997).

ACOT researchers summed up what they learned from this innovative project the following way: "Fundamental instructional changes such as these will have a positive impact on student engagement far more lasting than that of any technological tool in and of itself" (Sandholtz et al., 1995b, p. 30).

Findings from Other Studies

Any researcher would be thrilled to have a testing environment as extensive as an ACOT classroom in which to thoroughly investigate the effect of an extreme amount of technology on teachers and learners. The question that remains is whether the resulting changes are transferable to other, more typical classroom settings. An overview of recent research conducted in non-ACOT classrooms will begin to define the roles of teachers and students in the classrooms of the future.

Computer-Using Teachers and Students

Becker (1994) looked at how "exemplary computer-using teachers" differ from other teachers in the environment in which they teach, their personal computer experience, and their teaching habits. Using information from surveys of third- through twelfth-grade teachers, this study found four main requirements of a school environment in order to make it more conducive to exemplary computer users. First, teachers need to be surrounded by other teachers who use computers. Whether expert or novice, teachers can benefit by the collegial sharing of ideas, resources, and teaching strategies with other computer-using teachers in their building. Next, teachers benefit by working in an school where computers are used for authentic, meaningful purposes, such as for writing for a real audience. Exemplary computer-using teachers are more likely to come from a setting like this than from one in which word processing is only used to accomplish predetermined skills or one where computers are used primarily for games. Another component of the setting that makes for more proficient computer users is financial support for technology at both the school and district levels. Schools where exemplary computer users were found frequently had a school or district computer coordinator who assisted teachers in getting started with technology integration. In addition, these teachers had available to them sufficient staff development opportunities, to instruct them in computer applications and integrating the computer into the content being taught. Finally, the fourth common requirement for the support of expert computer users was a "resource-rich" environment. Teachers often had smaller class sizes and less students per computer. It is unclear whether teachers were able to become exemplary computer users because they had smaller classes or if they were given smaller classes because they were exemplary computer users.

When surveyed about their personal backgrounds, researchers found that these exemplary computer-using teachers, more than other teachers, spent a great deal of their personal time working on computers, staying after school, or bringing computers home. These teachers on the whole also had more training with using computers, higher levels of education, more experience teaching their current subject, and tended to a large degree to be male. In practice, the teachers surveyed who fell into the category of exemplary computer users more often than others made conscious decisions to alter existing curriculum, eliminating less important topics to allow room for more computer-related endeavors. They allowed students some choice in their learning and encouraged teams of students working together on computer assignments. Together, these data imply that both increased personal interest as well as greater amounts of experience, with computers and with general content knowledge, make for a teacher more apt to be successful in computer integration in the classroom.

Becker's finding that the proportion of exemplary computer-using teachers who are male is greater than the male proportion of teachers on the whole might be strengthened by other research results. Whitley (1997) found that boys and men are more likely than girls and women to see themselves as computer users and to see the world of computer use as male-dominated, although behaviors related to computers do not generally vary according to gender. Boys were more concerned with mastery of computer work, and were also felt more relaxed while working with computers, possibly leading them to feel better about their performance of work on the computer. It is believed that differences in how boys and girls perceive their computer competence stem from boys having more opportunities, at home and at school, to use computers (Nelson & Cooper, 1997).

Environmental Requirements for Change

In a study of the perception of the computer's role in schools, both teachers and administrators stressed the need for training to update teachers' knowledge of new technology and its use in education (Yaghi, 1996). They felt that this training should not be limited to specially designated computer teachers, but must be extended to all teachers involved. Respondents with more experience integrating computers into the curriculum saw greater benefits of computers in motivating students and increasing their self-confidence, thus furthering the indicated need for teaching training. A challenge to getting teachers the needed experience is highlighted by responses indicating that many teachers and administrators thought that using technology in the classroom was not really necessary until mandated by district-level authorities.

A study of how the processes of teaching and learning are changing in computer-based classrooms (Swan & Mitrani, 1993) produced some intriguing results. In looking at the actual amount of time spent on educational activities in classrooms with traditional instruction versus classrooms where instruction was presented via the computer, it was initially found that teachers and students interacted slightly less in the computer classrooms than in the traditional classrooms. However, when the time students are interacting with the computers, also considered instructional time, was factored in, it was concluded that students in the computer-based classes spent at least as much time in instruction than did students in the traditional classes. The times that students and teachers interacted were far less often initiated by teachers in the computer-based classes than in the traditional classes, and all activity on the computers was student-initiated. Further, students in the traditional classes learned in whole groups 17 times more often than students in the computer-based classes, suggesting that students learning from computers have a greater opportunity for individualized instruction than in traditional classes. It was thus determined that computer-based environments foster more individualized, student-centered learning than do traditional learning environments. The teachers in these classrooms saw their roles evolve from dominant to supportive of student-centered learning. The authors hypothesize that learning in computer-based classrooms is becoming a three-way partnership between the teacher, the student, and the computer, facilitated by the computer's interactive nature.

Specific Academic Effects

Those involved with educational policy decisions regarding technology issues are frequently concerned with one issue: Do the academic gains brought by the addition of computers into classrooms outweigh the financial expenditures necessary to equip classrooms? Unfortunately, those looking for quick answers will find none. The results from research into the effects of technology on language, math, science, and social studies are mixed. Whereas a large proportion of researchers are able to demonstrate positive academic results, others have shown no effects or even slightly negative impacts on achievement.

Language Arts.   Research into the effects of technology on student achievement in language arts has resulted in widely disparate findings. Jones (1994) found that the quality of writing produced by second-graders on word processors improved over writing they produced using paper and pencil, and, in addition, their stories were longer than those that they wrote by hand. The positive effects of word processors were not limited to the work done on the computer, however. Students who first had experiences writing with the help of word processors showed signs that they maintained a higher level of writing even when they later wrote with paper and pencil. These results may occur because word processors allow students to think about the language they use in composition rather than the physical requirements of handwriting. Generally, attitudes regarding writing may also improve while working on the computer, and students may keep this positive attitude when writing away from the computer (see Figure 2-4).

FIGURE 2-4   Changing teaching and learning behaviors as a
result of the addition of technology in a classroom.

Another study (Nichols, 1996) found few differences between sixth-grade students
who wrote compositions on word processors and students who wrote compositions by hand.
The quality and complexity of compositions, as well as the accuracy of grammar, were comparable between the two groups. The main difference found was in length of writing. Those
students using word processors, provided they had ample keyboarding experience, wrote
significantly longer compositions that those writing with paper and pencil. The authors suppose that this may be a result of students being able to think clearer and easier when using
the word processor.

Dybdahl, Shaw, and Blahous (1997) show that using computers has no conclusive
effects on either the quantity or quality of the writing of fifth-graders. They suggest that the
difference in students' writing abilities will stem from their teachers' beliefs and dedication
toward teaching writing rather than from the decision to use or not to use computers.

In a review of research on the effects of word processing programs on students' writing abilities, Reed (1996) highlights research that shows that writing using word processing
programs improves students' attitudes toward writing, produces longer and more fluent written products, and allows students to revise their writing easier and quicker than with paper
and pencil. Despite this success, Reed points to the potential problem that word processing
programs as they stand are not completely aligned to writing process theory. The programs
offer an open area for drafting compositions, but do not prompt student writers to consider
prewriting thoughts or specific revision activities. Although this low level of writing assistance is beneficial to older and more advanced ability writers, because they tend to already
have in place the writing process habits of prewriting and revision, younger and lower-ability
writers may benefit from using composing software that provides a greater level of writing

guidance, combined with outside, noncomputer writing assistance. Using word processors as one tool in a complete writing program is clearly indicated by these findings.

As well as examining the use of word processors in writing instruction, research has also been done regarding how reading electronic storybooks effects comprehension. Matthew (1997) and Greenlee-Moore and Smith (1996) found that students had higher comprehension scores after reading the electronic texts versus reading printed text. The interactive effects of the sound, animation, narration, and additional definitions that make up the electronic stories motivate students to want to read the stories again and again, something researchers found to occur less often with printed books. Teachers must guide and support students as they learn how to best use the features available in electronic stories. Matthew cautions that the educational potential of these stories is jeopardized when insufficient teacher guidance is given and students lapse into using the programs solely for the entertainment value of the interactive features.

Fitzgerald and Koury (1996) reviewed literature on technology-assisted instruction for students with disabilities. In the areas of composition and reading, the body of literature has shown positive effects from using technology with students with mild and moderate disabilities. Improved comprehension, spelling, and collaborative practices were found. Positive attitudes were promoted in students who used multimedia tools to compose. Current advancements in voice transcription technology do not allow students to compose a piece of writing completely via dictation, but other gains show promise.

Mathematics.   Research into how computers have affected mathematics learning and teaching can be reviewed in the three main areas: programming, computer-assisted instruction (CAI), and tool software (McCoy, 1996). McCoy found that programming, which requires students to actually write computer programs that help develop logic and reasoning proficiency, is the area covered the most in the research. Students from primary to secondary grades who have programming experience score higher on measures of geometry knowledge and problem solving. Unexpectedly, other studies found gains in nonacademic areas, such as creativity and self-concept.

CAI software is related to mathematics generally comprised of drill and practice, tutorial, and simulations. A review of research (McCoy, 1996) found that experimental groups of students from third grade to high school, using fraction software, problem-solving software, and estimation software, scored significantly higher than control groups. Simulation programs that allowed students to actively explore mathematical environments were shown to be effective in helping students understand geometric notions and develop intuitive understandings of graphing. The author cautions that without appropriate teacher guidance, students using these types of software may not fully benefit from the intended experiences.

Finally, students using mathematical tools, such as programs designed to aid in algebra, geometry, and calculus work, were shown to have gained a better understanding of the topic (McCoy, 1996). The tools allowed students to actively participate in mathematical topics that otherwise might be considered stagnant or outdated (Blubaugh, 1995). Students were more motivated and self-confident about subjects like calculus, finding them to be more meaningful than previously thought (Rochowicz, 1996). Students in math courses where computers were used were able to tackle more complex problems without spending time on routine exercises. High school geometry students using problem-solving software as part of their mathematics program scored significantly higher in both problem-solving and general performance areas than students not using the software (Funkhouser, 1993). In addition, students found enjoyment in what they were learning, which motivated them to put more effort into their work. Other studies, however, found no difference between the achievement levels of students using computers in mathematics and those who were not, yet noted improved motivation and participation of the computer users (McCoy, 1996).

Science.   Computers have been used in science classrooms in a variety of ways aimed both at helping students learn scientific facts and at giving them experience with the scientific process. As with other studies of academic achievement, results in the area of science are mixed. In one review of current literature on the topic (Weller, 1996), results span the range from showing that work with computer-assisted instruction packages allowed students to learn more than they would working in only a traditional lab setting, to computer instruction acting as a supplement to traditional instruction, to, finally, computer programs being not more effective than some styles of instruction, such as self-paced.

Simulation software, and the more complex science "microworld" simulations, offer students opportunities to change understanding at the conceptual levels. A number of studies of students in middle grades found that simulations did facilitate change and growth in conceptual understanding. Students were often able to transfer their understanding to written tests, on occasion outperforming students at much higher levels who had not had the benefit of learning with technology. Secondary students learning from simulations were shown to score higher on standardized science tests and to be capable of sharing rich scientific dialogue about the topic of a simulation.

Studies on the effects of other technologies, such as interactive video and microcomputer-based laboratories, where actual data are measured and converted into digital information, and a number of others show similarly variable results (Weller, 1996).

Social Studies.   In a review of recent research involving the effectiveness of computers in social studies (Berson, 1996), drill-and-practice programs were found to be the most prevalent of applications used in social studies education. Use of this type of software was studied primarily with secondary students, and results showed modest gains in recall-type skills and motivation. Simulation programs allowed students to go beyond the basic knowledge level to explore environments to which they might not normally be able to go. Although working with these programs appeared to increase a student's ability to recall facts, as well, students additionally showed improvement in problem solving, curiosity, and personal initiative and control. Willis (1996) concluded after a review of the literature that computerized simulations resulted in students who could communicate better and at higher levels than those who did not use simulations in social studies. Other findings on the use of social studies simulation programs show little or no difference in achievement, and some go so far as to say that the computers proved distracting to students' established learning processes (Berson, 1996). Berson continues his research review by summarizing research on the use of databases in social studies classrooms. He found that databases were encouraging to the development of students' abilities to search for and analyze the extensive collections of current and historical data. Overall, computers allowed students access to information and motivated them to inquire and to learn.

Future Trends

Every indication we have tells us that computers will continue to affect larger portions of our lives as we head into the next century. The research presented in this chapter has shown that educators still do not have a clear picture of how technology impacts teaching and learning processes, yet new challenges are already pushing to the forefront. Every day, new schools are connected to the Internet, which begs the natural question: How will online opportunities improve or impair learning? At this formative stage of the Internet and the World Wide Web, empirical research on how immediate access to information around the world will change education is sparse. Roblyer (1997) has indicated some early trends that might guide our understanding of this new phenomenon. It appears as though teachers, and likely students, will become more proficient and natural users of online resources if they have access at home as well as at school. E-mail has risen to the top of the most used applications, connecting learners and colleagues everywhere. Of course, the teachers who have begun experimenting with online technology are commonly those who typically takes risks in other instructional areas as well. It is hoped that the easy communication possible with e-mail, coupled with continued training and time to practice, might serve to make all teachers eventually feel moved to examine and improve teaching practices. It remains to be seen how these initial trends will play out in the results of future research.

Caveats

Before educators get swept up into this wave of technology, they might do well to take heed of the advice of critics and from lessons learned during research. A growing concern among critics is that the charm of technology might not be so magical after all. Some argue that students become so focused on learning the tricks of the particular software packages that they are prevented from learning what the package is designed to teach (Oppenheimer, 1997). Oppenheimer continues with the equally troublesome goal of fostering group computer work. In reality, only one student is centered in front of the computer screen with control of the mouse at any one time. Other students may or may not be attending and participating in the decision-making process, and depending on the management of the computers in a particular classroom, may or may not get a turn in the "driver's seat" with any regularity. Another concern is the student that may have difficulty learning or even paying attention in a classroom filled with the variety of noises, activity, and distractions common to technology-enhanced rooms (Sandholtz et al., 1995b). What might bring success for some may prove detrimental to the learning of others.

The successful results shown to have come as a result of technology may themselves be suspect because of faulty experimental designs (Becker, 1994; Weller, 1996). Another hypothesis is that students using technology in their learning may show gains in academic achievement simply because more time and effort is devoted to students because of the newness of the medium (Weller, 1996).

A practical problem that could arise is with schools and districts that do find the money to purchase needed technology. The rate of technological advancement is staggering, and in order to provide the best education possible to students, hardware must be maintained, software must be upgraded, and staff must be kept trained in the most current practices. These

FIGURE 2-5   Students often spend more time working to complete projects when working with technology.

issues might prove to be too great of a financial burden for the schools and districts to regularly face. Oppenheimer (1997), directly quoting Jane David, a consultant heavily involved with the ACOT project, says, "There are real dangers in looking to technology to be the savior of education. But it won't survive without the technology" (p. 62). There are clearly no easy answers for schools, so it follows that the best advice would be to consider these potential drawbacks as part of a complete and ongoing decision-making process regarding technology integration.

Conclusions

As each new media type has become available to classrooms, educators, along with the general public, have been quick to jump on the bandwagon, hoping that *this* time, real change in education may be possible. Much of the past research on technology integration has focused on incorporating computers into traditional teaching methods (Berson, 1996) and allowing teachers to do what they normally do, but faster (O'Neil, 1995). Educators are discovering that it is no longer enough to merely place a computer into a classroom and say that students are "using" technology. It is the way computers are used rather than the actual machines themselves that contribute to learning (Proctor & Burnett, 1996; Roblyer, 1996). Researchers are beginning to look more at how technology might change basic teaching and learning processes, moving away from simply investigating whether students have higher test scores with computer-based instruction (Roblyer, 1996). The questions now focus on whether it is the technology itself that is making these changes or if it is instead the unique ways the technology is used in each teaching and learning situation that make the differences.

Because teachers generally do not have a say in district-level hardware and software purchasing decisions, it falls to them to determine how to best utilize what is available in the classroom. With thoughtful planning by trained educators, computers might be integrated into the curriculum effectively (Waxman & Huang, 1996). Taking cues from current research findings will inform teachers and allow them to change long-held attitudes about how they should teach and their students might learn. Educators need to discover the role technology plays in learning, the new roles to which teachers may need to adjust, and how this all will be managed in schools already overwhelmed with financial, social, and educational demands (Clark & Salmon, 1986).

The interaction between the technology and the users is actually beginning to be seen as a conversation that is different with every user in every situation (Kozma, 1994). This idea presents difficulties for neat, convenient research. More qualitative, ethnographic-type studies are called for, but the dilemma is brought up that no easy, all-encompassing answer is available to apply to every situation (Roblyer, 1996).

The issue with research is one of timing. Research cannot keep up with the rapid evolution of new technology. Teachers, who generally are on the forefront of innovative methods, often do not write their findings so that others can learn from their insight (Willis, 1996). The novelty of computers and the physical adaptations that must be made to classrooms to incorporate the computers into the physical space is often what proves to teachers that other ways are not only possible, but frequently better (Ringstaff et al., 1995a, p. 35). Computers force teachers to look more closely at individual students and their needs rather than addressing the class as a whole with one blanket method or technique. Learning can then become driven by student needs rather than by teacher or curriculum requirements. It is with this constant experimenting, striving to help each learner find his or her best learning techniques, coupled with an awareness of the research that academics and practitioners alike are conducting, that teachers will indeed bring about positive change in the nature of teaching and learning.

Summary

With growing societal pressure to meet the goals of a technological future, educators are making a prominent place for technology in schools. To prepare for the changes technology will inevitably make in teaching and learning practices, teachers must remain aware of the current educational research findings in the area. How teachers perceive the benefits and barriers new technology presents to education will directly impact practical day-to-day integration.

Apple Classrooms of Tomorrow (ACOT), an innovative research project designed to investigate the effects of regular, convenient access to technology over an extended time period, gives each student and teacher a computer to use at school and another to use at home. Although researchers found that the technology was initially used to accomplish traditional tasks, this extreme level of technology integration ultimately produced noticeable changes in both teaching and learning. Teachers began to recognize expertise in students, to shift away from traditional classroom space utilization, and to discover the benefits of good collegial communication. As the study progressed through the years, teachers advanced through similar stages of familiarity with and reliance on technology in their jobs. ACOT research indicates that teachers need to be ready to change and take risks over the time it will take to fully incorporate technology as a teaching and learning tool.

Students displayed better attitudes toward school and more willingness to work together. Although using computers was not the best learning plan for each and every student, overall increased exposure to technology leads to more developed problem-solving abilities and greater skill at working collaboratively.

Other studies about the effects of technology in education reveal trends about teachers and environments necessary for successful integration. Teachers who are considered exemplary computer users appear to share, among other qualities, a greater interest and level of experience with both computers and with their own subject areas. They tend to work in supportive environments where colleagues also use computers frequently for innovative and authentic purposes. It is a widely held belief that teachers need continued training to increase their motivation to use technology and their confidence in their ability to make technology a meaningful part of their educational plan.

In classrooms where technology is used, students initiated communication more often and have more opportunity for individualized instruction than in other classrooms. Teaching roles change to allow for student-centered learning. Effects on specific academic areas, like language arts, math, science, and social studies, are mixed. The indication is that continued research in these areas will help to isolate the effects of technology from those of other instruction improvements. Educators will be challenged to look for ways to integrate technology for new uses, to address individual learning needs rather than simply using new technology in old ways.

LEARNER ACTIVITIES

1. Watch both the local and national newspapers and popular news magazines over a month's time for news on educational technology. What are the current issues? How is research on technology's effectiveness being portrayed to the public?

2. Visit a local school and observe the level and amount of technology available. What is the school or district plan for integration? What evidence do you see of its progress?

3. Interview a teacher who has incorporated technology to some extent into his or her instructional plan. According to the teacher, what challenges have been faced?

4. Research technology's effectiveness in your intended area of specialty.

5. Make a list of how teaching in a classroom like ACOT will be different or similar than the education you had growing up. How will it change daily classroom activities?

6. How might universities and other teacher preparation programs better ready future teachers to take advantage of the technology they will surely have in their classrooms? How are

strategies that will be used to introduce technology to students similar to those that can be used to familiarize teachers?

7. Write a note to the parents of your future students explaining your philosophy of technology integration.

8. How would you convince a colleague to utilize computer technology in his or her teaching repertoire?

9. What are your predictions for the future of technology use in education? Will schools always attempt to emulate the degree of technology integration that society achieves?

10. Play the devil's advocate role. Compose a brief argument against the purchase and use of computers in schools.

BIBLIOGRAPHY

Apple classrooms of tomorrow. (1995). *Changing the conversation about teaching learning and technology: A report on ten years of ACOT research.* [Brochure]. Cupertino, CA: Apple Computer.

Becker, H. J. (1994). How exemplary computer-using teachers differ from other teachers: Implications for realizing the potential of computers in schools. *Journal of Research on Computing in Education, 26,* 291–321.

Berson, M. J. (1996). Effectiveness of computer technology in the social studies: A review of the literature. *Journal of Research on Computing in Education, 28,* 486–501.

Blubaugh, W. L. (1995). Use of software to improve the teaching of geometry. *Mathematics and Computer Education, 29,* 288–293.

Clark, R. E., & Salomon, G. (1986). Media in teaching. In M. C. Wittrock (Ed.), *Third handbook of research on teaching* (pp. 464–478). New York: MacMillan.

David, J. L. (1995). Partnerships for change. In *Apple education research reports* (pp. 45–46). Eugene, OR: International Society for Technology in Education.

Dybdahl, C. S., Shaw, D. G., & Blahous, E. (1997). The impact of the computer on writing: No simple answers. *Computers in the Schools, 13*(3/4), 41–53.

Fitzgerald, G. E., & Koury, K. A. (1996). Empirical advances in technology: Assisted instruction for students with mild and moderate disabilities. *Journal of Research on Computing in Education, 28,* 526–551.

Funkhouser, C. (1993). The influence of problem-solving software on student attitudes about mathematics. *Journal of Research on Computing in Education, 225,* 339–346.

Greenlee-Moore, M. E., & Smith, L. L. (1996). Interactive computer software: The effects on young children's reading achievement. *Reading Psychology, 17*(1), 43–64.

Jones, I. (1994). The effect of a word processor on the written composition of second-grade pupils. *Computers in the Schools, 11,* 43–54.

Kozma, R. B. (1994). Will media influence learning? Reframing the debate? *Educational Technology Research and Development, 42*(2), 7–19.

Matthew, K. (1997). A comparison of the influence of interactive CD-ROM storybooks and traditional print storybooks on reading comprehension. *Journal of Research on Computing in Education, 29,* 263–275.

McCoy, L. P. (1996). Computer-based mathematics learning. *Journal of Research on Computing in Education, 28,* 438–460.

Nelson, L. J., & Cooper, J. (1997). Gender differences in children's reactions to success and failure with computers. *Computers in Human Behavior, 13,* 247–267.

Nichols, L. M. (1996). Pencil and paper versus word processing: A comparative study of creative writing in the elementary school. *Journal of Research on Computing in Education, 29,* 159–166.

O'Neil, J. (1995, October). On technology and schools: A conversation with Chris Dede. *Educational Leadership, 6–12.*

Oppenheimer, T. (1997, July). The computer delusion. *The Atlantic Monthly, 280,* 45–62.

Proctor, R. M., & Burnett, R. C. (1996). Computer attitude and classroom computers. *Computers in the Schools, 12*(3), 33–41.

Reed, W. M. (1996). Assessing the impact of computer-based writing instruction. *Journal of Research on Computing in Education, 28,* 418–437.

Ringstaff, C., Sandholtz, J. H., & Dwyer, D. C. (1995). Trading places: When teachers utilize student expertise in technology-intensive classrooms. In *Apple education research reports* (pp. 35–37). Eugene, OR: International Society for Technology in Education.

Roblyer, M. D. (1996). The constructivist/objectivist debate: Implications for instructional technology research. *Learning and Leading with Technology, 24*(2), 12–16.

Roblyer, M. D. (1997). Predictions and realities: The impact of the Internet on K–12 education. *Learning and Leading with Technology, 25*(1), 54–56.

Rochowicz, J. A., Jr. (1996). The impact of using computers and calculators on calculus instruction: Various perceptions. *Journal of Computers in Mathematics and Science Teaching, 15,* 423–435.

Sandholtz, J. H., Ringstaff, C., & Dwyer, D. C. (1995a). The relationship between technological innovation and collegial interaction. In *Apple education research reports* (pp. 37–38). Eugene, OR: International Society for Technology in Education.

Sandholtz, J. H., Ringstaff, C., & Dwyer, D. C. (1995b). Student engagement revisited: Views from technology-rich classrooms. In *Apple education research reports* (pp. 29–30). Eugene, OR: International Society for Technology in Education.

Sandholtz, J. H., Ringstaff, C., & Dwyer, D. C. (1997). *Teaching with technology: Creating student-centered classrooms.* New York: Teachers College Press.

Stuebing, S., Celsi, J. G., & Cousineau, L. K. (1995). Environments that support new modes of learning. In *Apple education research reports* (pp. 27–28). Eugene, OR: International Society for Technology in Education.

Swan, K., & Mitrani, M. (1993). The changing nature of teaching and learning in computer-based classrooms. *Journal of Research on Computing in Education, 26,* 40–54.

Tierney, R. J., Kieffer, R., Stowell, L., Desai, L. E., Whalin, K., & Moss, A. G. (1995). Computer acquisition: A longitudinal study of the influence of high computer access on students' thinking, learning, and interactions. In *Apple education research reports* (pp. 31–32). Eugene, OR: International Society for Technology in Education.

U.S. Department of Education. (1996). Getting America's students ready for the twenty-first century: Meeting the technology literacy challenge. [Online]. Available: <www.ed.gov/TechnologyPlan/NatTechPlan/title.html>

Waxman, H. C., & Huang, S. L. (1996). Classroom instruction differences by level of technology use in middle school mathematics. *Journal of Educational Computing Research, 14,* 157–169.

Weller, H. G. (1996). Assessing the impact of computer-based learning in science. *Journal of Research on Computing in Education, 28,* 461–485.

Whitley, B. E., Jr. (1997). Gender differences in computer-related attitudes and behavior: A meta-analysis. *Computers in Human Behavior, 13,* 1–22.

Willis, E. M. (1996). Where in the world? Technology in social studies learning. *Learning and Leading with Technology, 23*(5), 7–9.

Yaghi, H. (1996). The role of the computer in the school as perceived by computer using teachers and school administrators. *Journal of Educational Computing Research, 15,* 137–155.

3 Electronic Messaging

FOCUS QUESTIONS

1. What basic e-mail skills are transferable among various software programs?
2. How can e-mail be used to enhance communication in educational communities?
3. What privacy issues must be considered when communicating electronically?

Professional isolation is an unfortunate hallmark of teaching. Traditional school practices require teachers to work alone with their own groups of students, inside the four walls of their classrooms, with little contact among colleagues on any given day. The technology that has the most potential to bridge physical distances between teachers and learners and to provide a method for collegial collaboration is electronic messaging. As easy as it is to learn to use, e-mail can quickly be mastered even by novice computer users. With a little awareness of the privacy issues that could affect its use, e-mail can successfully be used for planning and instruction among teachers, students, and experts worldwide.

Electronic-Mail Fundamentals

Electronic mail, commonly known as e-mail, is a way of sending paperless "letters" from one computer user to another. With a few keystrokes and a few seconds, messages can be sent and received, allowing for nearly immediate written communication. The concept of e-mail is often compared to the familiar traditional mail to better understand its similarities and differences. For instance, an e-mail message must be sent to a unique address, and the recipient "opens" his or her mail once it has arrived in a "mailbox." The similarities end there, however. The speed and ease with which messages can be sent and organized using e-mail software truly separate this communication medium from anything seen previously. A number of e-mail software packages are currently available, but once the basic procedures of sending, replying, forwarding, and organizing messages are mastered, they can be easily transferred for use in any e-mail program.

Sending a Message

To mail someone a regular message, you must first write the message on a piece of paper, put it in an envelope labeled with the person's full address, add a stamp, and drop the letter into a mailbox for the Postal Service to deliver. To send a message electronically, you must follow very similar steps.

Using an e-mail software program, you first choose to compose a message. Messages are written in the form of a business memo. The *header,* a collection of pertinent information at the beginning of a message, opens with the recipient's address.

Everyone who has an e-mail account has a unique e-mail address that allows mail to be sent directly to that address, either to a desktop computer or to a server account that the recipient may access remotely. An e-mail address has two parts that are separated by the @ sign, which essentially represents a particular person at a particular location. An address begins with a person's name or user ID, often a shortened version of a name, such as the first initial and the last name (see Figure 3-1). Following the @ sign is the domain name, which identifies the server that houses the person's e-mail account and may consist of a number of subdomain names. Finally, the address is ended with an extension identifying the type of organization sponsoring the account, such as *edu* for an educational organization and *gov* for a government account. All components of the domain name of an e-mail address are separated by periods, and there are no spaces in the entire address. Some e-mail systems use addresses that are case-sensitive, meaning that a capital letter in an address means something very different than a lowercase letter, whereas case makes no difference at all with other systems. With traditional mail, if one of the parts of an address is left off the envelope, it is possible that some diligent postal employee might track down the recipient. Unfortunately, electronic messages require all of the components of an address to be present. A message

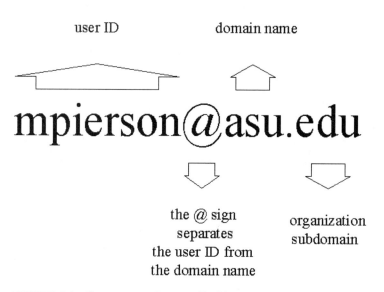

FIGURE 3-1 Components of an e-mail address.

sent to an incorrect or incomplete address almost surely will not reach the person for whom it was intended, but instead will be returned to the sender as "undeliverable mail" or lost forever in cyberspace.

Since accuracy is so critical, it is helpful to use an e-mail program's capability of saving addresses to an *address book.* Generally, you can save the e-mail address of a person to whom you frequently write under a simpler nickname, so that instead of remembering a long, multidomained address, you can type a nickname, and the address of the person will automatically be inserted.

Completing the header information, the sender can list other addresses of people who should be sent copies of the message, usually marked *CC* for "carbon copy." Other files, such as word processing documents or spreadsheet worksheets, can be sent along with an e-mail message. In the *attachment* line, the desired file is identified or linked to the message according to the procedures of the e-mail program. Finally, a brief *subject* can be listed, giving the recipient some idea of what the message contains. The subject is not required to be completed in order for the message to be sent, but it is a courtesy to the person reading the messages to not have to guess at a message's content.

Composing is essentially the same as using a word processor, as errors can be easily corrected and text can be manipulated to some degree. Most programs come with spell-checkers to proofread messages for accuracy, and some allow text to be formatted, such as boldfacing or changing the font. E-mail conventions do not demand strict adherence to formal letter writing rules.

One distinct advantage that e-mail holds over traditional mail is the ability to easily send identical messages to more than one person. By simply adding the additional addresses to the header, the message is sent out to all parties listed. If you find that you frequently send messages to the same group of people, you can make a *distribution list* of the addressees so they will not need to be inputted each time. The distribution list can be given a name, and from then on, only the name has to be entered into the address line in the header to send the message to the entire list.

Responding to a Message

When you log-in to your e-mail account, the first thing you will want to do is check your *mailbox,* also called an *inbox,* to see if you have any messages. Although the procedures vary slightly with each program, the messages can generally be viewed in a list form with the date the message was sent, the name or e-mail address of the sender, and the subject line. New messages that have not yet been "opened" are marked as such so they can be easily distinguished from messages you have already read. Clicking on the message line will bring up the complete text of the message. After reading the message, a decision can be made as to what to do next.

If after the message is read it is determined that it requires an answer, you can send a *reply.* When you choose to reply, you can usually choose whether to include a copy of the original message along with your response, to remind the sender what was said, or you can simply send the answer by itself. The header is supplied automatically with the recipient's return address already listed, and the subject line usually includes a prefix of *RE:* indicating to the recipient that this message is a reply to the earlier message.

Sometimes a message you receive might be of interest to another party. In this case, you can *forward* an exact copy of the message to that other person. When you choose to forward a message, a new header appears with a blank address line. You supply the address of the person to whom the message will be forwarded. The subject line contains the original subject with the addition of a *fwd* affix, indicating to the recipient that this message has been forwarded.

Whether a message has been replied to or forwarded, two more options remain. If the message is important, it can be saved. Saved messages can be organized into folders, like other computer files, so that they will be easy to retrieve at a later date. A message can also be saved by just leaving it where it is in the inbox, where it can stay until it is removed. If a message is no longer needed, the inbox can be cleaned out by *deleting* the message. When you choose to delete, the program prompts you to confirm this is the action you want to take. If it is, the message is removed to a "trash can." Of course, as with a real letter that is thrown away in a trash can, if you change your mind, you can usually rescue a deleted message by taking it out of the trash can, provided you have not yet closed the e-mail program.

Advanced Features of E-Mail Software Applications

The e-mail software packages available today range from the very basic to those with the "bells and whistles" found in high-end software tools, although the end product, an electronic message, is virtually the same. New programs rapidly appear on the market, each bringing new and improved features to e-mail users. The best advice is to investigate the program to which you will have access to make yourself familiar with the options available to you.

One of the earliest e-mail programs is PINE (Program for Internet News and Mail). It offers very basic features in a text-based, or command-driven, environment (see Figure 3-2). This means that in order to send or respond to a message, a user must input the commands using the keyboard, rather than with the mouse. The program contains an address book, a spellchecker, and the ability to organize messages into folders. Because PINE is available free from the University of Washington, many universities use it as their main e-mail package.

Most Internet browser programs (see Chapter 4) offer an e-mail component to give their users a more complete communications package. Netscape Communicator, for instance, contains Messenger Mailbox, which presents a graphical interface to the user (see Figure 3-3). Icons, or pictures, show whether messages are new or have already been read and give navigational clues to perform standard e-mail functions. High-priority messages can be marked with a *flag* as they are sent, so that the recipient is aware of messages that should be answered right away. The text of a message is easier to manipulate in the graphical programs such as Netscape, because you can highlight and drag text just like in a word processor. The advantage to using an e-mail program that is part of your Internet browser is that you can check for new messages while you are already online using the Internet. URLs, or Internet addresses, sent within an e-mail message are hotlinked to take the user directly to that website with just a click.

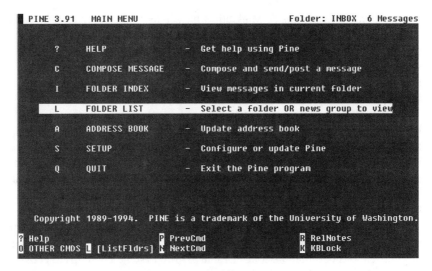

FIGURE 3-2 The main menu of PINE e-mail application.

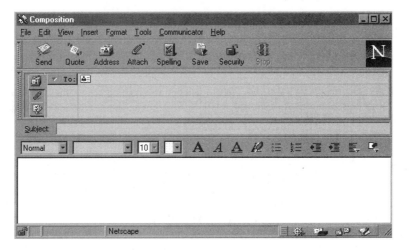

FIGURE 3-3 Composing a message in Netscape Communicator's Messenger Mailbox. *(Copyright 1998 Netscape Communications Corp. Used with permission. All Rights Reserved. This electronic file or page may not be reprinted or copied without the express written permission of Netscape)*

Microsoft Internet Mail, the e-mail component of Internet Explorer, allows the user to customize the interface, or what the user sees on the screen, to fit the individual's purposes. An "inbox assistant" lets you organize your messages even before you receive them. For instance, if you get quite a few messages from a listserv to which you subscribe, you may want to have those messages automatically sorted into a separate folder so you can go through them at your leisure without having them get in the way of your other messages.

Other programs, like Lotus cc:Mail, allow the sender to easily attach files, such as spreadsheets or graphic files. As programs continue to evolve, new models for the navigation and organization of mail will appear, as well as multimedia capabilities that include audio and video e-mail options. Fancy features aside, though, whichever e-mail program you will have access to will always be able to perform the basic functions of sending, replying, forwarding, and saving.

E-mail sent between people using the same software application often works with the least problems, but most programs are now able to cooperate with each other through electronic gateways, or bridges, between systems. Occasionally, you may notice some cryptic lines at the beginning of an incoming message from another system, identifying the minor alterations that were necessary to make the message readable under your e-mail software. These alterations generally do not change the body of the message in any way, and so can be ignored.

As you become more familiar with e-mail programs and more comfortable communicating through this medium, you will start to pick up on some of the standard practices and conventions of e-mail discourse. Table 3-1 offers some good tips to get you started.

TABLE 3-1   Good E-Mail Habits

- Check your e-mail regularly. Once people know you have e-mail, they will start using it and expect you to do the same.

- Include a subject line so the person who is receiving your message can quickly prioritize the messages in his or her inbox.

- Use all capital letters sparingly, only when what you are saying is extremely important. When an e-mail message written in all capital letters is read, it appears as though the sender is "SHOUTING!"

- Read your messages before you send them. Spelling and grammatical errors make a message seem poorly written and can reflect on your intelligence.

- Give yourself time to calm down before responding to a controversial or inflammatory message. Sometimes the written message does not appear on screen the way it sounded in your head. Virginia Shea, author of *Netiquette* (1994), suggests asking yourself whether you would say to the person's face what you have written in the message. If not, you should rewrite it until you are sure it is acceptable. Once you send a message, it cannot be retrieved, and once it arrives at another person's inbox, it is out of your control and can be easily forwarded on to others you may not have intended to see it.

- Use sarcasm with caution, and preferably with people who have personally met you or are familiar with your sense of humor. Facial gestures that help give meaning to a sarcastic remark made in person do not transmit through e-mail, and sarcastic words alone could easily be misinterpreted.

- Remove the previous headings from messages that have been forwarded several times so your recipient does not have to scroll through a lot of useless text trying to find the message.

- If you are replying to just the sender of a message from a listserv or distribution list, be sure to choose the option to reply to the sender only. Others on the list will appreciate the courtesy of not cluttering their inbox with personal messages intended for other people.

Listservs

Once you have an e-mail account and are comfortable with the basic e-mail procedures, you might want to try participating in a *listserv*. A listserv is like a giant conversation among many people with a common interest. The ongoing dialogue that listservs facilitate keep teachers in touch with the most current educational issues. When you subscribe to a listserv, your e-mail address is added to the list of members. Any time a message is sent to the list address, a copy of the message is sent to every e-mail address on the list.

Joining a Listserv

Subscribing procedures vary slightly with each list, but generally you send a regular e-mail message to the address of the list manager, who may be a person who moderates the list screening messages to see if they are relevant to the list topic, or may be a computer that automatically distributes an identical copy of every sent message to every member. In your request, leave the subject line blank and in the body of the message, type:

subscribe listname firstname lastname

Since you are most likely "talking" to a computer, your instructions must be exact or they might not be interpreted correctly and you will not be subscribed. Most listservs will send you a confirmation message asking you to reply within a certain time frame confirming that you do want to be a member of that list. Once you have subscribed, expect to start receiving messages, sometimes quite a few messages, every day. The level of participation in the discussions will vary depending on the topic of the list and the individuals involved. Listserv members have the option to be active participants, contributing opinions and advice to the list regularly, or to remain passive observers, or "lurkers," who read all messages without actually sending a message. Any level of participation with which a person is comfortable is acceptable on a listserv. Keep in mind, however, that the information and viewpoints presented on the listserv come from other members of the list. These people are not necessarily experts in the field and may or may not be relaying accurate facts.

Many lists have rules, both formal and informal, for participating. As a courtesy to those who have already subscribed, participate in the list at first in a silent mode. Watch for the "code of conduct" that is accepted and for the type of information and comments that are typical. Pay attention to the tone of the messages. Regular listserv members are often intolerant of newcomers who do not play by the rules, and they may *flame* you, or send you a message that in no uncertain terms lets you know what part of your message was not welcome.

When you are ready to participate in the list, just send a message to the list address. This address should have been given to you in the information sent when you subscribed. Note that it is not the same address as the list manager's address to whom you subscribed. Try subscribing to a listserv for a while. If you find the topic or tone of the discussion is not quite what you had expected, you can take yourself off the list at any time. Again, the procedures for unsubscribing vary by list, but for most lists, you send a message to the list manager with the word *unsubscribe* substituted into the body of the original subscribe message.

Be very sure not to send this message to your list address or everyone on the list will receive it. There is not anything the list members can do to take your name off the list, although they may want to by that time!

Conversations for Everyone

Lists are available for every conceivable interest area, from professional or personal. Public lists cover topics from medicine and politics to religion and recreation and allow anyone with an e-mail address to subscribe. Private lists restrict membership to just certain groups, like particular college graduating classes or groups that use the list to stay in touch between annual meetings. Performing an Internet search (see Chapter 4) on "listservs" will yield a staggering array of lists that might be of interest. A more defined search can be done at websites like the Liszt site (<www.liszt.com>, see Figure 3-4). Table 3-2 provides a selection of general education and subject-specific listservs that might be of professional interest to educators.

The Issue of Privacy

Mail tampering is a federal offense. Barring any unforeseen natural disasters or lawbreakers, we feel safe that our mail will arrive to its intended receiver unmolested. Once that letter is in the hands of that person, he or she owns it and can throw it away or save it, thus ending the story of the letter. Not so with an electronic message. An e-mail message is not the sole property of the person who sent it or the person who received it, and, in fact, if it is sent from a school, which is a public institution, it may even be considered to be public information (Descy, 1997). Just because you send your message to one person's e-mail address, it is possible for any of a number of people to read your supposedly confidential message. Building

FIGURE 3-4   Liszt's search website on available listservs.

TABLE 3-2   General Education and Subject-Specific Listservs

Under each list description is the listname in capital letters followed by the e-mail address of the list manager.

General Education	Subject Area
Educational Software Discussion CSOFT-L listserv@wuvmd.wustl.edu	Computer Applications in Science and Education APPL-L listserv@vm.cc.torun.edu.pl
Educational Administration Discussion ADMIN listproc@bgu.edu	American String Teachers Association List ASTA-L listserv@cmsuvmb.cmsu.edu
Media and Technology in Education AMTEC mailserv@camosun.bc.ca	Biology and Education Discussion BIOPI-L listserv@ksuvm.ksu.edu
Discussion of Computers in Teaching CTI-L listserv@irlearn.ucd.ie	Special Education Discussion CHATBACK listserv@sjuvm.stjohns.edu
Early Childhood Education (8–9 years) ECENET-L listserv@postoffice.cso.uiuc.edu	Creative Writing for Teachers and Students CREWRT-L listserv@missou1.missouri.edu
Updates from the U.S. Department of Education EDINFO listproc@inet.ed.gov	Center for the Study of Reading CSRNOT-L listserv@uiucvmd.bitnet
Legal Issues in Education EDLAW listserv@ukcc.uky.edu	Foreign Language Teaching Forum FLTEACH listserv@ubvm.cc.buffalo.edu
Education Policy Discussion EDPOL listproc@wais.com	Teaching Social Studies in Secondary Schools H-HIGH-S listserv@msu.edu
National Science Foundation Grants List GRANTS-L listserv@onondaga.bitnet	High School Journalism HSJOURN listserv@vm.cc.latech.edu
Collaborative Learning Project Ideas List IDEAS_LIST listserv@acme.fred.org	International Society for Education Through Art INSEA-L listserv@unbvm1.csd.unb.ca
Using the Internet in the Classroom INCLASS listproc@schoolnet.carleton.ca	Technology in Mathematics Education MATHEDCC listserv@vm1.mcgill.ca
Integrating Technology in the Schools ITS listserv@unm.edu	Minds-On/Hands-On Science Teaching MINDSON-NET majordomo@igc.apc.org
Educators K–12 Discussion KIDSPHERE kidsphere@vms.cis.pitt.edu	Music Education Discussion MUSIC-ED listserv@artsedge.kennedy-center.org

(continued)

TABLE 3-2 Continued

General Education	Subject Area
Support and Information for K-12 Teachers LRN-ED listserv@suvm.syr.edu	National Council of Teachers of Mathematics NCTM-L listproc@sci-ed.fit.edu
Discussion of Middle School–Aged Children MIDDLE-L listserv@postoffice.cso.uiuc.edu	Teaching Science in Elementary Schools List T321-L listserv@mizzou1.missouri.edu
Multicultural Education Discussion MULTC-ED listserv@umdd.umd.edu	Talented and Gifted Education Discussion TAG-L listserv@vm1.nodak.edu
Teaching Whole Language Discussion TAWL listserv@listserv.arizona.edu	Teaching English as a Second Language TESL-L listserv@cunyvm.bitnet
Ideas, Research, and Questions about Teaching TEACHNET listserv@byu.edu	Vocational Education Discussion VOCNET listserv@cmsa.berkeley.edu

administrators, district network supervisors, even people operating computers through which your message passes on its way to its final destination, all may have access to your message. Unlike the laws that govern tampering with traditional mail, it is perfectly legal to monitor the content of your e-mail messages. Even messages that have been deleted from the receiver's account can be recovered if necessary because the files on server computers are regularly saved on backup files. The advice e-mail users should heed is to be very cautious about writing anything in an e-mail message that you would not want other people to see. If you hear a rumor that your principal is peeking into people's messages, believe that it is indeed possible! When instructing even young students how to use e-mail, the issue of privacy must be discussed. Once they click on *send,* the message is out of their control.

Implications for Education

With access to e-mail in their classrooms, teachers have the opportunity to communicate with colleagues at their school, educators at other schools, parents, administrators, and educational contacts worldwide. The ease and immediacy of e-mail can have an enormous impact on the sharing of ideas, the making of requests, and the completion of other daily communication, both educational and managerial. E-mail allows teachers to be more productive and time-efficient, leaving more time that can be spent working for and with students. It cuts down on the stacks of papers teachers find in their box at the end of the day. Meetings can now be organized through e-mail, mailing out the plans to several people at once. Consensus on decisions between a group of teachers can be made without even dragging the plastic school chairs together to sit down. The opinions and contributions of even shy participants can be given equal weight in the final decision. Some schools are now sending attendance in via e-mail, making it possible to very quickly identify students who

FIGURE 3-5 Students communicating through e-mail.

are absent. Parents with e-mail access can contact a teacher with a question without having to wait until after school to call. Because e-mail is asynchronous, meaning that the messages do not have to be answered the moment they are received, teachers can respond at their convenience.

Students, too, can make use of e-mail. Some schools have set up accounts for each of their students, and others allow students to e-mail using their teacher's account. The possibilities for e-mail to support and inspire educational inquiry are virtually endless. Activities such as the following demonstrate the authentic uses of technology in the classroom.

■ Classes can participate in telementoring projects that connect experts in every conceivable field of knowledge to students in classrooms everywhere, all through e-mail. The Electronic Emissary Project out of the University of Texas at Austin was begun in 1993 (Harris, O'Bryan & Rotenberg, 1996) and acts as matchmaker between students and experts. The teachers, students, and experts work as a team to design projects that are goal-oriented and curriculum-based, with the teachers and students sharing their work with and looking for guidance from the experts. This program utilizes online facilitators that serve as liaison between the classes and the experts, bridging the gaps between the ages of participants and the different environments. Students in such relationships with real-life mentors gain not only content-oriented knowledge, but authentic communication skills, career encouragement, and motivation to learn.

■ Much of the collaboration needed for projects with students in other classes can be accomplished via e-mail messages. Students can interact with other students from other grades without having to leave their classrooms and walk around campus by themselves. Writing can be sent through e-mail by one student, modified by a student at the other end, and sent back for a continuous cooperative effort. Older students might even submit complete assignments and receive teacher feedback entirely electronically, all without using a single sheet of paper (Dowden & Humphries, 1997). Teachers having assignments turned in this way have less paperwork and an accurate documentation of when assignments were received.

Classroom Vignette

The classroom door is pushed open and the hot, sweaty fifth-graders pile inside after lunch recess. Ms. Beckwith calls out to the class as she stands at the door talking to a student, "Let's continue where we left off before lunch. If you need to check your e-mail, you may wait at the computers." One or two still-chattering students have already plopped down at each of the four computers in the room,

"I probably won't have an answer yet from Mr. Carter because I just sent my message this morning," Rebecca says to Lindsay as she confidently clicks her way into the e-mail program and her own inbox. "Sometimes he doesn't check his mail until the afternoons because he has so many meetings."

As she says this, she sees the one, lone message sitting in her mailbox, the envelope icon still unopened. "He did write!" she exclaims, and quickly opens the message from Mr. Carter, their class Emissary match. Mr. Carter is a state senator and he is working with students in Ms. Beckwith's class to understand the election process and to help them to plan their own mock campaigns. Rebecca had asked him just that morning whether he got nervous during speeches, since she had one scheduled in front of another class for the next day, and she is starting to get butterflies in her stomach.

In his brief e-mail reply, Mr. Carter says that he does, in fact, still feel nervous right before he has to speak in public, but that it usually goes away after he sees the audience become interested in what he has to say. He gives her a couple of ideas that always work for him so she can rehearse that night. Rebecca immediately clicks on the reply button and thanks him for the advice, promising to let him know how it goes after the speech the next day.

On the next computer, Antonio and Blake have just read the latest installment of their cooperative e-mail story and are discussing what twist the plot should take next. The two take turns with students in four other classes, two of which are not even at their school, adding a paragraph or two each time to a continuing story. When they are finished with each installment, they forward the updated story on to the next group. So far, the two fictional boys in the story entitled, "Escape from the Jungle" have made their way down a mountain, dodging gold smugglers and enemy aircraft in the process, only to find out that they forgot their walkie-talkies back by the bridge.

Antonio's eyes light up. "I know! They could hike back up the mountain, but come up to the bridge by a different trail, just in time to see some gorillas trying to eat their walkie-talkies!"

"Yeah!" agrees Blake, "But maybe the gorillas are really spies undercover!" The boys type in what they have come up with, make a few minor modifications, and send the story on its way to the next authors.

As they finish, Ms. Beckwith looks up from the groups of students she is working with. "Boys, could you send an e-mail to Mrs. Dillon to ask if we can schedule a time to use the art room to paint our campaign signs? I didn't see her at lunch today."

- Students in classes across the country and around the world can be "key pals," the electronic version of pen pals. Even young students are able to work on writing skills in a fun, meaningful activity, without the problems of deciphering developing handwriting or even paying for postage. Students learn that they have to use conventional spelling in order for their key pals to be able to understand their message. Key pals can serve as cultural guides to their part of the state or country or world, exchanging pictures and brochures, and making faceless parts on the globe come alive. Because electronic messages are communicated through text, students with different racial, ethnic, or religious backgrounds can learn to meet the person inside rather than perpetuating any stereotypes about outside appearances. Thinking critically about the circumstances of lives in other places or cultures helps students to identify and better understand what they believe to be important in their own lives (Rice, 1996). Key-pal programs can be set up privately between two teachers, or teachers can apply for key pals for their students through teaching magazines or even listservs such as KIDINTRO (subscribe to *<listserv@sjuvm.stjohns.edu>*).

Summary

E-mail has the potential to provide for regular and quick communication among all members of the educational community. Those new to using e-mail will quickly notice some similarities to the concept of traditional mail, such as the need to address a message with a person's unique location, but the speed and ease of sending electronic messages soon becomes apparent. All software programs allow for the basic operations necessary to compose, open, respond to, and save electronic messages. Higher-end software allows for more control over a user's mail management, such as graphical icons, direct links to the World Wide Web for URLs included as part of a message, and automatic mail sorting according to categories.

By joining a listserv, you can use e-mail to participate in ongoing conversations with people on an unlimited array of topics. Once you have subscribed by sending an appropriate message to the list manager, you will begin receiving copies of all messages sent to the list. You can either sit back and read passively or actively participate by sending your own contributions. Attention to the implicit and explicit rules of the list community will make the experience productive and pleasant for you and for other list members.

Educators should remain aware of and make sure their students are aware of the privacy issues related to the use of electronic messages. With thoughtful use, e-mail can provide a forum for quality collaborative work among students, teachers, colleagues, and the resource-rich community outside the walls of the school.

LEARNER ACTIVITIES

1. Experiment with two different e-mail packages. Compare features and evaluate the effectiveness of each.

2. Address an e-mail message *incorrectly* and send it. What happens?

3. Find a listserv of either a professional or personal interest. Join and watch the messages passively for several weeks, or until you feel comfortable to contribute a message of your own.

4. Research contacts for student key pals. Are there many organizations or individuals that exist to set up such relationships? Are there key pals available for all ages of students?

5. Begin an address book of professional colleagues, student family members, and community contacts.

6. Brainstorm a list of all the ways electronic communication can facilitate quality learning.

7. Research current privacy laws governing electronic communications. How often does your school or university back up e-mail files?

8. Write a lesson plan that incorporates the use of e-mail for the level student you plan to teach. What special help might they need to be successful? To what extent will e-mail be a part of your comprehensive educational plan?

9. Organize a virtual meeting between professional colleagues entirely through e-mail. Include sending out an agenda, encouraging discussion on the topics, summarizing key points, and providing a summary of conclusions reached. Then solicit reaction from those involved as to how e-mail might contribute to or detract from decision-making processes.

10. Find addresses of educational experts or community leaders in newspapers or journals. Send an e-mail message with a comment or a concern to several people and compare the response rates between different professions of people. Do those in the educational community tend to respond more readily? Are there any similarities among those from whom you never heard back?

BIBLIOGRAPHY

Abilock, D. (1996). Integrating e-mail into the curriculum. *Technology Connection, 3*(5), 23–25.

Besnard, C. (1996). Students' empowerment: E-mail exchange and the development of writing skills. *Mosaic, 3*(2), 8–12.

Descy, D. E. (1997). The Internet and education: Some lessons on privacy and pitfalls. *Educational Technology, 37*(3), 48–52.

Dowden, R., & Humphries, S. (1997). Using e-mail in computer assisted freshman composition and rhetoric. *T.H.E. Journal, 24,* 74–75.

Ekhaml, L. (1996). Making the most of e-mail: How to be concise, courteous, and correct online. *Technology Connection, 2*(10), 18–19.

Fargen, T. (1996). Surfing the Internet in gym class: Physical education e-mail keypals. *Teaching and Change, 3,* 272–280.

Hackett, L. (1996). The Internet and e-mail: Useful tools for foreign language teaching and learning. *On-Call, 10*(1), 15–20.

Hamilton, M. C. (1996). The trouble with e-mail. *CUPA Journal, 47*(2), 1–5.

Harris, J., O'Bryan, E., & Rotenberg, L. (1996). It's a simple idea, but it's not easy to do! Practical lessons in telementoring. *Learning and Leading with Technology, 24*(2), 53–57.

Rice, C. D. (1996). Bring intercultural encounters into classrooms: IECC electronic mailing lists. *T.H.E. Journal, 23*(6), 60–63.

Rogers, F. (1996). E-mail to the neighborhood. *TECHNOS, 5*(4), 33–36.

Scott, J. (1996). Creating your own Internet projects with e-mail. *School Library Media Activities Monthly, 12*(9), 43–48.

Shea, V. (1994). *Netiquette.* San Francisco: Albion.

4 Feeling at Home on the Internet

FOCUS QUESTIONS

1. How does the hypertext structure of the World Wide Web facilitate nonlinear, dynamic access to information?

2. What search strategies make it easier to find exactly what you are looking for on the World Wide Web?

3. How can you keep your students safe while they explore the Internet?

From its humble beginnings as a government experiment to provide connections among military and research institutions that were transparent, yet impenetrable enough to withstand a nuclear attack, the Internet has grown to be an incomprehensibly strong and far-reaching information network that bonds computers virtually everywhere. Someone sitting at one computer screen can travel to any computer that is connected to the Internet in mere seconds. The dynamic nature of the Internet, however, implies a future of continual growth beyond even what can be imagined today. Even with the understanding that the Internet may yet be in its developmental infancy, educators cannot ignore the limitless resources available from the worldwide community. They must become familiar with its basic operation in order to make the most of its benefit to students. This chapter gives an introduction to what the Internet is and how it is structured, and later chapters in this book invite educators to explore resources available online and to participate in designing their own web-based instruction.

In its most simplistic form, the Internet can be seen as a network of networks. Two or more computers linked together by wires and having the capability of communicating, or sharing information, form the base unit of a network. Most offices and many schools have found that by linking all of their computers together to form a *local-area network* (LAN), they can increase communication and thus increase efficiency. These LANs connected to other LANs connected to yet other LANs make up the basic structure of the Internet. But the Internet is more than just the physical wires and machines. It is also comprised of the resources available through these connections. Information on any topic, no matter how specialized or obscure, can be found somewhere on some computer connected to the Internet, and clearly these pieces of information are made possible by the people who create them. It is people who choose to make connections to others. It is people who place information online for others to access. Finally, it is people who make decisions on how to use the resources available to them. The Internet, then, can be really seen as a partnership among physical, informational, and human elements.

In the true spirit of this partnership, and as a key feature of the original military design, there exists no central Internet entity. There is no "home" computer at which all of the wires ultimately converge; instead, each host computer shares equally the authority and the responsibility for successful connections. Because of this, the network is perpetually strong, able to bypass any wires or machines that are not functioning by routing information in other directions. The Internet also lacks a main receptacle of knowledge and information. Its users both provide and draw from the vast selection of resources that make the Internet dynamic and rich with substance. Finally, there is no presiding human authority in charge of maintaining the Internet. It is a cooperative environment, with its participants governing themselves for the most part. The Internet Society (ISOC) is a nonprofit organization of volunteers that tasks itself with the responsibility of guiding the technical and practical growth of the Internet. Members of the ISOC make recommendations regarding what protocols will be necessary to support communication with new technology and also organize and assign unique addresses to Internet host computers. Other than these "housekeeping" functions, the ISOC does nothing to regulate, rate, or otherwise rule on the kinds of information that bounces throughout the world connections. The absence of a central overseer leads to quite an excess of duplicated, poor-quality, and even objectionable material that can be accessed online, but it also has created a democratic environment, for the people and by the people, the likes of which the world has never seen.

Unfortunately, for simplicity's sake, computers around the world are not all manufactured by the same company or with the same speed and capabilities, so there exists a need for a consistent way that they all can communicate. The Internet allows for standard communication by operating according to standard rules, or *protocols*. Every bit of information that is sent through the Internet must be broken down into manageable pieces, or *packets*, that can fit through the phones lines that are used to connect. These packets must conform to the *Transmission Control Protocol/Internet Protocol*, or TCP/IP. By formatting messages according to this protocol, any computer with the ability to connect to the Internet will have the ability to receive and reassemble the packets, resulting in a complete message. It is in this way that the Internet is able to be platform-independent.

The World Wide Web

There are a number of "entrances" onto the mighty network of networks known as the Internet. One is through e-mail, as was discussed in Chapter 3. Another, which is quickly becoming the most popular way to locate many types of information, is through the World Wide Web (WWW).

Hypertext

The web is an attractive, graphically arranged, nonlinear way to access information available on the Internet. The key to navigating through the World Wide Web is *hypertext*. The prefix *hyper* means "above" or "beyond" and *text* refers to words on a web *page*, which is the basic unit of the web structure. Hypertext, then, is the word or words that when clicked on, present some information beyond the word itself. In today's increasingly multimedia-enhanced web environment, that information might be audio or video, but the most frequent use of hypertext is to *link* one web page with another. By clicking on a word identified as hypertext, usually underlined and of a different color than other text, you can jump to another page of information. You might even be taken to a completely different *website.* A website is a collection of a number of web pages at one address location introduced or organized by a *homepage.* The *hyperlinks,* or hypertext that links to other pages, allow you to immediately see additional information on just exactly what you choose, rather than having to page through irrelevant information as you might need to in a reference book. It is exactly this freedom to explore documents in a three-dimensional way that gives the web its appeal.

The Purpose of Web Browsers

In keeping with the goal of consistent accessibility of the Internet, documents on the World Wide Web are accessible to any computer that has *browser* software. Browsers do two things that allow you to see World Wide Web documents. First, the software seeks out and retrieves a document requested by clicking on a hyperlink or by entering a web address, called a *Universal Resource Locator* (URL). A URL is similar to an e-mail address in that it identifies the specific location of the requested document by computer-domain designations separated by periods. The address does not include a person's log-on name followed by the @ sign, as in an e-mail address, but instead may identify a particular document name at the end of the address (see Figure 4-1). Additionally, a URL must begin with *http://,* which shows that this document follows the *hypertext transfer protocol,* or the specific rules that are set up for transferring documents in the World Wide Web environment.

The second thing a browser does is to allow you to see the document you have requested. Documents on the web must be written in *hypertext mark-up language* (HTML), which is a coded language that gives the directions necessary for documents to have specific layouts, including graphics and formatted text (see Chapter 8 for more information on

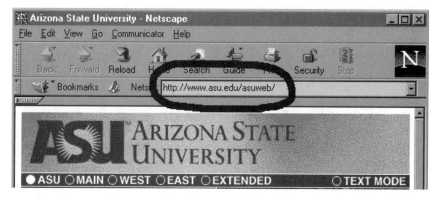

FIGURE 4-1 The hypertext transfer protocol prefix and URL displayed in Netscape. *(Copyright 1998 Netscape Communications Corp. Used with permission. All Rights Reserved. This electronic file or page may not be reprinted or copied without the express written permission of Netscape)*

creating HTML documents). HTML allows any document on the web to be viewed by any computer that has a browser. The browser interprets the HTML code in which the page has been tagged and displays the page on your computer screen as the person who wrote the page intended (see Figures 4-2 and 4-3).

How to Use a Web Browser

When the browser software is launched, it first shows the website that has been identified as its homepage, or starting point. This starting page can be changed to be any website, but often is the homepage of the school where the computer is located or can even be someone's personal homepage. From here, there are two main ways a browser helps you to see World Wide Web documents: simple browsing, or "surfing," and going directly to a website.

Surfing is quite simple and intuitive. From that very first website you see, you can begin surfing by simply clicking with the mouse on any of the hyperlinks. You will notice that when your pointer is poised over a hyperlink, the arrow changes into a pointing hand, indicating that this is indeed an active link. Clicking on that link points your browser to the location of the requested document, and once found, the document is loaded so that you can see it. When you "arrive" at that next site, you can read the information there, click on another link, or go back to the page you just left by clicking on the **Back** button. The browser remembers where you have been, so that even when you have wandered from site to site,

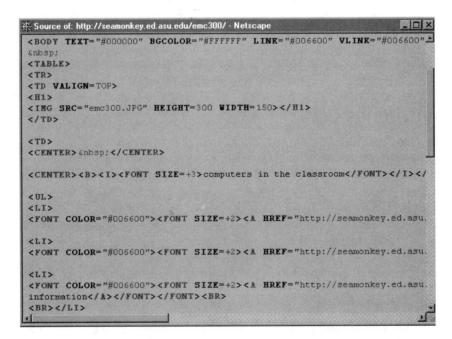

FIGURE 4-2   A portion of the source document for a web page. *(Copyright 1998 Netscape Communications Corp. Used with permission. All Rights Reserved. This electronic file or page may not be reprinted or copied without the express written permission of Netscape)*

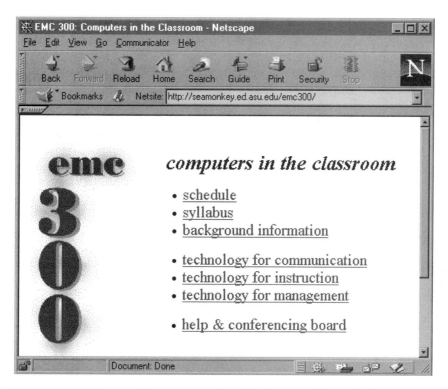

FIGURE 4-3   The same document as rendered in a browser. *(Copyright 1998 Netscape Communications Corp. Used with permission. All Rights Reserved. This electronic file or page may not be reprinted or copied without the express written permission of Netscape)*

you can always step back until you arrive back to where you started. If you want to go back to a particular site you have seen, rather than stepping back page by page, select the name of the site from the **Go** pull-down menu. If you would like to start again from the beginning, click on the **Home** button to take you back to your home site. Browsing is best when you are not exactly sure what you are looking for because you can take the time to slowly investigate all of the related links. If you do know where you want to be, you will probably want to go directly there.

    If you have the URL for the site you wish to visit, you can click on the **Open** button and type it into the window, or you can just type it directly into the **Location** text box and then press **Enter.** If the address is correct and the site is still current, you will be taken directly to it. If you have mistyped the URL, or if the site is no longer being maintained by its operator, you will be taken to a page that says that you have requested an invalid address. If this happens, check the address you typed to see if you made a mistake.

    To avoid having to continually input the long address to a favorite site you visit frequently, you can click on **Bookmarks** and **Add** to add a bookmark at that site, thus saving the URL. The next time you want to go to that site, click on **Bookmarks** again, and just choose the name of the site you want to automatically go there.

Searching the World Wide Web

Sometimes you do not have the URL for the website you need, and surfing from link to link would be too time-consuming and haphazard of a way to find it. In this case, you will want to perform a web search. There are essentially two approaches to searching for information on the Internet (Pierson, 1997). The first is to use a hierarchical subject directory, like *Yahoo,* which first shows a list of very general subjects. Choosing from these subjects will narrow the search until actual web-page links are given. Be prepared to spend some time looking through the threads of topics to find what you want since the directory designers may have a different idea of the organization of information than you do. A subject directory is handy if you want quick, general information.

The other, more directed, approach to finding information on the Internet is to use a search engine, such as the currently popular Excite, Lycos, AltaVista, or HotBot. Clicking on the search button in your web browser should take you to a site with links to all of the largest engines, or look at Table 4-1 for the URLs to take you directly to the engine websites.

Search engines are actually enormous indexes of information locations that have been amassed by computer programs designed to automatically go out and find these sources. Search engine sites allow you to input keywords, or *search strings,* to guide the search of the indexes. All of the available search engines vary according to size, speed, options, and how documents are actually indexed. Some engines, for example, search for terms only on the headers or page titles, whereas others thoroughly inspect the entire page text for the requested keywords.

Searching Strategies

Once you have located a search engine site, the best thing to do is to check the help section available on all sites for search tips specific to that engine. Being aware of an engine's features will help you to perform more efficient searches. With the constant updates and improvements being made to each engine, however, it is nearly impossible to be an expert on every feature of every engine. It makes good sense, then, to become familiar with general properties and basic search strategies common to most search engines. Table 4-2 describes some helpful search tips and gives examples of the search strings you would enter into the

TABLE 4-1   World Wide Web Search Engines

AltaVista	\<www.altavista.com>
Excite	\<www.excite.com>
HotBot	\<www.hotbot.com>
Infoseek	\<www.infoseek.com>
Lycos	\<www.lycos.com>
Magellan	\<www.mckinley.com>
NetGuide Live	\<ms.netguide.com>
WebCrawler	\<www.webcrawler.com>
Yahoo!	\<www.yahoo.com>

TABLE 4-2   World Wide Web Search Strategies

Search for the singular form of a term. This search will give you both *convertible* and *convertibles*.	**convertible**
Enter all of the spellings you think might apply for a given term, separating each by a space.	**Hanukkah Hanukah Chanukah**
Enclose a phrase in double quotes, otherwise the engine will find every occurrence of each individual word.	**"Grand Canyon"**
Be as precise as possible. Entering a common word, such as "book" would give you far too many useless sites. Include the word in a specific phrase to help narrow the search.	**"antique book dealer"**
Require that a term must be contained in every document by preceding it directly with a + sign.	**+mineral**
Prohibit a term, meaning that no documents found will contain it, by preceding it with a – sign.	**–music**
Require some terms and prohibit others within one search string. This example will give you documents about rocks that are minerals, but will not include anything about rock music or rock bands.	**"rock" +mineral –music –band**
Use wildcard characters at the end of a phrase to substitute for several missing letters. AltaVista, for example, uses the asterisk (*) as a wildcard character. This search will give you *vegetable, vegetarian, vegetation,* etc.	**vege***
Use Boolean operators AND, OR, AND NOT, and NEAR to narrow searches.	
• Use AND to find documents containing more than one term occurring together.	**scholarship AND loan**
• Use OR to specify one term or the other found separately.	**Kansas OR Illinois**
• Use AND NOT to exclude a term from the search.	**farming AND NOT wheat**
• Use NEAR to find documents that contain two terms in close proximity to each other, usually within 10 words.	**"United Nations" NEAR Bosnia**
Combine Boolean operators and phrases into logical groupings with parentheses.	**(African OR Asian) AND elephant**

search engine. Figure 4-4 shows the results of a simple query using one popular search engine. There is no one best search engine that will serve your needs every time. For the best results, enter the term you want into several different search engines to ensure a complete and well-rounded search.

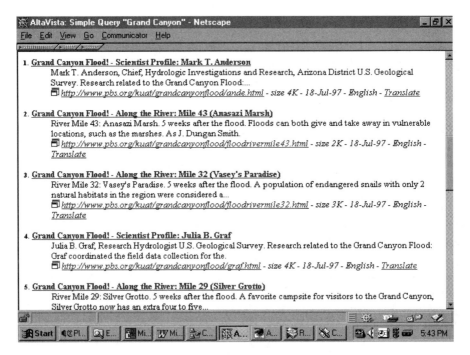

FIGURE 4-4 Results from using the Alta Vista search engine to search for the string "Grand Canyon." *(Digital, Alta Vista, and the Alta Vista logo are trademarks or service marks of Digital Equipment Corporation. Used with permission.) (Copyright 1998 Netscape Communications Corp. Used with permission. All Rights Reserved. This electronic file or page may not be reprinted or copied without the express written permission of Netscape)*

In the ever-evolving search engine market, there are now available specialized search engines that allow you to focus your search on documents related to very specific topics (Vaughan-Nichols, 1997). A list of the most current specialized engines, such as ones that locate health-related sites or information on buying and selling cars, to name a couple, can be found by clicking on the search button on your browser.

Other Internet Services

In addition to presenting hypertext web documents, browsers also offer easy access to resources available through the older, text-based services. Access to services like transferring files, logging on to systems remotely, and reading news are so seamless that you might not even realize you have left the World Wide Web.

File Transfer Protocol (FTP)

If you want to send or receive an entire file, such as a database or graphics file, you will want to use *File Transfer Protocol* (FTP). FTP is the set of Internet rules governing the sending of files from one computer to another. You can use FTP through the World Wide Web, to *download files,* or copy them to your system from another remote system. You can also use an FTP program, such as WS-FTP for Windows and Fetch for Macintosh (see Figures 4-5 and 4-6).

The software window on either program prompts you to log in and give your password to gain access to files on the remote system. Some systems allow you to use FTP anonymously by giving the word "anonymous" for your log-in name and your e-mail address as your password, if you do not have an account on that system. This will give you access to the archives of files that the institution has made available to the public. FTP also lets you *upload* files from your computer to a computer on another system.

Telnet

Another way of accessing remote systems is through *Telnet,* which is yet another Internet protocol. Rather than just letting you download files like FTP, Telnet actually lets you log-in to other systems, using programs they have, searching databases, such as library holdings, or even checking e-mail from remote locations. Some versions of Telnet come preloaded as part of Windows or Macintosh operating systems, and others are available for free download at numerous websites. Telnet can also be accessed through most web browsers by typing in *telnet://*

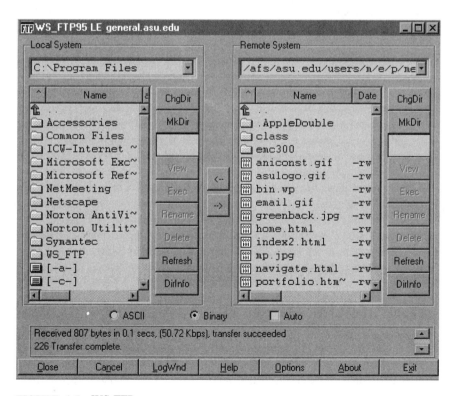

FIGURE 4-5 WS-FTP.

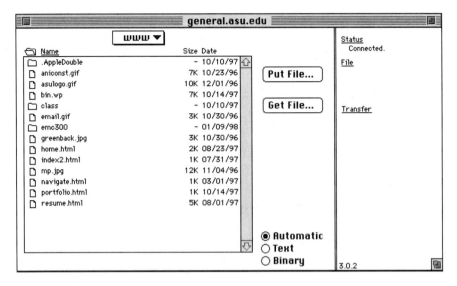

FIGURE 4-6   Fetch.

followed by the host computer name in the location text box. As with other communication applications, an online connection must already established in order to use Telnet to connect to remote locations.

Newsgroups

Newsgroups, like listservs (see Chapter 3), are a way to discuss timely issues related to a topic of your choice with other people who share similar interests. The difference with newsgroups is that the messages are not automatically distributed to each member's e-mail account, but rather "posted" on something like an electronic bulletin board for others to see at their leisure. You can look at messages only, or choose to post a reply for all to see. Most browser software also includes a news-reader component that allows you to choose which newsgroups you wish to peruse on a regular basis. When you enter a newsgroup, you will see the messages listed by subject, the name of the author, and the length of the message in lines. These messages are arranged in threads, with replies to particular messages listed underneath the originals so you can follow the line of dialogue. You can click through the messages, reading only the ones that interest you and skipping the others.

Privacy and Security

Because the Internet has become a true community of people, it faces some of the same serious issues that plague real communities. Just as people put up fences around their yards and alarm their cars to protect their families from outside harm, so will they also need to take care to protect themselves from potential privacy invasions and other dangers lurking within the Internet society.

Privacy

Even though you may be sitting by yourself at your home computer, if you are exploring the Internet, many people may know exactly who you are and what you are doing. Some of the information they find out about you is given by you voluntarily, when you fill out an online registration form, such as to receive complimentary software. This personal information is often sold to marketing companies, who will probably begin sending you piles of junk e-mail. To keep your information from being sold, inspect online registration forms carefully to see if they have a policy of not selling the information that they receive. If you do not see any type of disclaimer, you might want to resist divulging your personal data.

Other information can be collected from you without your even knowing about it. Websites are able to detect what type of computer you are using, what browser software you have, and what other sites you have recently visited, all from your browser (Mann, 1997). After some sites get this information, they are happy to leave your computer with a little treat, called a *cookie*. Cookies are pieces of text that a website you visit actually stores on your computer. The next time you visit that location, the site requests the cookie from your hard drive, getting the information on who you are and the specifics on the business you might have done with them in the past. Although there are instances when it is helpful to have particular sites know who you are, like when a frequently visited site can customize the path it presents to you to fit your particular interests. It may be a little unsettling, however, that this information exchange is being done right under your nose without you even smelling it. All of these privacy issues can be dealt with by using a variety of software tools, available online or commercially. The first step to understanding the potential privacy invasions is being aware that you are not alone out there.

Security

Because the Internet operates in an essentially unregulated arena, material that is objectionable or inappropriate to students can be stumbled upon. Parents and educators alike will need to make proactive choices to ensure that the computer world is a protected place to explore. Supervision is unquestionably the best way to know what students are coming across on the Internet. Additionally, Internet "filtering" software gives varying amounts of control over the sites students can access. The software can be programmed to keep students from venturing to sites with certain objectionable words in their titles and some can keep track of what sites have been visited. Even as these programs progress in their sophistication, none of them is designed to be a substitute for watchful, responsible adult supervision while children are using the computer. The frequency with which new and potentially dangerous sites are added to the Internet makes that goal a practical impossibility. Instead, this software is meant to provide some convenient safeguards to keep students safe in their pursuit of information on the Internet.

Classroom Vignette

Norman Richards has faced the unique challenges of teaching the middle school grades for over 22 years. He is an expert in his content area. He knows how to keep students motivated and inspired. He even makes an effort to keep informed of current trends and practices of today's young adult culture. All in all, he feels that he does a good job in his teaching responsibilities.

He learned today that one of his top students, Chad, has been diagnosed with a rare brain disorder. It is operable, but the surgery is going to be postponed until the Winter Break so that Chad can finish the semester. Norman recalls the worried look on the face of Chad's mother as she explained the situation to him this afternoon. It would be a struggle for her to keep her spirits up, as well as those of her son.

This disease was unknown to Norman, and Chad's mother had very little information from the doctor. The teacher wanted to be sure he was doing what he could to help Chad get through these last few weeks successfully. On his way back to his classroom after the last hour's class, he had stopped by the school media center to see if they had any information on the disease. The media specialist, Sue Jaffries, could find nothing that they had actually on campus; it was apparently a little known, and fairly recently discovered ailment. She recommended that he do a search on the Internet to see if he could find some recent information.

As he walked through the door of his classroom, he glanced at the "computer corner," boasting of one dust-covered Macintosh computer. He had used it a few times, and he had some basic computer skills from his machine at home, on which he kept his personal finances. Students typed reports on the word processor occasionally, but other than that, he had not incorporated computer technology into either his teaching or his planning. Within the last year, he vaguely remembered some technicians coming in after school hours to install some wires, and he heard that every classroom was now connected to the Internet. There had been a couple of in-service training sessions on computer integration, but he had skipped them in favor of getting other work finished. A colleague had chided him for missing the training and had said, "Hey, if you ever decide to join the Information Age, just click on Netscape and you'll figure it out!" Well, no time like the present, thought Norman, and he flipped on the power strip and wiped the dust off the screen.

When he had logged on to his account, he found the Netscape icon and hesitantly double-clicked on it. An unfamiliar screen opened up, and he took a few minutes to study it. He saw a selection of buttons, like **Back** and **Home,** as well as a menu bar at the top that looked pretty much like the one he had seen in word processing programs: **File, Edit, Help,** etc. In the center part of the screen, he saw a white background with his district's familiar logo, as well as a list of topics, like "District Mission Statement" and "List of Schools." He poked around experimentally for several minutes, learning that clicking on the blue words took him to other pages, and that the **Back** button at the top brought him back to the first page.

Intrigued, and actually finding out things he didn't even know about his own district, he remembered what his goal was today. Sue had mentioned that he needed to do a "search," and he took a chance on clicking the button that was labeled, "Search." After several seconds, he was shown a screen that said "AltaVista," and after a few minutes of examining the screen, he tentatively typed the name of the disease into the text box and began his first Internet search.

By the time he looked at his watch, it was 6:30 p.m., and he had been surfing the Internet for almost three hours! He had discovered a couple of references to the disease from which Chad suffered, as well as a whole host of other topics that had attempted to distract him from his mission. From what he had seen so far, there indeed appeared to be plenty of information available on the Internet, but he was not sure he was going about finding it in the right way. He came across countless pages that had nothing to do with what he was looking for, even though he had typed in the right term. He made a mental note to ask Sue tomorrow for some advice on searching. He hoped to find some information to share with Chad's mother, and he also had his curiosity piqued as to what kind of educational resources he might be able to locate. He closed out of Netscape, logged off the computer, and stood up and stretched, inspired after having survived this first trip into the online world.

Summary

The Internet is essentially a large network linking together all of the smaller networks that connect computers around the world. The physical wires that form the Internet carry information composed by and for people. There is no central authority that governs Internet activity or operation, nor is there a central information repository. The spirit of the Internet requires its users to monitor the quality of their own contributions to the collective information whole.

The World Wide Web offers nonlinear access to information through hypertext links. Web browsers allow you to travel to other sites either by clicking on a hyperlink or by inputting a Universal Resource Locator. The browser then displays the requested document as the page designer intended it to look.

You can search for sites on specific information by using a search engine, a web application that indexes websites and allows you to search for information by inputting keywords. A number of strategies let you narrow your search to more efficiently find what you are looking for.

Other Internet applications let you transfer files (FTP), access another computer remotely (Telnet), and discuss topical issues with others (Newsgroups). All online activity should be undertaken with the understanding that it is not entirely secure or private. With the open community inspired by the Internet, some available material may be inappropriate for some audiences. Being aware of such issues will help educators constantly seek ways in which to allow students to safely explore the Internet.

LEARNER ACTIVITIES

1. Open a web browser application, such as Netscape, and familiarize yourself with its components. Where can a URL be inputted? What kind of information can you get by passing the mouse arrow over a hypertext link?

2. Beginning at your home website, follow a path of hypertext links that interest you. How far away from your home site did you venture?

3. Refer to the URLs given for the popular search engines given in this chapters. Enter a very general keyword in a search engine of your choice. Using the strategies described in this chapter, along with any noted in the search engine's help section, continue to narrow your search. How many modifications to your search string did it take until you were satisfied with your search results?

4. Choose one keyword string that interests you and enter it into at least three different search engines. How do the search results compare? What types of information would you have missed by only using one engine? What opinions are you forming about the features that define a good engine?

5. Add a bookmark for each site you find that interests you during your searches. For the browser you are using, determine the method for saving bookmarks, and save your bookmarks to a file. Import this file into the browser on another computer to use for future searching.

6. Find out what Telnet and FTP applications your school's system uses, and learn how to operate them.

7. Search for a remote computer location that has software for free download. Follow the directions on the site to download a program to your computer.

8. After exploring the World Wide Web for a period of several weeks, check to see if any "cookies" have been left on your hard drive by any of the websites you have visited. Set the **Preferences** on your browser to notify you if any site wishes to place a cookie on your system, and keep track of how often you are alerted. Try visiting a site without giving it permission to place a cookie and then go back again after accepting the cookie. Do you notice any differences in the information you see there?

9. Draft an acceptable use policy that schools could adopt to protect students during their Internet exploration. Search for online information on how other schools are handling acceptable use issues.

10. Review an Internet filtering application. Test it thoroughly to see what types of objectionable material it intercepts and what is allowed to pass through its screens. Does the software live up to its claims of safety?

BIBLIOGRAPHY

Anderson, B. (1996). The Internet: Trends and directions. *Behavioral & Social Sciences Librarian, 15,* 59–64.

Bjorner, S. (1997). Day tripping to Internet world. *Searcher, 5*(2), 50–61.

Bogyo, J. (1997). So you want to use the Internet in the elementary school. *Technology Connection, 4*(2), 10–12.

Brandt, D. S. (1997). What flavor is your Internet search engine? *Computers in Libraries, 17*(1), 47–50.

Carroll, R. (1997). Documentation of electronic sources. *Business Education Forum, 5*(4), 7–10.

Collis, B. (1996). The Internet as an educational innovation: Lessons from experience with computer implementation. *Educational Technology, 36*(6), 21–30.

Cowan, G. (1996). How the web works. *Social Education, 60,* 113.

DeZelar-Tiedman, C. (1997). Known-item searching on the World Wide Web. *Internet Reference Services Quarterly, 2,* 5–14.

Falk, H. (1997). World Wide Web search and retrieval. *Electronic Library, 15*(1), 49–55.

Hill, J. A., & Misic, M. M. (1996). Why you should establish a connection to the Internet. *TechTrends, 41*(2), 10–16.

Kafai, Y., & Bates, M. J. (1997). Internet web-searching instruction in the elementary classroom: Building a foundation for information literacy. *School Library Media Quarterly, 25,* 103–111.

Laverty, C. Y. C. (1996). Internet primer: Workshop design and objectives. *Internet Reference Services Quarterly, 1*(3), 35–53.

Lindroth, L. (1997). Internet connections. *Teaching PreK–8, 27*(5), 68–69.

Mann, B. (1977, April). Stopping you watching me. *Internet World, 6,* 42–44.

Mondowney, J. G. (1996). Licensed to learn: Drivers' training for the Internet. *School Library Journal, 42,* 32–34.

Pierson, M. E. (1997). The honeymoon is over: Leading the way to lasting search habits. *Technology Connection, 4*(4), 10–12, 25.

Reed, J. (1995). Learning and the Internet: A gentle introduction for K–12 educators. *Distance Educator, 1,* 2, 8–11.

Sanchez, R. (1996). Students on the Internet: Can you ensure appropriate access? *School Administrator, 53*(4), 18–22.

Simpson, C. (1996). Full speed ahead on the Internet. *Book Report, 15*(2), 3, 5–7, 9–11, 13–14.

Tobiason, K. (1997). Tailoring the Internet to primary classrooms. *Technology Connection, 4*(2), 8–9.

Truett, C., Allan, S., Tashner, J., & Lowe, K. (1997). Responsible Internet use. *Learning and Leading with Technology, 24*(6), 52–55.

Vaughan-Nichols, S. J. (1997, June). Find it faster. *Internet World, 8,* 64–66.

5 Educational Software Types

FOCUS QUESTIONS

1. What are the defining characteristics of each type of software?
2. Why are the software types not the only thing teachers have to consider?
3. How can educational software be effectively integrated into an established curriculum?

Understanding the Categories

When schools allocate funds to bring technology into classrooms, one of the next purchases that quickly follows the hardware buys are those of educational software. Each piece of software, in its own unique way, allows a computer to help students learn specific things. Some software is designed to be used with large groups of students aided by much teacher involvement, and others are best used with small groups or individuals interacting directly with the computer. One of the most difficult challenges teachers face is meeting the individual needs of all students. With a varied assortment of educational software at hand, teachers are able to individualize instruction to enrich or remediate as is necessary for student success.

To understand how software might best be integrated into an established academic curriculum, it helps to be aware of the different types of software that are available. This chapter defines and illustrates some of the commonly referred categories. In order to be an effective facilitator of software use in the classroom, however, it is not necessary for teachers to discern exact differences among the categories; in fact, most of the descriptors of the categories overlap and most software titles can be easily classified in a number of different software categories. In an attempt to provide full-service educational solutions, newer software includes components of most of the different software types compiled together in one integrated learning environment (see Figure 5-1). Distinctions can be further blurred by the different terms used in the software industry to describe very similar categories. Use the alphabetical listing of software types in this chapter as a guide to understanding the terms that are used when discussing software, but do not misunderstand this to be a definitive list of all that is possible in software. Most of the software titles that are featured in Classroom Vignettes could also be classified in other categories, but they are used here to illustrate spe-

FIGURE 5-1 Bug Explorers by Compton's NewMedia combines a number of different software-type components to create one integrated learning environment. (*Courtesy of Compton*)

cific characteristics of each type. Many of the software titles highlighted in this chapter are reviewed on the Only the Best CD-ROM that accompanies this book.

Drill-and-Practice Software

Category Description

In general, drill-and-practice software allows learners to come in contact with facts, relationships, problems, and vocabulary that they have previously learned until the material is committed to memory or until a particular skill has been refined. The best drill-and-practice software possesses an interesting format that encourages repeated use by students, thus establishing the stimulus-response association required for memorization of certain facts. Sequential learning tasks and immediate feedback assist the student in the mastery of the skill.

Drill-and-practice programs are written in a range of sophistication. Simpler programs offer students the same type of practice they might receive using flashcards. Students receive a series of items, answer each one in order, and receive feedback based on how they responded. If students receive a mastery score on the selection, they move on to the next harder set of problems.

More advanced drill-and-practice programs attempt to serve each student with questions that are at the appropriate level of difficulty. A program might begin with some sort of a pretest in order to place a student at a proper beginning location. As the student answers questions correctly, the program automatically branches to more difficult subject matter, and students answering incorrectly are quickly brought to material at a lower level. This adaptive design allows students to work as closely to their own developmental level as possible so that they are constantly challenged to perform tasks that are not too frustratingly simple or complex.

Quality drill-and-practice programs utilize brief, effective feedback for both correct and incorrect responses, either giving students another chance for incorrect answers or giving positive, motivating reinforcement for correct responses. Students should be able to control the rate of the program, taking as long as they need to answer a question. They should also have the ability to quit the program at any time and resume at the place they left off when they return.

Practical Integration

Critics of classroom computer use often aim the brunt of their skeptical comments toward drill-and-practice software. Many of the early drill-and-practice programs were known as "drill and kill" because they presented the same isolated skills in the same way to every user, creating boring, impersonal learning environments. Because drill-and-practice were the first type of educational software brought into regular use by teachers, it was often used as a learning device rather than as a practice device by teachers unfamiliar with the potential of the media. As educational philosophy steers away from behaviorist principles toward more constructivist views of students making their own meaning, the practical use of all educational software must follow suit.

Drill-and-practice software is ideal when students need to practice discrete skills. The electronic mode can be more motivating than a paper-and-pencil counterpart, and the feedback to student responses is immediate. It can be used repeatedly without the need for teachers to grade papers or keep direct track of progress.

Drill and practice is usually thought of for aiding math skills because the largely unambiguous nature of basic math facts lends itself to the right or wrong format. It can also be effective in the area of vocabulary development. For example, the computer displays a definition, and the student types in the appropriate word. This process can be repeated until the associations between words and their definitions are complete. The association method can also take advantage of gamelike formats, contextual clues, rhymes, and riddles.

Students learning foreign languages or those who are learning English as a second language can use computer software to strengthen associations between corresponding words,

Classroom Vignette

Michael, Whitney, Jessica, and Cari, kindergartners in Mrs. Stevens's class, began the year well above other students in their mathematical abilities. By midyear, they could count by 1s, 2s, 5s, and 10s with fluency and could write numbers past 100.

To encourage their continued progress, Mrs. Stevens began introducing them to some basic place value concepts. She used base-10 blocks to illustrate the relationship between 1s, 10s, and 100s, and within a short amount of time the four were trading place value digits with confidence. Following the work with the concrete manipulatives, Mrs. Stevens connected what they were capable of with the blocks to numerical writing.

When the four students reached an independent level of familiarity with place value concepts, they began working with Mighty Math Carnival Countdown. With the Bubble Band, they could trade ten bubbles for one big tens bubble or trade ten tens bubbles for a hundreds bubble. The students were able to practice place values at their own pace, allowing Mrs. Stevens to work with other students on other math instruction.

expressions, and grammatical constructions. Sound and pictures can illustrate relevant vocabulary and can make some potentially ambiguous expressions more understandable. Thus, the language learner can benefit from computerized, individual instruction and may be able to communicate proficiently in the target language in a shorter amount of time than would be possible otherwise.

Instructional Game Software

Category Description

Instructional games can be very similar to drill and practice, but have added increased motivation by having game rules, an entertaining environment, and competition to be the winner. Students may be more willing to work at practicing skills if they know they can do so by playing a game. Depending on the particular game, students can compete against the computer or against other students. Some instructional games take on the form of many traditional games, such as board games, logic games, adventure games, or word games, whereas others are originally created as software.

Practical Integration

Educational games can be used just as drill-and-practice software might be. Skills that have already been introduced can be practiced and strengthened. Although it is true that students may be more motivated to use instructional games, you must constantly evaluate whether the learning experience is purposeful. Students may have mastered the instructional objectives of a game long ago, but may still enjoy playing. Too much playing might lead to an abuse of the game format. Take time to make sure that the use of gamelike software is balanced with other relevant learning opportunities. Because many games may be violent or may tend to encourage aggressive playing behavior in the classroom, preview all content and monitor program use to see that it is serving a meaningful place in the instructional sequence of your classroom.

Integrated Learning Systems

Category Description

Integrated Learning Systems (ILSs) have offered schools comprehensive instructional and management features for decades. Largely traditional in methodology, the expensive ILSs are networked software compilations that address objectives in the core curriculum areas. Pretests, instruction, practice, and posttests are designed to be aligned with national or district curriculum goals. Students typically work independently, and their progress is tracked and reported automatically. When they have mastered a particular set of objectives, they advance to the next section. Teachers can monitor students' performance by examining records printed out by the system, and can choose to supplement the electronic instruction as becomes necessary.

Classroom Vignette

Mr. Hegland's third- and fourth-grade multiage class has been working hard over the last several weeks to learn basic multiplication facts. They have looked for equal groups of items in their everyday world, compared the patterns they found to fact patterns on a times table, and practiced with flash cards. Students have gained varying amounts of fluency with the facts and will continue to do so over the course of the rest of the year.

Today, Mr. Hegland has set up several stations through which students will spend the morning rotating in order to gain even more experience and confidence with the facts. One of the stations is located at the two classroom computers, on which he has loaded Mega Math Blaster. This program allows students to practice, among other topics, multiplication facts in an arcade game format. Students compete in an outer space environment to solve problems at one of six difficulty levels (see Figure 5-2).

Because this is new software for students, Mr. Hegland explains it briefly to the whole class. He sets up the context of the program by explaining the need to rescue the main character from Gelator, the Brain Drainer. He then goes over to show the first group at the station some of the basic operations, such as how to log-in, what levels might be most appropriate, the training on the game rules, and how to view the high scores. He has looked at the program himself a couple of times, and so knows the general layout enough to get the students started. This group's job will then be to train the group that follows them how to operate the software, a peer-teaching strategy Mr. Hegland frequently uses when introducing new software.

Matthew, Sara, Donna, and Jimmy play at the game for the half hour they are at that station. They're animatedly involved, building strategies as they go. Sometimes they are so excited with winning that they yell out loud, and then quickly shush each other, giggling as they look around to find Mr. Hegland. When their time is up, they reluctantly give up their seats at the computer and show the next group how to play.

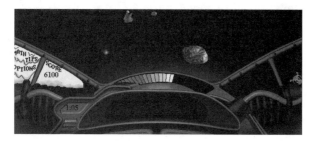

FIGURE 5-2   Mega Math Blaster. (*Courtesy of Davidson & Associates*)

Practical Integration

The adoption of ILSs often make the transition to using technology easier for schools because the curriculum is completely prepared. This packaged approach, however, may not always allow for easy integration into other outside curriculum. The software systems are generally intended to stand alone as the sole source of instruction. The systems follow a typically behaviorist approach to learning, funneling all students through a linear presentation of the curriculum. The easy mistake many schools make is assuming that when technology is brought into their classrooms, these curriculum delivery systems will adequately replace their teachers. Care must be taken to ensure that the instructional format and content provide the best learning opportunity for each student. Current beliefs about the variety of learning styles found in any group of students lead to the understanding that any one method will likely not be sufficiently individualized to be successful. The human teacher is needed to orchestrate ILS use so that the most instructional benefit can be derived by each student.

If your school has adopted an ILS, be prepared to assume the role of an instructional facilitator. Be aware of the content and format of the software so as to anticipate student needs and questions. Rather than relying solely on the automatic records of each student's progress, investigate further to be sure that students are getting the instruction they need.

Problem-Solving Software

Category Description

Problem-solving software requires students to apply higher-order strategies and synthesize knowledge from multiple curricular areas in order to solve problems. Students can test hypotheses, learn from mistakes, and refine skills as they gain mastery of problem-solving techniques. Software of this type can provide practice in solving problems by modeling general critical thinking steps, by focusing on specific subject-area issues, or by creating an open environment in which students can discover their own strategies. Whatever the method, problem-solving software affords the user more freedom than does drill-and-practice or tutorial software, but does not necessarily present the real-world context that characterizes simulation software.

A useful framework for understanding the definition of problem-solving software classifies programs in terms of *learner control.* Some programs give little control to the user beyond the ability to make logical guesses, one at a time. Other programs provide for full learner control, with the user deciding exactly what he or she will do next and moving freely from one activity to another. Good problem-solving programs promote the development of systematic thinking patterns and transcend the boundaries of simple tutorial or drill-and-practice software.

Practical Integration

People who are adept with using problem-solving strategies did not become that way merely by using one or two software packages. Effective problem solving is built by continuous practice and experience in a variety of meaningful situations. This understanding must be clear in teachers' minds as they plan a place for problem-solving software in the daily workings of a classroom. No software can be used as the sole tool for developing students' critical thinking abilities. Instead, software should be an seen as one effective component in a repertoire of activities that promote the acquisition of higher-order thinking skills. Whether a piece of software is used to appropriately extend a lesson or a particularly strong program inspires continued class work away from the computer, teachers must plan for extensive electronic and nonelectronic chances for students to think critically.

Classroom Vignette

Ms. Johnson always stresses problem-solving strategies to her primary students. She does not believe in having students work out of context, but rather always tries to relate concepts in any subject to the real world.

When five of her students consistently had trouble understanding early geometry concepts, and all began to have poor attitudes about their own abilities, Ms. Johnson turned to problem-solving software as another tool to provide a useful context for their learning (see Figure 5-3). Over the course of two weeks, she introduced the group to the problem-solving activities in Snootz Math Trek. She took time to show the students through the program because she wanted them to become familiar with the characters and the settings. She felt that if she just pointed them in the direction of the computer, these particular students would view their work as only one more waste of time and therefore miss the potential growth in their thinking strategies. The extra time spent paid off, because she soon saw students excited about the program and heard them talking about Snootz well after they were finished using the computer.

The students concentrated on only one of the five thinking activities in Snootz, the one that dealt with the shape puzzles in Al's Garage. The Snootz characters engaged students, and the exposure to the quality problem-solving activities made light bulbs start going on in their heads.

Speaking with them individually over the next several weeks proved to Ms. Johnson that not only were the students demonstrating proficiency with problem-solving strategies, but they were feeling confident about what they knew. One student even offered to show one of the top math students how to use the software.

FIGURE 5-3   TesselMania! by MECC allows students a great deal of control as they work to design their own puzzles. (*Courtesy of MECC*)

Reference Software

Category Description

In years past, when students needed to conduct research, they were required to go all the way down to the library to peruse heavy encyclopedic tomes. Technology has brought both the storage capabilities to gather volumes of facts onto one small CD-ROM, and the media variety with which to effectively bring life to static reference material. Reference software can take the form of any traditional reference works, such as dictionaries, encyclopedias, and thesauri. Other reference software presents extensive collections of information on a focused topic.

Practical Integration

Electronic reference works can be utilized just as traditional reference material would be. Depending on the particular learning activity, students might refer to software as needed to answer specific questions. They also might openly explore a multimedia reference without specific goals to guide their learning. The multimedia components of reference software present information in graphic, audio, video, or other alternate formats that allow uniquely unlimited access to students who might not be developmentally able to contend with the text version of the information (see Figure 5-4 and 5-5). You will want to plan for all the diverse learning possibilities these resources might offer your students.

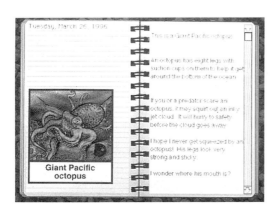

FIGURE 5-4 One Small Square, Seashore by Virgin Sound and Vision gives students access to illustrations, animations, and video on over 200 plants and animals from the seashore. (*Courtesy of Virgin Sound and Vision*)

FIGURE 5-5 Zak's Look it Up! by Compton's NewMedia lets students find facts on a host of different topics in its reference collection. (*Courtesy of Compton*)

Classroom Vignette

Max had chosen to study dinosaurs for his independent project. He remembered learning about them when he was in kindergarten, but he just saw a movie about them, and now he really wanted to become an expert. He already knew a lot of dinosaur names, and he now wanted to learn more about how each type of dinosaur lived.

He was now sitting in front of Eyewitness Virtual Reality: Dinosaur Hunter, the new software his teacher had sent him to the library media center to use (see Figure 5-6). An older student just showed him how to move around in the program, and now he is exploring on his own. He hungrily studies the bright pictures and watches the videos and animations. He sees how paleontologists dig for and piece together fossilized bones, and he feels like he is actually participating in the field project. He remembers a few times to write down some notes, but he mostly just takes in the wonder of the multimedia-designed research environment.

The next day and the day after that, Max heads down to the media center to research dinosaurs. After just a couple of days, he knows his way around the "dinosaur museum," and can name a great number of dinosaur facts. He is even starting to think of ideas for how he might show his class what he has learned in his research.

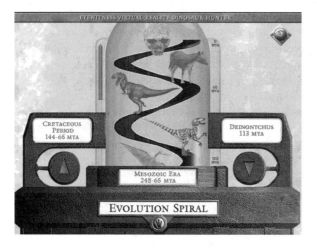

FIGURE 5-6 Eyewitness Virtual Reality: Dinosaur Hunter. (*Courtesy of DK Multimedia*)

Simulation Software

Category Description

Educational simulations allow students to experience events or phenomena that they are not able to witness personally and that would be too difficult or too dangerous to duplicate in a classroom setting. Software can simulate manipulating objects, performing a set of procedures, or acting in a given situation. Real processes can be slowed down or speeded up to study the effects of artificially tinkering with the variables.

Simulations provide contexts rich for meaningful individual learning construction. Like life experiences, simulations require the synthesis of many skills and understandings, making for true cross-curricular learning. Students must use what they know in ways that force them to confirm and expand their understanding. Simulations allow students to make and be affected by their own decisions. Guided by data provided by the software, the student becomes an active player in the scenario, selecting certain options or taking risks, and then witnessing the results of their decisions. Their involvement in a simulated situation lets them experience some of the feelings and problems associated with participating in the actual situation. They see the reasons for developing good strategies and therefore begin to think in a more organized fashion.

Good simulations build realistic, yet appropriately unpredictable environments. They combine text with a selection of media elements that create engaging, content-rich situations.

Practical Integration

Simulation software prompts active discussion and encourages cooperation toward common goals. Depending on the situation being simulated, the software can be effective with a variety of student groupings. Entire classes can work together, collaboratively making key decisions. Small groups of students can explore situations separately and then later compare notes to see how others performed under the same circumstances.

In science labs, student can pour and mix dangerous chemicals via simulation, and mistakes do not blow up the classroom. Through the simulation, students can begin to make the fine discriminations needed for proper handling of chemicals. It is also possible to simulate experiments that are too expensive, complicated, or time-consuming to replicate in school laboratories, such as building models of the systems in the human body (Coleman, 1997). Simulations provide for more student involvement than is possible through a reading assignment or lecture.

Social studies simulations can help students reenact historical events, learn about other societies, or experience governmental procedures, such as elections and lawmaking (see Figure 5-7). When running simulation software, students must first understand certain information and concepts so that they can then analyze situations and make wise decisions; therefore, learning becomes more relevant and useful to them.

Simulations can also be used to train students in the operation of tools and different types of equipment. Such training allows students to practice skills and procedures needed to operate the equipment safely and accurately—without danger to themselves or to the equipment.

Social studies, science, business, and vocational simulations can be valuable learning devices if their use is wisely integrated into the curriculum at appropriate times. Simulations do not serve as stand-alone units, but are most effective when used to illustrate and use skills, ideas, and experiences that have first been explored by other means. Students must be prepared with both knowledge of the content and an understanding of how to operate the simulation itself, preparation they would undoubtedly receive in advance of the corresponding real-life situation.

FIGURE 5-7   Students can imagine what life was really like in the Old West with the realistic images, video, digitized speech, and original music of Oregon Trail II. (*Courtesy of MECC*)

When having students work in a simulated environment, you must ensure that they understand the shortcomings of the software. No matter how realistic the representation of the life situation, it remains merely a simulation, and is thus not entirely accurate or sufficiently complex. Discussing decisions and consequences with others who have used the program can help students to connect the simulation with reality.

Tool Software

Category Description

Software tools help teachers and students become efficient and productive managers of textual, numerical, and graphical information. Because tools are not as content-specific as other software types, they can extend what humans are able to do in virtually any curricular or management area. Just as teachers and students use pencils, for example, as tools in innumerable daily activities, so, too, can the word processors, spreadsheets, databases, graphics, and authoring programs be used. Other tools lend themselves to a particular content area, but allow users of many different ages to create or do something unique. Tools such as these

Classroom Vignette

The new student was expected in class next week. Mr. Saunders had explained to his primary class that Troy was moving here from Alaska, and this had initiated an impromptu, week-long study all about the state of Alaska. So far students had read books, watched videos, and talked about it incessantly; they were fascinated with this far-away and radically different place. Somehow every child in class had decided that it was important to know what it was really like in Alaska before Troy came to class.

Mr. Saunders remembered a new piece of software that the technology specialist had introduced at the last staff meeting called Zurk's Alaskan Trek. Among other things, like solving math problems and writing stories, it allowed students to create their own scenes of animals and plants of Alaska, and then observe how the environmental characters would interact in real life. Animations simulated the wildlife as set up by the students. Mr. Saunders decided that the program would be perfect to keep his students' interests high and answer some of their more difficult questions. He would check it out to bring to class tomorrow.

Along with the software, Mr. Saunders brought to his room a computer projector so that he could demonstrate Zurk to the whole class at once. He wanted to model some of the thinking processes that students would need to be successful using the program, and he also wanted to give his students a chance to learn from each others' ideas.

He brought them to the Animal Theater first and showed them how easy it was to manipulate the environment, adding plants and animals to the screen. As he added each item, he asked for volunteers to name them and tell what they had learned about each. When he had built a simple scene, he asked students to predict what they thought could happen with the given variables. He played the movie, watching students' faces as they found out how close their predictions were. Students offered suggestions for how various changes to the planned environment would change the actions of the setting.

The class spent the afternoon illustrating Alaskan scenes, which they would have the chance to try out using the simulation program later that week. Mr. Saunders encouraged them to explain why they chose the scenes they did and how they thought they would play out. They all couldn't wait to ask Troy if he had seen anything like that in Alaska.

will be used by students all their lives in most professions, and the general skills and habits they learn by using software for various learning tasks will be transferable to other software they will be required to use in their future.

Practical Integration

Software tools afford quite a bit of freedom to teachers in how technology can be integrated into various learning tasks. Whereas other content-specific software, such as drill and practice or tutorials, is appropriate only for a particular subject area and developmental level, productivity tools can be used across grade levels and across subjects. Children using this type of software are more in control of the operation of the program than they might be with other types of software. The processes and products can be more customized.

Classroom Vignette

One of the most difficult areas of the eighth-grade language arts curriculum to teach effectively, according to Mrs. Hancock, is poetry. Students just are not interested. She has tried reading well-known selections, and they do not want to listen. She has told personal facts about the poets, and students do not take time to remember their names. It seems that short of bringing in actual poets to share the passion and the artistry that poetry can bring out in people might be the only way to make students understand the art of poetry. She was, therefore, most interested when she found the program In My Own Voice: Multicultural Poets on Identity.

Mrs. Hancock feels that all good writers have a writing environment that is comfortable to them and inspires them to write, and she was amazed that this software simulates such a rich environment. In the Writer Space, students can access all of the program resources. A gallery of artistic images can be visited and the poems that were inspired by the art can be heard. Students can study one poet's style by reading a collection of his or her poems and hear in the poet's own words how each poem was created. Even the actual text of each poem can be examined to see examples of the unique capitalization, punctuation, and physical layout that is acceptable in poetry. Budding poets can even choose from a selection of background music to further frame the writing mood.

Over the next several weeks, students worked individually or in pairs to write and rewrite their own original poems using the writing tool In My Own Voice (see Figure 5-8). When they all had a poem they were proud of, Mrs. Hancock planned for one more extension to the project.

The students used another tool program called Blocks in Motion to design an electronic illustration to accompany their poems. They used the various backgrounds and motions to create a scene they envisioned when they thought about their poem. Once each student had finished experimenting and each had designed a finished visual representation of their poem, a recording was made of each student poet reading his poem. The audio recordings would play in an electronic slide show of the student creations.

The class held a gallery day when Ms. Johnson invited other classes to visit the poets. Not only had students learned about poetry, but they had personally experienced what it feels like to be a poet.

FIGURE 5-8   In My Own Voice: Multicultural Poets on Identity. (*Courtesy of Sunburst Communications, Inc.*)

Your students might use word processors to record information they have researched or to write creatively. They may compose letters directly on the word processor or may type in field notes after having scribbled them down on paper. With spreadsheet programs, students can study the relationships between amounts of money or can learn to schedule time. Students might organize research content using a database program. With graphics software, students can explore geometric relationships, geographic features, and artistic representations.

Internet tools, such as the HTML editors described in Chapter 8, are making up an increasing share of the tool software. The creative production versatility of authoring software is developed to a great extent in Chapter 13.

Teachers should also be using productivity tools to support their efforts as teachers and managers of student information. Specific tips for using software as an aid to classroom administration can be found in Chapter 11.

Tutorial Software

Category Description

Tutorial software utilizes written explanations, descriptions, questions, problems, and graphic illustrations for concept development. Concepts are intended to be learned without any other instruction efforts, thus existing as a stand-alone form of instruction. This presentation of instruction differs from drill-and-practice software that only provides practice and assessment. Students are given opportunities in tutorials to gain experience with new concepts much like they would when learning with a living and breathing teacher. Often computerized or traditional written pretests are included with tutorial software to determine the most appropriate level of lessons for a particular student. After the tutorial portion of a lesson has been presented, drill-and-practice exercises are offered. In some cases, the student has total control of the number of exercises. Finally, a posttest for each objective or group of objectives determines mastery. Student scores may be displayed as the lesson ends, as well as suggestions for further study and practice.

Very basic tutorial programs present information and practice in a strictly linear fashion, similar to ways students would learn by themselves using a book. *Linear tutorials* present a series of screen displays to all users, regardless of individual differences among the students (see Figure 5-9). There are very few reasons for these "page-turner" programs to be in electronic form since they utilize little of the technical capacity of computers. *Branching tutorials,* on the other hand, do not require all users to follow the same path, but direct students to certain lessons or parts of a lesson according to results of computerized pretests and posttests, or to student response to embedded questions within the program (see Figure 5-10).

Tutorial programs that are designed to take full advantage of the medium should allow for the student to interact with the program continually as they practice new information. Good tutorials also allow individual students to work at their own pace, reviewing material as needed and moving ahead quickly when they fully understand a new concept. It does the learner no instructional good when a program advances to the next screen if the learner is not ready to go on. Adequate practice must be given following instruction, but prior to assessment. The author

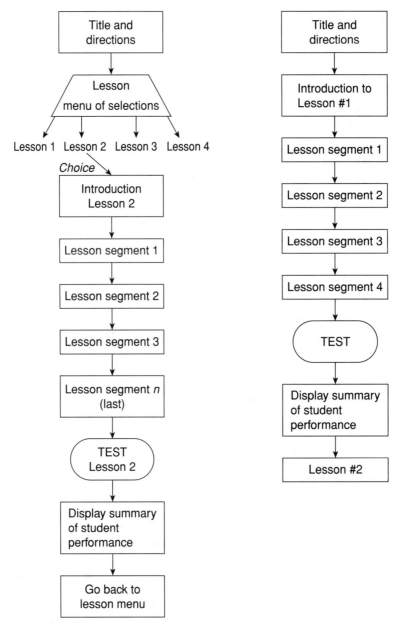

FIGURE 5-9 Linear tutorials.

of the tutorial must try to predict all possible correct responses and allow for insignificant misspelling and capitalization errors. The program must respond intelligently to incorrect answers, predict the most common incorrect answers, and offer specially tailored explanations

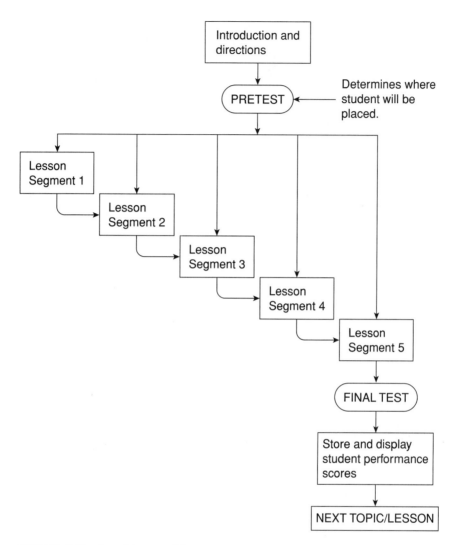

FIGURE 5-10 Branching tutorials.

and learning experiences according to which incorrect answers were chosen by the student. In addition, computerized tests must be as valid and reliable as their written counterparts, so that students are not subjected to material they have already learned and so that learning can be evaluated fairly and accurately. A management feature allows teachers to track student progress and step in if human instruction or redirection is warranted. In short, tutorial software requires the thorough instructional design that would be required of any good lesson a teacher would present in a traditional manner.

FIGURE 5-11 Discovering Music by Voyetra Technologies presents a complete introduction to the world of music. *(Courtesy of Voyetra Technologies)*

Practical Integration

In a busy classroom with dozens of different learning levels and styles, teachers can use tutorials to supplement their instructional efforts. Tutorial programs can teach students who require additional instruction on a topic, or can allow those who need more time to work through concepts at a slower pace. Instruction can be planned in a presentation style that complements what is available in a tutorial, so that students for which one style is not effective will have an alternative method to learn. Tutorials can open up learning opportunities to students in smaller or rural schools. If there are no teachers trained to provide instruction in higher-level math or science courses or certain languages, students can use tutorial software to learn what they would otherwise miss (see Figure 5-11).

Summary

Educational software allows teachers to use computers as versatile instructional aids to meet the individual needs of their students. Teachers can get a better understanding of how to incorporate software into their established academic curriculum by considering the types of software that are available: drill and practice, instructional game, Integrated Learning Systems, problem solving, reference, tool, and tutorial. Although knowledge of the software types is helpful for planning, teachers should know that the categories tend to overlap and many software pieces can be easily described by the descriptors of several of the categories. Drill-and-practice software allows students to work with information they have previously learned, getting immediate feedback to assist in skill mastery. Instructional games provide practice similar to that found in drill-and-practice software, but structures it in a game format, with rules and a competitive environment. Integrated Learning Systems offer complete, networked instructional, assessment, and management packages. Problem-solving software requires logical thinking on the part of students and assumes that some previous concept development has taken place. The continuing development of logical thinking is an important goal for problem-solving software. Reference software brings together great amounts of facts and illustrates them with a variety of media elements, such as graphics, animations, video, and audio.

Computer simulations allow students to experience real-life events in the safety of the classroom. Decisions must be made to affect the outcome of the simulation, so the student tends to become an involved and interested learner. Software tools are not as content-specific as other types of software, meaning students and teachers can use them across the curriculum to manage all types of information. Tutorials attempt to aid concept development by carefully presenting instruction and feedback. Students can utilize tutorials for remediation or enrichment, and they are especially useful when teachers for a specialized topic are not available.

LEARNER ACTIVITIES

1. Look at some newspaper ads and make a list of the features that appear most desirable in the educational software that is advertised. Do these features appear educationally sound or does flashiness seem to be selling more software?

2. Identify all of the software currently available on the market that could be used for your intended teaching area or grade level. Comment on the selection available to learners in your area.

3. Choose one specific piece of software and write a lesson plan for how you would integrate it into a complete instructional sequence. Be sure to include the instruction or other preparation that would precede the software use and how your students would follow up their experiences with the software.

4. Summarize the advantages and disadvantages of teaching a particular concept with and without educational software.

5. Describe the different strategies that would be needed to facilitate effective use of educational software by different-sized groupings of students.

6. Observe a traditional lesson taught to students of the level you plan to teach. What type of software would be appropriate to assist students with practicing or extending this topic? How might you convince the teacher to include educational software in his or her instructional repertoire?

7. Discuss how educational software changes the roles of teachers and students.

8. List five software companies and describe the apparent educational philosophy of each based on an examination of a selection of their current software.

9. Review the literature on the effectiveness of educational software since 1990 and summarize the research results.

10. List all the sources you can identify that teachers and students can use to find out information on how to use specific software.

BIBLIOGRAPHY

Adams, P. E. (1996). Hypermedia in the classroom using Earth and space science CD-ROMs. *Journal of Computers in Mathematics and Science Teaching, 15*(1–2), 19–34.

Allen, D. (1996). Teaching with technology: Problem-solving strategies. *Teaching PreK–8, 27*(3), 14–16.

Coleman, F. M. (1997). Software simulation enhances science experiments., *T.H.E. Journal, 25*(2), 56–58.

Frye, B., & Frager, A. M. (1996). Civilization, Colonization, SimCity: Simulations for the social studies classroom. *Learning and Leading with Technology, 24*(2), 21–23, 32.

Ivers, K. S. (1996–1997). Desktop adventures: Building problem-solving and computer skills. *Learning and Leading with Technology, 24*(4), 6–11.

Jenkins, D. (1996). Have more fun teaching physics: Simulating, stimulating software. *MultiMedia Schools, 3*(5), 42–47.

Johnson, J. M. (1996–97). Software for an evaluation workshop. *Learning and Leading with Technology, 24,* 48–50.

Mobley, E. D. (1996). Interactive multimedia in the music classroom. *Music Educators Journal, 82*(4), 22–24, 54.

Schatz, S. (1996). Show/Do/Cue: A model for training use of software tools. *T.H.E. Journal, 24*(2), 86–89.

White, C. S. (1996). Multimedia products for U.S. history. *Social Education, 60,* 379–83.

SOFTWARE BIBLIOGRAPHY

Blocks in Motion. Don Johnston, Inc.

Eyewitness Virtual Reality: Dinosaur Hunter. DK Multimedia.

In My Own Voice: Multicultural Poets on Identity. Sunburst Communications, Inc.

Mega Math Blaster. Davidson and Associates.

Mighty Math Carnival Countdown. Edmark Corporation.

Snootz Math Trek. Theatrix Interactive.

Zurk's Alaskan Trek. Soleil Software, Inc.

CHAPTER

6 Selecting Educational Software

FOCUS QUESTIONS

1. What are the differences among software selection, review, and evaluation?
2. What considerations must a district make when forming a plan for software review?
3. What are the benefits and drawbacks to using a checklist-type form to review software?

Now that it is clear what types of software are available on the market for instructional purposes, it is appropriate to discuss just how teachers and other school personnel make decisions regarding what software should be used for the benefit of their students. The list of newly published software titles expands monthly, but many times, software publishers forsake strong instructional design for colorful graphics and packaging (Hoffman & Lyons, 1997). In order to avoid wasting valuable teacher time and district money on advertising hype, educators must have in place effective, planned processes for the investigation and acceptance of software packages for use in their classrooms. This chapter first highlights some of the considerations that must guide any software choices educators make, and then it suggests an assessment process that takes into account the purposes for which the software is intended. An example review form is offered, with extensive descriptions of how it can be used and adapted to individual school and district needs. Sources of outside software reviews by evaluation organizations are given, along with contact information and related websites. Finally, alternate review approaches are proposed that may provide both more useful and accurate information about potential software uses as well as better accommodations of new multimedia software.

Software Assessment Terminology

To understand completely the very important job that must be undertaken in order to give students the best possible instructional products, distinctions must first be drawn among several similar and potentially confusing terms. McDougall and Squires (1995a) note the frequently interchangeable uses of the terms *selection, review,* and *evaluation* in the literature on educational software, and have, for clarity's sake, provided working definitions that separate the three. *Evaluation* is a specific process that aids in the actual development of software, occurring either during or immediately following the software development. *Reviewing* refers to the more formal assessment of the performance and characteristics of a piece of software, usually for the purpose of disseminating the results of the review to an audience of fellow educators. Organizations that exist solely to provide reviews of software to teachers are discussed later in the chapter. Finally, *selection,* according to these authors, describes the informal decisions teachers make daily with regard to what learning materials they will use in their classrooms. Based on their own experience and teaching styles and on what they know about the abilities and needs of their students, but without actually performing any structured review, teachers select what they think will work best. Because the audience reading this book will be most interested in strategies they themselves can use to make informed decisions about what software will work best in their classrooms, this chapter will focus primarily on district review procedures and individual software selection.

Guiding Principles behind Developing a Software Review and Selection Plan

Depending on the extent of its use in the classroom, educational software has the potential to make quite an impact on the delivery and even the interpretation of a school or district's curriculum. For this reason, districts must have a clear plan for reviewing and selecting educational software for use with students. In creating that plan, some basic principles must be considered.

At the outset of the entire selection process for educational software, it must be understood that merely sitting a child in front of a computer with an educational software title plugged into it does not constitute a sound educational plan (see Figure 6-1). Doing this would allow a software publisher's goals and intentions to override those of the district and the classroom teacher, thus taking thoughtful control out of the hands of those closest to students. Software use first must be consistent with the goals and objectives of not only individual classrooms, but also those of the school, the district, and the state. In addition, national curriculum standards, such as the National Council of Teachers of Mathematics (NCTM) Standards, should be consulted in formulating a plan for software use. Not only should the content be compared to local scope and sequence guidelines, but also the instructional design and the way in which the material is presented should be considered. The learning theories that underpin the content of a piece of software should match what is accepted in current educational literature, and should correspond to what is accepted in the local communities where the software is to be used. If a district embraces a constructivist educational philosophy, for example, it should seek educational software that allows students to come to their own understandings based on their experiences. Often, an implicit set of values are embedded into the structure and content of a piece of software, and these values must also be carefully examined to see if they fit with the intended learning environment. In essence, the software, like any other learning tool or activity, must match the purpose for which it will be used, and it must represent the best way to accomplish those particular educational goals.

FIGURE 6-1   Merely sitting a child in front of a piece of
software does not constitute a sound educational plan.

Some basic understanding of the idea of evaluation is also helpful from not only those involved with district review, but those who will be interpreting the reviews for classroom use. Evaluation is a highly subjective process, no matter how specific and criteria-based it aims to be. We make evaluations every day, such as whether we enjoyed a new restaurant or how well a tie looks with a shirt; evaluations that are based on our own individual tastes. Whoever is evaluating a software package is viewing it through the filter of her or his own unique perspective. The person's background experience, educational philosophy, and even personal interests play a role in determining how they will rate the software. Because we are human, there is simply no way around this natural subjectivity. The important point to make is that anyone who reads a review of software, or hears of an opinion on anything for that matter, must always consider the source of the review and again filter it through her or his own perspective. Because one evaluator dislikes a program, for example, does not necessarily mean that it is completely unusable for all purposes. Take all reviews under consideration and proceed according to your individual beliefs.

A Software Review and Selection Process

With the regular influx of new software to educational markets, school districts must have an organized process for how new software will be assessed and how decisions regarding purchase and usage will be made. One of the first steps is to obtain software copies for review purposes. This can generally be done by contacting the software publishers directly (Appendix A gives a list of publisher contacts). Many universities and state departments of education maintain review sites with software packages available for checkout.

The next part of the process that should be considered is who will actually have the first look at a new piece of software. Will curriculum policy administrators review software for the entire district? Will a committee of teachers representing their curricular areas or grade levels serve as reviewers? What role might parents or community members play in the process? Will students be observed using programs or will their opinions or comments be elicited? Although involving students in reviewing will add an extra step to the process, it promises the benefit of a very different rating than those which teachers or parents will provide (Reiser & Kegelmann, 1994). It is important for this flow of evaluative information to be made clear to the teachers who will have the direct experience of planning for and using each piece of software. Every teacher should have a clear understanding of how diligently and by whom a new software package has been reviewed. If there are comments available from district reviewers, a plan should be in place for disseminating the review information to teachers. If little local review has been performed, teachers should likewise be made aware of how much of the burden of selection and review falls to them.

Reviewers need some kind of a standard form on which review comments can be recorded and compared to comments about other programs. The easiest and most common method of assessing software is to use a checklist. The checklist form might contain any number of criteria to be examined and rated, sometimes with a simple yes or no and sometimes by choosing from a range of scores for each area. Forms can provide space to encourage longer answers regarding specific problem areas or ideas for integration of the program into curriculum. Later in this chapter, some objections to the checklist method of reviewing software will be raised, but it still remains the most straightforward way to compare results from several evaluators on several software titles.

Finally, a district software review plan needs to include some way of getting the review information for accepted packages into the hands of the teachers who will be using the software to teach. Knowing that the package was accepted is not enough. Teachers have a right to all information known about a program so they can make informed decisions about how to best use the program to facilitate student learning.

A good general review sequence like the one shown in Table 6-1 will ensure the best use of evaluator time and at the same time will result in the most consistent and reliable results.

Software Review Organizations and Other Review Information

To assist educators in making software selection decisions, a number of organizations exist solely to review and share information about new software packages. The *Educational Software Preview Guide* (Educational Software Preview Guide Consortium) is distributed annually by the International Society for Technology in Education (ISTE). The ESPG Consortium members, representing over 12 review sites, meet annually to compile reviews and to make specific recommendations that guide educators in purchasing and using software

TABLE 6-1   Sequence of Software Review

1. As a software package is received, first check it briefly to determine that there are no major technical flaws and that it includes complete documentation. If there are such technical problems, send the program back to the vendor with specific information describing the encountered problems.

2. If no problems are discovered, proceed by reading the program documentation thoroughly. To completely test the program's capabilities, run it three additional times: once to determine the program flow; next making as many mistakes as possible; and finally responding exactly as instructions indicate, making as many correct responses as possible. Test all program options, such as printing or playing video segments, and try every navigable path.

3. Try software with an appropriate student audience, if desired. As the students participate in the evaluation process, note both their actions and their comments.

4. Record the evaluation on a standard review form, such as the one presented later in this chapter, to encourage comparable results.

5. Make evaluation information available to teachers. One efficient way to organize these reviews is to compile evaluations into one cohesive database of titles. Distribute the database to teachers in either print or electronic form.

packages. Although the *Guide* is not meant to be a guarantee for educators to purchase the recommended software without first reviewing it themselves, it does provide a comprehensive and accurate starting point, based on established subjects, modes, and a rating system.

The *Only the Best* annual software guide, sponsored by the Association for School Curriculum Development (ASCD, 1998), compiles reviews of the 100 highest-rated software titles to aid educators in making selection decisions. The 30 evaluating contributors hail from across the United States and Canada.

Table 6-2 gives purchase contacts for these two guides, along with the Internet addresses for a number of additional review sites available on the World Wide Web (see also Figures 6-2 and 6-3).

An Example Educational Software Review Form

This form is appropriate for district review purposes and allows software reviewers to assess the complete software package, including both content and technical considerations. It is easily modifiable so that districts can match it to their existing district goals and curriculum objectives. For the more informal software selection that classroom teachers perform, a form as detailed as this would most likely not be time-efficient. Teachers, however, should be familiar with the review categories and types of items that are considered here as they make those important decisions in selecting software.

This form was designed to be easy to use, yet be descriptive enough to provide true indications of quality software. It first solicits basic identifying information that should be readily apparent from the program packaging and accompanying documentation. The form

TABLE 6-2   Educational Software Reviews

Print Resources

ASCD
Only the Best
1703 N. Beauregard St.
Alexandria, VA 22311-1714
800-933-2723
www. ascd.org

ISTE
Educational Software Preview Guide
Customer Service Office
480 Charnelton Street
Eugene, OR 97401-2626
Order Desk: 800-336–5191
Order Fax: 541-302-3778
www.iste.org

World Wide Web Resources

EPIE Institute Courseware Review Form
<www.columbia.edu/~jhb27/epieeval.html>

The School House Review
<www.worldvillage.com/wv/school/html/scholrev.htm>

Software Evaluation Clearinghouses
<www.netc.org/software/clearinghouse.html>

SuperKids Educational Software Review
<www.superkids.com/aweb/pages/reviews/reviews.html>

Way Cool Software Reviews
<www.ucc.uconn.edu/~wwwpcse/wcool.html>

then asks the evaluator to rate how well the package satisfies a series of criteria statements grouped by category. These category groupings do not imply that these often interrelated areas are independent of each other, but rather they are intended to aid the evaluator in understanding the structure of the evaluation process. The final section of the form provides for a graphical summary of all the section evaluations. It allows the evaluator not only to see in an instant the overall rating for the program, but to compare two programs with just a glance.

Identifying Information

The first few items you will need to complete are the obviously necessary title, publisher, and price of the software package, without which the evaluation process would become an unlabeled mess. Giving the date the package was reviewed helps to ensure that the most recent versions of software are being considered, and providing the reviewer's name becomes important when a number of different people are participating in the review process. Depend-

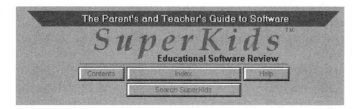

FIGURE 6-2   SuperKids Educational Software Review.
<www.superkids.com>

**Welcome to the
Way Cool
Software Reviews Project**

Note: This site was as an Editor's Choice A+ for the summer '96 issue of
<u>Classroom Connect.</u>

FIGURE 6-3   Way Cool Software Reviews. *(The Way Cool
Software Reviews Project is sponsored by the A. J. Pappanikou
Center: A UAP, at the University of Connecticut)*

ing on the process, there may be a need for more information on each evaluator's background or experience.

System Requirements.   The list of system requirements is important to include, and is usually listed on the software package or in the installation directions. If the minimum hardware requirements for the software to operate correctly are beyond that which the district possesses, the software may need to be put aside and reviewed at a later date, if, and when, more advanced equipment is purchased. Be specific when listing this technical information so that if there are problems with the operation, you will have a handy reference describing the system with which you are working. Most districts have a selection of computers with a range of capabilities, so evaluators may want to try each piece of software on a number of different machines to get a complete performance picture.

Grade Levels.   The grade level that is posted on the package documentation should only be used as a general guide for use. Often, what your students are able to accomplish may fall above or below the listed grade levels. Reviewers, therefore, should always consider how each package might be used with students outside the stated grade-level range. Sometimes students might not benefit from the intended task at their level, but may be able to use the program to accomplish some other goals. For instance, a reading program might be below the reading levels of some fourth-graders, but the program might be creatively used with the students to explore writing in a particular genre.

Subjects.   The subject section is extensive and is based on the subjects considered in reviews for the *Educational Software Preview Guide* (ESPG Consortium, 1998). Providing the evaluator with an entire list of subjects, as opposed to just a blank line on which to fill in the subjects, prompts the full consideration of the range of possible subject areas. Because many software packages cross curricular lines, check all the subject areas that apply. Other subjects that apply to a particular district or purpose can also be added to customize this list.

Modes. The purpose for which the software was designed is described by the modes, a concept also based on the *Educational Software Preview Guide* (ESPG Consortium, 1998). One piece of software can be classified under several modes because most software can be used in several different ways.

Program Description. Describe briefly the content that is covered by the program and the ways in which it is covered. Include here information on the setting as well as on any special features the program offers. This description is generic, omitting any evaluative opinions, and is similar to the description that might be found on the back of the software package. This type of description might be helpful if compiling a database of all of the software reviewed to give teachers some idea of what this program is about.

Content and Technical Information

This section consists of a series of criteria that describe what might be expected in a quality software program. Read each statement carefully, and circle the number that best describes your rating of this program for each indicator. Scores represent a range from 0 meaning Poor to a score of 5 meaning Excellent. Circle *N/A* if the indicator is not applicable to this program for any reason. For each section, then circle the score that best summarizes the program's performance on all of the indicators. This gives the evaluator a quick summation of a program's performance in each area.

Documentation and Supplementary Materials. Software is generally sold with some accompanying materials, including installation procedures, teacher's guides, student workbooks, and even the box itself. Theoretically, these items should make the use of the program easier and more effective. The indicators in this section ask you first to assess the thoroughness of the technical documentation. Were you able to install and operate the program successfully according to the supplied directions? In order for the program to be effective, it should have some stated educational objectives. Even if teachers can think of alternate instructional purposes for the program, objectives that are clearly stated give the program credibility and give teachers a starting point. With the understanding that software will not be used in isolation, activities should be suggested that can help integrate the software into the existing curriculum, as well as activities that can be used to extend or remediate instruction.

Program Content. The content is the heart of the program, and it therefore determines in many ways just how useful the program will be. Indicators here ask you to consider how well the program authors have matched the content to the stated objectives. Does the way in which the instruction is presented reflect current research, and does it allow for a variety of learners? You must also decide if the content appears up to date and is free from errors and unwanted stereotypes. More specific indicators could be added here to customize the content rating to district or state guidelines.

Presentation.   The way in which the instruction is presented can make or break a program. If the content is developed logically, with relevant examples and illustrations, students have a better chance of making meaning connections. It is a given that spelling, punctuation, and grammar be correct, but what a student sees on the screen must also be clear and shown with enough variety to keep the interest of the intended audience.

Effectiveness.   What ultimately matters with any instructional tool or strategy is whether it leads to student learning. This category is best judged by incorporating student participation into the review process. Do students appear to have a grasp on the concepts covered in the program following its use? Are they able to apply what they have learned, and does it seem that they are now interested in the topic? If students cannot participate in the review, the reviewers might be asked to use what they know about students that age to try to see the software from the student perspective. A very important indicator in this section asks you to decide whether the instructional software medium is appropriate in teaching this particular content. Remember that computers are not automatically the remedy for all educational ailments. Some nontechnical solutions do a better job of encouraging the learning process than do many software programs.

Audience Appeal and Suitability.   For this section, you will want to consider how closely what the program offers fits the needs of the intended audience. Rate whether the way the content is organized and presented will hold the interest of these students, and if once their interest is piqued, they will be able to read and respond as needed. Decide if the visual aids are appropriate for this audience, and if the time spent on content instruction fits with what you know about the attention span of your student group. Finally, assess whether the program customizes instruction by offering remediation or enrichment in response to student input.

Practice/Assessment/Feedback.   How does this program account for the learning it promotes? Good instructional design demands that the practice and the assessment be aligned with both the stated objectives and with the instruction. Feedback should be related to student responses and should occur immediately after a response in order to reinforce or remediate as needed. Depending on your personal or district philosophy of education, you may want to note the inclusion of alternative practice and assessment methods, such as portfolio compilation or collaborative learning.

Ease of Use.   The most well-designed instruction is rendered meaningless if a student cannot access it easily. For this section of the evaluation, reflect on how easy it is to work through the program. Are there directions and a **Help** screen available from every screen? Are these items thorough and easy to understand? Consider, also, how much control the user has to navigate at his own speed and to go wherever he wants to go. The final indicator is especially important with young or novice users who may not have yet developed competent keyboarding skills or mouse control.

User Interface and Media Quality.   Ideally, all of the media elements, such as graphics, audio, video, and animations, combine to create a virtual learning environment. Rate whether the environment created is appropriate for the intended learning audience. Are these media elements used to heighten student interest and promote instruction, or are they merely decorative? Additionally, evaluate the quality of those media elements. Do they appear to utilize the latest technical capabilities? Do the media elements function without technical problems?

Evaluation Summary

The last two sections of this evaluation form ask you to summarize the ratings you have made so far. Frequently, the only part of an evaluation that an end user might see is the final rating, so it is helpful to boil down the information from a longer form to a more concise format. This review instrument offers both a graphical and verbal summary. At the end of each section, you circled a summary score that best illustrated how the program performed on those particular indicators. Now, simply transfer those scores to the Section Summary Graph by shading in the score for each section. This creates a visual representation of the overall program rating, making it easy to see at a glance how the program rates and allowing for easy comparison of multiple programs. A district may want to set a rating minimum for acceptance of a package.

The other evaluation summary is an open area for you to record your Overall Evaluative Comments. This gives you the chance to explain the strengths and weaknesses of the program, including any areas that might not have been represented by the indicators on the evaluation form. These comments might be the deciding factors between two programs with very similar numerical ratings, so be persuasive and complete.

The form in Figure 6-4 can be duplicated and modified for educational software review purposes.

Objections to Current Review Practices and Future Trends

Checklist review forms, like the one presented in this chapter, have historically been the most common way of recording software evaluations performed by multiple reviewers. In recent years, however, voices in the research field related to educational software have raised concerns over the validity of relying solely on these checklist evaluations in light of modern educational philosophy and with regards to new multimedia technology.

McDougall and Squires (1995a) suggest that checklists are only truly useful in the *evaluation* of software, which has previously been defined as the specific process that aids in the development of software and occurs either during or immediately after the software development. Generic checklists, they contend, are not helpful in the review or selection of software because checklists are incapable of describing the context and surrounding activities to which a software program might contribute. In their critique of software, the researchers summarized other problems found in research on checklist use to include the main focus with checklists on technical issues rather than educational issues, the difficulty in assigning importance to certain items over others, the obstacles in recognizing a variety of teaching strategies, and the inability of one set of criteria to effectively define a number of different subject areas.

A review plan they propose instead of the checklist method is the "Perspectives Interactions Paradigm," which stresses the consideration of classroom activities, teaching and

FIGURE 6-4 Educational Software Review Form.

Software Title:		
Publisher:		Price:
Reviewer:		Review Date:

SYSTEM REQUIREMENTS:	GRADE LEVELS:
Platform:	Pre Kindergarten
Processor:	K–2
RAM:	3–5
Hard Drive:	6–8
CD:	9–12
Other:	Adult
	Teacher Tool

SUBJECTS

Art:	Keyboarding	Science:
☐ Music	☐ Language Arts	☐ Biology
☐ Performing Arts	Math:	☐ Chemistry
☐ Visual Arts	☐ Advanced	☐ Earth Science
☐ Cross Curricular	☐ Algebra	☐ Environmental Ed./Ecology
☐ Computer Science	☐ Geometry/Measurement	☐ General Science
☐ Early Childhood/Preschool	☐ Number	☐ Physics
☐ Health/Phys. Ed./Recreation	☐ Probability/Statistics	☐ Scientific Method/Lab Equip.
☐ Internet/WWW	☐ Multimedia Production	☐ Space Science
Instructional Tools:	☐ Problem Solving/Logic	☐ Social Studies
☐ Authoring Systems	☐ Reference Library	☐ Test & Testing
☐ Comp. Assisted Drafting	☐ School to Work	☐ World Languages (non-Eng.)
☐ Class Management		
☐ Computer Utilities		
☐ Desktop Publishing		
☐ Image Generator		
☐ Personal Productivity		

MODES

☐ Authoring System	☐ Education Game	☐ Problem Solving
☐ Bilingual	☐ Exploration	☐ Reference
☐ Creative Activity	☐ Guided Practice	☐ Simulation
☐ Computer Programming	☐ Internet	☐ Tool
☐ Demonstration/Presentation	☐ Limited English Proficient	☐ Tutorial
☐ Drill & Practice	☐ Multimedia	

PROGRAM DESCRIPTION: (Briefly describe the content and context of the program.)

(continued)

FIGURE 6-4 Continued

DOCUMENTATION & SUPPLEMENTARY MATERIALS:							
Necessary technical documentation is included.	N/A	0	1	2	3	4	5
Objectives are clearly stated.	N/A	0	1	2	3	4	5
Learning activities that facilitate integration into curriculum are suggested.	N/A	0	1	2	3	4	5
Materials for enrichment and remedial activities are provided.	N/A	0	1	2	3	4	5
Section Summary:	**N/A**	**0**	**1**	**2**	**3**	**4**	**5**
PROGRAM CONTENT:							
Instruction matches stated objectives.	N/A	0	1	2	3	4	5
Instructional strategies are based on current research.	N/A	0	1	2	3	4	5
Instruction addresses various learning styles and intelligences.	N/A	0	1	2	3	4	5
Information is current and accurate.	N/A	0	1	2	3	4	5
Program is free of stereotypes or bias.	N/A	0	1	2	3	4	5
Section Summary:	**N/A**	**0**	**1**	**2**	**3**	**4**	**5**
PRESENTATION:							
Information is presented in a developmentally appropriate and logical way.	N/A	0	1	2	3	4	5
Illustrations and examples are relevant.	N/A	0	1	2	3	4	5
There is appropriate variety in screen displays.	N/A	0	1	2	3	4	5
Text is clear and printed in type suitable for target audience.	N/A	0	1	2	3	4	5
Spelling, punctuation, and grammar are correct.	N/A	0	1	2	3	4	5
Section Summary:	**N/A**	**0**	**1**	**2**	**3**	**4**	**5**
EFFECTIVENESS:							
Students are able to recall/use information presented following program use.	N/A	0	1	2	3	4	5
Program prepares students for future real-world experiences.	N/A	0	1	2	3	4	5
Students develop further interest in topic from using program.	N/A	0	1	2	3	4	5
This is an appropriate use of instructional software.	N/A	0	1	2	3	4	5
Section Summary:	**N/A**	**0**	**1**	**2**	**3**	**4**	**5**
AUDIENCE APPEAL & SUITABILITY:							
Program matches interest level of indicated audience.	N/A	0	1	2	3	4	5
Reading level is appropriate for indicated audience.	N/A	0	1	2	3	4	5
Examples and illustrations are suitable for indicated audience.	N/A	0	1	2	3	4	5
Required input is appropriate for indicated audience.	N/A	0	1	2	3	4	5
Necessary completion time is compatible with student attention.	N/A	0	1	2	3	4	5
Program supplies remediation or enrichment when appropriate.	N/A	0	1	2	3	4	5
Section Summary:	**N/A**	**0**	**1**	**2**	**3**	**4**	**5**

FIGURE 6-4 Continued

PRACTICE/ASSESSMENT/FEEDBACK:								
Practice is provided to accomplish objectives.	N/A	0	1	2	3	4	5
Practice is appropriate for topic and audience.	N/A	0	1	2	3	4	5
Feedback corresponds to student responses.	N/A	0	1	2	3	4	5
Feedback is immediate.	N/A	0	1	2	3	4	5
Feedback is varied.	N/A	0	1	2	3	4	5
Feedback gives remediation and reinforcement.	N/A	0	1	2	3	4	5
Remediation and reinforcement is positive and dignified.	N/A	0	1	2	3	4	5
Assessment is aligned with objectives.	N/A	0	1	2	3	4	5
Open-ended responses and/or portfolio opportunities are promoted.	N/A	0	1	2	3	4	5
Collaborative learning experiences are provided for.	N/A	0	1	2	3	4	5
Section Summary:	**N/A**	**0**	**1**	**2**	**3**	**4**	**5**

EASE OF USE:								
User can navigate through program without difficulty.	N/A	0	1	2	3	4	5
Screen directions are consistent and easy to follow.	N/A	0	1	2	3	4	5
Help options are comprehensive and readily available.	N/A	0	1	2	3	4	5
Program responds to input as indicated by directions.	N/A	0	1	2	3	4	5
Title sequence is brief and can be bypassed.	N/A	0	1	2	3	4	5
User can control pace and sequence.	N/A	0	1	2	3	4	5
User can exit from any screen.	N/A	0	1	2	3	4	5
Only one input is registered when key is held down.	N/A	0	1	2	3	4	5
Section Summary:	**N/A**	**0**	**1**	**2**	**3**	**4**	**5**

USER INTERFACE AND MEDIA QUALITY:								
Interface provides user with an appropriate environment.	N/A	0	1	2	3	4	5
Graphics, audio, video, and/or animations enhance instruction.	N/A	0	1	2	3	4	5
Graphics, audio, video, and/or animations stimulate student interest.	N/A	0	1	2	3	4	5
Graphics, audio, video, and/or animations are of high quality.	N/A	0	1	2	3	4	5
Section Summary:	**N/A**	**0**	**1**	**2**	**3**	**4**	**5**

SECTION SUMMARIES:

Documents	Content	Presentation	Effectiveness	Appeal/ Suitability	Practice/ Assessment	Ease of Use	Interface/ Quality
⑤	⑤	⑤	⑤	⑤	⑤	⑤	⑤
④	④	④	④	④	④	④	④
③	③	③	③	③	③	③	③
②	②	②	②	②	②	②	②
①	①	①	①	①	①	①	①
⓪	⓪	⓪	⓪	⓪	⓪	⓪	⓪

OVERALL EVALUATIVE COMMENTS

Classroom Vignette

Kathy Donegan is one of three teachers at her high school that serve on the District Technology Review Committee. Her experience as a journalism and creative writing teacher allow her to select software that effectively handles the instruction of composition and other related topics, a combination she finds too infrequently in the software that has been coming in for review over the two years she has served on the committee.

The committee meets once a month and brings together teachers from around the K–12 district. Every third Tuesday, the teachers meet to see what new software review copies have been received by the district technology coordinator that month. The coordinator, Amy Ramirez, introduces each program by reading to what is listed on the package box and documentation, and from these descriptions, teachers volunteer to take the titles with them to review. Sometimes the teachers who take a program have students in the stated grade-level range and other times teachers are enticed by the flashy packaging or program features.

Software that has been reviewed during the last month is also brought back for discussion. At this time, the reviewing teacher offers a few brief comments and then suggests what other teachers might want to review it. Sometimes the reviewer does not like the software package and wants a second opinion. Other times, the original reviewer may feel that the program might apply to grade levels or subject areas other than those listed on the package. According to the official district review process, a piece of software must receive at least three "Excellent" reviews to be accepted, so a minimum of three different teachers must find value in a program in order for it to be proposed to the school board for purchase.

This week, a fourth-grade teacher has a multimedia production program that he highly recommends. He wants a middle or high school teacher to consider it, also, because he has thought of some other uses for it, such as script writing and dramatization. Kathy volunteers to take it with her to look at, remembering that the program sounded interesting when it was introduced at the last meeting. As she walks out of the meeting, she is already planning for how she can perform a thorough review by having students assist her in looking at this software.

---

learning roles, and curriculum issues over the attributes of software packages (Squires & McDougall, 1996). By examining the interaction of the perspectives of the student, the teacher, and the software designer, this new paradigm allows for a comprehensive view of learning, curriculum, and pedagogical issues, promoting new ideas, rather than mere descriptions (McDougall & Squires, 1995b).

Squires and Preece (1996) propose that when checklists separate evaluative categories, it implies that issues of program usability and learning are separated. The authors propose a "Jigsaw" model that provides for software to be evaluated with the ideas of learning interrelated with how a program is actually used.

With another view of how the review of educational software might be updated, Nicholls and Ridley (1997) posit that the new interactive multimedia programs that are becoming the norm in the software industry are so different than text-based learning materials that accordingly they need different methods of review. They contend that these types of programs allow such a range of navigational freedom throughout a variety of media and information that the software creators cannot actually predict just what type of learning experiences are possible. Multimedia software must be looked at like a work of art in the way that there is the potential for interpretation of a higher level of intellectual meaning. The authors are exploring ways in which the potential for these unpredictable individual learning experiences might be assessed.

The lesson educators should take from this shift in evaluation thought is that existing checklists might need to be modified to include more consideration of the learning contexts and the specific types of media being evaluated. Once the experts in the field propose workable models, school districts may want to make decisions as to how well the models can be assimilated into their existing district curriculum goals. Educators need to remember that they are the consumers. If software publishers want to continue to sell new products, they will have to fit the curriculum demands of the end users.

Summary

To ensure the purchase and effective use of quality educational software, districts and schools need to formulate an established plan. Whether it is a committee reviewing the software at the district level or a teacher selecting the best software to fit with a particular lesson, it is imperative to consider the way the software addresses the goals of classrooms, schools, districts, and states. National curriculum standards and current learning theories should also be kept in mind.

Many outside organizations publish reviews of software, both in print and on the Internet, but educators will want to examine all electronic curricular material closely to see if it fits their needs. Everyone involved in the process of evaluating software for educational purposes must understand that all evaluation rests to a large degree on subjective methods. Having a set process and a standard review form of which all participants are informed will help to make the results of reviews somewhat comparable across reviewers.

Checklists are the most common method for recording observations on software strengths and weaknesses. Generally, checklists require reviewers to respond to a range of questions from discrete yes-or-no items to longer narrative descriptions. Checklist review forms should be modified to fit the specific needs of the evaluation purpose.

Some experts say that using checklists to evaluate software focuses the reviewer unnecessarily on technical issues rather than educational concerns. Proposed alternative review methods involve the consideration of instructional context and potential for individual learning.

LEARNER ACTIVITIES

1. Have at least three people in different positions in the educational system (such as a student, parent, administrator, or community member) review the same piece of software. How do their reviews compare and contrast? What does this comparison tell you about the necessity of including different perspectives in educational planning?

2. What modifications would be needed to use the review form in this chapter with students as the reviewers? Choose a target student audience, and make a list of the changes you would make to allow students to use the form to review software independently.

3. Beginning with the indicators on the review form included in this chapter, design a very brief checklist that a classroom teacher could use to make decisions on which software to select for classroom use.

4. Go to the software review websites listed in this chapter. Bookmark them for easy return. How do these review sites compare with the information presented in this chapter?

5. Look up reviews of educational software published in educational technology journals. What are the review procedures? Are the reviews comprehensive enough to convince you to purchase the recommended titles?

6. Write a complete review of a piece of educational software and submit it to the software editor of an educational technology journal.

7. Research a school or district software review process. What types of people are involved in the process? How is review information disseminated to teachers?

8. Examine the current literature discussing educational software evaluation. What trends are emerging?

9. Host an e-mail forum with several peers or colleagues on the overall quality of educational software being produced today. Have participants send their responses to all in the "conversation" to keep everyone involved. Direct the ongoing discussion by sending questions soliciting perceived strengths and weaknesses of software that people have seen or used.

10. Is it possible to review one piece of software for all audiences and purposes? Compose a position paper on the topic, discussing the problems with generic software reviews.

BIBLIOGRAPHY

Association for School Curriculum and Development. (1998). *Only the best.* Alexandria, VA: Author.

Educational Software Preview Guide Consortium. (1998). *1998 educational software preview guide.* Eugene, OR: International Society for Technology in Education.

Graf, N. (1996). Making the CD-ROM choices. *Book Report, 15*(2), 13, 15, 23.

Hakkinen, P. (1996). Software designers and teachers as evaluators of computer-based learning environments. *Machine-Mediated Learning, 5*(2), 135–148.

Hoffman, J. L., & Lyons, D. J. (1997). Evaluating instructional software. *Learning and Leading with Technology, 25*(2), 52–56.

McDougall, A., & Squires, D. (1995a). A critical examination of the checklist approach in software selection. *Journal of Educational Computing Research, 12,* 263–274.

McDougall, A., & Squires, D. (1995b). An empirical study of a new paradigm for choosing educational software. *Computers and Education, 25,* 93–103.

Nicholls, P., & Ridley, J. (1997). Evaluating multimedia library materials: Clues from hand-printed books and art history. *Computers in Libraries, 17*(4), 28–31.

Reiser, R. A., & Kegelmann, H. W. (1994). Evaluating instructional software: A review and critique of current methods. *Educational Technology Research and Development, 42,* 63–69.

Shade, D. D. (1996). Software evaluation. *Young Children, 51*(6), 17–21.

Squires, D., & McDougall, A. (1996). Software evaluation: A situated approach. *Journal of Computer Assisted Learning, 12,* 146–161.

Squires, D., & Preece, J. (1996). Usability and learning: Evaluating the potential of educational software. *Computers in Education, 27,* 15–22.

Sturm, J. M. (1997). How to select appropriate software for computer-assisted writing. *Intervention in School and Clinic, 32*(3), 148–161.

7 Integrating World Wide Web Resources

FOCUS QUESTIONS

1. What considerations must be made to successfully integrate an online resource into a comprehensive lesson sequence?
2. How can understanding a framework of information make it easier to categorize and use Internet resources?
3. In what ways are the capabilities of the Internet reforming distance education?

As schools around the world establish connections to the Internet, and teachers and students gain proficiency with navigating through the vast quantities of readily available information, the true educational potential of the World Wide Web can finally begin to be understood. The web can be a dynamic tool capable of assisting educators in propelling learning to exciting and relevant levels and of bringing education to any students, anywhere, at any time (Ellsworth, 1997). Students can learn from experiences and communication that would never be possible within the scope of an isolated classroom. But instructional resources on the web should never be mistaken as substitutes for the skill and intuition of human teachers, or even thought of as replacements for traditional methods of instruction. Instead, these resources, when used appropriately, should be considered as rich enhancements of a complete educational plan.

Planning for the Instructional Use of Online Resources

The key to the effectiveness of any instructional tool lies partly in the tool's unique attributes, but to a larger degree in how the tool is actually utilized. This is very much the case with educational Internet resources. As was discussed regarding the use of educational software, merely having students sit in front of a computer connected to the Internet will not automatically result in a valuable educational experience. No matter how flashy or cute or seemingly educationally relevant a website or other resource is, if time is not taken to carefully plan for

TABLE 7-1   Questions to Consider When Planning for the Use of Internet Resources

1. What is the educational goal I want my students to achieve?

2. Is this a worthwhile educational goal, whether it be accomplished using electronic or traditional means?

3. Am I trying to make my educational goals conform to the available technology, or am I using these tools to more effectively meet my instructional goals?

4. When compared to other available tools, does this electronic tool effectively assist in obtaining this goal?

5. Can this goal be reached just as effectively using more traditional methods?

6. Is this electronic medium an effective way to teach an educational goal, or is this activity just a skill-building exercise in the use of the tool?

its use as part of an entire instructional sequence, the potential benefits to learners may be squandered. The first step in planning learning experiences that involve online resources is to consider the goals not only for one specific activity, but for the class and even the school as a whole. Ross (1995) offers the questions in Table 7-1 as starting points to the planning.

Understanding the place of an Internet-based activity within the larger scope of an entire curriculum will help teachers plan meaningful and effective learning experiences. Projects should be organized and well defined, just as a traditional lesson taught without technology would be (Barron, 1996). The structure of the lesson should fit with an individual teacher's teaching style and philosophy. If child-centered work is common in a particular classroom, for instance, then child-centered work should be considered for an Internet-based lesson. Of course, this should not discourage teachers from exploring new methods and letting the technology facilitate change in their teaching. It simply must be understood that any change that occurs is not the sole result of the use of any technologies. The Internet can supply the resources to motivate teachers and open their minds to the world around them available online, but this will happen only with the conscious participation of the teachers themselves.

Preparing a Learning Experience

The planning that is necessary to make the most out of an Internet-based lesson is virtually the same as the thoughtful planning that goes into any other quality lesson (Tomei, 1996).

First, define the goals of the lesson. Understanding exactly where a lesson fits into a curricular sequence, taking into account what experiences students have had prior to this lesson and what expectations are held for them following the lesson, will make more efficient use of your time spent searching for Internet resources.

After lesson goals are solidified, locate the online information that will be necessary for the lesson. This can be done by locating a site that has been recommended to you or by conducting a web search for information relating to your topic (see Chapter 4 for searching strategies). Because the quality and age appropriateness of websites vary, you will want to thoroughly explore the entire site prior to ever having students use all or parts of it. Be aware of the reading level and links to other sites that may be off the topic or even inappropriate for your students. Select several sites to provide a well-rounded information base. At this point, you also may want to consider nonelectronic information sources to complement the online information.

Next, plan the lesson, including specific learning objectives, content locations, procedures, and assignments. The form of the lesson plan can vary, from something extremely structured to something with flexible parameters, again according to the teacher's philosophy.

Finally, you are ready to facilitate the lesson. Be aware of some simple logistics, such as whether the online portion of the lesson will be conducted with the whole class together or whether groups will be working independently. Throughout the lesson, be cognizant of student reactions to this learning tool and in what other ways it might be used. Note areas of confusion or exceptional interest for follow-up lessons with other websites.

Assessing an Online Learning Experience

Assessing students' learning with Internet-based lessons is a new area, but it is conceivable that the assessment can come in a variety of forms, from traditional to something that reflects the most current educational research. As students are working through a website or other online resource, they might keep track of their progress. Keeping either a preprepared workbook with content-specific questions, or recording facts and thoughts in a less-structured journal, will provide direction to students in their online exploring. These records can also be used as an ongoing assessment of what students are learning. Ideas for presentations or authentic projects will arise through online searching, and traditional tests or quizzes could also be designed.

Recently, electronic evaluations have become more common on the World Wide Web. Interactive websites designed with special HTML forms working with *Computer Gateway Interface* (CGI) (Dickinson, 1997) allow students to send their answers to questions directly to a server computer. That computer either stores the answers or compares them to the correct answers and provides the students with instant feedback. Teachers will want to monitor these automatic results to see if they will be useful in their own evaluation. Being aware of these new types of evaluation will help teachers get the clearest ideas of how students are learning with the addition of Internet-based activities to the curriculum.

A Framework of Educational Resources

The task of sifting through and sorting out online resources can be a daunting one for teachers with often overwhelming professional responsibilities. Finding useful online information and understanding where it might be integrated into an established curriculum can be accomplished by examining the sites according to some sort of a categorical framework. Although no model can provide definitive organization of the unruly World Wide Web, one metaphor might provide some conceptual understanding. Berenfeld (1996) proposes comparing the scope of the information environment of the Internet to that of the natural environment of living things, commonly referred to as the "biosphere." Because the information environment grows and changes and is based on interdependence of its components, just as is the biosphere, he has coined the term "infosphere" to encompass all of the technology and communication advances in their environment. Extending this metaphor, it can be seen that just as with the reciprocating life processes that occur in nature, the processes that sustain the infosphere entail giving, taking, and nurturing. Based on this systemic view of the information environment, as well as on the proposed organizational models of both Berenfeld and Ellsworth (1997), this chapter presents examples of World Wide Web resources organized into an understandable framework of infosphere processes: planting information, harvesting information, and cultivating information. The ideas for use suggested here should not be taken as comprehensive, but are only meant to spur thinking about integration.

Planting the Information

Any natural cycle survives only with regeneration. That which will eventually be harvested can be so only because it was once planted. The environment of the Internet was built on the idea of the free contribution of ideas, and even students can help in this regenerative process by planting their own seeds of information that will propagate the online resource supply.

Students crave authentic audiences for their work. When they have learned something, it only makes them understand it better to show someone else. The potential size of the World Wide Web audience has taken student sharing to a higher level. Rather than being limited to writing for classmates or family members to read, students can easily publish their work for the world audience. Reports, stories, poems, and school periodicals can be published easily on a server at the school or district (see Chapter 8 for information on creating educational websites). These sites may be presented as a collection of factual information, such that other learners might use it as a resource, or pages could serve the purpose of portfolios, presenting a collection of the products of one student's learning.

There also exist websites dedicated to publishing the writing of students. Because such sites are already created and require only following directions to submit a piece of writing, they are easy ways to let students see their work published.

KidPub: <www.kidpub.org/kidpub/>
KidPub provides a forum for sharing of writing. Students can read stories that others have written and can in turn put their own stories online. By following a simple form, students, either independently or with the help of their teachers, can submit their own writing. Written pieces are placed on the website for others to see, so students gain an authentic audience without having to wait for the long time lines associated with publishing in a traditional magazine.

KidStuff Children's Publishing: <www.worldchat.com/public/kidstuff/a.htm>
This site is dedicated to publishing the writing of authors 14 years of age and younger. The writing must be space-related and can include stories and reports. Students are asked to e-mail their finished products to the website manager to be placed online.

Harvesting the Information

Life is made possible in our biosphere because of the ability of each living thing to gather, or harvest, what is needed for survival. In the information world, the information we need to serve our learning purposes is becoming more readily available and more easily obtainable. Educators using the Internet for educational purposes have at the click of a button the ability to harvest general educational information, content information, insights into what others have experienced that is unusual or different than a present situation, and complete lesson plans. Although examples are given to illustrate each category, most web resources could in actuality be classified in a number of categories.

Jumping Off Sites

The vastness of the World Wide Web can be intimidating, discouraging many novice computer users from venturing forth to investigate the valuable information that can be found. Many times, teachers simply need a safe, informative place to get started. These "jumping off" sites each in turn provide links to a great variety of educational resources, from very general to topic-specific. Someone at each sponsoring organization has done the searching "footwork," meaning that you can benefit from a convenient organized collection.

U.S. Department of Education:
The homepage of the U.S. Department of Education provides timely news regarding the state of education in our country, answers to frequently asked questions, links to related governmental officials, updates on legislation, application information for federal grants, and links to federally funded publications (see Figure 7-1). There are hints for teachers and researchers who use the site, and a search feature allows you to search the expansive site for specific information.

EdWeb:
EdWeb provides links to resources on educational reform and information technology. Success stories about real teachers using computers in classrooms are available, and a discussion area allows for the sharing of topical information among educators.

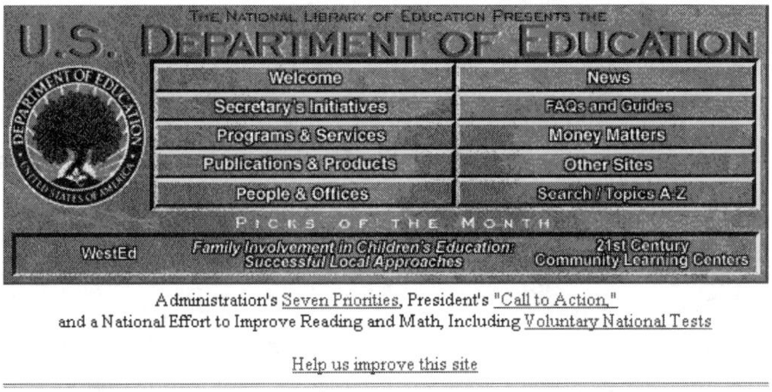

FIGURE 7-1   U.S. Department of Education.

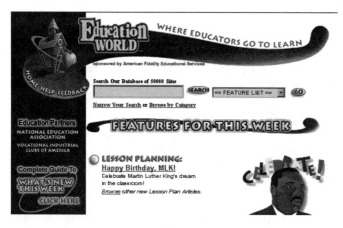

FIGURE 7-2   Education World™. *(Education World and the Education World logo are registered trademarks of Concourse C, Inc. All Rights Reserved)*

Education World: <www.education-world.com/>

Education World boasts a searchable database of over 50,000 educational resource sites (see Figure 7-2). In addition, the site maintains current features on monthly lesson plans, timely education-related news items, administrator articles, curriculum ideas, educational books, and reviews of online educational resources.

The Global Schoolhouse: <www.gsh.org/>

The Global Schoolhouse is organized to provide extensive Internet resources, including teacher activities, software guides, examples of exemplary school computer uses, and classroom Internet projects. The site is searchable and is well-maintained to provide current links to a large variety of educational resources.

Busy Teacher's WebSite: <www.ceismc.gatech.edu/BusyT/>

Compiled by Carolyn Cole of the Georgia Institute of Technology, this site lives up to its name. Organized alphabetically by curricular topic areas from archeology down to social studies, this page leads the way to a wealth of content resources and lesson plans.

InSite: <curry.edschool.Virginia.EDU/insite/>

The Information network of the Society for Information Technology and Teacher Education (InSITE) lists as its goal "Envisioning the integration of technology and teacher education." In pursuit of that goal, the website includes content links and other Internet resources for all levels of educators, including electronic publications, professional organizations, and paths to schools of education across the country (see Figure 7-3).

Content Resources

The largest category of educational resources on the World Wide Web, and those that are most easily incorporated into instructional plans, are those sites providing some type of content information. National organizations, research institutions, or even individual Internet users with

FIGURE 7-3   InSITE: Information Network of the Society for
Technology and Teacher Education.

a great interest in a particular topic might maintain these sites. The quality and extent of information will vary greatly between sites, necessitating thorough preview by teachers before students are asked to use them. These types of content sites can be used as minimally as a supplemental or enrichment resource or can supply the backbone of a series of lessons.

Language Arts

Children's Literature Web Guide:
<www.acs.ucalgary.ca/~dkbrown/index.html>
This is a complete resource locator for those who teach literature to children. The site compiles an annual guide to newly published literature, and points the user to annual award lists, such as Newbery and Caldecott. There are discussion areas, links to other children's literature online resources, a multitude of teaching ideas, and lists of current children's best-sellers. Still more links guide users to information on recommended books, authors, and movies based on books, as well as further resources for teachers, parents, and students.

Shakespeare Web: **<www.shakespeare.com/>**
Whether used to enrich an established curriculum or to spur an individual interest, many gems of information can be found on Shakespeare Web. Itineraries on a traveling Shakespearean theater company and tidbits on Shakespeare history are highlights.

Multicultural Book Review Homepage:
<www.isomedia.com/homes/jmele/homepage.html>
Maintained by students in Seattle University's Master in Teaching program, this site both lists and solicits qualitative book reviews to guide educators in planning for literature exploration. "Reviews of the Month" and links to other related resources complete the rich instructional tool.

Mathematics

Mega-Mathematics: **<www.c3.lanl.gov/mega-math/>**
Mega-Mathematics, a product of Los Alamos National Laboratory, brings very complex mathematical concepts to students in understandable, original ways. Lessons on such topics as colors, graphs, infinity, and algorithms are outlined completely so that teachers are prepared to facilitate the lessons. Lesson components include activities,

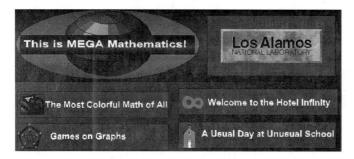

FIGURE 7-4   MEGA Mathematics. *(© 1992 Nancy Casey)*

vocabulary, background information, key concepts, evaluation ideas, relation to NCTM standards, preparation and materials, and indications for further study (see Figure 7-4).

Steve's Dump: Internet Resource Collection:
<forum.swarthmore.edu/~steve/index.html>
An enormous collection of all types of math-related resources, Steve's Dump is a great place for math educators to begin any Internet search. Links to resources are organized by type, topic, and grade level, and an on-site search engine allows for easy searching for specific items.

The Geometry Center: <www.geom.umn.edu/>
Funded by the National Science Foundation, the Geometry Center develops methods in which technology can be used to visualize and communicate mathematics and related sciences. Serving both academic and industrial fields, this site provides links to geometry references, software, course materials, and distance learning resources. Current projects include such areas as spacecraft design, solar system visualization, and satellite constellation visualization.

Science

VolcanoWorld: <volcano.und.nodak.edu/>
Learn about volcanoes from the experts! This NASA-supported site is loaded with everything you every wanted to know about volcanoes (see Figure 7-5). You can find the latest information on currently erupting volcanoes, observatories, and monuments, and research on the topic. Learners can access pictures, videos, stories, games, and activities, and they can even send a message to a real volcanologist. Teachers have available extensive lesson plans, and anyone can arrange to be alerted through e-mail of any new eruptions.

Arizona Mars K–12 Education Program:
<emma.la.asu.edu/neweducation.html>
An extension of the Mars Global Surveyor program, this page coordinates virtual visits to the Mars Global Surveyor TES facility, sponsors teacher workshops, and publishes

FIGURE 7-5   Volcano World. *(University of North Dakota)*

annual teacher guides, Spanish-language materials, and a quarterly, age-appropriate, newsletter for K–8 children, *Red Planet Connection.* There is access to current mission information, K–12 exercises, and even a Mars Global Surveyor paper model! The program is the longest-established Mars K–12 education project (see Figure 7-6).

SeaWorld/Busch Gardens Animal Information Database: <www.seaworld.org/>

Sea World and Busch Gardens maintain this vast website in order to provide an enthusiastic, imaginative, and intellectually stimulating atmosphere for students. Within the site, learners will encounter a list of animal information that spans from animal rescue to zoological park careers, hitting sea turtles, penguins, and even Clydesdales along the way. Teachers can depend on numerous lesson resources and activities designed by the Sea World Education Department. Current animal-related news and "Ask Shamu," a frequently asked questions area on animals, round out the resource.

Arizona Mars K-12 Education Program

Activities of the Arizona Mars K-12 Education Program include: student visits to the *Mars Global Surveyor* TES facility; biannual teacher workshops; workshops at national, regional, and state teacher conventions; visits to schools and community centers; annual teacher guides; Spanish language material; the quarterly newsletter, *TES News*; and a quarterly, age-appropriate, National Standards-based resource for K-8 children, *Red Planet Connection.* The program has been conducting outreach since 1992 and is the longest-established Mars K-12 education project.

FIGURE 7-6   Arizona Mars K–12 Education Program.

FIGURE 7-7   Congress.org. *(Capitol Advantage, McLean, VA)*

Social Studies

Congress.org: <207.168.215.81/>

This federal site links learners with information on activity in the legislative branch of the government. There is a directory of members, a calendar of events, and a list of legislative committees (see Figure 7-7).

The American Civil War Home Page:
<sunsite.utk.edu/civil-war/warweb.html>

The American Civil War Home Page gathers together in one place hypertext links to the most useful electronic files about the American Civil War (see Figure 7-8). The

FIGURE 7-8   The American Civil War Homepage.

lengthy list of links points to resources on time lines, photographs, specific battles, original documents such as letters and diaries, information on state participation, re-enactment groups, and other Civil War organizations.

Emulate Me: <www.emulateme.com/index.htm>
The mission behind Emulate Me's *E-Conflict World Encyclopedia and Simulation* is to eradicate conflict by increasing cultural awareness. The site contains detailed information about all the world's countries, including specifics about each country's economy, defense, geography, government, and people. National anthems are available on audio files, and maps are given as well.

Arts

ArtsEdge: The National Arts and Education Information Network:
<artsedge.kennedy-center.org/artsedge.html>
Operating under an agreement between the Kennedy Center for the Performing Arts and the National Endowment for the Arts, and supported by the U.S. Department of Education, this massive site is designed to help artists, teachers, and students communicate to support the arts in the K–12 curriculum. The listed projects, performances, and study guides are given to further the stated mission: to connect people to people, to connect people to information and resources, and to build a new base of knowledge in arts and education (see Figure 7-9).

Metropolitan Museum of Art: <www.metmuseum.org/>
The Metropolitan Museum of Art, one of the largest and best known art museums in the world, presents on this website collections of several hundred thousand exhibits at any given time. Exhibits cover world culture from prehistory to the present. The site features a calendar that details special exhibits, concerts, lectures, films, and other museum activities.

FIGURE 7-9   ArtsEdge: The National Arts and Education
Information Network.

FIGURE 7-10   Music Education Online.

Music Education Online:
<www.geocities.com/Athens/2405/index.html>
Music Education Online is designed to connect K–12 music educators to a variety of music education resources (see Figure 7-10). Links point to outside sites dedicated to instrumental music, choral music, educational music, musical institutes, and products. Ongoing music-related conversations are possible through an interactive bulletin board.

Experience Simulations

In these days of budget cutbacks, "frivolities" such as field trips are usually some of the first luxuries to go. Students, therefore, are not able to experience firsthand much of what their own community has to offer, let alone the richness and diversity that the world can show them. Through online communication, students can experience vicariously what they cannot see in person. Pictures and stories bring remote events and foreign parts of the world to vivid life through the screen of a computer.

Adventure Online: <www.adventureonline.com/>
From this site, students can follow modern-day explorers as they conquer the world's challenges. Current expeditions include a family retracing Magellan's original travel routes, the first attempt to circumnavigate the world's largest island by dogsled and kayak, and the first ever descent on kayaks down the Nile River. Students live the adventures through the explorers' journals, facts, and e-mail.

Global Online Adventure Learning Site (GOALS):   <www.goals.com/>
Through virtual field trips, GOALS lets students experience travel, adventure, science, technology, and nature (see Figure 7-11). Students can ride along with the first woman from the United States to sail around the world and the first transoceanic rowing expedition, among other adventures. Students can learn through reports, pictures, audio clips, and activities based on the actual exhibitions.

Welcome to the Global Online Adventure Learning Site. Explorers of all ages are invited to travel with us on a growing list of exciting and educational adventures. Our GOAL is to intrigue you with virtual field trips, travel, adventure, science, technology and nature. In addition to being an acronym for our name, the word 'GOALS' and our adventures are intended to inspire our readers to establish and strive for goals of their own, whatever they might be.

To learn More About GOALS click here.

FIGURE 7-11   Global Online Adventure Learning Site (GOALS).

Research Tools

AskERIC:

The Educational Resources Information Center (ERIC) is a federally funded national information system that provides a variety of services and products on a broad range of education-related issues. The *AskERIC* website gives access to education information to teachers, librarians, counselors, administrators, parents, and others (see Figure 7-12). Abstracts of professional journal articles and other educational documents can be searched in order to conduct research on hundreds of search terms.

Internet Public Library:

The Internet Public Library finds, evaluates, selects, organizes, and describes quality information Internet resources. It is arranged just like a real public library, with reference resources, special collections, and periodicals. A separate teen "room" directs teens to such information as arts and entertainment, books and writing, career and college, clubs, computers, and dating. The youth "room" has similar collections of information aimed at a slightly younger crowd.

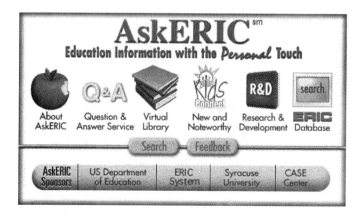

FIGURE 7-12   AskERIC Homepage.

FIGURE 7-13   Library of Congress.

Library of Congress: <www.loc.gov/>
The heart of America's library is its collection of documents, photographs, movies, and audio selections that tell the story of our country. There are also links from this site to legislative information, special national exhibits, and tips and tools for librarians and researchers (see Figure 7-13).

Cultivating the Information

The planting and harvesting that keep the natural life cycle going is not always composed of separate one-sided efforts. Often, cooperation is required to care for growing life. Bees work together to pollinate flowers. Birds carry seeds to help spread the growth. The most exciting aspect of the Internet is the potential for collaborative work between learners. Students in different geographic locations can combine thoughts and talents to learn and discover together. This exchange keeps learning alive and relevant while it opens students' minds to the possibilities for distant cooperation the Internet could provide for their future career paths. E-mail is one way this collaboration might occur. (See Chapter 3 for more information on the educational applications of e-mail.) A growing number of websites now offer the chance for classes to participate in organized online projects.

Quest: NASA K–12 Internet Initiative: <quest.arc.nasa.gov/interactive/>
This rich site brings teachers and students real opportunities to work with scientists, writers, engineers, and other professionals to authentically extend the walls of the classroom out into the real-world community. NASA has designed the activities to be both easy for teachers to set up and satisfying and relevant for students to engage in. Resources include biographies of NASA experts, chats and e-mail, lesson plans and student activities, ideas for collaborative work, areas for students to publish their writing, background and photo sections, and places where teachers can team with professional peers.

K–12 Internet TestBed: **<www.cpb.org/edtech/k12testbed/index.html>**

Sponsored by the Center for Public Broadcasting, the K–12 Internet Testbed has goals to create Internet-based educational networking projects with participants around the nation. The Testbed hopes to explore the potential of student electronic publishing in the classroom. Taking advantage of the experience of local public broadcasters, universities, museums, and other community institutions, it brings together the content development experience of the stations with the instructional experience of educators to foster new ideas and strategies in K–12 networking.

The Good News Bears: **<www.i2s.com/gnb/index2.html>**

The Good News Bears site is an ongoing project component of the Securities Exchange Simulation of the University of Illinois at Urbana–Champaign. Classes who subscribe for the project and pay a fee can participate in tracking and managing their own stock portfolios. Offered for free on the site are basic lessons about the stock market and other monetary issues.

Global SchoolNet Foundation Internet Projects Registry:
<www.gsn.org/project/index.html>

Global SchoolNet (GSN) collaborates with individuals, schools, businesses, and community organizations to design, develop, and manage hundreds of collaborative learning projects each year. This site is self-titled the "Stop-Looking" resource, meaning teachers can stop wasting valuable time looking for projects because all the important projects all listed here. The register includes both GSN's own projects and other Internet-based projects from other sources.

KIDPROJ: **<www.kidlink.org/KIDPROJ/>**

KIDPROJ is a site where teachers and youth group leaders from around the world can plan activities and projects for students (see Figure 7-14). It has been set up for the exchange of curriculum-based activities and other projects among a community of kids and a world of ideas.

FIGURE 7-14   KIDPROJ on the Kidlink Network.

Distance Education

As the availability of Internet resources ushers in changes in traditional forms of education, it simultaneously offers a new dimension to some alternative forms of education already moving past the four walls of a classroom. Distance education is literally defined as "the delivery of the educational process to receivers who are not in proximity to the person or persons managing or conducting the process" (Lewis, Whitaker, & Julian, 1995, p. 14). It has existed in some form for years, often serving students in rural areas who were not able to reach a school, or students who for some health or behavior reasons could not attend traditional school.

The correspondence model of distance education, which has served as the defining model of the field, was usually built around the teacher sending out course materials via regular mail. Upon receiving the materials, the student worked independently to complete the assignments, and then mailed them back to the teacher for grading. The technology that most aided this educational exchange was the telephone, giving students and teachers a chance to discuss necessary topics of concern. Although this arrangement allowed some school participation for large groups of students who otherwise would not receive educational at all, it amounted essentially to a strict delivery of education, with a minimum of guidance aimed at actually inciting learning (Berge & Collins, 1995).

With the advent of a global network of telecommunications, distance education has had new life and possibilities breathed into it. No longer is learning away from a traditional classroom the exception, but rather it is becoming a learner-centered standard many educational models strive to replicate. No longer are remote students left to struggle through learning on their own with only occasional phone contact with their teacher. E-mail and chat groups have provided a forum for relevant, content-rich, supportive online discussions between teachers and students as well as among students. Instead of sitting isolated at home working on assignments by himself, the distance learner can experience the feeling that he is part of a collaborative group of learners, a member of a class that is right there in the room with him. This feeling is called "social presence" (Mason, 1994). The rich assortment of resources that can be found on the World Wide Web augments static distance learning materials and creates an indefatigable research environment.

As students gain greater access to computer hardware and connections to the Internet, the chances for them to learn at a distance from one another increases. Students in small districts who would normally have a limited selection of courses available to them will soon be able to learn from content experts anywhere in the world. Adults who desire additional education will be able to fit the courses they need into a time schedule that fits with their work constraints. Parents who choose to teach their children at home will have available a world full of content and the chance for social contacts that will enrich their children's learning environment.

The near future holds promise for virtual schools, at the university, secondary, and even lower levels. Countless university courses are currently web-supported, offering some portion of their content online, and many are rapidly moving toward complete operation from a distance. A number of high schools are also now offering curricula online. Through a challenge grant funded by the U.S. Department of Education, the Virtual High School project is offering 30 online courses to 600 high school students in 13 states (Harrington-Lueker, 1997). By pooling resources and educator expertise, the range and number of courses

Classroom Vignette

"How many of you have ever been to the ocean?" Mr. Pace asked his third-graders that morning. Five or six sure hands went up, along with a few other tentative ones, and the teacher proceeded to elicit stories from the experiences of these students. Other children said they had seen the ocean on TV and still others had read about it and seen pictures in books.

"Well, I have a way to take you to the beach, without even leaving our classroom." And as sounds of disbelief filled the classroom, Mr. Pace proceeded to explain their new project.

He told them about the teacher from California he met at the conference he attended last month. She also teaches third-graders, and her school just happens to be very near the beach. The two teachers agreed to try a collaborative project to have their students teach each other about their respective climates, Mr. Pace's class about the mountain region in which their community was nestled and Ms. Dillon's class about their beach. He explained how each class would research the other environment, using information from the World Wide Web, as well as more traditional media like books and videos, and report on what they think it is like to live there. Then the classes would read each other's work and use their own personal experiences to help them edit for correctness.

Mr. Pace's class began that day with brainstorming a list of everything they knew about the beach and the ocean. They offered ideas on what they thought kids did for fun and even what kinds of clothes they probably wear. Based on these ideas, the teacher later spent the afternoon searching the Internet for beach-related informational sites, and bookmarking those sites that were appropriate for his students' reading and understanding levels. Combined with the books he had already gathered from the library, and two videos that he reserved from the district media center, he was ready to begin facilitating his students' exploration into life on the beach.

Over the next several weeks, students worked in pairs to investigate what the selected web pages had to offer. They took notes, and they discussed and argued over what the most important information was. Eventually, students wrote, individually and as a whole class, what their impression of what living near the beach must be like. When their thoughts were complete, Mr. Pace posted their drafted text onto their class website.

While Mr. Pace's class had been researching life on the beach, Ms. Dillon's class had been doing the same regarding life in the mountains. Now, each class had an initial report posted on the web, and their jobs switched from researchers to editors. Students in both classes spent time reviewing the other class's site in detail, writing up a list of comments and suggestions to send to their partner class. Each class also gathered pictures showing themselves in their surroundings to be scanned in and sent to the other class for their final website. The comments were e-mailed with the image files as attachments.

Mr. Pace's class eagerly listened as he read Ms. Dillon's class's comments about their research. They found that they were accurate about most of the facts, but needed to add some details regarding the specifics about the particular beach Ms. Dillon's class was most familiar with. They were surprised at how many things were similar even though they lived in such different places. Within several days, the class had amended their website and had developed a fairly complete vision about what it was like to live on the beach.

---

that can be offered to students are greatly enhanced. What a student can learn is no longer limited by the knowledge of individuals who are employed at one particular school building. As people experiment with the types of learning that are possible through the Internet to students at a distance, and as it becomes easier for educators to use and contribute to the online world, the structure of learning undoubtedly will change. Where now many distance courses are designed to closely resemble instruction that occurs face to face, new learning theories will be depended upon to guide new forms of learning for the online world.

Summary

The World Wide Web can be a source of unlimited resources that can bring exciting learning opportunities to students anywhere at anytime. In order to effectively and meaningfully integrate an online resource, teachers must first thoroughly plan a place for it in the comprehensive curricular sequence. Similar to preparing to teach a traditional lesson, it makes sense to first consider the goals of the lesson. Once appropriate websites are found that will help meet those goals, they can be included the lesson plan. Thought should also be given to ways in which technology will affect the facilitation of the lesson and can assist the assessment of learning.

Categorizing available web resources according to a framework makes planning for their use a more realistic task. The Internet can be thought of as an information environment, similar in process to the biological world in which we live. Learners can participate in processes of planting, harvesting, and cultivating information on various websites with potential educational application.

The information environment of the Internet also holds promise for the expansion of opportunities to learn from a distance. Student in rural areas, or those who for various other reasons cannot or choose not to attend traditional school, can now share in content-rich, supportive virtual learning environments. Virtual schools that offer all curriculum online are becoming common. With continued exploration into the possibilities presented by using online resources to facilitate learning, new forms of learning surely emerge.

LEARNER ACTIVITIES

1. Using the questions given in Table 7-1 of this chapter, list a lesson that could be taught effectively using Internet resources and one that could just as effectively be taught through more traditional means. What lesson characteristics might indicate an easy, successful use of Internet resources?

2. Write a lesson plan that integrates information from at least two web resource sites.

3. Visit the content sites listed in this chapter. How are these sites set up? What level of involvement should a teacher have for your intended level of students to successfully use each site?

4. Do a web search for resources that would give contact information. How applicable are these types of sites to your area of teaching interest?

5. Look in the popular educational technology journals. What type of guidance do the articles supply for teachers? Are there complete lessons that you could use unaltered? How much customization will other ideas take to put them into practice?

6. Find an online interactive project for students at your level. How much participation does this project involve? How many suggestions are there for outside activities?

7. What schools in your area offer courses through distance education? Are there single courses available and can entire degrees be completed from a distance?

8. Research the growing field of distance education. What trends are being explored by the leaders in this field?

9. What styles of teachers would not seem to lend themselves to easy integration of online resources? How might these teachers be convinced that such quality information is available on the web?

10. How can the "infosphere" metaphor be used to teach students about the Internet as a learning tool?

BIBLIOGRAPHY

Barron, A. E. (1996). *The Internet: Ideas, activities, and resources.* Tampa, FL: Florida Center for Instructional Technology.

Battle, R., & Hawkins, I. (1996). A study of emerging teacher practices in Internet-based lesson plan development. *Journal of Science Education and Technology, 5,* 321–342.

Berenfeld, B. (1996). Linking students to the infosphere. *T.H.E. Journal, 23*(9), 76–83.

Berge, A. Z., & Collins, M. P. (Eds.). (1995). *Computer mediated communication and the online classroom* (Vol. 3). Cresskill, NJ: Hampton Press.

Bogyo, J. (1997). So you want to use the Internet in the elementary school. *Technology Connection, 4*(2), 10–12.

Dickinson, K. (1997). Distance learning on the Internet: Testing students using Web forms and the Computer Gateway Interface. *TechTrends, 42*(2), 43–46.

Education World™. http://www.education-world.com.

Ellsworth, J. B. (1997). Curricular integration of the World Wide Web. *TechTrends, 42*(2), 24–30.

Harrington-Lueker, D. (1997, September). *Web high.* Electronic School, A26-A29.

Kalmbacher, S. (1996). The Internet: Logon to lesson planning. *Schools in the Middle, 5*(3), 19–22.

Kimeldorf, M. (1995). Teaching online: Techniques and methods. *Learning and Leading with Technology, 23*(1), 26–31.

Lewis, J., Whitaker, J., & Julian, J. (1995). Distance education for the 21st century: The future of national and international telecomputing networks in distance education. In A. Z. Berge & M. P. Collins (Eds.), *Computer mediated communication and the online classroom* (Vol. 3, pp. 13–30). Cresskill, NJ: Hampton Press.

Mason, R. (1994). *Using communications media in open and flexible learning.* London: Kogan Page.

Milheim, W. D. (1997). Instructional utilization of the Internet in public school settings. *TechTrends, 42*(2), 19–23.

Nicholson, D. (1996). Class projects on the Internet. *Education in Science, 170,* 10–11.

Norman, K. (1996). Introducing students to the World Wide Web. *Teaching Music, 3*(5), 34–35.

Ross, P. (1995). Relevant telecomputing activities. *The Computing Teacher, 22*(5), 28–30.

Tobiason, K. (1997). Tailoring the Internet to primary classrooms. *Technology Connection, 4*(2), 8–9.

Tomei, L. A. (1996). Preparing an instructional lesson using resources off the Internet. *T.H.E. Journal, 24*(2), 93–95.

8 Designing Instruction for the Internet

FOCUS QUESTIONS

1. What planning is necessary prior to establishing web-based instruction?
2. What are some strategies for keeping the documents of a website organized?
3. Why is regular maintenance vital to a quality website?

Teachers everywhere are discovering the possibilities for facilitating meaningful learning with World Wide Web resources. Students working at a distance or at a different pace than others, as well as those in a more traditional learning environment, are able to use the web as the actual method of instruction. The more time educators spend working with this instructional and informational mode, the clearer it becomes what types of interactive lessons and communication are conceivable using the web. Once teachers know what can be done, it is only a matter of time before they become comfortable enough to want to start planting their own seeds of information in the web environment. If your school district has server space in which you can publish a website, this chapter gives all the information needed to create well-planned, meaningful web-based instructional or informational sites.

Getting a Mental Plan

Creating a website requires more than just the task of tagging it with the HTML code. There are countless websites accessible now in the online world whose usefulness is questionable. Some prove to be difficult to navigate through, others are visually confusing, and still others contain inaccurate or outdated information. Rushing out and posting just any old website for the sake of saying you or your school has a website does not contribute to the cooperative information base of the web. Instead, it will ultimately serve as a waste of your valuable professional time. You will want to take care that the instructional site you are considering serves your intended purpose in a way that is appropriate for your anticipated audience.

Begin first by asking yourself some questions that will help to define the goals you have for this instructional site. Harris (1997) has suggested the following starting points:

1. Who will be interested in exploring the site?
2. What types of information should be available at the site to address the interests of different audiences?
3. How should this information be presented so that it is maximally helpful to identified project participants and/or to those just browsing through the site?

Audience

If you are designing a site that will provide content information for your students to use for instruction, it will be organized very differently than will a site meant to update parents or other outside community members on school announcements. If you are considering showcasing your students' writing, your site will have distinctive characteristics if the writing is done by kindergartners as compared to that done by sophomores. A website can serve many audiences by directing visitors to different sections. Think carefully about who will be accessing your site most often so that your planning can be efficient and audience-specific.

Types of Information

Primary to the planning of any website should be a consideration of the content the page is being designed to present. Without this forethought, the collection of pages you will be creating will resemble an art project more than the meaningful informative base it could be (Tennant, 1997). A classroom homepage will likely be viewed by parents or others interested in what students in the class are learning and doing. This type of page might include descriptions of projects, pictures of classroom events, or possible ways parents can extend the learning at home. A website meant to provide a thematic starting point for other classes would need to dedicate a certain amount of space to background information and facts pertaining to the project. If people find what they are looking for on your site, they will be more likely to come back to visit again. Inviting comments from visitors about the site and suggestions for what else they would like to see will help you to keep your site updated and relevant.

Presentation Strategies

There is an infinite number of ways to arrange the information on a website. Viewers may be required to scroll down the page through long chunks of text, or links can take viewers directly to other pages of information. Sometimes, your students might want to write the text of the page themselves, and other times, it might make more sense to provide a link to another established site that has already compiled an excellent treatment of the topic.

Based on your answers to these types of planning questions, you will begin to define the purpose of your proposed website. A website can take many forms in order for it to serve your identified purpose. One of the easier sites to begin with is a class homepage providing information to parents. A page such as this might be organized, as would a newsletter that might be sent home, with such items as homework assignments and upcoming announcements.

In addition to these basic inclusions, website functions will also fall into the categories of web resources presented in Chapter 7. Written stories can be published for all to see and collaborative projects with other classes can be managed via your website. You might design an instructional site that provides content information your students need for class, or you might supply thematic information to keep parents apprised of what is happening in school. Field trips and other experiences can be documented though digital photographs and written reflections to share with other classes who may not have made the same trip or who may not be familiar with your area of the country. Unlimited amounts of online resources can be compiled by and for your students.

Sketching Out a Visual Plan

With a good mental plan for what your site needs to include, your next move is to plan how you want the site to appear to others who will be viewing it. It would be easy to skip this planning step in favor of getting right to the HTML programming, but your valuable time could be wasted trying to visualize what you want the site to look like at the same time you are creating the site documents. A small amount of planning time up front will not only save time later, but will make for a more organized and easy-to-use website.

Begin by closely examining other websites you visit. Look at how the designer has laid out the text and graphics. Is it aesthetically pleasing or does it appear that page elements were just dropped in randomly? Are the graphics serving an obvious educational purpose or do they appear to be there for decoration only? Is the font size and style appropriate for the content? As you move around from page to page, is the navigation intuitive and well-organized, and once you get to another page, is it easy to get back to where you started?

When you have seen what is being shown on others' pages, sketch out what you envision for your page on a storyboard or a sequence of screen layouts. Your storyboard can be very rough or extremely detailed, as long as it gives you an idea of where text will be located, what size and other formatted text will be used, where graphics will be integrated, and how the navigational path is planned (see Figure 8-1). A simple, clean layout is the best place to start, as more complexity can be added later if desired.

Use specially formatted text, such as **bold-face** or *italics,* judiciously. An overly formatted page is difficult to read, and your user might spend more time concentrating on the abundance of special text rather than on the content of the page. Images should also be chosen carefully. Large graphics take a long time for the browser to load, which slows down the use of your website. Make sure that every picture serves a purpose in your layout and overall goals, rather than

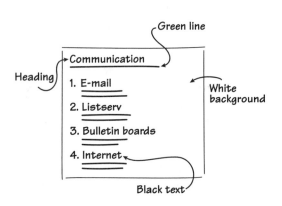

FIGURE 8-1   Sketching a storyboard for a web page.

just providing meaningless clutter. Your page will appear even more organized if you plan all the pages to have a consistent look and feel, such as by using the same background color or coordinating graphics throughout the entire site.

List in your storyboard the URLs for any hypertext links you would like to create. Good web design calls for fitting the link seamlessly into the text, rather than telling the user to "Click Here." Include links that enrich the information on your site, but not so many that the user is constantly thrown offtrack. The linked resources should directly pertain to the goal of the lesson or informational piece.

Just as you create hyperlinks to other outside resources, you can also link your home-page to other pages in your own website. Connect pages within your storyboarded site with arrows showing the paths for how the user will be able to travel through the pages (see Figure 8-2). Plan a simple navigational path. You do not want people who visit your site to be lost wandering around between your pages. Make sure you include a link back to your home-page on every other page in your site. Add to your storyboard any custom colors you plan on using to help you get an idea of whether the color scheme is visually pleasing and appropriate for your intended audience. The background color or image should be in high contrast to the text, such as light text on a dark background or dark text on a light background. Your students will be less likely to succeed in their web learning experience if they must struggle to make out what the page says. Finally, plan to place your name or school name and the date in a prominent place on the page so that people accessing your page will know how current the information is and how to contact you should they have comments or questions.

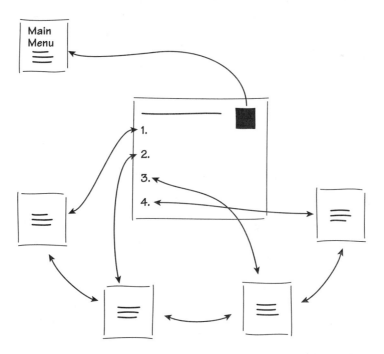

FIGURE 8-2   A storyboard showing the navigational path for a website.

To ensure an organized and easily modifiable website, it makes good sense to keep a record of the files names of the HTML documents you create. Cafolla and Knee (1996–1997) recommend documenting the following information to create a complete record:

- page titles
- source of each link and the reasons it was selected
- source of the graphics
- size and type of graphics
- width of horizontal lines

Even as you storyboard, jot down filenames you plan on giving to these pages. Keep to brief, logical filenames so you will remember what each page is by the name alone. Always use lowercase filenames to make it easier for your users to access your site with a browser. Web addresses are case-sensitive, so someone trying to find your site at "myhomepage.html will not get there if it is actually named "MyHomepage.html." At this point in your planning, this record will serve as a checklist to guide your page creation. Later, when you are updating your site, it will streamline your job by reminding you of the filenames and the organization of the files.

Tagging the Website

Now that you are armed with both a mental concept and a visual plan, you are ready to begin creating the actual documents that will make up your instructional site. Remember from Chapter 4 that a web page is a text document that uses HTML tags to tell the browser software how to display the page (see Figure 8-3). There are two main ways to create a web document. The original way, and some purists would say the only right way, is to type the text and HTML tags using a word processing software. A quicker and less tedious way is to use a software application called an HTML editor.

Either way you choose for your page creation, you will want to save your document, either to a disk, hard drive, or some other location, using the document names you planned on your storyboard beforehand. Save each file as "text-only" with an ".html" extension so that a browser will be able to display it. You can instantly view what your page will look like on the web by opening the file you saved in your browser. Your page should be fully functional when run off a disk or other local drive, but must be put online by transferring the files to a Web server for others to be able to access it.

Text by itself on a web page would appear plain and unformatted without using HTML tags to tell the browser exactly how you want the document to appear. Browsers are designed to only interpret the HTML tags, while ignoring other formatting, like from a word processor. Clicking on the **Return** key several times while creating the document, for example, may make a nice space in your document as it appears in your word processor, but the browser will just run all of your text together if it does not see specific tags telling it to put several blank lines in between the text. This can be frustrating the first few times you work with an HTML document because the tagged document looks very different than the browser-rendered page.

Tags are identified to the browser by the symbols < >. When the browser comes to these symbols, it knows that it is about to get specific instructions for how to display some

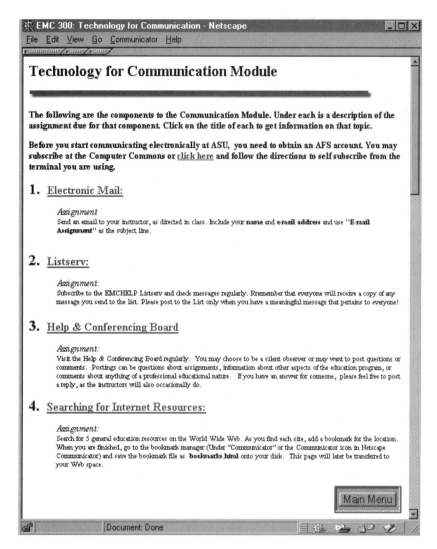

FIGURE 8-3 The finished web page. *(Copyright 1998 Netscape Communications Corp. Used with permission. All Rights Reserved. This electronic file or page may not be reprinted or copied without the express written permission of Netscape)*

part of the page. Many of the tags come in pairs, with a beginning tag and an ending tag, and whatever text or graphic lies between the two tags will be formatted according to those directions. These tags are sometimes referred to as "container" tags because the pair of tags contain the text to be altered between them. Several different levels of tags can operate on the same text. They should be arranged in a hierarchical manner, with the outermost tags applying to the larger portion of text and the innermost tags formatting the more specific text. Refer to Figure 8-4 for examples of how the HTML tags appear in a document and Figure 8-5 to see how the same page would look when presented on a browser screen.

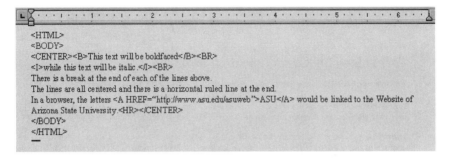

FIGURE 8-4   A sampler HTML document showing document, paragraph, character, and hypertext reference tags.

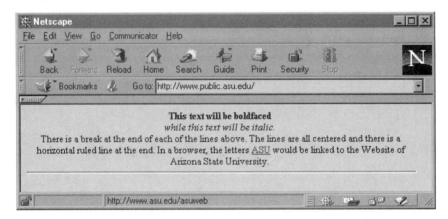

FIGURE 8-5   The way the tagged document would appear in a browser. *(Copyright 1998 Netscape Communications Corp. Used with permission. All Rights Reserved. This electronic file or page may not be reprinted or copied without the express written permission of Netscape)*

Document Tags

Document tags set the parameters for the entire document. These tags identify the document as an HTML document (**<HTML>, </HTML>**), define the two parts of the document, the head (**<HEAD>, </HEAD>**) and the body (**<BODY>, </BODY>**), and name the title of the document that will be seen in the menu bar of the **browser** (**<TITLE>, </TITLE>**). In the hierarchical order, the **<HTML>, </HTML>** tags are outermost, at the very beginning and the very end, because they affect the entire page.

Paragraph Tags

Paragraph tags give directions to the browser for displaying different sections within the body of text. Remember that simply returning to start a new line will not affect the way the text appears in the browser. To force the text to go to the next line, use the break return (**
), or to skip two lines, use the paragraph tag (<P>**). Notice that these two tags are only one-sided, because they create a space rather than contain any piece of text to be formatted. Section headings are automatically centered and boldfaced. They can be formatted in one of six heading sizes by using one of the levels of tags (**<H1>, </H1>** through **<H6>, </H6>**) with H1 being the largest. A paragraph or other section of text can be centered (**<CENTER>, </CENTER>**) and a horizontal-ruled line can be added to separate text sections (**<HR>**). Numbered or ordered lists can be identified (**<OL>, </OL>**) as can unordered or bulleted lists (**<UL>, </UL>**). Each item in a list is preceded individually with a tag to identify it as a list member (**<LI>**).

Character Tags

Character tags format individual letters or words. Any group of characters can be enclosed between beginning and ending tags that identify the text as boldfaced (**<B>, </B>**), italic (**<I>, </I>**), underlined (**<U>, </U>**), typewriter style (**<TT>, </TT>**), superscript (**[,]**), or subscript (**_,**). The font size can be assigned (**<FONT SIZE="1">, </FONT>**), and more recent versions of browsers allow the font style to be assigned (**<FONT STYLE="ARIEL">, </FONT>**).

Hypertext Anchor Tags

Hypertext anchor tags define words or images that when clicked on serve as pathways to other pages. The anchor tag is two-sided (**<A>, </A>**) and includes the destination address of the link. Enclosed between the two sides is the object that will be linked, such as a selection of text or an image. Anchors can indicate directions to three different places. First, links can be created to other websites anywhere in the world. The first half of the tag includes the hypertext reference modification as well as the URL of the destination site. The text or image that will comprise the hyperlink follows this beginning tag and the ending tag completes the code (**<A HREF="URL here"> text to be linked here</A>**).

Hypertext links can also be created from your homepage to other pages within your own site. The tag is identical to the previous, except that the URL will point to your own site address ending with the precise path of the file as it resides on your system (**<A HREF= "http://URL/filename.html">text to be linked</A>**).

If your document is long, you might want the user to be able to jump ahead to a later part of the same page rather than needing to scroll down the entire page. Go first to that later part, and give it a name by using the anchor tag with the NAME modification. In this example, **<A NAME="chapter3">How to Use E-Mail</A>,** an anchor point called "chapter3" has been placed at that document location. Now, the place you want to insert the link to this location must be identified. Use the same anchor tag, but with a hypertext modification to identify this as an active link. If at the beginning of your document you want the user to be able to click on the Words "Chapter 3" to jump to that already named location, use the tag **<A HREF="#chapter3>Chapter 3</A>.** The pound sign indicates that the destination is within this same document.

The hypertext tag can also be used to give people a way to communicate with you through e-mail. The e-mail tag automatically opens the e-mail client of the browser they are using when it is clicked on. Use the hypertext anchor tag, but with the "mailto" modification and your e-mail address (**<A HREF=mailto:e-mail address here>text to be linked</A>**).

Multimedia Tags

Images, audio files, and video files can be used to create an effective learning environment for your website. In order to use one of these three aesthetic enhancements, you must have the actual file saved in the same directory in which your website documents are stored. When the browser sees the tag directing it to display an image or play an audio file, it will look for it in that local directory. If the file is not located in that directory the browser will show a generic image with a question mark indicating the absence of the graphic file.

For an image to be viewable on the web, it must be saved in a format with either a **.gif** or **.jpg** extension. There are several ways to obtain useable images for your web pages. You can first save an existing image from another website. To save an image from another website, click the right mouse button over the image (or hold down the button for a second or two with a Macintosh). You will be given the option to save it and will be asked to choose where you want it saved. Using images from another person's website is very easy, but also very risky. Unless otherwise stated, all images are assumed to be copyrighted. If you save an image of a well-known commercial entity, and put it on your own website, expect to be served with a "Cease and Desist" order to stop violating their copyright by removing the image from your site. Use only images from sites maintained specifically for the purpose of providing copyright-free graphics for web development. Performing a web search for the search string "graphics" or "clipart" should yield several websites dedicated to this purpose.

You can create suitable graphic images by using a graphics software application. Be sure to save the file with the .gif or .jpg extension. Graphic files can also created by digitally scanning a photograph or other print-based picture using a scanner, which can save an image in either of the two formats.

To insert an image into your web-page document, use the one-sided image source tag identifying the file name of the image (**<IMG SRC="filename.gif">**). An image can also be used as the page background. Go back to the BODY tag earlier in the document and give the background modification, along with the name of an image file (**<BODY BKGRND= "filename.gif">**). This image will then be "tiled" or repeated over and over to fill the entire screen background.

Audio (**.wav**) and video (**.avi**) files are coded with the same tag that identifies a hypertext link (**<A HREF="filename.wav">put text to be linked here</A>**). Browsers interpreting this tag will automatically begin the media application that is necessary to run the file. If a file is very large, as some multimedia files can be, it is good etiquette to tell your users the approximate file size so they know how long they may need to wait.

Tagging text is not difficult given this list of tags, but it can be very tedious. An errant space or missing bracket means your tag is incomplete, making it impossible for the browser to interpret it correctly. For instance, using the beginning **<B>** tag to mark text as boldfaced and using the ending **</B** tag with a missing bracket will make the browser interpret the rest of the document after the boldface tag as *all* boldfaced. Because the HTML conventions

must be adhered to exactly, software designers have found a way to make this programming easier by creating HTML editors.

HTML Editors

HTML editors are to web-page creation as calculators are to computation, or even as electric mixers are to baking. The results are quicker and easier with the tools of convenience, although there are those who might say that those basic skills you learn doing it the "old-fashioned" way lead to a better end product. When HTML editors first hit the market, they were able only to format with the basic tags, but could not be counted on to produce some of the more advanced formatting. As is always the case with innovation and progress, however, the more recent editors are able to handle most of the more complex HTML programming, making web-page creation accessible to even those with no HTML knowledge whatsoever. This is good news for teachers who want to try their hand at designing web-based instruction but fear their busy professional lives will prevent them from learning a complicated coding language.

HTML editors look and act very much like word processors. The ease of operation is based on a convention called WYSIWYG, which is an acronym for "What You See Is What You Get." Rather than seeing a mess of tags identifying various types of formatting, you see on the screen the actual formatted results. If you want a title to be centered, for example, the program shows it to you centered. Without you realizing it, the **<CENTER>, </CENTER>** tags are being added into the actual HTML document behind the scenes. Editors automatically insert the document formatting and allow you to choose any other of the paragraph and character formatting that is available by clicking on toolbar buttons for each of the procedures. Images can be easily inserted by clicking on the image button and identifying what image file you want. To create text that is hyperlinked, simply highlight the text, click on the link button, and type in the URL or other destination location. Whenever you want to view the actual HTML tags, you can usually click on a button to view the source of the document, and here you will notice all of the tags that have been inserted into the document (see Figure 8-6).

Editing software allows you to create documents in two ways. Brand new documents can be written just as a word processing document would be and can be saved with a filename of your choice. If you are not sure how you want to lay out a page, but you have seen someone else's page on the web that you like, you can actually save their page onto your hard drive and bring it into the editor as a starting point for your page, using it as a template. Copyright laws are ever-evolving with regard to online information (see Chapter 14 for more information on copyright law), so caution must be taken to ensure that you are using only the page layout or formatting and not unlawfully using someone else's original text information. Many pages now come with copyright information listed at the bottom giving specific guidelines for what on their page can be used and what is protected, so be sure to check this citation before you use any part of an existing web page.

Editing software is available from a number of sources. The original, and many of the still current, editors are designed as stand-alone products, meaning that they are packaged as

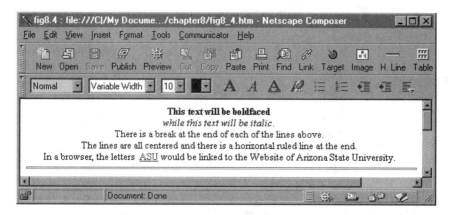

FIGURE 8-6 The sampler HTML document in Netscape Page Composer. *(Copyright 1998 Netscape Communications Corp. Used with permission. All Rights Reserved. This electronic file or page may not be reprinted or copied without the express written permission of Netscape)*

a complete application. Browser software, such as Netscape, now comes with a competent HTML editor as one feature, meaning that pages can be instantly viewed as they would appear online. Finally, newer versions of word processing programs, like Microsoft Word, allow the user to save a document as an HTML file, making it web-ready without even having to know what an HTML tag is. Some knowledge of basic HTML does come in handy if there is an error in the way the editor has tagged your page, but as the software genre improves, skills with HTML may go the way of the abacus and the slide rule.

Maintaining a Quality Website

If you are taking the time to design and create a website, you will want to be sure that you are posting a quality product and that the pages stay in good condition as time goes by. Make the time to check your site when you think you are finished constructing it, and then set a regular schedule of making updates and improvements.

Check Your Site

Just as you might have someone proofread something you have written, have someone who has not seen your website previously and who is able to provide candid comments navigate completely through the site. Have them first check for basic spelling and grammatical errors. Putting a page on the Internet with these types of errors is reprehensible and reflects poorly on both you as a web designer and on your school as a quality educational institution. Have your test user also check all of the navigational paths to make sure that every link goes where it says it does and that the routes are intuitive and allow for easy return to the homepage. You may have forgotten along the way to add a URL or check to see if resource sites were still operable. This way you will find it before your students or parents have the chance to become confused. It is important, also, to get an outside opinion on the page layout and color scheme. When you have worked with a page for quite a while, you may not even realize that the graphics make it hard to follow or that the font color is difficult to see on your chosen background.

Update Your Site

In the online world, information frequently changes, making it necessary for you keep up or risk letting your site become antiquated. Skeletons of websites that are no longer functioning or current litter the Internet, slowing down search engines and proving endlessly frustrating to busy people looking for timely information (Tennant, 1997). Websites to which you have linked may be there one day and may vanish the next. If your links go nowhere, the learning goals you have for your students will not be achieved. Go through to check your links regularly, deleting or adding any as necessary. If your site contains content information, be on the lookout for any new developments in the field that should be included in your selection. New research or discoveries keep the site current and keep your audience motivated. As your class changes its thematic concentration, change your page to fit its studies. Any other timely data, such as announcements of upcoming events or homework calendars, must be kept up to date for the site to be fully functional.

Improve Your Site

As you browse through other websites, you may notice design features or instructional sequences that might add to your site's functionality or appearance. Do not be afraid to make changes, either subtle or drastic. Just because you liked that lime-green background when you originally designed the site does not mean it still serves your purposes today. Any good instruction must be flexible enough to accommodate new ideas. Changing the look and feel of your site will keep it fresh and keep regular visitors coming back.

Involving Students in Web Design

What better way to teach students about the Internet and instill some pride and confidence in their own work than to have them participate in the designing of a website. All of the aspects of website creation discussed in this chapter can be accomplished by students as well as by adults, and at times might even be handled better by students. The complete process can prove to be a valuable cross-curricular project. Depending on the abilities of the students, they can gain practice with written language and with measurement, such as with graphic sizes as they work with the page design and layout. They can do the background research, both on the content to be presented on the site and on websites to which links will be created. Participating in the process from the beginning through completion will teach students about follow-through and accomplishment. Some schools are even able to offer students their own individual homepages on which they can publish their writing for an authentic world audience.

Classroom Vignette

The fifth-graders from Mrs. Tabor's class are settling in on the floor next to their first-grade "buddies" in Miss Kennedy's room. For five weeks, each of the classes has been studying "Habitats," both with age-appropriate assignments in their own rooms and integrated projects together. They are now preparing to go on their field trip to the museum next week. Mrs. Tabor and Miss Kennedy have decided that a great way to share their trip experience with the other classes at school, as well as with the students' families, would be by putting up a website detailing what they have learned and what they see at the museum. They plan on taking the digital camera on the trip, so any pictures they take on the trip can be automatically inserted into the web page.

Prior to meeting together, each of the two classes separately has already brainstormed long lists of what they have learned so far in this habitat unit. Now, the two classes sit looking at both charts of data, ready to make some decisions on what they want to include in their website. The teachers lead the discussion, with students from both classes offering their ideas. Finally, through much discussion, a list of core learnings is decided upon.

Now comes the job of designing their site. Using a projection system with her classroom computer, Miss Kennedy shows several different websites she has found that are useful in pointing out to students layout features and color combinations. The classes talk about what types of pictures they will be able to use and how to best showcase student writing. Working with their buddies, the students then sketch out on chart paper their ideas for how their website might be arranged. It is too large of a job to finish in one sitting, but over the next couple of days before the field trip, the classes compare all of the proposed page designs to decide on a final layout. It is also decided that each student will contribute some of his or her writing for the project, and several students have artwork on habitats that will be scanned in using the scanner down in the media center.

Back in their own classroom following the field trip, the fifth-graders learn how to use an HTML editing program. Together with Mrs. Tabor, they make a class practice website to get the feel for how to use the program. Over the next several weeks, the fifth-grade students bring their first-grade buddies in to work on converting their writing to HTML and laying out their individual pages. When the website is finished, the two classes have a dynamic record of their trip and all that they have learned that can be viewed and used by other classes and even parents at home.

Summary

Once teachers are familiar with integrating online resources into traditional instructional modes, they are ready to try exploring how to design web-based instruction. Planning ahead of time will ensure a site that serves your intended purpose for your anticipated audience. Sketching out a storyboard will help to visualize what the website will look like and how it will be organized. To be helpful in the planning process, a storyboard should include text location, text attributes, graphics, and color. Arrows connecting the cells of the storyboard show the possible navigational paths.

A document that will be seen on the World Wide Web is created using hypertext mark-up language (HTML) tags, which tell the browser how to display the page for the viewer. Documents coded with HTML can be created either in a word processor by inserting the raw tags or by using a type of software application called an HTML editor.

HTML tags describe formatting for the entire document, a paragraph, or individual characters. Other tags instruct the browser to insert hyperlinks or images.

Completed websites must be maintained to ensure they remain quality learning and information tools. On a regular basis, inspect your site for accuracy and functionality. Replace outdated facts or linked sites and determine if improvements are needed.

LEARNER ACTIVITIES

1. Create a simple storyboard of a lesson that incorporates at least two thematic online resources.

2. View the source code on a website. Compare the tagged document to the browser-rendered page. Can you follow the code?

3. Bookmark ten thematic websites that could be used to teach a concept. Check these websites periodically to see if they are being maintained with current information and if they are still functioning. How many of the sites are still quality instructional resources after one month? Six months? One year?

4. Using an actual newsletter that a classroom teacher has sent home in printed form as a template, create an electronic newsletter website.

5. Find a classroom homepage on the World Wide Web. What types of items are included? How well is it organized? Is there quality instruction or mainly just informational items?

6. Find an educational website. Have two students from your level of interest go through the website following all of the instructions that are given. Record their progress and their comments. What improvements do you think would be warranted based on their results? What improvements do they suggest?

7. Survey a group of parents to see how many would make use of an informational class website if their children's classes had one available. Do this group's responses seem to fit with the impression the media gives of parents' attitudes toward technology integration in the schools?

8. See if you have access at your school to a web editing application. Familiarize yourself with the software operations, and save a sample HTML document.

9. Find out the procedures at your school for saving web documents to a web server.

10. Research what the experts recommend when designing web-based instruction. What considerations make for good instruction across grade levels and topics? What specific attributes are relevant to your chosen level or area?

BIBLIOGRAPHY

Barkhouse, N. (1997). Grasping the thread: Web page development in the elementary classroom. *Emergency Librarian, 24*(3), 24–25.

Burgstahler, S. (1997). Teaching on the Net: What's the difference? *T.H.E. Journal, 24*(9), 61–64.

Cafolla, R., & Knee, R. (1996). Creating World Wide Web sites. *Learning and Leading with Technology, 24*(3), 6–9.

Cafolla, R., & Knee, R. (1996–1997). Creating World Wide Web sites. Part 2: Implementing your site. *Learning and Leading with Technology, 24*(4), 36–39.

Cafolla, R., & Knee, R. (1997). Creating Educational Web sites. Part 3: Refining and maintaining the site. *Learning and Leading with Technology, 24*(5), 13–16.

Descy, D. E. (1997). Web page design. Part one. *TechTrends, 42*(1), 3–5.

Descy, D. E. (1997). Web page design. Part two. *TechTrends, 42*(2), 3–5.

Descy, D. E. (1997). Web page design. Part three. *TechTrends, 42*(3), 7–9.

Harris, J. (1997). Content and intent shape function: Designs for web-based educational telecomputing activities. *Learning and Leading with Technology, 24*(5), 17–20.

Hill, J. R., Tharp, D., Sindt, K., Jennings, M., & Tharp, M. (1997). Collaborative web site design from a distance: Challenges and rewards. *TechTrends, 42*(2), 31–37.

Monahan, B., & Tomko, S. (1996). How schools can create their own web pages. *Educational Leadership, 54*(3), 37–38.

Quinlan, L. A. (1997). Crafting a web-based lesson. Part two: Organizing the information and constructing the page. *TechTrends, 42*(1), 6–8.

Richardson, E. C. (1996). Site construction. *Internet World, 7*(4), 62–64, 66.

Scigliano, J. A., Levin, J., & Horne, G. (1996). Using HTML for organizing student projects through the Internet. *T.H.E. Journal, 24*(1), 51–56.

Tennant, R. (1997). Web sites by design: How to avoid a "pile of pages." *Syllabus, 11*(1), 49–50.

9

Designing Lesson Plans

Subject Areas

FOCUS QUESTIONS

1. What types of thoughts must go into planning for any lesson that will integrate the use of technology?
2. How can technology be integrated into your own content area?
3. What clues can teachers use to decide when a particular technology lends itself well to the teaching of a particular topic, and when other nontechnical strategies might be more appropriate?

Chapter 1 presented profiles of technology-literate students. Of course, it is ideal when children are introduced to computer literacy topics and computer-assisted instruction in their earliest school experiences. The knowledge they gain early on then serves as a foundation for continued computer learning through high school and even into adulthood.

Perhaps the most important concept for students to grasp is that the computer is a powerful tool for getting work done. When computers are used across the curriculum, students begin to appreciate the vast range of tasks that can be accomplished with computer power. The computer no longer appears to be a technological enigma that can be understood only by science and math wizards. Students come to understand the computer as a manageable and multifaceted tool for writing essays and stories, performing sociological and scientific research, solving mathematical problems, and learning more about any subject they wish to study.

Teachers of all subject areas can foster this attitude in their students by introducing computer learning into their curricula. This presents quite a challenge to teachers who are themselves novice computer users or who specialize in subjects that are not traditionally associated with computer usage. To assist teachers in designing workable lesson plans that will maximize the time their students spend working with computers, this chapter presents sample lesson plans for five major curriculum areas: mathematics, science, language arts, social science, and special education. It is our hope that teachers will use these lesson plans as a springboard for their own creativity.

Formulating Lesson Plans

Teachers will find that the process of designing lesson plans that include computer media is very similar to designing traditional lesson plans. Many of the same factors must be taken under consideration, whether students work with computers or with pencil and paper. In formulating lesson plans, the teacher tries to answer a series of questions:

- For what ages or grade level is this lesson appropriate?
- What is the objective of the lesson? What will students know or be able to do after completing the lesson?
- What materials are required to perform this lesson?
- What preparation is required on the teacher's part? On the students' part? What knowledge, skills, and concepts are necessary for students to complete the lesson successfully?
- What activity is most effective in teaching the lesson?
- How will student learning be evaluated after the lesson is completed?
- What follow-up activities may be useful in reinforcing or expanding knowledge gained through the lesson?
- What special notes will contribute to greater success of the lesson?

Most teachers are accustomed to considering these factors in creating lesson plans. There are additional factors that can make or break the computer learning experience. Other questions a teacher might address are

- Which technology is best suited for meeting the learning objective?
- What aspect of the computer's capabilities make it the best tool to use?

To a large extent, lessons must be tailored according to the hardware and software resources available in the individual teacher's classroom, school, or district.

- Do students have access to computers in the classroom so that the only person controlling the amount of computer time is the classroom teacher?
- If so, how many computers are available?
- Can the entire class participate in the lesson at the same time or will students need to work in shifts?
- Will students work individually, in pairs, or in larger groups?
- If computers are available in a central setting such as the media center, what constraints are placed on computer time for students?
- Will students work during normal class hours or will they schedule computer time outside of normal class hours?

These factors will determine how practical a given lesson plan is for a particular class.

All the lesson plans presented here have been designed for flexible use. That is, they can be tailored easily to meet the special needs of an individual teacher or class. Teachers can simplify a complex lesson for younger or less experienced students by providing or even inputting data before the lesson begins. On the other hand, a relatively simple lesson becomes more challenging if students are required to research and key in data on their own. Teachers can also customize lesson plans by changing the topic of a lesson. For example, the lesson plan for researching computer scientists is also useful for researching chemists, biologists, zoologists, and so forth.

Another feature of the lesson plans in this chapter is that they are uniform in format. It is recommended that teachers decide on a standard format for designing lesson plans. Doing so makes it easier to share lesson plans with other teachers who want to introduce computer-based instruction in their own classrooms.

The format of the lesson plans incorporates the following subheads:

- Grade level
- Objective
- Materials
- Preparation
- Activity
- Evaluation
- Follow-up
- Special notes

Grade Level.   This is an indicator of the age or grade level for which the lesson is considered appropriate. It should be used as a guideline only, not as a hard and fast rule. The level of difficulty of the lessons can be adjusted for different grade levels or even different ability levels within the same class. Gifted students and those with prior computer experience will probably be quite successful with lessons aimed at higher grade levels.

Objective.   A simply stated goal or set of goals that the lesson should accomplish should be established. The objective indicates what knowledge or skill the student will acquire or strengthen by completing the lesson. Of course, in a very real sense, all computer-based lessons share an important objective: to help students become comfortable and competent in using the computer as a tool.

Materials.   This is a broad category that covers the hardware, software, and other teaching materials required to facilitate the lesson. The teacher needs to determine whether sufficient hardware exists to run the software called for in the lesson.

- Do computers have enough memory to run the software?
- Is the software readily available or must it be ordered externally?
- Does the course material to be used include other teaching materials such as textbooks, workbooks, ditto masters, and so on? A critical consideration under this category is whether there is an available source of data that students will need to complete the assignment.
- Do students have access to a database through telecommunications or will they be required to do library research before beginning computer work?

Preparation.   This section of the lesson plan lists the preparation required before the lesson is presented. In most cases, preparation included background information, concepts, skills, and vocabulary that students need to have mastered before attempting the lesson. But there are also other factors. Does the teacher need to format disks, copy files, or enter data before students can perform the lesson? Do students need to perform research or conduct polls to generate the data they will need?

Activity.   This section of the lesson plan is a step-by-step description of the activity in which students will participate. Often, much of the activity does not require hands-on work on the computer but rather it calls for research, polling, completing data entry sheets, and other activities that are part of the learning experience.

Evaluation.   After completion of the lesson, students should be evaluated to determine whether they have in fact accomplished the objective(s) of the lesson. This section indicates the most practical method of evaluating results of the activity.

Follow-Up.   The follow-up section of the lesson plan lists classroom activities that can occur after completion of the lesson to reinforce or expand skills and knowledge gained during the lesson. Follow-up helps ensure retention of mastery and can also help students see relationships among various activities in the classroom and how these activities relate to the world outside.

Special Notes.   Teachers may want to include special comments or notes in the lesson plan that indicate potential problems and solutions. This section can also be used to record ideas for varying the lesson plan so that it can be used in another subject area or with a different group or level of students. Any additional information that is pertinent to the success of the lesson is included under this heading.

Under each of the five subject areas included—mathematics, science, language arts, social science, and special education—two lesson plans are given. The first is recommended for elementary classes; the second is recommended for secondary classes. Again, the level of difficulty of the lessons can be adjusted to classroom needs by the teacher. None of the lesson plans calls for a specific software package, unless the package is available in the public domain at no cost or at a nominal cost. In some instances, commercial software has been suggested as a possible alternative or enhancement to the basic lesson. Thus, teachers with limited software budgets can make use of these lesson plans.

Lesson Plans for Mathematics

Because of its number-crunching ability, the computer is an excellent tool for use in teaching mathematics. Much of the educational software on the market today was written to teach mathematical principles. For that reason, the classroom teacher should have little difficulty in locating effective math packages. The lesson plans in this section enable the teacher to use applications software—spreadsheet—to solve mathematical problems in much the same way that a businessperson uses a spreadsheet to make predictions and plans.

Lesson Plan 1: Matthew's Skateboard

Grade Level: 3 to 6

Objective: Students will perform simple spreadsheet operations to solve word problems.

Materials Required: Spreadsheet software, handout with statement of problem.

Preparation: Students need to be familiar with the spreadsheet concepts of *row, column,* and *cell.* They also need to have a basic understanding of the spreadsheet as a tool for solving mathematical problems. Teachers should develop formulas for solving the problem if working with younger students. Older students will benefit from developing their own formulas as part of the activity. Teachers will also need to prepare a handout with a clear statement of the problem.

Activity: Present a clear statement of the problem: "Each week Matthew receives an allowance of $5. He wants to save part of his allowance to buy a skateboard, which will cost $60. But he also wants to spend part of his allowance on candy and part on video games, which cost 25 cents a game. If Matthew plays six video games each week and spends $1 for candy, how many weeks will he have to save in order to buy his skateboard? How many weeks if he stops buying candy and plays four video games each week?" Assist students in inputting numerical data and formulas. Then instruct the spreadsheet to solve the problem.

Evaluation: Verify the results. Do students understand that the computer made no problem-solving decisions on its own but rather followed their instructions?

Follow-Up: Allow students to create their own allowance budgets by supplying information that applies to them. Lead the class in a discussion of potential uses for the spreadsheet. How might their families use it as a tool for managing the household budget?

Special Note: An interesting variation of this lesson is to divide the class into two groups. One group will use the spreadsheet to solve the problem while the other group uses pencil and paper. This helps students appreciate the tremendous speed at which computers can perform mathematical calculations.

Lesson Plan 2: Slippery Oil Prices

Grade Level: 7 to 12

Objective: Students will use a spreadsheet to examine patterns in oil pricing and to predict trends for the future.

Materials Required: Spreadsheet software, data entry sheet, source of data for history of oil prices.

Preparation: Students need to be familiar with basic operations of a spreadsheet package. This can be introduced along with an historical overview of the spreadsheet from its invention in the 1970s as an accounting tool to its continually expanding applications as a prediction instrument and decision-making tool. This discussion should also explore the wide range of current uses of the spreadsheet in business, government, and research.

Activity: Have students research the pattern of oil prices for a prescribed period of time (e.g., six months, one year, five years). Instruct students to record their findings on a data entry sheet. After data have been keyed into the spreadsheet, have students assess the trend in oil prices. They can also discuss possible reasons for patterns that they detect. (If graphing software is available, the data can be shown by means of a line graph.) Finally, have students use the spreadsheet to predict patterns of oil prices for a prescribed period of time in the future and speculate on how this trend might affect gasoline prices.

Evaluation: Compare the results of student spreadsheets. Do they agree? Assess the reliability of predictions of pricing patterns.

Follow-Up: Lead the class in a discussion of possible uses of the spreadsheet as a prediction and decision-making tool. Invite a guest speaker to explain how he or she uses a spreadsheet in business, government, or research. If students have a graphics package, they can use the results to generate line graphs of pricing trends and predictions.

Special Notes: This lesson can be adapted for a class in geography, political science, or economics as part of a study of major oil-producing nations.

Comments: A WWW search can provide students with more information regarding oil sources that can be built into a spreadsheet file.

Lesson Plans for Science

There are many applications of computer power in the science laboratory and classroom. In fact, some of our most innovative technological developments have come from computers that were designed for scientific applications. Therefore, it is appropriate that science teachers demonstrate to their students what a powerful tool the computer can be in furthering scientific investigation.

Lesson Plan 3: The Weather Report

Grade Level: 2 to 6

Objective: Students will gather data on weather conditions and display the data with graphs or charts.

Materials Required: Graphics software, student worksheet for data collection, printer for generating hard copies of student graphs and charts.

Preparation: Students need to be familiar with the process of generating bar graphs or pie charts. They should also understand the rudiments of systematic collection of data. The teacher should prepare a student worksheet listing the types of weather to be observed (sunshine, rain, clouds, snow, wind, and so on) and the days of the month during which weather will be observed.

Activity: At the beginning of class each day, remind students to observe the weather and record the data on their worksheets. Encourage them to record weekend weather conditions at home and add these data to their worksheets as well. Students should collect data for a prescribed period of time (e.g., one month).

After students have completed data worksheets, assist them in entering the data into the graphics program as the basis for a pie chart or bar graph showing the number of sunny, rainy, cloudy, windy, and snowy days during the month. Display students' graphs on a bulletin board for easy comparison.

Evaluation: Compare the students' graphs. Are they similar? What accounts for differences between graphs?

Follow-Up: Discuss how climatologists use computers to gather, calculate, and display weather data. Invite a local climatologist to speak to the class and bring samples of computer-generated displays of weather data. Encourage students to continue collecting data over a longer period of time so that their body of data is larger. The WWW is an excellent source for up-to-date information for class projects and research.

Special Note: Older students may enjoy trying to predict the weather. Have students contact a WWW site of your region of the National Weather Service for normal and record-setting weather conditions in your area within the past year. Students can use data to make weather predictions and then observe the actual weather to determine the reliability of their predictions.

Comments: Check with your local television station for possible software. Using a weather radio and an LCD panel will allow students opportunities to be classroom meteorologists and give weather reports just like on television.

Lesson Plan 4: Computer Pioneers

Grade Level: 7 to 12

Objective: Students will use a database to store and organize information about pioneers in computer development.

Materials Required: Database software, WWW access to sources of biographical information on scientists.

Preparation: Students need to be familiar with basic operations of database software. Vocabulary terms that must be presented are *template, record, field,* and *key.* With younger students, teachers may want to design a template including fields such as

> Name
> Nationality
> Field
> Born
> Died
> Contribution

Older students can benefit from designing their own templates since this will give them experience in naming fields and designating keys.

Activity: Have students research the library and the WWW for biographies of scientists who have contributed to technological development. As a class, determine which people will be included in the database. Of course, names can be added as students perform their research. Students should keep note cards with pertinent information to be keyed into the database later.

After records have been keyed in, students can access the database to share information they have uncovered or to answer questions on a quiz prepared by the teacher (e.g., "Where was John von Neumann born?").

Evaluation: How many records are contained in the database? By which keys can records be retrieved? Do students understand the sorting capabilities of the database?

Follow-Up: Ask students to give brief reports to the class on the figures they have researched. Lead the class in a discussion of relationships among computer pioneers. Is there evidence that some of the scientists were influenced by others?

Special Note: Students may wish to make use of the database to generate a time line that illustrates the prehistory of the computer as well as the generations of computer development.

Lesson Plans for Language Arts

There may have been a time when teachers of language arts thought that the computer had nothing to offer their students. Fortunately, this is no longer the case. Many teachers and students have discovered that the computer is a wonderfully patient tutor of reading and writing skills. There is an abundance of word processing and desktop publishing software programs on the market for students of all ages. In addition, there are programs that assist with spelling, grammar, and word choice.

Lesson Plan 5: Write a Story

Grade Level: K to 6

Objective: Students will use basic functions of a word processing package to create a class story.

Materials Required: Word processor with illustration capability to tell a story (for younger children).

Preparation: The teacher should format a disk and create a document file with a story title. Students should also have had some practice with typing on a keyboard. It is helpful if students understand the basic elements of a story—plot, setting, and characters.

Activity: The teacher should explain to the children that the class is going to use the computer to write a story. The teacher will begin the story by typing the first sentence or simply an introductory phrase such as "Once upon a time. . . ." After that, each student will add a sentence of his or her own. Once all the students have had an opportunity to add a sentence to the story, the teacher can read the finished story to the class.

Evaluation: Were students able to formulate and type in original sentences? Were they interested in the story? Did the story have basic elements such as plot, setting, and characters?

Follow-Up: Students can print the story and take copies of it home to share with family members. Lead a discussion about cooperating with others and sharing ideas.

Special Note: With very young children, it might be a good idea to provide illustrations that spark ideas and lend a coherent plot to the story. An interesting variation of this lesson is for the teacher to create a form in which students can fill in their own names and other information to create a story about themselves.

Comments: Most major software companies have specific writing software programs that allow students to write and illustrate their own storybooks. The Key Caps accessory allows for foreign-language stories. Some programs are also available in a second language.

Lesson Plan 6: Research Notes

Grade Level: 7 to 12

Objective: Students will use a database to store and organize research notes and to format a bibliography.

Materials Required: Database program that includes report formatting capability, printer, bibliography style sheet such as the MLA's *Handbook for Writers of Theses and Dissertations.*

Preparation: Students should be familiar with basic operations and applications of databases. Also necessary are vocabulary terms such as *template, record, field,* and *key.* Middle school teachers may want to design a database template including the following fields:

> Author
> Title
> Publisher
> City of publication
> Year of publication
> Topic(s)
> Notes

High school students may benefit from designing a template of their own and designating keys such as author, title, and topic.

Activity: Working with a common topic or with individual topics, students will conduct library research. They should keep notecards with information to be keyed into the database. After all the records are keyed in, students can retrieve information or print listings of it.

Depending on the report formatting capabilities of the database, assist students in formatting a bibliography with correct placement and punctuation of information. Provide a standard style sheet to aid students in formatting the bibliography. Print the bibliography to demonstrate how the computer saves the tedious work of typing.

Evaluation: Check the bibliography for correctness and style. What have students learned about the process of research and the use of the computer to expedite research?

Follow-Up: If students have created individual bibliographies, have them work in small editing groups to proofread and revise their bibliographies. Lead a discussion of other ways that databases simplify the research process, for example, allowing direct access to up-to-the-minute information. Explore ways in which the computer is likely to change the way we do research. Discuss the advantages of formatting various reports of the same data for different purposes.

Special Note: This lesson can be used as an effective prelude to writing a research essay since students have created a working bibliography while completing the lesson.

Comments: The WWW has access to most writing guidelines as well as step-by-step approaches for writing papers with projected time lines.

Lesson Plans for Social Studies

Disciplines within the social studies area have benefited greatly from computer applications such as database and spreadsheet. Especially in fields such as psychology and sociology, where large bodies of statistical data contribute to a greater understanding of human behavior, the computer has made life easier for both teachers and students. Simulation programs can bring history to life by placing students in the midst of historical situations. Social studies teachers can choose from a wide range of computer applications to challenge their students.

Lesson Plan 7: Computer Attitudes

Grade Level: 3 to 7

Objective: Students will use a spreadsheet to calculate totals on a poll of computer attitudes.

Materials Required: Spreadsheet software, survey instrument.

Preparation: The teacher should prepare a survey instrument to be used by students to poll friends, classmates, parents, neighbors, family members, and so on, to discover their attitudes toward computers. The grade level of the students will determine the number and complexity of survey questions. Suggested questions are as follows:

> Do you like computers?
> Do you work with a computer?
> Do you own a computer?
> Do you think computers can help people?
> Do you think a person has to be a genius to work with computers?

Older students will benefit from designing their own survey. They may want to use a word processor to generate a survey form. Students must have mastered certain vocabulary terms in order to work with the spreadsheet—*column, row, cell,* and *formula.* The teacher may want to design the spreadsheet in advance to simplify the data entry process for students.

Activity: Have students poll 10 people to determine their attitudes toward computers. Then assist each student (or have more experienced students assist less experienced students) in entering the resulting data. After data have been keyed in, have the spreadsheet calculate totals.

Evaluation: Were students successful in conducting the poll? Did they develop a sense of the importance of correct data in statistical calculations?

Follow-Up: Lead the class in a discussion of the results of the survey. What did they discover about people's attitudes toward computers? Were young people more open to computers than were older people? Do students think that computer attitudes will change in the future?

Special Note: If graphics software is available, students can display their data in bar-graph or pie-chart form for a more dramatic presentation. Students can also write a report of their findings.

Comments: Data and Decisions: Bar Graphics by Wings for Learning is a graphics program that can be used to introduce data manipulation.

Lesson Plan 8: Career Decisions

Grade Level: 8 to 12

Objective: The student will make a career decision after researching several major U.S. cities.

Materials Required: Database software, access to current statistical data on major U.S. cities via the WWW or library.

Preparation: Students must be familiar with basic database operations and terminology, particularly *template, record, field,* and *key.* Middle school teachers may want to design a template that includes fields such as

City	State
Population	Population under 35
Per capita income	Unemployment rate
Average temperature	Average rainfall
Number of colleges	Number of hospitals
Popular sports	Number of churches

Older students may benefit from designing their own template to include factors they consider important in making a career decision.

Activity: Tell the students to imagine that they have completed their education and are ready to enter their chosen career field. They have received three job offers in three different cities. Before making a decision about which offer to accept, they are to conduct research about the three cities.

Either have the class choose three cities for research or have individual students select three cities that appeal to them. Encourage students to select major cities so that current data will be readily available. After students have conducted research on three cities, assist them in entering the data into the spreadsheet. Students can then print a listing of their data for easy comparison.

After students have had an opportunity to review their listings, ask them to choose one of the job offers based on their findings. Have them list the factors that most influenced their decision.

Evaluation: Were the students able to locate all of the information called for in the database? Did the students suggest additional characteristics that could be included? Were students able to reach decisions with which they felt comfortable?

Follow-Up: Have students write an essay explaining their decision and the factors on which it is based. Lead the class in a discussion of the different factors people consider in relocating and how these factors are prioritized differently by different people.

Comments: The Carmen Sandiego series by Broderbund may be used to build a classroom database on countries, states, and cities. Several commercial software programs and some WWW sites provide maps as well as related information.

Lesson Plans for Special Education

The computer is an extremely effective tool in the special education classroom because it is infinitely patient. Students can work at their own pace without feeling threatened or rushed. Also, the computer seems to motivate many students to repeat lessons and exercises, thereby reinforcing the knowledge they have gained. In effect, the computer provides the student with limitless individual attention that the special education teacher cannot always provide. Much of the educational software on the market for the traditional classroom can be adapted for use in the special education classroom as well.

Lesson 9: Budgeting Time

Grade Level: K to 6

Objective: Students will determine a typical daily schedule and create a pie chart to show how much time is spent on various activities.

Materials Required: Graphics software, student worksheet.

Preparation: The teacher should make sure that students understand terms that refer to time such as *today, tomorrow, yesterday, last week, next month,* and so on. Students also need to understand how to interpret a pie chart. Students should give thought to the fact that most people follow a daily routine of awakening in the morning, working or attending school during the day, sleeping at night, and so on. The teacher should prepare a worksheet of typical daily activities.

Activity: Have the students list the activities they perform each day. Then have them estimate the amount of time they spend on each activity. Assist the students in entering their data into a graphics program to create a pie chart. Have the students share their pie chart and explain their daily routine.

Evaluation: Did the students include all common daily activities? Were their time estimates reasonable? Did they spend time talking with classmates about their daily schedules?

Follow-Up: Students may enjoy writing a story about their daily routine. An interesting variation would be to ask students to write a story about a day in which they did everything backward.

Comments: TimeLiner (Tom Snyder Productions) may also be a helpful software program for this activity.

Lesson Plan 10: First Aid

Grade Level: 6 to 12

Objective: Students will create a database of common emergencies and first-aid measures to be taken when these emergencies occur.

Materials Required: Database software, access to library or WWW first-aid information, printer.

Preparation: Invite emergency service professionals (police, firefighters, paramedics, etc.) to speak to the class on common emergency situations and first-aid procedures.
  Student should also be familiar with basic database operations and terminology, including *template, record, field,* and *key.* The teacher may want to create a database in advance, including fields such as

  Emergency situation
  Phone numbers and agencies
  Immediate steps to take
  Appropriate first-aid measures, if relevant
  Other useful information

  Older students may benefit from designing their own database template with teacher assistance.

Activity: Lead the class in a discussion of common emergencies that occur in the home, in public, on the job, in automobiles, and so on. Have the class create a list of emergencies; the list will serve as a basis for student research. Suggest appropriate sources of information (including personal interviews of professionals), WWW, and have students choose an emergency to research. The students should be sure to gather the type of information necessary for the database. After students have conducted their research, assist them in keying data into the database. If a printer is available, it may be useful to print a listing of the database that the students can take home and use as a reference manual.

Evaluation: Have students learned how to handle common emergency situations? Do they know whom to contact in case of an emergency? Is there a 911 emergency phone number in the area? If so, do students understand when to use this number?

Follow-Up: Students can give oral reports on their research so that other students in the class develop a sense of how to handle a range of emergency situations.

Summary

Teachers of all subject areas can incorporate computer-based education into their traditional curricula. This increases the number of students who have experience with computers when they finish school. It also increases the amount of technology in use in the classroom and serves as a bridge to the future when computer-based education will be the rule rather than the exception. The first step in incorporating computers into the curriculum is to be able to develop effective computer-based lesson plans.

In general, computer-based lesson plans must account for the same factors that all lesson plans depend on:

- Grade level
- Objective
- Materials required
- Preparation
- Activity
- Evaluation
- Follow-up

The lesson plans presented in this chapter follow a format that includes all these features as well as allowing for additional notes that may lend to the success of a particular lesson plan.

With computer-based lesson plans, there are additional factors that must be taken into consideration. Most of these factors have to do with availability of software and hardware. Will students have unlimited access to several microcomputers with connectivity to the WWW? This situation allows the teacher to plan more extensive use of the computer than a situation in which students must go in pairs to a media center where they can use the computer for no more than half an hour. Are there programs available to handle the activities planned?

This chapter presented 10 sample lesson plans. There are two lesson plans for each of the five curriculum areas—mathematics, science, language arts, social science, and special education. Under each curriculum area, the first lesson plan is for use by elementary teachers, the second for use by secondary teachers. It is the authors' hope that teachers will use these lesson plans as a springboard for creating their own innovative and effective computer-based lesson plans.

LEARNER ACTIVITIES

1. Present one of the lessons in this chapter and report on the results.

2. Write a lesson plan for your subject area following the format suggested in this chapter.

3. Research the WWW, books, and periodicals that include computer lesson plans. Develop a bibliography of these resources.

4. Adapt one of the lesson plans in this chapter for use with a specific software package.

5. Adapt one of the lesson plans in this chapter for a higher or lower grade level.

6. Write a lesson plan that develops a thematic learning environment and integrates several content areas.

7. Write a lesson plan that includes the WWW for data collection.

8. List the essential elements of a lesson plan.

9. Integrate cooperative learning into one of the lesson plans. Try the lesson with a class.

10. Modify one of the lesson plans to include portfolio-assessment procedures.

BIBLIOGRAPHY

Allen, D. (1994a). A spring software sampler. Teaching with technology. *Teaching PreK–8, 24*(8), 20–22.

Allen, D. (1994b). Teaching with technology: Byte into math. *Teaching PreK–8, 24*(4), 22–27.

Allen, D. (1995). Teaching with technology. Software that's right for you. *Teaching PreK–8, 25*(8), 14–17.

Anderson-Inman, L. (1987). The reading-writing connection: Classroom applications for the computer, Part II. *The Computing Teacher, 14*(6), 15–18.

Anderson-Inman, L. (1990–1991). Enabling students with learning disabilities: Insights from research. *The Computing Teacher, 18*(4), 26–29.

Balajthy, E. (1988). Keyboarding, language arts, and the elementary school child. *The Computing Teacher, 15*(5), 40–43.

Barnes, S., & Michalowiczs, K. D. (1994). Now & then: From cashier to scan coordinator; from stones to bones to PC clones. *Mathematics Teaching in the Middle School, 1*(1), 59–65.

Bayliffe, J., et al. (1994). Tech time: Using technology to enhance "my travels with Gulliver." *Teaching Children Mathematics, 1*(3), 188–191.

Berlin, D. F., & White, A. L. (1995). Using technology in assessing integrated science and mathematics learning. *Journal of Science Education and Technology, 4*(1), 47–56.

Bitter, G. G., & Frederick, H. (1989). Techniques and technology in secondary school mathematics. *NASSP Bulletin, 73*(519), 22–28.

Braun, J. A., Jr., & Kuseske, T. (Eds.). (1994). A teacher's perspective on what's ahead for technology. Media corner. *Social Studies and the Young Learner, 6*(3), 26–28.

Bristor, V. J., & Drake, S. V. (1994). Linking the language arts and content areas through visual technology. *T.H.E. Journal, 22*(2), 74–77.

Browning, R., & Nave, G. (1983). Computer technology for the handicapped: A literature profile. *The Computing Teacher, 10*(6), 56–59.

Cappo, M., & Osterman, G. (1991). Teach students to communicate mathematically. *The Computing Teacher, 18*(5), 34–39.

Collis, B. (1988). *Computers, curriculum, and whole-class instruction.* Belmont, CA: Wadsworth.

Connelly, M. G., & Wiebe, J. H. (1994). Teaching mathematics with technology: Mining mathematics on the Internet. *Arithmetic Teacher, 41*(5), 276–281.

Cuoco, A. A., et al. (Eds.). (1994). Technology tips: A potpourri. *Mathematics Teacher, 87*(7), 566–569.

Dickens, R. A. (1991–1992). Success with writing and the concept formation model. *The Computing Teacher, 19*(4), 27–29.

Faltis, C. J., & Devillar, R. A. (Eds.). (1990). *Language minority students and computers.* New York: Haworth Press.

Gagne, R. M. (1987). *Instructional technology: Foundations.* Hillsdale, NJ: Lawrence Erlbaum.

Goldberg, K. P. (1994). Applications: Using technology to understand the jury decision-making process. *Mathematics Teacher, 87*(2), 110–114.

Harvey, J. G., et al. (1995). The influence of technology on the teaching and learning of algebra. *Journal of Mathematical Behavior, 14*(1), 75–109.

Heid, M. (1995). Impact of technology, mathematical modeling, and meaning on the content, learning, and teaching of secondary school algebra. *Journal of Mathematical Behavior, 14*(1), 121–137.

Hoyles, C., et al. (1994). Learning mathematics in groups with computers: Reflections on a research study. *British Educational Research Journal, 20*(4), 465–483.

Hunt, N., & Afford, L. (1991–1992). Involving students in computer-based cooperative lessons. *The Computing Teacher, 19*(4), 34–37.

Johnson, D. C., et al. (1994). Evaluating the impact of IT on pupils' achievements. *Journal of Computer Assisted Learning, 10*(3), 138–156.

Kader, G., & Perry, M. (1994). Power on! Learning statistics with technology. *Mathematics Teaching in the Middle School, 1*(2), 130–136.

Kapisosky, R. M. (1990). Math and science: Vitality through technology. *Media and Methods, 26*(4), 59–61.

Kaput, J. J., & Thompson, P. W. (1994). Technology in mathematics education research: The first 25 years in the JRME. *Journal for Research in Mathematics Education, 25*(6), 667–684.

Kuechle, N. (1990). Computers and first grade writing: A learning center approach. *The Computing Teacher, 18*(1), 39–41.

Lampert, M., et al. (1994). Using technology to support a new pedagogy of mathematics teacher education. *Journal of Special Education Technology, 12*(3), 276–289.

Manes, M. A. (1994). Technology tips: A global electronic community. *Mathematics Teacher, 87*(8), 650–651.

O'Connor, J., & Brie, R. (1994). The effects of technology infusion on the mathematics and science curriculum. *Journal of Computing in Teacher Education, 10*(4), 15–18.

Pert, T. (1990). Manipulatives and the computer: A powerful partnership for learners of all ages. *Classroom Computer Learning, 10*(6), 20–29.

Phelps, M. V. (1994). The federal role in educational technology. *Educational Media and Technology Yearbook, 20,* 142–150.

Phillips, R. J., et al. (1995). Evolving strategies for using interactive video resources in mathematics classrooms. *Educational Studies in Mathematics, 28*(2), 133–154.

Resources on computer-based reading and writing instruction. (1988). *The Computing Teacher, 16*(1), 24–27.

Riddle, B. (1988). Computer-based astronomy: The opposition of Mars. *The Computing Teacher, 16*(3), 20–23.

Rowland, K. L., & Scott, D. (1992). Promoting language & literacy for young children through computers. *Journal of Computing in Childhood Education, 3*(1), 55–61.

Solomon, G. (1990). Learning social studies in a one-computer classroom. *Electronic Learning, 9*(7), 18–20.

Suddath, C., & Susnik, J. (1991). *Augmentative communication devices.* Reston, VA: Office for Special Education Technology.

Wicklein, R. C., & Schell, J. W. (1995). Case studies of multidisciplinary approaches to integrating mathematics, science and technology education. *Journal of Technology Education, 6*(2), 59–76.

Widmer, C. C., & Sheffield, L. (1998). Modeling mathematics concepts: Using physical, calculator, and computer models to teach area and perimeter. *Learning & Leading with Technology, 25*(5), 32–35.

Wresch, W. (1990). Collaborative writing projects: Lesson plans for the computer age. *The Computing Teacher, 17*(8), 19–21.

Young, M. (1995). Assessment of situated learning using computer environments. *Journal of Science Education and Technology, 4*(1), 89–96.

10 Designing Lesson Plans

Integrating CAI Software

1. What lesson contexts must be created to effectively integrate CAI software?
2. What other materials may be required to enhance the use of the software?
3. How might students miss learning opportunities by using a piece of software without a surrounding lesson context?

Chapter 9 presented a number of suggestions for introducing students to common computer applications such as word processing, database, graphics, spreadsheet, and the WWW. Teachers can adapt applications software easily to fit into virtually all areas of the curriculum. This chapter will demonstrate how computer-assisted instruction (CAI) software can be integrated into the traditional curriculum. CAI packages have been designed specifically for classroom use and can be a very effective means of introducing or reinforcing concepts. They require little if any modification and contain all the instructions needed to begin operation.

When creating lesson plans that include CAI software, the teacher needs to consider some of the same factors discussed in Chapter 9. The availability and location of computer hardware certainly affect the way lessons will be presented and whether students will work individually or in groups. Most CAI packages include suggestions for the teacher to assist in maximizing the learning experience. It is a good idea to review these suggestions carefully before presenting lessons.

If the CAI software being used has been used already in other classrooms in the district, the teacher may also benefit from talking with other teachers about their experiences with the software. For example, teachers who have used the software before can judge how much knowledge—both of computer usage and of the subject being presented—is required for the student to operate the program effectively. Are there bugs in the program that may hinder learning? Are some activities in the program more interesting, more useful, or more challenging to students than others? Experienced users of the software can answer these and other questions that the new user may have. Schools could build a resource bank of CAI lesson plans that include teacher comments.

The CAI software discussed in this chapter is actual educational software on the market today. Courseware episodes of some software presented in this chapter are on the CD-ROM included with this book. Teachers wishing to purchase this software should check local software retailers or contact the software publishers directly (Appendix A) for information on availability. Planning is the key in the CAI experience. For example, ordinary software may take several weeks to order and receive a CAI package if it is not available at a local software or teaching supply store. Teachers may face limited choices if their districts have not set aside sufficient funds for the purchase of software. In some cases, it is possible to rent software for a short period of time at much less expense than the purchase price of the package. But rental also requires planning and lead time.

The CAI software presented here is a representative sampling of the educational software available on the market. Software for the classroom has seen tremendous development in the past several years as publishers respond to the needs of today's teachers. This chapter attempts to give teachers an overview of CAI software packages available and the wide range of subjects such software can teach. Teachers are strongly urged to do some research of their own to see what other CAI packages are available for teaching all areas of the curriculum.

The sample lesson plans in this chapter have been designed for five specific areas of the curriculum: science, social science, language arts, mathematics, and special education. It should be noted, however, that many of the CAI packages described can be used in an interdisciplinary fashion. For example, a lesson in social science can be used as the topic for a writing assignment. In fact, CAI courseware generally includes teacher guides that offer suggestions for interdisciplinary activities.

The lesson plans all follow a uniform format that has proven useful in the computerized classroom. See Chapter 9 for a discussion of the lesson plan format.

Most software is on CD-ROM. Usually, they are hybrid versions, meaning that the CD will run on a Macintosh or PC computer. Be sure to carefully read machine requirements before attempting to run the software on your computer. In addition, be sure to read the read-me file; often, specific steps are required to have the software sound, video, and printing to work properly. One final note, some software is on a disk and requires making a backup. Backup disks should be done before the lesson is introduced so that class time is not taken up with this one-time procedure.

The same rule applies to CAI software that requires students to store their work on disks. Working disks must be formatted before their use and—especially with students too young to format their own disk—teachers can save valuable computer time by formatting or initializing disks in advance of the lesson.

CAI Software for Science

Lesson Plan 1: Dinosaur Hunter

Grade Level: 4 to 12

Objective: Students will travel back 250 million years and explore the world of Dinosaurs.

Materials Required: Eyewitness Virtual Reality: Dinosaur Hunter (DK Multimedia). A Macintosh computer with a CD player is required. A WWW connection can be utilized.

Preparation: Provide resources to investigate dinosaurs. Models of different dinosaurs are ideal for student comparisons.

Activity: Have students explore Excavation Site, Dinosaur arena and take guided tours. Small-group as well as class exploration is encouraged! Dino ONLINE accesses the program's website.

Evaluation: Observe student progress through discussions and successes using the activities provided by the software.

Comments: This is a virtual reality software program and students may need assistance to take advantage of all the features of the software. A WWW connection extends the capabilities of this software.

Lesson Plan 2: El Niño

Grade Level: 8 to 12

Objective: Students experience a simulated research mission that represents a real scientific mission. The mission is about a predicted El Niño event that may have disastrous effects for life as well as the economies of the world.

Materials Required: Ocean Expedition: El Niño (Tom Snyder Productions), Macintosh utilizing QuickTime Virtual Reality. A CD player is required.

Preparation: Groups of students are involved in the activity with various responsibilities.

Activity: Students first sign in as a crew member. Then students identify the climate variable the crew will study. Crew roles are determined by the booklet each crew member receives (navigator, data collector, data analyst, or communication expert). Students then learn how to navigate on the ship and follow mission goals. Specific information is provided throughout the mission. The program includes a HELP feature.

Evaluation: Student progress can be monitored by reviewing and grading the message files that they must complete during the mission investigation.

Comments: The program can be used with large groups, small groups, or individual learning. Science Court, The Great Solar System Rescue, and Rainforest Researchers (Tom Snyder Productions) are other project-type science software programs. A review of Blocks in Motion (Don Johnston, Inc.) is included on the CD-ROM accompanying this book.

CAI Software for Social Science

Lesson Plan 3: Create and Administer a Survey

Grade Level: 3 to 10

Objective: Students will learn to design a survey instrument, conduct a poll, and display the results in a table, circle graph, line plot, grid plot, stem and leaf plot, bar graph, etc.

Materials Required: Data Explorer (Sunburst Communications), Macintosh or PC computer, data disks.

Preparation: Students need to understand the basic principles of polling groups of people to discover their attitudes about a given subject. Teachers can maximize computer time by assisting students in designing their surveys on paper before using the computer. The class must also decide who will answer the survey and whether the survey will be administered on paper or on computer. Teachers working with younger students may want to format or initialize data disks in advance of the lesson.

Activity: Students use Data Explorer to create a survey of up to 50 questions of one or two lines each. Students also provide up to five possible answers for each question. Surveys can be edited and printed for distribution. The program also allows surveys to be taken on the computer. When surveys are taken on paper, students must key in results for tabulation by the computer. Survey responses can be edited in case of data entry errors. After all responses are tabulated, students can display the results in the most appropriate graphs to illustrate their findings.

Evaluation: Can students identify the advantages of taking surveys? Can students identify patterns or trends indicated by survey results? Can students suggest ways of honing or improving the survey process?

Comments: An interesting exercise is to divide the class into two or more groups so that their survey results can be compared. Other programs are MATH Worlds: Sampling (William K. Bradford Publishing) and MECC Graph (The Learning Company). Reviews of An Odyssey of Discovery: Geography (Pierian Spring) and Zurk's Alaskan Trek (Soleil Software, Inc.) are available on the CD-ROM accompanying this book.

Lesson Plan 4: Multicultural Poets on Identity

Grade Level: 7 to 12

Objective: Students will explore questions of identity through multicultural American poetry.

Materials Required: In My Own Voice: Multicultural Poets on Identity (Sunburst Communications), Macintosh with CD player. A review of this program is included on the CD-ROM accompanying this book.

Preparation: Students must be made aware of the Writerspace to create their own poetry.

Activity: Working individually or in pairs, students explore over 80 fine art selections and music compositions. In addition, they listen to authors read their own poetry and discuss their sources of inspiration through multicultural American poetry.

Evaluation: Students should be able to analyze the information and it is hoped to be inspired to write their own poetry.

Comments: The courseware includes many resources that encourage students to apply their knowledge to writing their own poetry. Other related software includes the Decisions, Decisions (Tom Snyder Productions) series of software programs, which encourage students to explore the thinking processes by looking at an issue from different perspectives. Social studies programs utilizing video discs are Martin Luther King, Jr.; Communism and the Cold War; Powers of the U.S. Government; and The '88 Vote all by ABC News Interactive; and Point of View and History in Motion by Scholastic New Media.

CAI Software for Language Arts

Lesson Plan 5: Write Your Own Book

Grade Level: 3 to 12

Objective: Students will begin authoring their own books while learning fundamentals of word processing.

Materials Required: Student Writing Center (The Learning Company), Macintosh or PC computer, data disks.

Preparation: Students should be aware of the basic procedures involved in word processing. A spell checker, bibliography maker, grammar tips, and over 150 graphics are included with the software.

Activity: Students can begin to create their own books by designing a cover page. Students can type in personal information including name, school, city, and year on the cover. Creativity is encouraged in creating the students' own book on a topic of their choice or a teacher-selected topic requiring research and a bibliography.

Evaluation: Continually review students' notebook and writing for progress to the final completed book.

Comments: Students should be encouraged to decorate their book covers further with their own artwork. This lends color and creativity to the book. Giant George and Ruby Robot, BIG and Little (Sunburst Communications) requires a Muppet Slate but also allows students to create and design various publications of differing sizes up to 5 feet tall. Clifford's Big Book Publisher (Scholastic New Media) provides graphics, clip art, and fonts for younger students to write their own big books. Other related programs are Print Shop Deluxe (Broderbund), Hyperstudio (Roger Wagner Publishing), Kids Works Deluxe (Davidson & Associates, Inc.), My Own Stories (The Learning Company), Children's Writing and Publishing Center (The Learning Company), and The Multimedia Workshop (Davidson & Associates, Inc.).

Lesson Plan 6: Readiness for School

Grade Level: PreK to 1

Objective: Students learn readiness skills of colors, counting, ABC's, reading, music, languages and vocabulary.

Materials Required: Preschool Mothergoose (Piranha Interactive Publishing), a Macintosh or PC computer with a CD player.

Preparation: Students must be able to use a mouse and understand the icons and their activity.

Activity: Students go through the activities. Teacher and parent information is provided to assist in the use of the program.

Evaluation: The program includes a childhood development chart. The teacher materials and activities provided on the CD can be used to determine understanding of the objectives.

Comments: The parenting information and activities are important to involve the parents in the education of their child. Other related programs are Discis Book Library (Discis), Spell It Plus (Davidson & Associates, Inc.), The Early Vocabulary Development Series (Laureate Learning Systems), The Sentence Master (Laureate), and New Talking Sticky Bear (Optimum Resources). A review of Discovering Authors (Gale Research) is included on the CD-ROM accompanying this book.

CAI Software for Mathematics

Lesson Plan 7: Math Explorations

Grade Level: 1 to 6

Objective: Students will practice mathematical skills through fractions, decimals, and percents.

Materials Required: Mega Math Blaster (Davidson & Associates), Macintosh or PC computer with CD player. A review of the program is included on the CD-ROM accompanying this book.

Preparation: Since Mega Math Blaster provides drill and practice, it is necessary that students already have learned the material being practiced before running the program. It is also useful for students to have minimal typing ability and familiarity with operating the computer. For younger students, the teacher may want to load the program and select the appropriate option from the main menu.

Activity: Mega Math Blaster covers basic math activities in a game format. Have the students go through the three levels of difficulty.

Evaluation: A student's success at the game will indicate mastery of the skills being practiced. Visual progress reports are provided as a student progresses through the math levels.

Comments: Many mathematics software programs are available. Blaster Learning System (Davidson & Associates, Inc.) includes all of the Blaster series of programs through algebra and geometry. Reviews of Snootz Math Trek (Theatrix Interactive, Inc.) and Mighty Math Carnival Countdown (Edmark Corp.) are included on the CD-ROM accompanying this book. Outnumbered (The Learning Company), Carmen Sandiego Math Detective (Broderbund), and Preschool Mothergoose (Piranha) are also programs that give students opportunities for practice.

Lesson Plan 8: Geometry

Grade Level: K to 5

Objective: Students will learn and practice concepts of spatial relationships, patterns, shapes, creating patterns and shape, shapes within shapes, and mirror symmetry through exploration.

Materials Required: Tenth Planet Explores Math: Level 1 Geometry (Sunburst Communications), Macintosh computer with microphone and printer.

Preparation: Review the basics of running the program, including using the microphone to record results into the student's notebook.

Activity: After loading the program, students can select activities from the program. Once a topic has been selected, the computer guides the student through the activity. The program is a series of interactive multimedia geometry units to develop students' understanding of geometry and spatial sense by building on the students' natural experiences. The program provides many activities for the students to manipulate objects to form shapes and patterns.

Evaluation: All results can be captured in each student's notebook, including written as well as verbal comments. Pictures of completed shapes and designs can be "photographed" into the student's notebook.

Comments: Other related geometry programs for various grade levels are Geometer's Sketch Pad (Key Curriculum Press), Geometric Presupposer (Sunburst Communications),

Elastic Lines (Sunburst Communications), Mathematical Modeling (Learning in Motion), and Hands on Math, Volumes I, II, and III (Ventura). These programs can be used for teaching as well as learning geometry concepts.

CAI Software for Special Education

Although there is limited CAI software on the market that has been designed specifically for use in special education, most CAI programs can be adapted to the unique needs of the special education classroom. It is especially easy to tailor CAI software that includes authoring components so that the teacher may create questions or problems that relate specifically to the subject area under consideration. The lesson plans that follow present CAI software that adapts well to use with exceptional students.

Lesson Plan 9: Logic Builders

Grade Level: Since Logic Builders allows the student to choose from three levels of difficulty, the game can be adapted to a wide range of skill levels.

Objectives: Students will improve their ability to follow directions by recreating spider webs according to computer-generated patterns.

Materials Required: Logic Builders (Scholastic New Media), Macintosh or PC computer.

Preparation: Students should understand basic operations of the computer and have minimal typing skill. Teachers should assist students in loading the program and selecting the appropriate game from the main menu.

Activity: In the first session, students select DRAW A WEB from the main menu. This game enables the student to experiment with the process of drawing a spider web with the help of on-screen spiders. In future sessions, students will play MATCH A WEB in which they are required to recreate a master design displayed on the right side of the screen. Still more challenging is RECALL A WEB, which requires students to recreate the master web from memory. Students achieve high scores for recreating webs in as few moves as possible. As students earn points, they receive promotions to the level of Big Boss.

Evaluation: The score maintained by the computer can be used as an indicator of student success in redrawing patterns. Do students select higher levels of challenge after gaining experience with the program?

Comments: Factory (Sunburst), The Oregon Trail 2 (The Learning Company), Lego TC Logo (LCSI), Carmen Sandiego series (Broderbund), and the Sim series (Maxis) of programs are alternative software approaches to this lesson. A review of Blocks in Motion (Don Johnston, Inc.) is included on the CD-ROM accompanying this book.

Lesson Plan 10: Recreation and Leisure

Grade Level: 8 to 12

Objective: Students will locate and participate in recreational and leisure activities in the community.

Materials Required: ClarisWorks (Filemaker, Inc.), Macintosh or PC Computer, a data disk, WWW connection, and reference materials on local recreational and leisure activities.

Preparation: Students should be introduced to the database concept and should have minimal typing skills. The teacher can design a template to include the following fields: Activity, Organization, Address, Cost, Services, Hours, and Eligibility. The data disk should be formatted in advance of the lesson. Students need to be familiar with collecting data from the WWW.

Activity: Ask students to compose lists of recreational and leisure activities that they enjoy. As a class, discuss what opportunities are available in the local community. Then have students search the WWW, contact public agencies, and conduct research to discover other leisure activities offered in the community. After students have completed their research, have them key their data into the database. This is an excellent opportunity to teach students about retrieving and sorting records in the database. If a printer is available, have students print a copy of their database for a referral list.

Evaluation: Have students uncovered valuable information about leisure activities available to them? Are students able to enter and access their information quickly and easily? Do some of the students participate in any of the activities included in the database?

Comments: As an ongoing class project, ask students to bring in information about new activities, schedule changes, and so forth to keep the database up to date. Students who participate in community activities can report their experiences to the class. Microsoft Works (Microsoft) and Hyperstudio (Roger Wagner Publishing) are popular applications programs.

Where to Find Out More about CAI Software

For further details about the CAI software presented in this chapter or other CAI software, the authors recommend that you contact the software publishers directly at their addresses listed in Appendix A. A current listing of recommended software can be found in the *1998 Educational Software Preview Guide* (<www.iste.org>) and the CD-ROM accompanying this book.

Summary

This chapter presented a number of practical suggestions for integrating prepackaged CAI software into the traditional classroom. Following hints for the teacher were 10 lesson plans, two for each of five curriculum areas: mathematics, science, language arts, social science, and special education. For each curriculum area, one lesson plan is aimed at elementary students and one is designed for secondary students. Refer to the *1998 Educational Software Preview Guide* (<www.iste.org>) and *Only the Best* (<www.ascd.org>) for related software.

The lesson plans presented in this chapter are intended to serve as guidelines for the teacher who is in the process of selecting and implementing CAI software packages. The lesson plans follow a format that has been designed to aid teachers in planning, carrying out, and evaluating computer-assisted lessons effectively. Several of the software programs have demonstration versions on the CD-ROM that accompanies this book. A list of educational software publishers and their addresses is also included on the CD-ROM accompanying this book as well as Appendix A. The CD-ROM should be helpful to obtain further details on the packages discussed in this chapter as well as this book.

LEARNER ACTIVITIES

1. Complete a software evaluation form from Chapter 6 on each of the demonstration CAI packages on the CD-ROM accompanying this book.

2. Prepare a detailed lesson plan on one of the demonstration software included on the CD-ROM accompanying this book.

3. Develop a plan for storing software, manuals, and student diskettes in the classroom.

4. Connect to the EDUCAST site at <www.educast.com> and research the resources available through this web site. Download several lesson plans for class discussion.

5. Adapt one of the lesson plans in this chapter to a higher or lower grade level.

6. Create a new lesson plan for software not included in this chapter. Follow the same format as the lessons in this chapter.

7. Prepare a lesson plan based on several software packages, emphasizing one content area. Correlate the objectives of the curriculum to the software objectives.

8. The National Council of Teachers of Mathematics (<www.nctm.org>) has established curriculum standards (<www.enc.org>). Develop a lesson plan using CAI software that correlates to one or more standards.

9. Prepare a lesson plan integrating mathematics, science, and social studies into the lesson utilizing a CAI program.

10. Select two or more lesson plans from this chapter and integrate new methods of assessment such as portfolios.

BIBLIOGRAPHY

Cerrito, P. B. (1994). Writing, technology, and experimentation to explore the concepts of elementary statistics. *Mathematics and Computer Education, 28*(2), 141–153.

Cuoco, A. A., et al. (1995). Technology tips: Technology and the mathematics curriculum: Some new initiatives. *Mathematics Teacher, 88*(3), 236–240.

Cuoco, A. A., et al. (Eds.). (1994). Technology tips: Technology in perspective. *Mathematics Teacher, 87*(6), 450–452.

Educational Software Evaluation Consortium. (1998). *The 1998 educational software preview guide.* Eugene, OR: International Society for Technology in Education.

Frederick, B., & Frederick, H. (1988). What's in it for me? An inservice approach to help integrate computers. *SIOCC Bulletin, 4*(3 & 4), 16–17.

Gerber, M. M., et al. (1994). Computer-based dynamic assessment of multidigit multiplication. *Exceptional Children, 61*(2), 114–125.

Hoyles, C., & Noss, R. (1994). Technology tips: Dynamic geometry environments: What's the point? *Mathematics Teacher, 87*(9), 716–717.

Hsu, L., & Lee, G. D. (1991–1992). Providing access for students who are visually impaired. *The Computing Teacher, 19*(4), 8–9.

Johnson, D. L., Maddux, C. D., & Candler, A. C. (Eds.). (1986). *Computers in the special education classroom.* New York: Haworth Press.

Johnson, J. M. (1998a). New software releases. *Learning & Leading with Technology, 25*(5), 42–44.

Johnson, J. M. (1998b). Software reviews. *Learning & Leading with Technology, 25*(5), 45–51.

Lehman, J. R. (1994). Technology use in the teaching of mathematics and science in elementary schools. *School Science and Mathematics, 94*(4), 194–202.

Mason, M. (1983). Special education: A time of opportunity. *Electronic Learning, 2*(8), 54–55.

Milone, M. N., Jr., (1990). Painless grammar: Revising with the help of a grammar checker. *Classroom Computer Learning, 10*(6), 18–23.

Nelson, T. B., & Rogel, J. (1995). Operation Sluggie and other software products from the fourth grade. *Computing Teacher, 22*(5), 39–41.

O'Connor, J., & Brie, R. (1994). Mathematics and science partnerships: Products, people, performance, and multimedia. *The Computing Teacher, 22*(1), 27–30.

Only the best. (1997–1998). Alexandria, VA: Association for Supervision and Curriculum Development.

Phillips, R. J., & Pead, D. (1994). Multimedia resources in the mathematics classroom. *Journal of Computer Assisted Learning, 10*(4), 216–228.

Rice, M. (1995). Issues surrounding the integration of technology into the K–12 classroom. *Interpersonal Computing and Technology Journal, 3*(1), 67–81.

Schipper, D. (1991). Practical ideas: Literature, computers, and students with special needs. *The Computing Teacher, 19*(2), 33–37.

Selby, L., et al. (1994). Teachers' perceptions of learning with information technology in mathematics and science education: A report on Project Prometheus. *Journal of Computing in Teacher Education, 10*(3), 24–30.

Solomon, G. (1989). Computers help students see art in a different hue. *Electronic Learning, 9*(2), 16–18.

Stahl, G., et al. (1995). Share globally, adapt locally: Software assistance to locate and tailor curriculum posted to the Internet. *Computers & Education, 24*(3), 237–246.

Thompson, E. O. (1989). Using the Geometric Supposer: Triangles. *The Computing Teacher, 17*(1), 30–34.

Vernot, D. (1987). New power in social studies software. *Electronic Technology, 6*(8), 36–37.

Watkins, M. W., & Abran, S. (1985). Reading CAI with first grade students. *The Computing Teacher, 12*(7), 43–45.

Waring, B. (1998). The 1998 New Media Hyper Awards. *New Media, 8*(3), 36–49.

Wepner, S. B. (1990). Computers and whole language: A "novel" frontier. *The Computing Teacher, 17*(5), 24–28.

Widmer, C. C., & Sheffield, L. J. (1994). Putting the fun into functions through the use of manipulatives, computers, and calculators. *School Science and Mathematics, 94*(7), 350–355.

WWW SITES

<www.ascd.org>

<www.educast.com>

<www.enc.org>

<www.iste.org>

<www.nctm.com>

<http://tblr.ed.asu.edu>

11 Administrating with Technology

FOCUS QUESTIONS

1. How can basic software tools be used to facilitate print-based communication?
2. What types of planning and scheduling can be aided with the use of technology?
3. How can teachers use technology to record assessment observations?

The one aspect of a teacher's job description that rarely makes it into most discussions in college teacher preparation programs is that of being an administrator. Many new teachers arrive in their first classrooms ready to get on with the job of "teaching" and instead discover that they are poorly prepared to manage the day-to-day operation that a bustling classroom community requires. It is unrealistic to see modern teachers solely in the role of instructors, and, in fact, their necessary administrative duties require them to wear many of the hats that most leaders in the professional world must also don. Noninstructional activities make up a large segment of a teacher's typical day, and those daily responsibilities could easily infringe on the time allocated for actual instruction. Administrative duties must therefore be carefully managed. Although teachers are often ready to consider ways in which students can benefit from technology, they sometimes are not aware of how technology can help them in accomplishing administrative duties (Office of Technology Assessment, 1995). Technology can aid greatly in making time spent in these routine administrative tasks effective and efficient, and this undoubtedly can lead to more minutes available for meaningful contact with an educator's clients, the young learners.

Because computerizing these basic administrative affairs can make for more consistent and accurate management systems as compared to the handwritten and figured approach, more democratic leadership patterns can emerge in the classroom. Gone are the days when teachers' carefully handwritten gradebooks are hidden away under lock and key, for fear of tampering from little prying hands. Instead, teachers are finding that students of all ages are capable of some degree of responsibility for the routine tasks that surround and make possible the learning environment of the classroom. This shift in policy necessarily accompanies the general shift from teacher-directed learning situations to productive, child-centered learning contexts. Technology facilitates greater student participation by providing safe, predictable organizational systems.

By reflecting and modeling this shift in pedagogical and organizational focus, this chapter will serve to provoke thought and experimentation on the part of teachers in how they might best use technology to ensure their daily efforts are faster and more efficient. The ideas here should not be construed as comprehensive nor should every idea be assumed to be vital to successful classroom management in the Information Age. A teacher's individual management style and the unique composition of each individual class will determine the extent to which technology might streamline administrative tasks, just as unique management styles influence the operation of corporations elsewhere in the business world. There remains little doubt, however, that the classroom microcosm now has smart options to help it function.

Step-by-step instructions will not be given in this chapter on the operation of software tools, such as how to create a document using a word processor or how to write a formula in a spreadsheet; proficiency with common productivity tools has begun to be considered a baseline skill for employment in any professional field. (See Appendixes C, D, and E for introductory information on using word processors, spreadsheets, and databases.) The purpose of this chapter, rather, is to suggest beginning points for implementing a technologically-organized plan of action. The chapter is arranged according to administrative purpose, with ideas for those software choices that might best be used for each task. Uses for productivity software tools that come packaged on most computers are primarily discussed because teachers are more likely to have access to these basic programs in their classroom computers. Features of some specific-purpose tools that are applicable to particular administrative responsibilities are also described.

Communicating

Inherent to the role of a classroom teacher is the need to act as a liaison between many groups of people: parents, administrators, students, other teachers, students from other classes, and community members. Strong, organized strategies are a must to pull off communication that often rivals corporate public relations campaigns. The Information Age has brought with it the ability to communicate electronically, such as through e-mail, as discussed in Chapter 3, however paper-based communication forms remain a necessary component to a teacher's communication arsenal. Many of the stakeholders that make up a classroom community do not have the capabilities to communicate electronically, and many items, such as those giving parent permission, require handwritten signatures. Basic productivity tools to which many teachers have access can prevent the job from becoming a correspondence nightmare. The suggestions that follow may seem like obvious uses of computer technology, but will serve as basics on which to build a strong communication platform.

Letters

Whether it is a lengthy summary of a semester's work or a brief response acknowledging a note received, writing letters to parents is a daily requirement of most teachers' jobs at the K–12 level. With teachers having little time in the daily routine to sit and compose an intelligible letter, a word processor can prove invaluable. Letters can be generally typed faster than they can be handwritten, especially if a computer is available in the classroom. Time can further be saved by beginning with a previously written letter as a template and modifying it to fit the current purpose. Many word processing programs also supply templates for this same timesaving purpose.

Letters that are sent home can be saved in case a parent does not receive it or there are questions regarding what was said (see Figure 11-1). Spelling and grammar can be checked, formatting adjusted, and personal touches, such as a class or school logo, can be inserted to design a professional-looking letter. Parents will appreciate the legibility of a typed letter and therefore may actually be more likely to respond to it. As with any typed letter, always be sure to sign it by hand. A letter with a typed signature implies that little care was taken to elevate it past the status of a mere form letter, lowering the letter's importance in parents' eyes to that of junk mail. Word processors can also be used to create thank-you notes and solicitations for help or information to other teachers, community members, and content experts.

Newsletters

Keeping all parents up to date on classroom and school occurrences is vital to the creation of a strong parent-school network, and the job can easily be done by publishing a weekly newsletter. Publishing a professional looking newspaper-type document right on the classroom computer is possible with most word processors. Parents can be notified of class study topics, upcoming events, new policies, and anything else of concern.

Depending on the ages and abilities of students, class "reporters" can actually write much of the text of the newsletter. This gives students an authentic writing purpose with a real audience, and the student participation guarantees a newsletter with the appeal of personality and variety. Many classrooms come up with a catchy title for their weekly publication and find

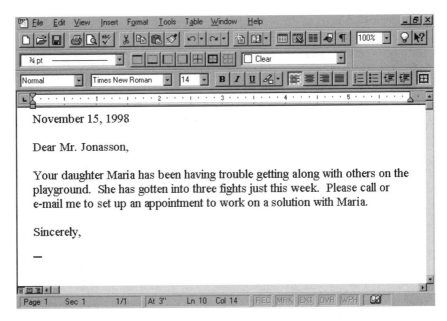

FIGURE 11-1   A word processed letter to parents. *(Screen shot reprinted by permission from Microsoft Corporation)*

or create relevant graphics with which to personalize the final product. The basic layout can be saved as a template to be used week after week, minimizing time spent to simplify what it takes to insert the new information each week. Many schools where teachers do have convenient access to word processors now require teachers to produce a newsletter of some sort to send home on a regular basis.

Official Correspondence

Parent permission is frequently required for participation in anything from field trips to Internet usage. Creating, printing, and copying these types of releases to send home makes for consistent, professional-looking records of parent responses. Although most schools, or even districts, have in use standard forms for these purposes, occasions may arise for which there is no set form in place, such as requesting permission to take home a class pet, for example, or notifying families of an end-of-semester recital. Teachers should make sure any forms that are sent home are easy to understand and provide ample writing space for parents.

Student Contact Information

Keeping in touch with your students' families is made easier by keeping up-to-date student records. Schools often provide teachers with printed lists of student information, but these pages represent a static form of keeping this information. If a family changes phone numbers, or a parent gets a new job with different hours, a printed list can be modified only by hand, leaving a messy record-keeping system.

Creating a database record for each student in class allows for a neat, easy-to-update filing system. The fields in a database can be customized to allow for information specific to particular students and situations. A database for a class in which most students ride the school bus may need to include a field identifying the bus number in order to be complete. A database on older students might include students' after-school work numbers. Larger text fields can be used to add anecdotal comments. Databases not only provide for a convenient, consistent compilation of information about students, but that information can also be searched and sorted. If, for example, all of the students who have other siblings attending the same school need to be contacted, students with completed "sibling" fields can be sorted and printed out. Student information can be entered into a database by teachers, or the task can be shared. Having the database open on the computer screen, along with an example of a student record, as parents come in for a "Meet-Your-Teacher" night at the beginning of the school year can serve as an invitation for parents to fill in their own child's data. Not only does this spread the workload, but it also introduces parents to some of the many ways technology is being used to perform administrative tasks in the classroom.

Planning

Teachers, like any great executives, need to envision what the future might hold, planning for the educational goals of their students. Regardless of the personal teaching style and philosophy of each teacher, most create some sort of plans to reach both long- and short-term objectives. Plans that are sketched out on paper may grow messy and unreadable through subsequent modifications. Productivity software can aid in planning activities by saving teachers' time and making quality, functional, final products.

Lesson Plans

When a newly graduated and employed teacher heads to the teaching supply store, the first item placed into the shopping cart is usually a "Teacher's Plan Book." These books contain blank weekly calendars, with the days identified down the left side of the page and half-hour increments clearly marked across the top. As schedules of special activities and class times are mapped out, changed, and finalized throughout the weeks before the start of the school year, and sometimes well into the first days of school, the neat order of most plan books begins to suffer. Handwritten schedules get crossed out, erased, and modified. Even when weekly plans do settle down into routine schedules, daily activities must still be handwritten into the book. Regularly scheduled activities must be repeatedly entered over and over again, week after week. Many times activities take longer than the time planned and must be carried over into other time slots. All in all, handwritten plan books are messy, redundant, and generally not an effective utilization of a teacher's time.

Productivity software, such as word processing or spreadsheet software, can make some of this hassle more manageable. Using a spreadsheet, teachers can easily map out a generic weekly schedule (see Figure 11-2). If activities change, they can simply be deleted or moved. Classes that occur predictably at the same time every day or week can easily be copied over to the next cells. Teachers who require more space to plan for lessons can format their planning pages to allow for large blocks of planning space. Tentative plans can be printed out on a daily, weekly, or longer basis, or plan templates, with recurring activities blocked in but learning time left blank, can be printed out to allow for handwritten adjustments.

Planning for days when a guest teacher will be in is also simplified. Typed plans supply the guest teacher with accurate information on all necessary special student and schedule considerations and can be prepared ahead of time to lessen the busy work of preparing to be absent for a day. The planning options are as endless as the variety of teaching styles and circumstances.

Longer-term planning can be accomplished using software tools as well. Monthly calendars can be created manually using a spreadsheet, with help from templates or "Wizards" that come packaged with most word processing software, or even by using software especially intended to create calendars. An entire school year can be mapped out ahead of time, making it possible to see how thematic units might interrelate or how required curriculum elements can be coordinated into the allotted school days. As plans change, calendars can be easily modified accordingly.

Visually aided planning can also be facilitated with the use of basic productivity software. It is common for teachers to plan for various related curriculum areas at the same time, using a "web"-type graphical representation so connections between topics or activities can easily be seen. Using a simple drawing program, teachers can map out thematic units or entire semester plans, making it possible with one glance to see how learning might be structured. Software tools make staying organized an easy reality for teachers.

	Monday
8:00-8:15	Opening (Attendance, Lunch Count, Calendar)
8:15-9:30	Language (Literature, Writing)
9:30-10:00	Music
10:00-11:30	Math
11:30-12:15	Lunch
12:15-1:30	Science/Social Studies
1:30-1:50	Recess
1:50-2:30	Group Work
2:30-3:00	Journals, Storytime

FIGURE 11-2   A custom weekly lesson-planning page.

Planning for Individual Student Needs

As plans for reaching both long- and short-term goals are made, customizing plans to meet the educational needs of individual students can be facilitated by referring to a database of individual student concerns. Whether added to a main database of student information, or created as a separate file of learning characteristics, comments on everything from student learning modalities to special classes required can be recorded, making planning to meet the needs of students as easy as clicking a mouse button. If, for instance, three students leave to go to work with a speech pathologist every Tuesday at 1:00, a guest speaker can be scheduled around that time so that the students would still be able to participate. Whereas scheduling around one or two students' special schedules or planning for ways in which they will learn best might be possible without any help from a computer, effectively planning for the instruction of 30 students or several times that many for teachers who see a series of different classes throughout the day, by considering their individual needs, could become problematic. A database created for this purpose will maximize planning and teaching time by helping to manage the specific characteristics a teacher must remember about every student.

Designing a Classroom Layout

How the furniture in a classroom is physically arranged reflects both the personal style and the teaching style of a teacher. Not only does the placement of desks or bookshelves contribute to the aesthetic atmosphere, but it determines the functional traffic patterns of the room. Desks pushed into groups are conducive to different learning experiences than desks that are organized into measured rows. Regardless of the desired learning atmosphere, graphics software can be of great assistance. All available furniture can be mapped out and moved. Student names can be assigned to desks or tables and shuffled to achieve a workable mix of personalities and learning styles. These types of modifiable seating charts are especially helpful for guest teachers to become familiar with students (see Figure 11-3).

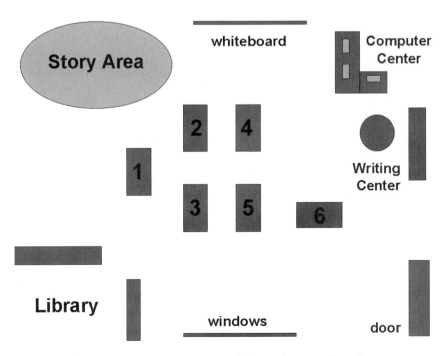

FIGURE 11-3   Using a graphics program to design a classroom floorplan.

Scheduling

Along with the educational planning that the creation of quality learning environments necessitates, much attention must also be paid to the fundamental scheduling of activities and other arrangements, scheduling that is in many ways similar to that which many good office managers regularly undertake. Budgeting money, booking guest speakers, and making arrangements for field trips can all be simplified with the use of classroom technology.

Budgeting Money

Operating a classroom frequently involves the planning, collecting, accounting, and distributing of money. Money might be collected to pay for a field trip, raised by having a school candy sale, or saved to reach a class goal. When students begin bringing in wrinkled dollar bills and handfuls of coins, an orderly system of money management is vital. The features of a spreadsheet are best designed for the purpose of budgeting money. Columns can be organized to account for who has brought in what amount, and formulas can be written to calculate the total amounts. Time estimated to reach monetary goals can be planned, relying on calculations based on an anticipated income from a money-raising event. A legible spreadsheet accounting for every penny is a much superior method of tracking classroom expenses than a handwritten list of names and amounts scrawled on the back of an envelope full of dollars and change (see Figure 11-4).

Booking Classroom Guests

Despite the perception of isolation that four walls give to most classrooms, there are, in reality, often enough visitors moving in and out of classrooms to give teachers plenty of practice in the role of talent booking agents. Guests may range from parent helpers to community experts, but the appearances of all visitors must be carefully choreographed to fit in seamlessly with the natural flow of classroom learning. Teachers and students can use word

Total Cost for Field Trip to Mexico				
Cost per student X	# of Students =		Total Cost	
$900.00	27		$24,300.00	
Candy Sale			$14,000.00	
Car Washes			$2,500.00	
Bake Sales			$800.00	
Remaining Personal Contributions			$7,000.00	

FIGURE 11-4 Budgeting classroom expenses with a spreadsheet.

processors to compose initial letters inviting guests to come to the class. These letters might even be based on generic letter templates written to include all of the basic information about the class that a visitor might need to know. Scheduling visitors can be done with either a spreadsheet or a calendar program, making accurate work of keeping track of who can be expected each day of school. Consulting online schedules regularly will remind teachers of upcoming visits so that if any unexpected schedule changes occur, guests can be contacted and rescheduled in a timely manner. Guest contact information should be carefully recorded into a database, so that it can be quickly accessed. Finally, word processors and possibly even graphics programs can be utilized to easily write thank-you notes to any guest that has helped students in some way.

Generating

Teachers generate learning documents every day, no matter the subject or age of students taught. Even teachers who adhere closely to a packaged curricula have frequent cause to supplement commercial materials with those that are teacher-made. Working from what is known about individual and collective abilities of students, as well as on the pace and climate of learning; workpages, recording sheets, quizzes, tests, dictated stories, and an unlimited number of other materials need to be created. Many teachers have scribbled down a handwritten quiz at the last minute only to have students run into problems trying to read the handwriting. The variable widths of handwriting make for poor-quality copies. When students are faced with a handwritten page with which to work, they may not put forth their best effort since it does not appear as though a great effort was shown in the creation of the assignment itself. Word processed documents are professional, neat, and customizable (see Figure 11-5). Topics that come up on the spur of the moment can be quickly added to an existing document, and an appropriate amount of space on the page can be left for students to write depending on the size handwriting with which students of that particular age are capable. Any special grading practices employed by a class can be accommodated by creating custom documents.

Another strength of using technology in generating learning materials for the classroom is that it facilitates sharing of ideas among teachers. So often, a teacher who wants to use a page that another teacher has created is left to merely copying the document, making due with any portions that do not directly pertain to the class, or attempting to cut and paste to customize it to fit a unique purpose. Word processed documents are superior in this case because they can be shared either on disk or through a network and can be easily modified to reflect class needs.

Evaluating

Any instructional effort is undertaken by both the instructor and the learner with the hope that the learning of something new will be the end result. Almost continuously, teachers arrive at various forms of evaluative conclusions, conclusions that shape and guide plans for future instruction. The recorded products of evaluative activity can take a number of forms, but can generally be discussed in two chief categories: quantitative and qualitative records.

Quiz

1. What was the main point our speaker was making today?

_____

_____

_____

_____

2. How will this message help you in your life?

_____

_____

_____

_____

_____

3. How might you find out more about this topic?

_____

_____

_____

_____

_____

FIGURE 11-5   A teacher-made quiz generated using a word processor.

Classroom technology can assist teachers with both types of record keeping, making the tedious, potentially error-prone activities easy and accurate, thus facilitating the straightforward report of progress to parents.

Quantitative Record Keeping

Traditionally, students have been assessed according to standard, established criteria, and their achievement compared either to each other as in norm-referenced assessments or according to their mastery of the objectives themselves as is the case with criteria-referenced conclusions. In either case, scores received on evaluative assessments must be recorded and compiled so that a longer-term assessment of an individual can be accomplished. A teacher's gradebook has always been thought to hold all the answers regarding a child's progress. The story was told in the neat columns and rows of handwritten names and numbers.

Although this manner of assessment remains the preferred method of measuring students' learning, the way in which records can be kept has received a helping hand from spreadsheet software (see Figure 11-6). Now, instead of entering student names by hand, names can be easily typed in. Records for new students can be inserted into the alphabetically correct position, rather than being tacked on to the bottom of the list out of order. Grades that are entered can be modified if assignments are resubmitted, for example, without creating a mess of erasings and blobs of correction fluid.

Mr. Brooks
8th Grade English
3rd Hour

	Assignment 9/14	Assignment 9/16	Assignment 9/18	Assignment 9/20	Assignment 9/24	quiz #1	quiz #2	quiz #3	quiz #4		Total	%
Total Points	20	20	20	20	20	5	5	5	5		120	100%
Berland, C.	20	17	17	20	18	5	5	5	5		112	93%
Booth, D.	19	19	19	18	5	4	4	5			112	93%
Chambers, A.	17	16	19	20	18	5	5	5	5		110	92%
Davis, M.	17	17	19	20	18	5	5	4	3		108	90%
Gillis, L.	20	18	19	20	18	4	5	5	5		114	95%
Goetz, M.	20	18	19	12	18	3	5	4	3		102	85%
Hatten, A.	20	18	19	20	18	3	5	5	5		113	94%
Kinney, R.	19	18	20	20	15	4	0	4	4		104	87%
Landers, M.	20	20	20	20	20	3	1	3	5		112	93%
Levy, D.	17	19	17	20	19	4	2	2	5		105	88%
Livingston, P.	14	19	14	20	19	2	2	3	5		98	82%
Marshall, J.	10	19	20	19	19	5	4	2	5		103	86%
Nedley, H.	18	18	20	19	14	5	4	3	5		106	88%
O'Connor, M.	20	20	20	19	20	5	3	4	4		115	96%
Quesada, S.	12	14	20	19	20	2	3	5	5		100	83%
Scott, T.	17	19	20	19	20	2	3	5	5		110	92%
Steele, R.	13	5	20	19	20	2	5	5	5		94	78%
Tencer, J.	15	19	19	19	20	1	4	3	5		105	88%
Vanderpool, V.	20	20	20	20	20	5	5	5	5		120	100%
Wyatt, K.	20	19	19	19	20	5	5	1	5		113	94%

FIGURE 11-6 A gradebook created using spreadsheet software.

The most powerful advantage of using a spreadsheet to keep track of student grades, though, is the software's ability to perform computational functions on numbers. No longer does a teacher need to take time to enter each grade for a student into a calculator to calculate an average grade. With a drag to highlight a row of grades, and a click on a shortcut button, a simple average computation can be placed into a target spreadsheet cell. Formulas can be easily written to perform more complicated calculations, such as applying different weights to the scores received on different assignments. A further advantage of keeping grades on a spreadsheet is the ability to represent scores graphically. Most programs will produce any number of graphs and charts to present student achievement in ways that are readily understandable and comparable.

Several programs are available that are designed expressly for the purpose of recording and calculating grades. Formulas most useful in calculating grades are already written

Classroom Vignette

Margaret Anderson unlocked the door to the sixth-grade class in which she would be substitute teaching today. As a regular substitute teacher for the district, she had seen all types of teaching situations, and worked with all levels of preparation left by the classroom teacher. It was always a mystery as to how much information would be given to her when she walked into each new day of substituting.

Margaret could see that the day's plans, as usual, were left on the teacher's desk. Right away, she knew the outlook for a successful day was good. The plans were word processed and very explicit. It appeared as though these were the regular teacher's plans, but they had been modified to include notes especially for someone not familiar with the regular class routine. Where the day's plan listed the day's starting time as 8:00 a.m., for example, it was typed next to it, "You will find students lined up outside next to the large tree."

Such helpful details were sprinkled throughout the plans:

"Remember to send Peter to speech class at 10:35."

"Pick up students from lunch at the west side of the cafeteria."

"A guest speaker, Mrs. Abernathy, will be coming at 2:10 to speak about her job at the county courthouse. She is aware that you will be here, and she will bring everything she needs."

Margaret got the impression that not only was this teacher organized, but that she was also smart. Keeping her lesson plans electronically made it easy to make changes. Rather than having to handwrite directions thorough enough for a stranger to keep the class moving throughout the day, she only had had to modify her existing plans with a few pertinent notes. It left Margaret feeling confident that she had enough information to make the day a good experience for both the students and herself.

Her impression of this teacher's ability to use technology to keep a well-managed classroom was furthered when the students entered the classroom. The first girl to walk in turned on the computer by the doorway and launched a database application. She found her name, signed herself in, and entered her lunch order. One by one these jostling, active sixth-graders made their way through the door and independently used the computer to take their own attendance and lunch count. All that was left for Margaret to do was glance at the list to make sure it was complete and send it to the office via e-mail. It appeared that more teachers than just this one were using technology to their advantage to make this school run more smoothly and efficiently.

and made easily accessible in these programs, and graphical outputs are created especially for student progress reporting purposes. Despite these features, though, many teachers prefer the flexibility and customizability that a generic spreadsheet program gives them in creating their own system over these purpose-specific products.

Qualitative Record Keeping

As educational philosophy progresses with the times, views of what type of information provides indication of learning are changing as well. The steadfast belief that numbers can tell the complete story of a learner is giving way to a recognition that what a teacher observes in daily interactions with students is in fact telling of the growth of those students. Indeed, as educators embrace this new anecdotal method of assessment, at the same time they scramble to find a way to consistently and comparably report student progress in words instead of numbers. Although these more subjective observational methods may never share the reliability and validity that hard numerical measurements do, they can be made more manageable, and perhaps more meaningful, with the help of classroom technology.

By creating or adding to an existing database record for each child, teachers can record observations in a central, organized location (see Figure 11-7). Because it is not practical to run over to the computer to access the database whenever a student says or does something of note, teachers can develop notetaking practices that work with the technology-based record keeping. Keeping handy a notepad allows teachers to quickly jot down the name of the

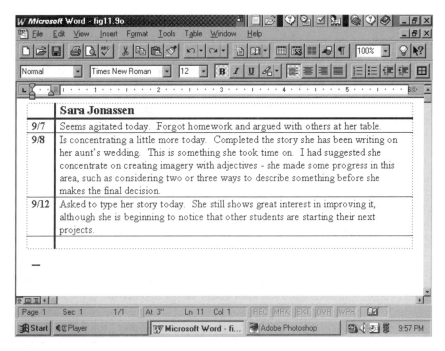

FIGURE 11-7 Anecdotal records kept on a word processor. *(Screen shot reprinted by permission from Microsoft Corporation)*

student and what indication of progress they notice. At a later time, just as a teacher would need to take time to record quantitative grades, a teacher can sit with the database application open and enter in the observations. This also gives a teacher opportunity to scroll back up through a student's record to track patterns or make predictions. Although this type of recording could, in essence, be done with paper and pencil, handwritten notes are static documents. The text of anecdotal records recorded in a database can be searched by keywords to see, for example, how frequently a student has offered an answer in class or has had a problem behaving with another student. These records can additionally be merged into word processed documents to create instant parent reports of student progress.

Conclusion

The few ideas presented here are only beginning thoughts of how technology can aid in the administrative duties of a teacher. Once teachers conquer initial fears that technology will only give them more work to do, they can start to understand how truly liberating technology tools can be (Sandholtz, Ringstaff, & Dwyer, 1997). Software is continually being improved, adding automatic features that perform functions that now must be done manually. Teachers should be aware of what software is available to them through their schools, and must always be ready to consider new ways that technology can make their jobs easier and more organized.

Summary

Along with their instructing responsibilities, teachers must serve as administrators of the day-to-day operations of their classrooms. Basic software tools can make it easy for teachers to create consistent, professional, and accurate products for communicating, planning, scheduling, generating, and evaluating management tasks.

In addition to electronic communication like e-mail, teachers still have many occasions when print-based communication is necessary. Word processing applications can be used to quickly send all kinds of letters, from newsletters to thank-you notes. Teachers can begin with a template form and can then save finished products for future use. Contact information on students' families and other community members with whom teachers and students need to communicate can be stored and organized in a database application.

Planning for both short-term lessons and longer-term curriculum maps can be done by using a word processor or a spreadsheet. Regular, predictable activities can be automatically scheduled, and individual student schedules can be planned. Seating charts designed with a graphic program can keep the classroom layout functional and can serve to inform guest teachers.

Teachers have a need to schedule a number of different items, and a spreadsheet application is ideal for keeping accurate records. Money for special activities or trips must be counted and accounted for. Classroom guests and helpers must be booked into the set schedule and then planned around it.

Regardless of the topic being taught, there are frequently teacher-made materials, including practice pages and quizzes, that are required. Word processing programs and graphics applications allow for nearly spontaneous generation of all types of professional-looking print materials. Documents are easy to share among colleagues and to modify to fit individual needs.

Finally, both quantitative and qualitative records of student evaluation are kept easy with basic software applications. Grades can be best organized and calculated by using a spreadsheet. Changed grades or new students are easy to insert while maintaining a neat record. Anecdotal records of progress can also be kept using a word processor or a database. As software applications continue to improve, they will make teachers' administrative efforts more effective and efficient.

LEARNER ACTIVITIES

1. Look for the templates that are included in the word processing software you generally use. What possibilities does the program present for the administrative tasks of teachers?

2. Using a spreadsheet application, design a simple gradebook for a fictitious class. Include scores for several assignments and formulas to calculate the final grades.

3. Make a list of ways in which the students you plan to teach can participate in administrative duties of their classroom.

4. Open a database program and experiment with creating a student database of information. What types of categories might be required to keep complete records of your students?

5. Using a template or beginning with a blank page, design a weekly newsletter for your class. Include a catchy title, any necessary graphics and all formatting to create a finished product. What types of information will you include on a regular basis? How much of the writing and compilation of the letter can realistically be done by your students?

6. Obtain a teacher's plan book after it has been used for several months. Study the types of activities that are written, as well as how much space is used and how many lessons appear to be moved around or otherwise altered after being planned. Based on this teacher's planning habits, how would you design a custom lesson planning page using a software application?

7. Create a calendar for scheduling classroom guests and other long-term special activities. Brainstorm a list of all possible visitors to your classroom, including those who will help on a regular basis as well as the types of people who might come only once.

8. Use a graphics program to design a classroom floorplan. Visit a classroom at the level you will teach to see the type of furniture that is used and in what ways it can be organized. Plan for smooth traffic patterns and varying size group work areas.

9. What does the research say on the use of anecdotal records? What are some methods that experienced teachers use to keep track of these types of observations?

10. Design an electronic form on which to record qualitative, anecdotal records on individual students. What will be the best way to keep these records updated?

BIBLIOGRAPHY

Huber, J. (1997). Gradebook programs: Which ones make the grade? *Technology Connection, 4*(1), 21–23.

Office of Technology Assessment. (1995). *Teachers and technology: Making the connection.* OTA-CHR-616. Washington, DC: U.S. Government Printing Office.

Sandholtz, J. H., Ringstaff, C., & Dwyer, D. C. (1997). *Teaching with technology: Creating student-centered classrooms.* New York: Teachers College Press.

12 Organizing with Technology

1. What are some considerations behind the choice to group computers together into labs versus putting them into individual classrooms?
2. How can collaboration with colleagues lead to more student opportunities to use technology?
3. How might the physical conditions of a classroom and educational philosophy of a teacher affect how computers are placed?

Some would say that in a perfect world, every student would have his or her own computer. Students could work whenever they wanted or needed, they could gather together to learn in groups, and they could use them as easily as they now use other learning tools, such as pencils or books. Since this dream is not yet a reality for the majority of schools, the question of how student learning can be organized in any given technology situation needs to be addressed. How can teachers make the most of what they have available, ensuring that students get experience with the types of skills that will be indispensable in their future academic and professional pursuits? Unfortunately, the simple logistics that are explained in teacher inservice trainings or in professional journals and books do not always prove simple when put into practical use.

Computer Labs versus Classroom Computers

In order to devise a workable plan for both student and teacher computer use, you need to begin with an understanding of how computers are distributed in your school. There is an ongoing debate among educators as to how computers can best be arranged to offer students the most equitable and effective access to technology. One school of thought values a model that places all of the computers into one computer lab, generally located in an extra classroom or other free space at the school (see Figure 12-1). This layout was the common practice during the early years when computers were still gaining an accepted place in our schools, and it still makes the most sense to many technology planners today. It is cost-effective in that it gives all students in all grade levels a chance to use the machines, and it

FIGURE 12-1 A school computer lab.

means that the expensive machines are used virtually all day. Each class typically schedules a weekly "computer time" when they can go down to the lab together to work. If a school is lucky, it may have a full- or part-time computer teacher to instruct with or about technology or to assist the classroom teacher with ideas and technical support.

Educators on the other side of the debate see advantages in breaking apart the traditional computer labs and distributing the machines out among the classrooms. They stress that in order for technology to be truly integrated into the learning process, it must be immediately accessible to learners. If computers are located in a lab, that may mean that students only place their hands on the equipment once a week, and then only in an artificial, unconnected way. Having a set "computer time" gives the impression that computers are some separate entity, a "field trip" on which students get to embark just once each week, instead of the idea that the machines are viable learning tools that can provide endless research and production possibilities each day.

Of course, lab advocates are quick to point out that a plan that involves sending all of the computers into the classrooms creates problems of its own. Although a small group of students can work on a timely activity in the classroom, the whole class cannot learn the same thing at the same time. Teachers may be forced to explain the same concept a number of times, as each group gets an opportunity to come to the class computer. Not having computers in one location also may preclude a designated technology teacher from presenting lessons, and instead might require the classroom teachers to assume the majority of technology instruction.

There are countless variations of computer distributions that fall somewhere in between these two extremes. Sometimes new computers are arranged together into labs so that all students have access to them, and the older computers are doled out to individual classrooms. Many schools are now experimenting with distributed computers in classrooms with the addition of "minilabs" of a small number of computers located in groupings around the school, possibly shared by two or three grade levels. Understanding the issues, and then considering which path your school has chosen to take and the thinking that went into making that choice will help you plan for the smartest computer use possible for your class.

Organizing Learning in a Lab Setting

If the majority of your students' time with computers will be spent in a computer lab setting, some forethought and well-planned procedures can make for successful utilization of the technology. Trooping your entire class down to the computer lab without any plan as to what will happen there will only waste your students' valuable time with computers and cause undue frustration for everyone involved. Consider each of the following areas as they relate to the real situation at your school.

Equipment

Being prepared is a motto teachers should live by, but when it comes to technology, that motto becomes a rule that simply cannot be broken. You need to be familiar with the equipment your students will be using so that you will be able to effectively facilitate their learning. Although this does not mean you need to be a technology expert, you need to be at least familiar enough with the operation to facilitate your students' learning experiences.

Skill with computers is a unique area that is leading teachers to reconsider the notion that they must be knowledgeable about everything that they teach in the classroom. Students may in fact know more about a particular piece of software or hardware, and may have less fear of exploring the unknown, than many of their teachers. Although there are a multitude of ways teachers can encourage and capitalize on these individual strengths and desires to experiment, they should at the same time be making an effort to acquire a personal level of familiarity with the present technology. A learning experience in the computer lab will be more closely integrated into the ongoing curriculum and be therefore of greater educational benefit to students if you have taken the time to walk down to the computer lab to become comfortable with how the computers are configured prior to bringing your entire class down for a lesson.

Preplanning and Preinstructing

To make the most out of a brief weekly computer lab experience, students must be primed for what they will be doing and what will be expected of them. Valuable time will be wasted if the class must wait until they are seated in the lab to receive instructions for how their time will be spent. A lesson that fits well into a curriculum sequence will be planned in advance. Any materials students will need should be brought along with them. If groups will need to do any note taking, for example, they should have paper and pencils available. If students will be using a productivity tool to finish a piece of work, such as a word processor to type a story they have written, that work should be out and ready to go when you leave for the lab. If possible and appropriate, instructions can be given and work strategies discussed prior to arrival in the lab. This will not only maximize available lab time and prepare students with a productive mind-set for the work period, but will stress to students the continuity between what they learn in the computer lab and what they are learning in class. This strategy reflects the view that technology is just another tool in your instructional arsenal, rather than a special, disconnected activity.

Assistance

One important consideration when planning class use of a computer lab is the extent to which you can depend on supplemental assistance. If your school or district employs a designated technology teacher, find out how often this teacher is available to help you. Depending on other responsibilities, some technology specialists may offer to plan with you for technology integration, may co-teach an activity with you, or may even teach entire technology-rich lessons. Sometimes several schools are forced to share a technology teacher, meaning that the teacher's time available for each individual teacher is limited. Unfortunately, other districts, whether due to lack of funds or insufficient teacher interest, do not have additional technology help available at all. This puts the onus on teachers in a situation like this to plan and implement lessons with technology on their own. An enormous number of educational journals now address technology issues, providing current and very practical suggestions for lessons and projects. Subscriptions to a few of these will encourage meaningful discussion about effective technology integration within the school. In any case, knowing what type of assistance you can expect will allow you to plan accordingly (see Figure 12-2).

FIGURE 12-2   A parent assisting students with work on computers.

Teamwork and Creative Scheduling

In the absence of additional assistance, or with the intention of capitalizing on the benefits of collaboration, teachers must seek out opportunities to team with colleagues at their school. Collaborating with peers leads to the expansion of ideas and more concise use of time with any teaching endeavor, but even more so with the new and potentially time-consuming possibilities presented by technology. There is no need to "reinvent the wheel" each time you plan a lesson that takes advantage of a computer. Talking about successes and challenges with other teachers will motivate you to grow and explore more than you might be moved to on your own.

Working closely with peer teachers also allows for creative scheduling of time in the computer lab. If each class is only allotted one time slot per week, two classes working together could conceivably get twice as much time in the lab. Working with a partner on the computer is often a great way to learn, and at the same time students benefit from having the combined teaching expertise of two teachers. If just one or two students are not able to go to the lab with the rest of your class, or if they require more time to work on a project, a cooperative plan with another teacher could allow them to join the other class during their time. The newness of technology in the school setting has the potential to prove the many benefits of collaboration to teachers who would not otherwise consider opening themselves to the idea.

Basic Lab Procedures

Just as your class lives by a set of basic classroom rules, so should they have some key understandings to help their time in the computer lab operate smoothly. Although most of your regular classroom procedures will apply, teaching in a computer lab is unique because of the sheer addition of a room full of machines. Depending on how the furniture in the lab is arranged, moving around the room might be challenging and even potentially dangerous, with the multitude of connection cables and power cords protruding from the backs of computers. Many labs push the computer tables around the perimeter walls of the room, meaning students can see and talk to other students sitting directly on either side of them, but must get up to speak to others. Labs with tables arranged in long rows may make it difficult to get from one point in the room to another just a few rows back. Small groupings of four computers pushed together have been shown to allow for good student communication and room navigation. Unfortunately, although the "best" arrangement might depend on your students' needs and your own teaching philosophy, these types of room arrangement decisions will likely not be left up to you. Teachers using a communal school lab are generally at the mercy of those who originally set up the lab.

Large monitors sitting on top of the tables tend to hide students' faces, making it difficult to make eye contact with a student or gain the attention of the whole group when you need to make a general announcement. The quiet hum of one computer does not seem at all intrusive to normal conversation, but yet an entire room full of computers can sound something like a roar when trying to get the attention of someone across the room. In addition, many educational software programs rely heavily on auditory effects, which can turn the room into a circus of beeps and bells. Finally, students simply might just be so intensely engaged in the interactive work they are doing that they may not even be paying attention to what is going on around them. The introduction of a number of simple behavior habits adjusted to fit the students you teach and your own personal management style can facilitate a more productive atmosphere in the computer lab. Explaining and modeling these habits to students before the computers are even turned on will encourage their adoption and continued use.

Traffic and Communication Patterns. Establish clear traffic and communication patterns with students. Consider the layout of the room, including where wires are located and the amount of space surrounding student work areas. You want students to be able to move through the lab safely and with a minimum of distraction to others who are working. Decide if it is best to have students be able to get up and move freely around the room when needed or if they need to speak only with those sitting directly next to them. Have a plan for where students can go during class to help ensure both their safety and the order of the classroom.

Help Signals. It is sometimes difficult to see a small hand raised for help between all of the computer monitors, so another way for students to attract attention is needed. Some labs have signs or other objects that students can place on top of their monitors so that you can see at a distance when someone needs help. Reminding students to use this method rather than raising their hands sometimes seems to counteract the hand-raising habit they have in the regular classroom, but it generally works better than having them yell out when they need you. In addition, it allows other helpers, such as parents or older students, to respond to the request for help.

Group Attention Signals. Because of the difficulty in attracting student attention in the lab setting, it is vital to have a highly visual signal to let students know you need their attention. Flickering the lights on and off works well. Having a set place for students to look to find you once you have given the attention signal can also help you focus their attention more quickly.

Time to Exit. The time spent in the lab often seems to pass very quickly, but the time needed to prepare to leave can be great. Students not only need to reach a good stopping point in their work, but they need to save their files, close the programs they were using, and possibly shut down the systems. Give students ample warning before it is time to leave so that they will have time to prepare. This will save the rest of the class from waiting too long at the door and prevent conflicts when the next scheduled class enters the lab.

Volunteer Helpers. To give your students the best chance for success while using the computer lab and to decrease the time they have to sit idly waiting for you to help them, solicit extra help during lab time. In addition to content instruction, students will need help operating new software programs and assistance with the ever-present technical problems. Many parents have experience with computers or are willing to volunteer despite their lack of computer knowledge. They can gain some computer familiarity of their own and at the same time can offer another set of hands to help students. Other invaluable help can come from older students who have some time between their own classes or can arrange to get away from class during your lab time. These students can reinforce their own skills and confidence by helping those younger than them. You might even have students in your own class take turns serving in the role of Technical Monitor, collaborating with peers on some problems and alerting you when your help is needed. Make sure that whoever is helping is introduced to the class so students know who is available to assist them. If you normally do not utilize outside helpers in your class, your students may need to develop a trust for the helpers before they stop waiting only for help from you. The combination assistance can combine to create a productive atmosphere in the computer lab.

File Storage

Encouraging students to use technology for authentic productive purposes often requires giving them the means to work on one project over the course of several class periods. Students therefore will need the ability to save their work for the next time through a number of storage methods.

If students will be sitting at the same computer each time they are in the lab, one storage solution is to have them save their work to a designated directory on that particular computer's hard drive. In this case, all teachers with students using the lab throughout the day would need to agree on a common directory structure. Directories can be made for each student on the machines they use, meaning directories for students in many classes could be found on any one computer. Students would need instruction on exactly where and how to save their work so as not to damage anyone else's files or any other application programs on the hard drive.

If a school is wired for a local-area network, student work may be saved into the network drive, making it accessible from other school computers. Students would then be able to sit in a different location each time in the lab or could also edit their work from a computer elsewhere on campus. An organized directory structure should be planned for a network, such as making directories for all students in one class under their teacher's name.

If no network exists or if saving work to the hard drive of a computer in the lab restricts future work on projects, students can also save work on disks. Each student should be taught how to insert and remove disks, how to save to them, and how best to care for them. Because of the somewhat fragile nature of disks, you may want to develop a system for group storage of the disks, such as keeping all students' labeled disks in one basket that can be brought to the lab each time. Older students may be able to keep and care for their own disks, but should be introduced to the concept of always saving a backup copy of any important files (see Figure 12-3).

FIGURE 12-3 Student disks organized together. (*Courtesy of Curtis Computer Products*)

Organizing Learning in a Classroom Setting

A great deal of thought must go into how you plan on utilizing your classroom computers, whether you have one or are lucky enough to have several. Many of the planning and operational procedures parallel those that have been discussed for lab use, but the differences lie with the increased freedom you have in room arrangement and scheduling. The use of the computer in your classroom should reflect your personal style and educational philosophies just as the use of any other learning tools do. Your very attitude about the computer's place in your instructional plan goes a long way in determining how your students will view its usefulness. If the computer sits in the corner under an inch of dust or if computer time is spent only "playing" games, students will naturally fail to see its potential importance in their learning. If, on the other hand, students see your enthusiasm for technology, if they see you using it as a tool to accomplish real goals despite your fear of learning something new, they will be drawn to learn and experiment with skills they must have to be successful in the future. For simplicity's sake, these recommendations will be directed primarily to the one-computer classroom, but they can be easily modified to fit the technology available to you as well as to fit the particular needs of your students.

Room Arrangement

The way your classroom is arranged is an expression of how you view the learning process, and how you integrate technical equipment into the physical space of your classrooms is an extension of these beliefs. Instead of pushing your classroom computers into the nearest corner, thoughtfully consider how they will be used by you and your students.

If you plan to have individuals or partners to use a computer while the rest of the class engages in other activities, you may want to put the computers off to one side of the room. Since what is seen on a computer monitor can be distracting to students working elsewhere, resist pushing the computers up against the wall, and instead turn them so that the monitors face away from the majority of the class. Bookshelves or other furniture can also be moved to create a more private computer area if desired. This, of course, makes it more difficult for you to view the computer screens to see how students are progressing, so be prepared to adjust your supervision habits.

If small groups will be using the computers, be sure there is enough room for several chairs to be pulled up and that there is easy access to other group work areas. If you plan to use the computer as one station in a series of learning centers to which students will be rotating, plan ahead for traffic patterns. Be sure students can easily get around the work area, even if others are sitting at the computer.

If you would like to try using your classroom computer as a presentation aid for the whole class (see Chapter 13 for more information on presenting and producing with your classroom computer), you will want to be sure the computer is located so that it is easy to connect to a projection device or can be easily moved. Avoid the temptation of placing the computer on your "teacher's desk" if you plan on having students regularly use it on their own. This location gives the impression that it is *your* computer and students are merely borrowing time on it.

As important as the learning purpose is to deciding how to arrange computers, what also must be considered is the reality of the physical situation of your classroom. Computers must be within reach of electrical outlets, for example. Care should be taken so that the glare from windows does not make seeing the screen impossible. The actual furniture on which the computer is placed should also be given some thought. Some schools purchase specially designed computer furniture. Others have gone as far as to ingeniously build the computer monitor right into the desk itself, allowing students to see it through a sturdy, waterproof glass top, but leaving a flat workspace across which students can easily see and be seen (Bozzone, 1997). If your school has not acquired any special furniture, you may be forced to creatively craft a computer workstation by pushing together existing desks and tables. Take the time to make this workstation as ergonomically appropriate for your students as possible, such as by raising or lowering the table legs. These preparations will make for a more functional technology classroom (see Figure 12-4).

Technical Procedures

When computers are distributed into classrooms, teachers must assume much of the responsibility for the day-to-day technical operation of the equipment. There may be a school or district technology specialist available, but you will want to be familiar with enough of the basic troubleshooting strategies to prevent long interruptions of student productivity. You will want to take time to study how the wires are connected to the computer and to other peripherals, such as a monitor and a printer. Organize software on the desktop with icons so

FIGURE 12-4 A classroom computer workstation.

that students will be able to quickly and easily find applications they need without disturbing other directories or programs.

Model appropriate care and use of the machine and software to prevent some potential problems. Dust the computer and the monitor weekly, for example. Keep floppy disks away from magnetic devices and excess heat or cold. Depending on students' ages or capabilities, they can be taught to handle many common operational and maintenance procedures, such as loading a new CD-ROM or replacing paper into the printer. When technical or other problems arise, think aloud to students as you consider your options, and demonstrate how you would solve them, thus providing a real problem-solving model. The more independently students can operate your classroom computer, the more confident they will be in using it.

Scheduling Computer Use

Students should be made aware of the expectations you have for their computer use just as they are aware of expectations for other academic and behavioral habits. Make it clear when it is appropriate to go to the computer and when other work should be focused on. This will prevent congregation around a computer every time a new sound is heard or your students enter the room at the beginning of the period.

Whether you have just one or several computers in your classroom, you can design efficient use strategies by scheduling time for students to work on the computers. Your students will need time to use the computer in two different ways. It is first essential to provide time for students to explore and learn how to use computer hardware and software. This might be an informal, discovery time or may be structured so that students work with one particular skill or program. Students also must have time to use what they have learned for productive purposes. These personal work times should allow students to use technology to work on class assignments or to pursue individual projects, but should be organized around an ultimate goal of a finished product.

A number of different strategies can be used to introduce new computer skills. To demonstrate some basic operational skills, such as manipulating text in a word processor or saving files to the school network, you may choose to show the entire class at once using a projection device. If you have received a new piece of software, you might decide to show it to a couple of students, and let them teach the next couple of students, and so on. You can also write some simple, developmentally appropriate directions and let students discover how to use a graphics program on their own using the directions as a guide. With any method, students must be allowed time to practice these ideas before they are required to use them for real purposes. Once students are confident with the basics, they can apply what they know to achieving other academic goals.

A sign-up sheet for computer time is one way teachers organize student computer use, but, unfortunately, if students can only sign up for time when they have finished their other work, only a select few students will ever get regular computer experience. Creating a set weekly schedule for computer use can help to ensure equity in opportunities for students in a one-computer class. Look at all of the available time when your students are in the room, and divide this time into workable blocks of perhaps thirty minutes each. Slot in students' names so that each has time for both practicing new skills and authentic technology use, ideally scheduled in two separate work times to give them the best chance for quality learning. Schedule students for times during the days when they can work on the computer without missing instruction that they need. Depending on your students' experience level and specific needs, having them work in pairs could be more beneficial than working by themselves. Post the schedule so that students know when their weekly times are and when there are open slots (see Figure 12-5). This allows them to plan when they will be working on the computer, and also shows open times that are available for spontaneous technology use. Students must feel that they have opportunity to word process a story or create graphics when they need to without necessarily having to wait for once or twice a week. The posted schedule also encourages student monitoring of computer use. When a student's computer time is over, he can alert the next person on the list, relieving you to work with students in other capacities.

Assistance

Successful facilitation of a technology-rich classroom requires the coordination of help from a number of sources. Parent volunteers with computer experience can provide needed technical support, and those who are computer novices can encourage and supervise as they learn along with the students. Older students who are able to donate time can teach younger students the finer points of a new piece of software or can help with some of the manual work that sometimes slows down little hands, such as typing text into a word processor. Peers can also serve as teachers to one another, sharing special skills or teaming to work out a problem. They often can fill in where teachers may lack the technical expertise.

Make your students aware of their options for assistance so that they learn not to depend on you alone. This is a difficult lesson, especially considering the inherent technical problems that come with regular use of computers. A simple paper jam in the printer or a malfunctioning CD-ROM can bring to a standstill the immediate continued use of the computer. Students' first reaction is to think that you alone will be able to remedy the situation,

	Monday	Tuesday	Wednesday	Thursday	Friday
8:00-8:30	Raymond	Jenny	Maura	Mary	Donna
8:30-9:00	Jonathon			Gene	Jeffrey
9:00-9:30		Ally	Tonya	Winston	
9:30-10:00	Rachel	John	Robin		
10:00-10:30		David			
10:30-11:00	Alex	Elaine		Harmony	Vonny
11:00-11:30	LUNCH				
11:30-12:00	RECESS				
12:00-12:30	Tricia	Joshua		Greg	Tommy
12:30-1:00			Gina	James	Shawna
1:00-1:30			Troy		
1:30-2:00	Marisa	Gwen		Jimmy	
2:00-2:30	Whitney		Travis		
2:30-3:00					

FIGURE 12-5   Weekly schedule of classroom computer use.

and, indeed, many teachers new to using technology fall into the trap of running to solve every technical glitch that springs up. If this habit continues, being the sole technical problem solver will monopolize your time. An independent, problem-solving atmosphere established in your classroom will help students to troubleshoot technical problems themselves and with those who are there for them.

Teamwork

As talented at scheduling the use of one computer a teacher may be, there remains considerable limitations to having only a single machine. This is an excellent time when teamwork among your colleagues can be invaluable to your students. One easy way to make the most of the computers in classrooms is to work out a schedule with other teachers so that your students can go to use their computers when their students are not using them and vice versa. When schools have such a low ratio of computers to students, the time computer keys are sitting idle should be minimized.

A more drastic, yet potentially more beneficial, act is to consider teaming with other teachers to pool your single computers together to create a minilab. One teacher can volunteer to house the lab in a corner of the classroom, and a schedule can be worked out so that small groups of students from all the classes involved can come together to work on projects or content software. As teachers everywhere strive to effectively integrate technology into everyday learning experiences, they must all be open to the creative possibilities that open up when they work together.

The Role of the Library Media Center

"Getting through the book" is no longer a goal for any but the poorest of America's schools. Becoming information managers and assisting students in becoming knowledge workers are newer roles for teachers and media specialists. Learning with multimedia technology maximizes the time available for discussion, thinking, and creating knowledgeable responses to the data, issues, and problems.

Storytelling as an instructional strategy is both timeless and effective. Elementary school library media centers often take full advantage of this strategy and offer special areas for booktalks, dramatic productions, storytime, student-authored works, and independent free browsing, viewing, and reading. Electronic storybooks on CD-ROM, books on tape, videotaped readings of popular big books, books and stories presented in other languages, pop-ups, and flip animations may all be available for enjoyment.

Living in a global village has diminished the distance between the world's countries, while simultaneously illuminating the differences between cultures. Library media centers may provide materials and resources in a variety of formats that learners may access. General reference material such as an encyclopedia (an example is The New Grolier Multimedia Encyclopedia by Grolier Electronic Publishing), almanac, dictionary, thesaurus, maps, globes, and charts are all available in electronic formats: videodisc, CD-ROM, and computer software. A library media collection may also include posters, multimedia kits, audio cassette recordings, films, videotapes, models, and microforms.

Having a shared production area available within the library media center allows both faculty and students to create and publish instructional and learning materials. Ideally, there might be two or three production areas for students, faculty, and the library media center staff. A production area might provide a scanner, a digitizer, copier, printer, book-binding equipment, VCR, video camera, audio equipment, and microcomputer. Software would include desktop publishing; spelling and grammar editing programs; clip art; font, graphics, and art programs; and video-enhancing programs such as VCR Companion (Broderbund), Slide Shop (Scholastic New Media), HyperStudio (Roger Wagner Publishing), and HyperScreen (Scholastic New Media). Fully outfitted production areas might also include a darkroom facility, a multistation computer lab, and a video studio with editing equipment.

The reference area should include both laser disc and CD-ROM players to facilitate the many informational resources available in these formats. It should be a large, flexible space to accommodate both large- and small-group presentations and for individual research. Online electronic networks and database services might be available as well as cable television. A microcomputer with large screen display capabilities should be available for instructional presentations. Some reference areas include display space for student-produced work as well as realia. In addition to laser disc and CD-ROM players, the reference area might contain equipment that facilitates video capture, scanning, and viewing.

Many new library media centers are being built to include either an adjacent computer laboratory and/or and area within the center for hands-on mathematics and science activities. Within these areas, introductory robotics might be available such as Lego Logo (LCSI), science materials in videodisc format, which may be interactive through Hypercard stacks or barcode weather-gathering equipment that may include an online database and simulation materials, and software such as PC Globe (Broderbund), Health: Understanding Ourselves (ABC News Interactive), Science ToolKit (Broderbund), Visual Almanac (Optical Data), and SimCity (Broderbund). Technological equipment might include microcomputers, printers, and graphing calculators with display capabilities. The instructional practice of using real-life models, patterns, data, and problems as the basis for learning activities is catching hold. Programs such as Voyage of the MIMI (Wings for Learning), which capture the interest of learners through topics, storyline, and situational problems, introduce math and science concepts and activities while integrating technology. Software that allows students the opportunity to study high-interest content while practicing skills is popular.

Simulation and data manipulation software that provides students with graphic displays such as histograms, bar graphs, and scatter plots are also available. Some schools have answers, decisions, and opinions that may be electronically polled and graphed by computer. The teacher may use the resulting information to make instructional decisions and to determine skill and concept attainment.

Having the library center's collection available through electronic catalog and computer terminals, which may be housed in other parts of the school as well as on site, provides faculty and learners with immediate means and the capability of enhancing and/or remediating the instruction through the availability of other resources and materials. If the school library media center is a participant in a resource-sharing project with other libraries, the quantity of resources is even greater.

Flexible use of space and the ability to electronically access information outside the center and school are the two key factors when designing or recreating school library media

Classroom Vignette

Shari and Adam sat together in front of the computer by the door in their classroom. This was their "Exploration Time" for the week, and this week's assignment was to explore the new software Mrs. Simmons had shown them last week, PowerPoint (Microsoft Corporation). She had said that they could use PowerPoint to make presentations, like for their history projects that were coming up.

Shari took the laminated page of activities called "Try This" that Mrs. Simmons had left next to the computer for them to work with during their 30 minutes. She read the first activity out loud to Adam, "Make a new slide."

The two continued working through the page of activities, creating a sample slide show. They reminded each other of how Mrs. Simmons had demonstrated the program and worked together to figure out how to do the couple of things she had not shown. The last item on the "Try This" page asked them to think of ways that they might be able to use this program in a real way.

"I think we could make some slides to show what we learned in history," began Adam. "Maybe we could put the words we want to say on the screen and then we could just read the screen when we are talking in front of the parents. Then if we forget what to say, we could just look up there at the screen."

"Yeah," said Shari. "And maybe we could put some pictures in so it looks good. My project is on the Colonists, so maybe I could find some picture of the *Mayflower* or of what the people looked like then. But I don't want to wait that long to try it. I think I'm going to make a slide show tomorrow during my "Production Time" or maybe when we're in the computer lab."

The two practiced showing their sample slide show for the rest of their time, trying to speak without looking at the screen like Mrs. Simmons had shown them.

---

centers. The library media center must house, circulate, and distribute information in all formats to hundreds of users on a daily, hourly, and minute-by-minute basis. Reading, viewing, accessing information, and learning are all encouraged to become pleasurable lifelong activities within the library media center of the twenty-first century. The dust on the old library warehouse of books has departed!

Summary

Because budget shortages in school districts preclude the purchase of a computer for each and every child, choices must be made regarding the best placement of the available machines. Schools can opt for grouping them together into a computer lab, doling them out into individual classrooms, or some variation between those two extremes. The debate between supporters of each end of the spectrum wages on, but teachers must be prepared with some strategies for teaching with technology no matter where it is located.

With computers installed in a lab, students can all work on the same thing at the same time, and all students in a school can get their hands on a computer every week. The drawback to the lab setting, however, is that each student in the school might only get a chance to use a computer once a week, turning technology into a special activity disconnected from other learning. A single computer in a classroom allows students to use the electronic tool in a spontaneous, integrated manner. With a single computer, though, only small groups of students can work at any one time. Teachers may be forced to reteach a concept a number of times so that everyone gets a chance to learn.

Educators must have strategies in place to make the most of teaching in either a computer lab away from their classrooms or with one computer in their classrooms. To keep work in a lab relevant and efficient, teachers need to be prepared and informed. Giving students the information they need on what the goal is for a lab session prior to setting foot in the lab allows them to have a proper mind-set. It emphasizes the connectivity between what they work on in the lab with other learning processes. The unique attributes of working in a room with multiple computers humming away demand that students be taught specific procedures for getting help, giving their attention, moving safely around the room, and storing their work files.

Teachers with a computer in the classroom should plan the machine's location carefully to reflect its intended uses. A schedule can ensure equity in student access of the computer. Modeling of basic technical procedures can make it possible for students to solve many simple technical problems.

Soliciting help from parents or older students provides for smoothly operating computer work in either setting. Creative collaboration with colleagues can create even more opportunities for students to use computers as a tool in authentic learning endeavors.

LEARNER ACTIVITIES

1. Visit several elementary, middle, or secondary schools, or speak with several teachers. How are the computers at these schools organized? How successful do the teachers appear to be at making the arrangement into an effective learning environment?

2. Using a weekly teaching schedule from an actual classroom as a guide, create a weekly computer use schedule for students at your intended level. Without having any student miss a required activity, how much time per week can each use one classroom computer? How must free space in the schedule is there available for spontaneous use?

3. List the pros and cons of both lab and classroom placement of computers.

4. Prepare a budget proposal for purchasing a computer for every student at a school near you. Include in your plan the number of students, the approximate price of computers based on current retail prices, and any furniture that would be necessary.

5. Write a lesson plan that effectively incorporates a trip to the computer lab. Include related preparation ahead of time and follow-up work afterwards, so that the use of the technology tools are framed in context.

6. Write a letter to convince parents to volunteer their time to help students with using technology.

7. Visit a computer lab at a local school. Based on the specifics of the room layout, make a list of procedures you think would be necessary for safe and organized use of the lab. How does your list compare with any procedures that are actually used in the lab?

8. Design a floorplan that would facilitate effective computer use in a one-computer classroom.

9. What are ways to propose team collaboration on computer use? How can cooperation be encouraged among new teams?

10. How do you envision classrooms of the future? How many of these procedures will still apply?

BIBLIOGRAPHY

Anderson, G. (1996). Setting up computer workstations in classrooms and libraries. *Media and Methods, 32*(5), 14–16.

Banaszerski, R. (1997). Strategies for the one computer classroom. *Learning and Leading with Technology, 25*(1), 32–33.

Bozzone, M. A. (1997). Technology for kids' desktops. *Electronic Learning, 16*(5), 47–49.

Buchanan, L. (1996). Planning the Multimedia Classroom. *MultiMedia Schools, 3*(4), 16–21.

Fraundorf, M. C. (1997). Distributed computers and labs: The best of both worlds. *Learning and Leading with Technology, 24*(7), 50–53.

Federico, C. (1995). In defense of dabbling: The case for drop-in sessions. *Technology Connection, 2*(7), 13–16.

Green, E. E. (1996). Fitting new technologies into traditional classrooms: Two case studies in the design of improved learning facilities. *Educational Technology, 36*(4), 27–38.

Schulz, C. D. (1997). Today's school library media center: Technology is key. *Educational Horizons, 75,* 78–82.

Scott, R. (1995). How to get your own computer lab in your classroom. *English Journal, 84*(6), 62–64.

Sills-Briegel, T. M. (1996). Teacher-student proximity and interactions in a computer laboratory and classroom. *Clearing House, 70,* 21–23.

Waddick, J. (1997). Physical considerations in the development of a computer learning environment. *British Journal of Educational Technology, 28,* 69–71.

Wright, D. (1997). Successful furniture solutions. *School Planning and Management, 36*(2), 34, 36, 38, 40.

Zeitz, L. (1995). Troubleshooting computer problems: A teachers' guide. *Learning and Leading with Technology, 23*(1), 16, 32–33.

13 Producing and Presenting with Technology

FOCUS QUESTIONS

1. In what ways might the specific purpose for a multimedia production guide the planning?
2. What forms of media can be used to enhance instructional presentations?
3. What preparations must be made in advance of giving a technology-aided presentation?

Putting It All Together

As current educational research touts the advantages of authentic, project-based instruction and assessment, it becomes apparent that educators and students alike can use the capabilities of technology to make these new goals a practical reality. Technology presents some amazing opportunities to compile quality, varied informational products and effectively present those products to groups of people in meaningful ways.

Multimedia productions are so named because they are designed by integrating different mediums of information, such as text, audio, graphics, video, and animation elements. As opposed to a traditional lesson or presentation, where the user sits passively and receives the information in only the one way it is presented, multimedia can cater to a whole range of learning and teaching styles. At one end of the spectrum, multimedia can enhance somewhat traditional presentations where the control for the sequence of the presentation of information lies primarily with the presenter. On the opposite end of the range, multimedia can form *hypermedia* environments, where the user has the freedom to make decisions as to how or in which direction to explore. A hypermedia structure creates an environment without the linear restrictions associated with many paper-based learning materials. These hypermedia environments let the user access information in any order they wish. This access simulates the natural, nonlinear ways in which humans learn and allows for individual construction of knowledge. The flexibility and interactivity that can be achieved by synthesizing information with these multimedia elements can create a sensory experience that matches individual thinking patterns of both presenters and learners.

The process of creating multimedia products ideally reflects the philosophy that teachers and students are at times both the experts and the learners in the classroom. Both groups can use technology to prepare and present cohesive lessons or to demonstrate what has been learned in a unit of study. As with any use of technology, multimedia projects should be seen as a natural part of the teaching, learning, and evaluating processes that occur regularly in classrooms, rather than as some separate, added-on requirement. This chapter will outline a practical process both teachers and students can follow when using technology to author informative products and present them to others.

Planning and Research Preparation

Defining the Purpose

Creating a multimedia production can provide not only for real acquisition and use of technology skills, but also for the practice of visioning, planning, and making purposeful choices. Just as with any lesson, you and your students can make the most of the preparation process and the unique attributes of the technology if you understand the distinctive purpose of each project from the beginning. For what audience will it be prepared? To what extent will technology play a role in the creation and presentation of the production? Putting together a quick lesson for your class on the differences between warm- and cold-blooded animals in your area of the country will require different preparation than a research project undertaken to convince the school board to purchase new, safer playground equipment. The following is a sample of types of multimedia projects teachers and students can design:

■ **Lessons:** Whether taught by teachers or peer students, new concepts can be presented to others with the variety of media required to ensure all learners have the chance to learn in ways that make sense to them. Lessons can be prepared for whole groups to view at once, for small groups, or even for individual tutorial purposes.

■ **Research Projects or Book Reports:** Resources can be collected and reports written as usual, but they can then be compiled with relevant media about the topic or author. These projects can be used as the sole form of holistic evaluation or as a comprehensive review for another, more traditional assessment.

■ **Stories or Games:** A simple story written by a student can be transformed into an interactive project by infusing media elements and giving the user some decision-making ability. This gives an alternative to simply word processing a story and drawing pictures to accompany it.

■ **Parent or Community Informational Works:** Both text and media elements can cooperate nicely to inform others of rules, current events, and policy. This type of project could be realized as continuously running slide shows as participants enter a room or even stand-alone, kiosk-type, self-guided tours.

- **Electronic Portfolios:** Just as artists collect samples of what they have produced, students can bring together choice bits of written work, scanned images, photos and videos of events, and explain the importance of each in their own voice by recording a voice-over narration. Students can choose work they most want to include, and may even be required to defend their choices in front of a group of teachers, parents, and peers. Electronic portfolios reflect the current educational philosophy that places value on what students can actively do rather than relying only on static scores they receive on a test to tell the story of what they have learned. Teachers might also maintain portfolios, documenting instructional and professional growth and providing some proof of accountability.

Background Research

Multimedia projects, like any traditional projects, require strong, accurate content. Students and teachers should never make the mistake of thinking that audio clips and pretty pictures can make up for flimsy descriptions or missing facts. If you are teaching a lesson to students, make sure you have solid objectives and examples. Students should follow whatever research techniques and writing processes they normally do, making use of both text-based and electronic resources. Notes and other text can be word processed during this stage or simply handwritten. It is helpful for later procedures if this text is proofread and ready to be made into a final draft form.

Storyboarding

The importance of visually planning for the organization of a project was stressed in Chapter 8 with regard to the design of websites, but it is as equally vital to the successful creation of other electronic projects. You and your students should list the titles of the final drafts of the written forms of projects and transfer them to storyboard form, such as onto 5" × 7" index cards. These cards can be easily arranged and rearranged in order to arrive at a visual, logical flow of information. Storyboards can be created with varying amounts of detail, from just sketches to full graphic plans. This detail will be determined, again, by your purpose, time constraints, and developmental levels of the project designers and the audience.

Screen Design

Considering some basic design features at this stage in the planning will help ensure clear presentations. Model examples and nonexamples of these recommendations to even very young students so they can make personal judgments about what guidelines would make for the clearest presentations. Always temper each of these general recommendations with an understanding of the audience for the presentation or instruction. If an instructional presentation would benefit from an unorthodox use of text or color, make the best call for the purpose. Whatever design choices you make, remember that consistency is key. Random design features will make for a busy, distracting presentation. (See Table 13-1 for additional design tips.)

TABLE 13-1   Multimedia Design Issues

1. Limit the amount of text on each screen. Different audiences of students can handle varying amounts of text, but leave some space around the text or use graphics to break up large text pieces.

2. Choose a font that will be legible to learners. Some fonts prove easier to read when viewed on a computer screen or when projected up on the wall. A sans serif font, one without any decorative letter features, in a size of between 18 to 24 points is the easiest to read from a distance.

3. Use phrases or just key words rather than complete statements.

4. Words written in all capital letters are difficult to read. Underlined text should be reserved for hypertext links only.

5. Use colors appropriate for the topic and audience. Be sure text color contrasts with the background color, such as light text on a dark background or dark text on a light background.

6. Use graphics or other media elements for a real purpose rather than for mere decoration.

Producing Multimedia Elements

Once the content of the presentation is mapped out, you and your students can begin to consider what media elements might lend themselves to creating a complete learning experience. Inclusion of these elements will depend on the extent and quality of the equipment available to you at your school, but as with any teaching endeavor, resourcefulness and creativity will take you past many of the technical limitations.

Graphics

Graphics can include any visual component, even the artful representation of text. Graphics in a presentation should serve an instructional purpose rather than merely providing aesthetic decoration or clutter. A picture can show concepts that words can only hint at, illustrating relationships that might remain unclear with mere descriptions. Graphics can come from a number of sources and can include drawings, paintings, graphs, and photographs.

Clipping. Premade clip art graphics can be "clipped" from a CD collection or a sample from another program and placed into your program. Although clip art is often a good place to start, especially for those who are hesitant to try their hand at creating their own artwork, clip art can only provide a generic illustrative component.

Drawing and Painting. Most integrated software suites contain some sort of a graphics program that allows you to create your own graphics. *Painting* programs provide a selection of tools that allow you to create pictures by assigning color attributes to the actual pixels that comprise the screen, similar to how you would use paint to create a picture on a canvas. *Drawing* tools allow you to create illustrations by combining different line-based objects. These objects can be selected individually and moved around to be placed in any desired position (see Figure 13-1).

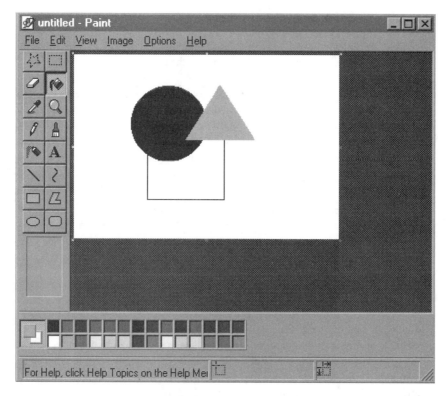

FIGURE 13-1   Paint, available with Microsoft Windows 95. *(Screen shot reprinted by permission from Microsoft Corporation)*

More advanced computer-aided design (CAD) software has carried the design of jet engines, automobile parts, circuit boards, tools, bridges, and homes to new heights of sophistication.

Scanning.   Scanning allows project designers to customize their presentation with a range of graphical elements. By using a flatbed scanner, you can convert any graphic into digital form that can be added to a multimedia presentation (see Figure 13-2). Traditional artwork, such as sketches and paintings, paper creations, magazine pictures, and even photographs, can be scanned in. If copyrighted graphics are used for a student learning opportunity, proper credit should be given to the original source, and if your presentation will have a potentially wide audience, obtain permission to use copyrighted material first.

Taking Digital Pictures.   Digital cameras can be used to take pictures just like traditional cameras, but instead of recording the image on film, they save the image electronically (see Figure 13-3). These cameras can then be plugged directly into a computer and the images can be downloaded right onto the hard drive. Pictures can be taken of students, families, surroundings, special events, or anything else of particular interest.

FIGURE 13-2   Viviscan DeskSaver Scanner. (*Courtesy of Vivitar*)

Video

The proliferation of camcorders has made novice video producers out of many families. Video segments can illustrate an event or a procedure so that a learner feels as though they were actually there. With the help of some special equipment, videos can easily be inserted into multimedia presentations.

Using Video Clips.   Like clip art in still graphics, prerecorded video is available for purchase on disk or CD-ROM. The quality of these clips is often high because they are professionally produced. They are often copyright-free and so can be used for educational purposes. These type of premade clips are ideal for presentations on topics that you would have no way of viewing personally, such as of exotic wildlife or historical events.

Digitizing Prerecorded Video.   Once a video clip is chosen from a videotape using a standard VCR or a camcorder, it must be transformed into digital form in order to be incorporated into a multimedia program. Digitizing applications can be used to perform this process and to produce as a result a movie in one of several formats, including QuickTime movies and AVI files (see Figure 13-4). The platform operating system you have will dictate what movie format is required. Once the video is digitized, it can be edited and saved using digital video editing equipment. The ability to digitize video allows personal experiences, such as a family trip or a school event, to become part of a presentation.

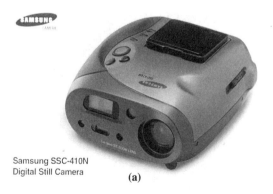

Samsung SSC-410N
Digital Still Camera   **(a)**

(b)

FIGURE 13-3   (a) Samsung's digital still camera. (*Courtesy of Samsung Electronics America, Inc.*) (b) Casio QV-300 digital camera. (*Courtesy of Casio, Inc.*)

FIGURE 13-4   Computer Eyes frame grabber. (*Courtesy of Digital Vision, Inc.*)

Recording Digitally.   There are now available digital video cameras that record directly into digital form. Although these cameras remain relatively expensive, they allow the video segments to be dropped directly into a multimedia presentation without the need for other preparation.

Audio

From voice-overs to sound effects to background music, the addition of audio elements has the potential to create any learning atmosphere you or your students can imagine.

Using Sound Effects and Music.   Digitally recorded sound effects, such as nature or other environmental sounds, are readily available on CD-ROM or as part of many authoring programs. Regular music that is digitally recorded on CD can also be used. Simple sound-mixing programs, some that come packaged on computers and others available as part of CD-ROM sound effects packages, allow you to easily record and edit clips of the music as you play it through the computer's CD-ROM drive. Experimenting with the combinations of lifelike sounds can help ensure a learner-friendly environment.

Recording Sounds.   Simple recording applications let you use a microphone to record voice-over narration or the reading of a favorite story. What is recorded can be saved, and then manipulated using a sound-mixing program (see Figure 13-5). Adding your own voice to a presentation personalizes it, as well as allows complete customization of what is being said.

FIGURE 13-5   Sound Recorder recording application, available with Microsoft Windows 95. (*Screen shot reprinted by permission from Microsoft Corporation*)

Creating Sounds.   Computer music synthesizers combine a pianolike keyboard with a music synthesizer and computer software. When using a synthesizer to create music, musical issues such as pitch, amplitude, special effects, tempo, note sequence and duration, and other important elements of music can be considered. During and after the composition process, music can be played back through the computer, and in some cases, through stereo speakers. Compositions can be stored on diskettes, and played and retrieved, at any time.

Animation

Animation shows a series of slightly different still graphics in quick succession to give the impression of action and movement, similar to the idea of flipping the pages of a pad of paper quickly to see the sketched figures appear to move. Animation can illustrate something happening that video may not be able to ideally portray, such as the completion of the water cycle or the activity of the inside of a volcano.

Using Premade Animations.   Like the other media mentioned, collections of premade animations are available on CD-ROM that can be dropped right into a multimedia presentation. Animations can be extremely time-consuming to create, because of the many numbers of drawings it might take to effectively simulate an action. Therefore, finding a ready-made animation that illustrates a desired effect will save time and allow those with little experience with the animation process to benefit from the usage of this media.

Animating.   Many sophisticated authoring and presentation programs now offer tools to facilitate animation. Still images can be made to appear to move without requiring the user to have extensive animation skills. The capabilities of these programs can only be expected to improve, allowing novice multimedia designers to incorporate quality effects with minimal effort.

Authoring Multimedia Productions

With the content planned and the media elements selected and prepared, the next step in the production process is to actually drop the text and media into a program that serves as a "shell" that comprises the final product. Although some programs work best in creating multimedia-enhanced presentations and others result in full nonlinear hypermedia programs, all share some basic properties that are important to understand. The procedures outlined here are general but are applicable to whatever software tools to which you will have access.

Building Blocks

What we are capable of doing with technology is often difficult for us to comprehend, so analogies to other things with which we are familiar are frequently used as a way of explanation. Multimedia programs are often built on basic units called "cards" or "slides" (see Figure 13-6). The analogy to index cards or transparency slides is deliberate. You can write pieces of information or notes for a presentation on index cards and put all the cards together into a stack. These index cards can then be moved around, arranged in any order, and rearranged as needed to fit the purpose of the presentation and the meaningful flow of the content. So, too, can the electronic cards and slides be ordered and reordered within the electronic "stack," thus providing a very editable presentation format.

Each card or slide has a background, which can be made to be a color or a design. Authoring and presentation programs offer a selection of premade backgrounds or you can

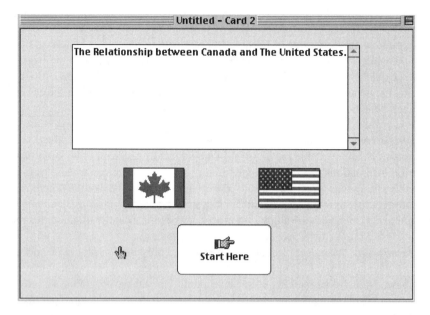

FIGURE 13-6 A card in a Hyperstudio stack. *(Hyperstudio® is a registered trademark of Roger Wagner Publishing, Inc. This Hyperstudio screen image is used with the permission of Roger Wagner Publishing, Inc.)*

use one of your own graphics. These backgrounds are generally designed to remain constant throughout the presentation, although the designer may choose to change the background color or graphic to fit the purpose of the content of each card. Any text that needs to be seen on every card or slide, such as the date or a school logo, can be placed on the background.

Objects

Onto each card or slide can be placed any number of objects. Objects can be text fields, graphics, or other media items in the form of buttons. Placing these objects on the cards or slides is like writing information on traditional index cards, except that the objects on these cards can be moved around easily to make for effortless layout editing. When the card or slide appears in the presentation, those objects appear superimposed on the background (see Figure 13-7).

Text Fields. In order to place text onto a card or slide, you must first create a text field. A text field is a rectangular tablet onto which text can be typed or imported from a word processing program, and then edited as needed. The field can be moved anywhere on the card or slide and can be resized and reformatted. Text can be arranged within multiple text fields on each card or slide.

Graphics. Prepared graphic items, including clip art, scanned images, and digitally produced pictures, can be placed anywhere on a card or slide. They can be moved, resized, and overlapped.

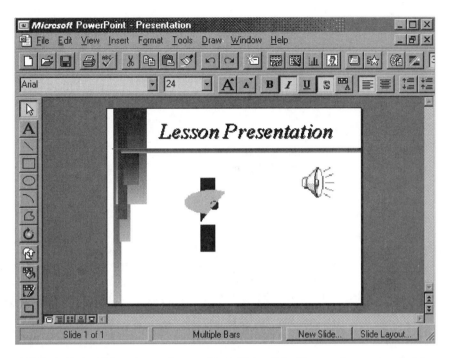

FIGURE 13-7   Objects inserted onto a PowerPoint slide. *(Screen shot reprinted with permission from Microsoft Corporation)*

Media Buttons.   Other media items, such as audio, video, and animations, can be placed on any card or slide. These types of objects can be accessed during a presentation by clicking on an icon or button, or can even be set to play automatically.

Transitions

The way in which a user moves from one card or slide to another in a multimedia program is the defining difference between presentation slide programs and hypermedia programs, and is one reason why an author might choose one type of production software over the other. Presentation programs that are comprised of a series of slides are typically intended for the sequential presentation of information. The presenter or user can view slides in ascending order by clicking the mouse button or can view the slides in order passively by using an automatic timed advance feature. A previous slide can be reviewed, and particular slides can be brought up by number from a navigational menu. You and your students may choose to use a slide program when designing an information product or a more traditional instructional lesson.

Hypermedia authoring programs capitalize on the concept of nonlinear movement among slides. Just as buttons can be added to a slide in order to utilize media elements, buttons can also be used to offer the user options for movement to other information. The project author adds a button to a card and assigns an action to the button. Some actions define media usage and others function as transitions to other specific cards. Rather than require a user to know a specific slide number in order to go directly to that slide, the author can make

TABLE 13-2   Example Presentation and Hypermedia Software Tools

Presentation/Slide Software

KidPix (Broderbund Software)
PowerPoint (Microsoft Corporation)
ClarisWorks (Filemaker, Inc.)

Hypermedia Authoring Systems

Hyperstudio (Roger Wagner Publishing)
Digital Chisel (Pierian Spring Software)
Authorware (Macromedia)

the button a direct avenue to any card in the stack. Depending on the complexity of the authoring program and the sophistication of the author, these buttons can be chosen from a selection of predefined actions or can be customized with special scripting languages. Hypermedia authoring programs offer unlimited interactive design for any type of research project, story or portfolio. Table 13-2 lists several popular presentation and hypermedia programs.

Presenting with Multimedia Technology

Regardless of whether your audience of learners fills an auditorium or fills one chair, or whether your presentation is intended to prompt a live presenter or is meant to function as a stand-alone product, computer hardware and software facilitates clear, effective presentation of ideas. Understanding the differences in possibilities technology presents over traditional presentation methods will make you and your students confident presenters of all types of information.

Hardware

The hardware that is needed to present information using a computer depends on the purpose of the presentation. If an individual or small group of students will be working through a hypermedia lesson, a standard computer monitor may be sufficient for all to see. Make sure the computer is located in an area with room to pull up enough chairs for all learners and other aspects of the setting, such as lighting, are such that everything on the screen can be seen without problem.

If your audience, however, is an entire class or even a larger crowd, you will need a compatible projection device. Some rooms are equipped with television monitors that can be interfaced with a computer so that the screen display can be displayed on the monitors. Liquid crystal display (LCD) panels are lightweight, flat devices that can be placed onto an overhead projector and attached to a computer to project an image of the computer screen. The clearest images are produced with projection devices that connect to a computer and shine the display directly up onto a wall screen in either a small room or a large auditorium. Become familiar with what is available to you at your school or district. Practice connecting the

Classroom Vignette

Tyler and Ashley's kindergarten class has just finished learning about dinosaurs, but none of them is going to be sitting down to take a test to assess what they have learned. Instead, each student will design one slide in a class multimedia presentation, highlighting facts and illustrations about their favorite dinosaur. The slide show will be presented to students' parents at this semester's "Open House," so everyone wants to do his or her best.

Tyler chooses to draw a picture of a Stegosaurus. He uses the drawing program to outline the dinosaur from a picture in a book his teacher had read to them. He has trouble drawing the tail, so he erases it and redraws it. When the picture is complete, he adds a text field to type in all the dinosaur words he knows. He finds the microphone on the computer shelf above the monitor, plugs it in to the computer, and records his slide narration, "This is my Stegosaurus. He's as big as the whole page and he just stepped on a little tree." When he is done with his slide, he saves it to his personal folder, because his teacher said she would put all the slides together when everyone was done.

That afternoon, Ashley starts her dinosaur slide. She has trouble deciding which dinosaur to choose, so she decides to split her slide in half and show the differences and similarities between carnivores and herbivores. She draws a detailed illustration of two dinosaurs she remembers from a CD-ROM her class used last week. She finds a book that tells about carnivores and herbivores, and because she does not know all the words herself, she slowly copies some of the sentences into two text boxes. When she hears that it is time to go to lunch, and she still has not finished the slide to her liking, she saves it to her folder so that she can complete it tomorrow.

When the night of the Open House comes, Tyler and Ashley walk excitedly though the door of the classroom, knowing that right inside is the computer on which the slide show is playing over and over, or "looping" as their teacher had called it. She had put all of the students' slides into one show and programmed it with an automatic timing option so that when parents entered, they could watch the entire show at their leisure. Parents commented on how good all of the slides looked. When Mrs. Satchell, the principal, looked in to check on the progress of Open House, she was able to see very quickly what students had learned and how technology was facilitating the instruction and assessment of students at all levels.

---

computer with the projection devices, becoming familiar with the physical layout of the cables and adapters. Note any adjustments that are needed to the screen resolution to make the image viewable on the larger screen. Connect and disconnect the peripherals several times with your students, if appropriate, so that they see what kind of preparation is necessary to pull off a successful presentation. Many preferences need to be set correctly for a computer to cooperate with a projection device to project its image onto a larger screen, so do not leave these types of preparations to the last minute.

Software

Each presentation or hypermedia program has specific procedures for showing the final product. Become familiar with these procedures, and use them to do a "dry run," advancing through every card or slide in a presentation using the mouse or keyboard as will be required in actual usage. When giving a lesson or presentation in front of a group, rehearse what you will say to accompany the program content. When students are using a program to learn independently, check all buttons to make sure they perform the planned action.

Preparation

The best advice you and your students could follow when planning to use your computers for presentations is to always have a backup plan. Even a thoroughly planned presentation can be thwarted by unforeseen technical problems. Something as simple as a missing cable adapter or an incompatible version of software can stand in your way of making a successful presentation. If it is essential that the instruction be carried off at a certain time, make transparencies of the slides so that you can make do with an overhead projector if necessary. If the instruction can be handled in another method or at another time, be ready to make an instructional switch at the last minute. Although we always hope our plans can be carried out smoothly, modeling this kind of quick thinking will teach your students invaluable, real-world problem-solving skills.

Summary

The capabilities of technology can be used to support authentic instruction and assessment by both teachers and students. Presentations for a variety of purposes can be created by combining different media with instructional or informational ideas.

A quality multimedia production must first begin with careful background research and planning. Consideration to details such as consistent screen layout and design will contribute to ease of learning. Accurate, comprehensive facts and examples will complete the presentation.

Graphics, video, animation, and audio are multimedia elements that can be used to frame the learning environment. There are a range of file formats that are acceptable for use in multimedia design. Any of these files can be adopted from premade media collections or originally created using a number of methods.

These media elements are then placed, along with any text, into an authoring or presentation program. Presentation applications are comprised of individual slides that can be shown in order, whereas authoring applications let the author create nonlinear productions of information and media placed on individual cards. Choosing which type of production is most appropriate requires considering both the intended purpose and the needs of the audience.

Either type of production can be presented in a number of ways using technology, from using a regular computer screen for teaching to a small group or projecting the program images onto a larger screen for many to see at once. Computers must be configured to work with projection devices. Checking connections and setting preferences ahead of the scheduled time for a class or presentation will help ensure a working presentation system. Being prepared with a backup plan, such as skipping ahead to another lesson or using transparencies of the slides to give the presentation, is vital to establishing the flexibility necessary to be a proficient in the skills of technology-enhanced presentations.

LEARNER ACTIVITIES

1. Find out what authoring applications are available on your schools' computer systems. Familiarize yourself with one of the programs by creating a sample multimedia production.

2. Write simple directions for creating a production using the authoring software. Include specific references that would be appropriate for students who are new to the concept of authoring.

3. Use a presentation slide application to create a simple slide show. Experiment with the colors and transition effects to arrive at an effective presentation environment.

4. Make a list of instructional or informational situations that would require a nonlinear presentation and those that would best be accomplished using a slide-type presentation.

5. How might a multimedia project be used to assess a student's understanding of a concept in your area of interest? Give specific examples and criteria that could be used in making a judgment of understanding.

6. A series of steps necessary to creating a multimedia product are outlined in this chapter. Adapt this list to a more specific step-by-step plan that could be followed with students at the level you are interested in teaching.

7. Design three example screen layouts for presentations with three very different end purposes. Include color, font size and placement, and graphics that would be appropriate for both the topics and the audiences.

8. Find a commercial collection of clip art or video segments. How extensive is the collection? When would it be appropriate to use these premade media elements and when would original creations be more suitable?

9. Borrow a digital camera or digital video camera. Record an event using the equipment and choose several pictures or video segments that would be useful in illustrating an informative presentation on the event. How does having the pictures or video already in digital form affect the job of compiling the product? What types of considerations would need to be made when using such equipment with students at the level you plan to teach?

10. Obtain a projection device that is compatible with an available computer. Learn how to connect the cables and configure the computer preferences in order to make it work. Practice projecting in different-sized rooms and in various conditions. How long does it take you to set up in preparation for a presentation? Make a list of the types of technical problems you think you could possibly run into?

BIBLIOGRAPHY

Allen, D. (1995). Teaching with technology: Enhancing student projects. *Teaching PreK–8, 26*(30), 20–23.

Barron, T. (1996). Getting friendly with authoring tools. *Training and Development, 50*(5), 36–46.

Clark, J. H. (1996). Bells and whistles . . . but where are the references? Setting standards for hypermedia projects. *Learning and Leading with Technology, 23*(5), 22–24.

Cross, L. (1995). Preparing students for the future with project presentations. *Learning and Leading with Technology, 23*(2), 24–26.

D'Ignazio, F. (1996). A multimedia publishing center from scratch (and scavenge). *Book Report, 15*(3), 19–22.

Downs, E., & Clark, K. (1997). Guidelines for effective multimedia design. *Technology Connection, 4*(1), 8–9.

Dunham, K. (1995). Helping students design hypercard stacks. *Learning and Leading with Technology, 23*(2), 6–7, 61.

Ennis, W., & Ennis, D. (1996). Ten tips to aid teachers creating multimedia presentations. *Journal of Computing in Teacher Education, 13*(1), 16–20.

Farmer, L. S. J. (1995). Multimedia: Multi-learning tool. *Technology Connection, 2*(3), 30–31.

Florio, C., & Murie, M. (1996). Authoritative authoring: Software that makes multimedia happen. *New-Media, 6*(12), 67–70, 72–75.

Gribas, C. (1996). Creating great overheads with computers. *College Teaching, 44,* 66–68.

Jordahl, G. (1995). School-grown videos. *Technology & Learning, 15*(8), 26–27, 30, 32.

LeCrone, N. L. (1997). Integrating multimedia into the curriculum. *Technology Connection, 4*(1), 14–15.

Lewis, S. (1995). Student-created virtual tours. *Learning and Leading with Technology, 23*(2), 35–39.

Mauldin, M. (1996). The development of computer-based multimedia: Is a rainforest the same place as a jungle? *TechTrends, 41*(3), 15–19.

Milone, M. N., Jr. (1995). Electronic portfolios: Who's doing them and how? *Technology & Learning, 16*(2), 28–29, 32, 34, 36.

Milone, M. N., Jr. (1996). Kids as multimedia authors. *Technology & Learning, 16*(2), 22, 24, 27–28.

Milton, K., & Spradley, P. (1996). A renaissance of the Renaissance: Using HyperStudio for research projects. *Learning and Leading with Technology, 23*(6), 20–22.

Monahan, S., & Susong, D. (1996). Author slide shows & Texas wildlife: Thematic multimedia projects. *Learning and Leading with Technology, 24*(2), 6–11.

Reese, S. (1995). MIDI-assisted composing in your classroom. *Music Educators Journal, 81*(4), 37–40.

Roblyer, M. D. (1997). Videoconferencing. *Learning and Leading with Technology, 24*(5), 58–61.

Sammons, M. C. (1995). Using in-house CD-ROM publishing to store and present classroom materials. *Educational Technology Review, 4,* 26–32.

Stafford, D. J. (1997). PowerPointing the way. *Technology Connection, 4*(1), 16–17.

Strasser, D. (1996). Tips for good electronic presentations. *Online, 20*(1), 78–81.

Taylor, H. G., & Stuhlmann, J. M. (1995). Creating slide show book reports. *Learning and Leading with Technology, 23*(1), 8–10.

Thorp, C. (1995). Choices and consequences. *Teaching PreK–8, 26*(2), 58–60.

Troutner, J. (1996). Yes, they put on quite a show, but what did they learn? *Technology Connection, 3*(1), 15–17.

Troxclair, D. (1996). Teaching technology: Multimedia presentations in the classroom. *Gifted Child Today Magazine, 19*(5), 34–36, 47.

Tuttle, H. G. (1997). Electronic portfolios tell a personal story. *MultiMedia Schools, 4*(1), 32–37.

Welsh, T. (1997). From multimedia to multiple-media: Designing computer-based course materials for the Information Age. *TechTrends, 42*(1), 17–23.

Woodward, M. (1997). Developing a multimedia product. *English in Education, 31*(1), 48–54.

14 Ethics, Equity, and Social Issues

1. What are the ethical concerns of technology in education?
2. What are the equity issues of technology in education?
3. In what ways can education overcome the ethical, equity, and social concerns in the schools?
4. What are the policies for software use?
5. What are the social issues of technology in society?

Introduction

We have only to look around us to see the myriad of daily applications of computers in our lives. Computers are now so pervasive in our society that the question of how they can be used most wisely, efficiently, and ethically is no longer academic. Instead, it is a lively issue that demands the attention of anyone interested in computer use. Although many of the purposes for which computers are used are extremely beneficial to the individual and to society, there is an unfortunately wide range of misuse as well. For the past several decades, science fiction writers, philosophers, educators, and many others have been warning us about the dramatic changes that computers will cause in our lives. What will these changes be? How will we adapt to such drastic reorganization of our routines?

Current research seems to offer more questions than answers about these issues, which we must grapple with now if we are to shape a productive and humane future. Indeed, issues such as computer fraud and invasion of individual privacy are no longer matters of speculation: They are immediate concerns that must be addressed as we move further into our technological future. In this chapter, we examine the contemporary problems of computer fraud, invasion of privacy, technological elitism, long range concerns of shifts in the workforce, and the role teachers will play in promoting ethical and equitable use of computers in the future.

Computer Fraud and Misuse

Hundreds of thousands of large mainframe computers are used in the United States alone. People directly involved with these systems number in the millions. Many others have access to mainframes through microcomputers. These figures add up to an alarming increase in the incidents of computer abuse, especially computer-related crime—a trend that will likely continue into the future. Let's look briefly at two examples of computer fraud before examining some ingenious schemes.

A computer analyst at a Wall Street brokerage house programmed a computer to sell nonexistent securities through fictitious accounts. The analyst pocketed $832,000 before the fraud was discovered.

A computer security consultant defrauded a Los Angeles bank of $10.2 million by requesting a funds transfer to an account in a Soviet bank in Switzerland through a computerized system.

What is the cost of this type of theft? Estimates are billions annually, and this may be conservative. Computer crime is big business.

One ingenious case of computer-related theft involved a bank employee whose only computer training was operating a terminal. The employee selected accounts with large amounts of money and few transactions and used a computer to change the balance figures. Pocketing the difference, he then made sure that the computer quickly "corrected" the error. Using his position as a chief teller to receive advance notice of audits and inspections, he was able to prevent the bank and the customers from becoming suspicious. During a period of three years, he transferred $1.5 million, enabling him to spend up to $30,000 per day to support his gambling habit.

In another case, the perpetrator never even touched a computer, although he apparently understood the computer system. After being granted a 12-month installment loan, he noted the codes on the installment payment forms he received from the bank. Instead of including the top form with his first payment, he sent the bottom form. The bank's computer generated a form thanking him for paying off the loan so promptly. He did not literally steal the money and when the error was finally discovered, he was not prosecuted since he claimed that he had simply made a mistake by sending in the wrong form.

Other cases involve indirect interaction with the computer as well. Several crimes have been committed by using the magnetic or specially shaped character codes placed on checks and deposit slips. In one such case, a man opened an account in the usual fashion and deposited several thousand dollars. After receiving his personalized checks and deposit slips on which his account number was printed, he obtained the blank courtesy deposit slips that are left on the bank's counters. Then he had his magnetic ink code printed on these deposit slips and returned them to the counters in the bank. A number of depositors unwittingly used these fraudulently imprinted deposit slips, expecting the money to be credited to their own accounts. However, the computer read the fraudulent coding and the money was sent to the thief's account instead. The error was noticed when customers complained that their checks were bouncing after they made deposits to their accounts. By this time, $250,000 had been diverted and $100,000 had disappeared.

Rounding is another technique for diverting funds from one account to another. Banks routinely round interest amounts up or down. Dishonest programmers can instruct the computer to place the rounded-down amounts into a separate account that they created for this purpose. If there are discrepancies, depositors often blame their own mathematical errors and do not complain to the bank.

Theft of Goods

Not only money but also goods are stolen via the computer. Often, goods are ordered in some way through the computer and are sent to a pickup point. For example, one case involved 217 railroad boxcars owned by a bankrupt railroad. Federal agents investigating the case found that a computer program had been altered to show that these cars had been sold to a fictitious company. This company would later "resell" or rent the cars, returning the profit to the owners of the bankrupt company.

Another story of computer-stolen goods began on a young man's way home from school. While rummaging through various trashcans owned by the telephone company, he acquired a library of operating manuals for telephone equipment, not especially valuable then but worth keeping. By this means, he also obtained discarded telephone equipment as well as the instructions for ordering new equipment. Through various ruses, he succeeded in getting the codes to access the ordering system. He then set up the telephone equipment in his home, in conjunction with an automatic remote dialer and his own terminal, and began ordering new equipment for resale. This project increased to such a grandiose scale that he hired several employees and organized a company to sell the equipment to private suppliers and users until he was caught.

Private industry and individuals are not the only victims of computer-related crime. There are numerous cases on record involving theft of government goods. It is a relatively simple matter for dishonest personnel to adjust computerized supply records so that huge quantities of food, vehicles, parts, fuel, and clothing are delivered to the wrong hands for later resale. Items less tangible than money and goods are also stolen or tampered with.

Theft of Information

Stealing information from a computer and using a computer to market stolen information illegally are not uncommon practices. Many private companies and government agencies maintain computerized lists of their customers and clients. Once unauthorized personnel access these lists, the information can be sold to others for various uses. For example, a department of motor vehicles employee was charged with adding more than a thousand names to a computerized list of approved applicants for driver's licenses. The employee then sold the licenses to unqualified drivers for a profit of more than $300,000.

Police personnel have been known to sell computerized lists of criminal records to be used as bribery or for blackmail. Tax calculation methods have been sold to those in high tax brackets that benefit from legally claiming deductions. Even health records have been sold. Some information has been held for ransom. The list goes on and on.

This is a serious concern to school personnel who store student records on computers. With access to a computer and the determination to break into confidential records, students have been known to alter the grades of their friends and enemies. Also, students or others can destroy data that are critical to school administrators. Even if the data can be recovered, school personnel must spend a great deal of time and money recreating lost records.

Theft of Time

The theft of computer time is another computer-related crime on the increase. In one case, a high school student who was an electronics enthusiast gained access to a company's computer system to play computer games. People who invade computer systems without authorization are called *hackers,* and their escapades are not always so innocent. In another case, a man used secret passwords to gain access to the computer owned by his former employer. Over long-distance phone lines, he used the computer to direct the operation of machines owned by his present employer. The total commercial value of the time consumed was $15,000. Another case of time theft involved an illegal bookmaker who used a university computer to make his betting calculations.

We have seen how computers can be used to commit crimes against individuals, banks, industries, and government agencies. Computers can also be used to commit crimes against other computer companies. This includes getting access to new computer specifications, future product details, customer lists, and marketing information.

Since computers can be very expensive to buy, rent, operate, and maintain, some users share computers to reduce cost. However, once users gain access to a computer, they have the potential to raid the computer's memory. Some cases on record involve millions of dollars in business and information stolen in this manner.

Theft of Programs

Software piracy, another very serious problem, is the theft of computer programs. Software piracy occurs whenever a person purchases a computer program and then copies it for friends or resale. However, piracy is not limited to individuals: It has spread to microcomputer users' clubs as well, some of which maintain libraries of programs. New members can copy or use these programs rather than purchase them from software retailers.

Some retailers are major perpetrators of software piracy. They buy copies of programs and then duplicate them for resale. These programs are either sold separately or offered as added sales incentives. Some unscrupulous retailers purchase programs at special group rates and then duplicate the programs and resell them, either at the individual rate or at a discount (which is less than the average retailer pays for the product wholesale). This is known as bootlegging software.

Software bootlegging occurs on such a large scale that it costs an estimated $2.5 million each month—$1 million in actual losses and $1.5 million in lost sales opportunities. Its success lies in the fact that it is quite easy to copy computer programs. Because of the wear and tear on program disks, most computer programs are written with the capability to copy programs onto tape or disk as backup to be used in case of loss of the original.

Unfortunately, piracy also occurs in the classroom. Many teachers are caught in a bind: They have a class full of students who want to use the same software at the same time, but there's not enough software to go around (usually because of budget limitations). Given the ease with which software can be pirated, it is tempting to make unauthorized copies.

Computer Software: Copyright Issues

Have you ever "borrowed" a computer program from a friend or co-worker? Are copyrighted computer programs currently installed on your home or office computer? If so, do you know whether those programs were borrowed or installed with the permission of the copyright owner? Federal copyright law gives the copyright owner the exclusive right to determine who can install or borrow copyrighted computer software. If you or an authorized University representative purchased software from a reputable vendor, then that purchase probably included the purchase of a licensee for the purchaser of the software. Before you use, share, or distribute the software, you should understand the terms of the license. If the software was purchased "off the shelf" or prepackaged, then the packaging will include the license terms. This method of disclosing the license terms is sometimes referred to as "shrink wrap" licensing, because the language often provides that by opening the (shrink wrap) packaging, the purchaser agrees to be bound by the terms of the licensee. If the software was developed or customized for a particular purpose, an underlying written agreement may contain the terms of the license. If University employees developed the software in the course—of or as part of their employment—then the copyright in the software will belong to the Arizona Board of Regents. This means that no one can distribute the software or license or allow others to use it without the express, written authorization of someone authorized to contract on behalf of the board. Agreement to licensee software created by ASU employees should be reviewed by the Technology Collaboration and Licensing Office or the Office of General Counsel. If the University hired a consultant or independent contractor to develop the software, the agreement with the consultant or contractor should either assign ownership of the copyright in the resulting software to the University or should contain the license terms governing the use and distribution of the software. All agreements with third parties (including students) for the purchase, lease, creation, or adaptation of software or other copyrighted materials for use by the University should be reviewed by Purchasing and Business Services or the Office of General Council. License terms may restrict the individuals or sites that are authorized to use the software. The term of the use, the purpose of the use, and the ability to distribute and copy the software may also be limited by license terms. The license may describe penalties for violation of its terms. Unauthorized copying or distribution of software may also result in civil criminal liability under federal and state laws. The University and the individuals involved in the unauthorized copying may be liable even if the software was copied for an educational or a nonprofit use.

Software publishers have taken aggressive steps to protect against infringement of their copyrighted software. These steps may include an audit of University computers to search for software being used without authorization. The presence of unlicensed software may result in considerable liability for the University and for individuals involved in unauthorized copying. In other words, unless you are an authorized user, that "free" copy of a copyrighted software program may not be free at all.

Source: Arizona State University Office of General Counsel, 1997.

Although the act of piracy takes only a few minutes, the ramifications are long-term. First, piracy sets a poor example for students, who are, after all, the computer users of the future. Second, it ultimately results in higher prices of CAI software since publishers must raise prices to compensate for losses through piracy. See <www.spa.org> for copying guidelines and other policies on software use.

Computer piracy results in higher software prices for the user. Software developers must divide the cost of writing, packaging, and marketing software among the many potential buyers of prepackaged software. Piracy results in fewer legitimate customers and, consequently, higher-priced software packages to guarantee a profit to the developer. Thus, software piracy affects all computer users. An ethical alternative to piracy is to purchase a software license, which permits the purchaser to make a designated number of copies of a program.

Now let's look at crimes in which the computer itself is a victim. We examine some of the reasons behind these attacks and then explore some of the methods of abuse.

Physical Abuse of Computers

Recently, several books and articles have attempted to explain the motivation behind physical abuse of computers. Many attacks result from persons who view the computer as a destroyer of personal identity. Some people regard the computer as a detested symbol of corporate capitalism. Computer users commit other acts in moments of frustrated, irrational outbursts. Sometimes attacks are planned for political reasons.

Computer equipment can be damaged in many ways. Instruments used to damage computers include guns, pointed objects, fire, and magnets. In 1986, students at a high school in Sacramento, California, fired numerous shots into a computer used to notify parents of student absences. Radical and revolutionary groups to express protest have also used computer sabotage. During the war in Vietnam, a number of computers at American universities were targets of abuse, especially those thought to be connected with Defense Department research. Many other examples have been cited. In 1970, in a bombing at the University of Wisconsin, one person was fatally injured; damage to the computer was estimated at more that $500,000. During the same year, a Molotov cocktail damaged a computer at Fresno State University in California, costing the school $1 million. In 1973, in Melbourne, Australia, antiwar demonstrators used a double-barreled shotgun to extensively damage a computer in the offices of an American computer manufacturer.

Demagnetization is another commonly used method of destroying data stored magnetically, as on magnetic tape and floppy and hard disks. By passing any magnetic material near the storage media, the data will be erased. In 1970, an antiwar group attacked data-processing facilities, destroying equipment, punch cards, and magnetic tape. Several magnets were found in the rubble, and since some of the tapes had been erased by demagnetization, it is safe to assume that these magnets were used to destroy the data. Reconstructing the lost information cost more than $100,000.

The latest danger to befall computers is called a *virus,* which is a destructive program that causes an undesirable action to occur, such as data loss. Programmer saboteurs bury virus programs within other harmless programs called Trojan horses. A user purchases a Trojan horse without realizing that it contains a virus.

It may take a considerable length of time to detect a virus in the computer. Virus programs are usually designed to lie dormant until triggered by a certain sequence of keystrokes or a particular date. But this is not always the case. For example, on November 1, 1988, a person entered into the computer a virus that was intended to live innocently and undetected in ARPANET, the U.S. Department of Defense computer network and the forerunner of the

Internet. But a design error in the virus caused it to replicate out of control. This virus ultimately jammed more than 6,000 computers nationwide, including computers at the Rand Corporation, SRI International, Lawrence Livermore Laboratories, the Massachusetts Institute of Technology, and military bases all over the United States. The virus spread by "mailing" itself to other computers under the auspices of a legitimate user. Since the program continued to replicate itself, it slowed down and then eventually shut down all the computers to which it gained access. In a case like this, the potential threat of a computer virus is no laughing matter, as it could have compromised the defense of the country.

To solve the problem, vaccine programs are being written to detect and eradicate virus programs. Though they are not always effective, vaccines help alleviate the problem.

Maintaining Security

There is a definite need for security of computer equipment and its data. This is true for a computer system of any size, from a large mainframe system with extensive peripheral equipment to a microcomputer on a student's desk. Whereas it is reasonable in large organizations to allow only authorized personnel to enter the computer room, in most schools such a security measure would be unrealistic. However, access to the administrative computer containing confidential records should be limited. Security measures in the computer lab and in individual classes would be necessarily broader.

Security measures are actions taken to prevent the fraudulent use or destruction of computer equipment. These measures include something a person has (a key or badge), something a person knows (a password), or something about a person (a fingerprint, a voiceprint, a facial feature).

Most large companies have security systems that one must pass through to gain access to the computer room. These systems may use special cards to insert or buttons to press on the outer door of the computer room.

However, according to many computer security experts, security needs to be even tighter. They advocate the use of many logical but frequently overlooked security measures.

One measure allows only the personnel necessary to perform certain functions to be in a certain place, for instance, in the computer room. Therefore, once programs are written and in place, computer programmers should not be allowed to go into the computer room and should never be allowed to run their programs. Another measure requires the investigation of staff and security clearances for those who work with confidential information. A third measure establishes a system for efficiently investigating suspected breaches of security.

No system is ever foolproof, but every effort should be made to ensure the security of both computer and data. Setting up controls helps to prevent unauthorized and fraudulent modification of data during processing and ensures the validity, integrity, and accuracy of applications and system software during design, programming, testing, and implementation.

Computer centers commonly use another popular measure—the *password*, which usually is a coded sequence. Passwords are frequently used to gain access to the computer via a computer terminal or a telephone hookup. Most users have limited access that allows them to perform specific functions. Other users require more flexible access. Authorization is granted to particular users at different levels, ranging from a particular group of items in the database to an entire data file, database, or program.

For example, student files set up for the teacher's use should not be accessible to students. By the same token, the teacher should not be able to access the personnel files available to the principal.

One effective security measure that organizations can use to minimize the possibility of computer crime is to screen potential employees carefully during the hiring process. Many private detective agencies have investigators who specialize in this area.

Although the security risks covered here threaten large computer systems, microcomputers are also at risk. These systems are even more vulnerable because they are transportable and more easily hidden. For instance, data files and programs can be stolen by simply slipping a disk into a coat pocket or a briefcase. In addition, disks can be destroyed easily by magnets or fire.

An effective security system drastically reduces computer crime. But, as we have seen in the beginning of this chapter, it is not always easy to eliminate fraud. Computer crimes have been discovered in a number of ways, including accidental exposure, careful audits, inside informants, and unfortunate circumstances (unfortunate, that is, for the perpetrator). Detection of crime is one matter; reporting crime is often quite another.

Teaching and regulating ethics are extremely difficult. Once breaks in security are discovered, many organizations become very reluctant to admit them. Consider what happens when a company reveals a fraud scheme involving its computer.

First, if customers see how easy it is to tap the company's records and accounts, the trust and integrity of the company might easily be undermined. Large amounts of business could be lost, costing the company more than the original theft. Second, the case would be reported in newspapers. The company executives would be embarrassed and seem foolish; they might even lose their jobs. Third, losses not covered by insurance would have to be made up from company profits, which would certainly displease stockholders and owners. Therefore, the reasons for keeping computer crimes secret are easy to understand. Fortunately, many industries, especially the banking industry, have federal controls that encourage reporting of such crimes.

Other factors cause businesses to hide computer crimes. Proving that someone has stolen materials or money using the computer is often difficult and, consequently, costly. It is sometimes cheaper to write off losses and then work to prevent such situations from occurring again. Indeed, it may even be cheaper to keep the crime a secret than to prosecute.

The problem associated with computer crime stems from the relative newness of handling large amounts of data by computer. In the past, data were handled in ways that provided physical evidence. Nowadays, experts must authenticate computer-generated physical evidence—printouts. Sometimes the originals must be located. The legal system is currently wrestling with this and other evidential issues.

Individual Privacy

Thus far, we have discussed crimes and abuses committed by individuals for their own personal gain. Many of these crimes affect us only indirectly, through increased prices and lowered standards of quality. However, one aspect of computer crime may have an impact on each and every one of us: invasion of privacy resulting from improper use of databases.

Until 1974, there was little concern about privacy with regard to data banks. Few data banks shared their information, since manual access was slow and inefficient. However, as technology has advanced and data banks have evolved into databases, so has concern for privacy of the individual increased. In 1974, President Gerald Ford signed the Privacy Act into law. Its purpose was to protect confidentiality of files generated by the federal government. Its principles are paraphrased as follows:

- There must be no personal data record-keeping systems whose very existence is secret.
- There must be a way for individuals to find out what information about them is in a record and how it is used.
- There must be a way for individuals to prevent information about them obtained for one purpose from being used or made available for other purposes without their consent.
- There must be a way for individuals to correct or amend records of identifiable information about them.
- Organizations creating, maintaining, using, or disseminating records of identifiable personal data must assure the reliability of the data for their intended use and must take reasonable precautions to prevent misuse of the data.

Let's examine the privacy issue with regard to several situations. First, consider credit checks. Today, we are a nation of borrowers. In fact, we have become so dependent upon credit that much business probably could not exist without it. Cars are bought on time payments, merchandise is charged to credit cards, and homes are mortgaged. All these items are bought on deferred payment plans requiring the establishment of credit.

Problems always arise whenever there is access to credit information. Questions range from who is authorized to access the information to how much information that person is entitled to know. In addition, the information available may or may not be accurate. For example, data might have been entered incorrectly, resulting in denial of credit purchases. Often, information is entered into a system but is never removed. A record of an arrest in a law enforcement database may be entered without indication of whether or not the person was acquitted of the charge. This same information may result in a university refusing an applicant admission. Another problem results from the unrestricted use of data. The large amounts of data available today often become accessible to more people than originally intended. The growth of government obviously increases the amount of data collected. In addition, data collected by one agency is often shared and used by other agencies for other purposes.

We submit tax forms to the Internal Revenue Service each year. The Census Bureau gathers information. Law enforcement data banks compile criminal records. Motor vehicle departments contain registrations of car ownerships and licenses. There are voter registration lists. With this wide range of information available, the possibility exists to merge these databases. Such a merger could produce a detailed picture of an individual, threatening the individual's right to privacy. Many doctors and other professionals are reluctant to store client information in computer systems because of such a threat.

With such capability, privacy has become a major issue that must be resolved by a thorough understanding of the implications of access to databases. The computer is invaluable in the proper collection and distribution of information. It is up to those with access to use this information legally, wisely, and ethically.

ncerns in Education

So far our discussion of computer crime and the drastic changes that computers are causing in our society have pointed out some of the new responsibilities that teachers are facing. Two questions in particular demand immediate answers.

First, how can we ensure equal computer access to all students? Educators are concerned that only students in more affluent school districts are receiving adequate computer literacy training. Those in areas where funding is more limited may receive little or no hands-on experience with computers. This creates a dangerous form of technological elitism. In a society where most desirable employment is technologically oriented, those with more computer training will enjoy higher salaries, better fringe benefits, and a generally superior lifestyle. Conversely, those who receive little or no computer training will be severely disadvantaged in a computerized society.

Educators have a responsibility to make certain that all students have sufficient access to computers, regardless of ethnic or socioeconomic background. To do less is to doom underprivileged children to an underprivileged adulthood. It is necessary to create and support programs that reach out to all students and prepare them equally for productive citizenship in our increasingly technological world. This issue and other ethical concerns are addressed by the International Society for Technology in Education (ISTE) in their *Code of Ethical Conduct for Computer-Using Educators.* See <www.iste.org> for information on this topic.

Second, how can we teach our students to use computers in an ethical manner? Educators share with parents and society at large the task of teaching ethical use of computers. There are two effective methods of accomplishing this. First, the teacher must set an example of ethical behavior whenever using or discussing the computer in the classroom. A lecture on the evils of software piracy becomes meaningless if the teacher practices piracy.

Also, the teacher can spend class time discussing ethical issues with students. There are many role-playing models that cast students as software pirates, software publishers, and so on. This gives students an opportunity to consider computer crime from all angles and can spark discussions that help students develop and clarify their own ethical codes.

Equity in Education

Equity issues are a major concern of educators utilizing technology. Gender and equal availability of technology for everyone are the main equity issues. Research has documented that boys are more interested and involved with technology. Participation in elective technology activities is less among girls. Software generally tends to emphasize male-dominated activities. Games often include violence and competition as motivation. These software characteristics tend to attract males. Therefore, careful student software selection is essential for addressing gender in the classroom.

Student access to computers is dependent on the financial capabilities of a school or school district. Although the ratios of students to computers are steadily decreasing, many low socioeconomic schools have limited access to computers and the World Wide Web. Although congress and state governments have taken steps to increase access through the e-rate as well as other technology grand programs, the gap is still significant. Parent groups fund raising, industry partnerships, and careful budgeting in schools can help improve access to technology. In addition, teachers must take advantage of the technology for students to be involved in more than drill-and-practice activities, which seems to be common in lower socioeconomic schools. Web designs often do not take cultural connotations such as language and color into consideration. A final concern for educators is what students are accessing via the WWW. Pornographic sites are common and schools use various approaches to block access. In addition, concern for plagiarism activities utilizing the WWW is becoming a major concern. Technology provides opportunities but also provides concerns to teachers and parents. All must work together to take advantage of this powerful tool!

Summary

We have only begun to experience the radical changes that computers will effect on society as we know it. Computer scientists and sociologists differ in their estimates of our technological future: Some foresee a stark "1984"-type world of humanoid robots and mechanized human beings; others, Toffler among them, predict a bright future in which humans, aided by advanced technology, function with greater freedom than ever before. Who is right remains to be seen, but this much is certain: Computers are bound to change our lives and our society in dramatic and irrevocable ways.

Computer fraud and abuse take many forms: theft of money and goods, unlawful use of information stored in computers' memories, and unauthorized use of computer time. Sometimes computers themselves are victims of sabotage. Hackers enter computer systems without authorization. Software piracy, which is the theft of computer programs, can cause software prices to increase. (The software license is an incentive to discourage piracy.) The computer virus is another major concern of computer security. The entry of a virus can destroy or damage records and shut down computers. Generally, viruses are difficult to detect, but vaccines are available to overcome them.

Computer crimes are on the increase partly because of the increasing number of computers in society. Computers affect more and more lives every day in many ways. Some people feel intimidated by a machine with so much influence. Perhaps with the advent of microcomputers, more people will see that the computer is a beneficial tool that can be controlled. There are various methods of maintaining security in the computer room, primarily by limiting access to the room to authorized personnel. The password is the most popular method of controlling entry into a computer system and limiting access to records. In addition, many organizations screen potential employees in the hiring process. However, computer crime is often difficult to detect. In many instances, the crime is not reported to law enforcement agencies for fear of losing customer confidence in the company and its services.

In addition to concerns for the security of organizations, there is concern for the rights of individuals. The Federal Privacy Act of 1974 was made into law to protect the confidentiality of files generated by federal government computers. Several state governments have passed laws to further protect the average citizen from illegal use of computer information.

Besides computer crime, the issue of changes in the labor force is another major concern.

Teachers face new challenges in computer-based education. First, they must strive to provide equal access to computers for all students, regardless of ethnic and socioeconomic background. Second, they must promote computer ethics in their classrooms. They can do this by setting an example of ethical computer use and by using tools such as role-playing and simulations to examine ethical questions. Educators and parents have a concern for student access to pornographic sites and schools are using various approaches to block access. In addition, plagiarism concerns on student assignments utilizing the WWW are becoming a major concern. Technology provides opportunities but also provides concerns to teachers and parents. All must work together to take advantage of this powerful tool!

LEARNER ACTIVITIES

1. List the major educational issues and concerns for the Internet and WWW.

2. Do the principles of fair information in this chapter seem reasonable?

3. List the major classroom ethical issues.

4. List the major classroom equity issues.

5. List ethical and equity issues related to the Internet and WWW.

6. Discuss the "gender-related differences in attitudes toward computers."

7. What are the dangers of technological elitism?

8. Describe recent cases of fraudulent uses of computers.

9. Discuss security measures necessary for a computer center.

10. Research violations of individual rights to privacy through unauthorized access to records.

11. Research the problem of training displaced industrial workers and suggest several methods of accomplishing such training.

12. Visit a local credit bureau and list the steps necessary for accessing your personal credit information.

13. List several recent cases of computer viruses and what was done to remove them.

14. Describe how the U.S. government maintains security on all records pertaining to individuals.

15. List all the local, state, and national government databases that contain data about you. Be as specific as possible.

16. Describe how a person could be characterized using all the information about them stored in computer databases.

17. Summarize the research on girls and attitudes toward computers.

18. Summarize the research on low-income technology access.

19. Review a popular educational software package and check for male-dominated roles in the software.

20. Review the methods of blocking pornographic web sites for eliminating student access in schools.

BIBLIOGRAPHY

Dietz, L. D. (1982). Computer security: Not just for mainframes. *Mini-Micro Systems, 15*(6): 251–256.

Eline, L. (1992). Safeguarding online systems. *Technical Training, 9*(2), 24–31.

Engler, P. (1992). Equity issues and computers. In Gary Bitter (Ed.), *Macmillan encyclopedia of computers* (pp. 359–367). New York: Macmillan.

Gordon, A. (1988). Viruses pose tricky threat to computers. *The Arizona Republic,* p. AA-1.

Hannah, L. S., & Matus, C. B. (1984). A question of ethics. *The Computing Teacher* 12(1): 11–14.

Keyboard bandits who steal your money. (1982, December 27–1983, January 3). *U.S. News and World Report,* 92, 68–69.

Lee, J. (1992). Hacking. In Gary Bitter (Ed.), *Macmillan encyclopedia of computers* (pp. 425–434). New York: Macmillan.

Legal bulletin. (1997). Tempe: Arizona State University Office of the General Council.

Lockheed, M. E., & Frant, S. B. (1983). Sex equity: Increasing girls' use of computers. *The Computing Teacher, 11*(8): 16–18.

Markoff, J. (1988). Computer "virus" linked to "bored students." *The Arizona Republic, 99*(171): 1–2.

McAdoo, M. (1994). Equity: Has technology bridged the gap? *Electronic Learning, 13*(7), 24–34.

Parker, D. B. (1981). *Computer security management.* Reston, VA: Reston.

Robyler, M., Dozier-Henry, O., & Burnette, A. (1996). Technology and multicultural education: The "uneasy alliance." *Educational Technology, 35*(3), 5–12.

Toffler, A. (1981). *The third wave.* New York: Bantam Books.

WWW SITES

SPA copying guidelines and related information: <www.spa.org>

ISTE guidelines and related information: <www.iste.org>

ADDITIONAL READING

Business Week	*Newsweek*
Communications of the ACM	*PC WEEK*
Computerworld	*Time*
eMediaweekly	*U.S. News and World Report*
Information Week	*USA Today*
InfoWorld	*Wall Street Journal*
NewMedia	

15 Emerging Technologies

FOCUS QUESTIONS

1. In what ways are emerging technologies helping computers to mimic human capabilities?
2. How might computer innovations impact classrooms of the future?
3. What effects will the increased storage capacities of computers have on the transmission of information in various media?

Technological advancement is constantly offering many challenges to teaching and learning. With the advent of computers in science and industry, technological developments occur almost daily. The present and future are sometimes hard to distinguish: What was science fiction 10 years ago is reality today and will be obsolete in 10 years. Engineering and computer science students are often told that their education will be outdated by the time they graduate and enter their professional fields. The lightning speed of technological advancements in our age makes predictions of the future tentative and difficult. However, some technological trends have emerged over the past several years that permit us to speculate about how technology will revolutionize our society and our daily lives in the future.

One fact is certain: Computers are here to stay! The work of our complex society could not be accomplished without the speed and accuracy that computers allow. Also, the multifaceted work of computers in research and development, coupled with the research of scientists and engineers, will produce the next generation of computers, more capable than those in use today. Their work is oriented toward several areas: continued miniaturization, greater memory capacity, speech synthesis and recognition, enhanced graphics displays, as well as many emerging technologies.

One of the most noticeable characteristics of computers during the past 20 years has been their decreasing physical size. Many of the powerful computers of the 1960s were room-sized; in the 1980s, a home computer owner could own and operate an equally powerful personal computer that could be set up in the corner of a study or family room! The 1990s saw the introduction of portable computers and notebook-sized computers that fit into a briefcase or backpack. What has accounted for this decrease in size of computer hardware?

Integrated Circuitry

The first generation of computers (1944–1958) relied on vacuum-tube technology, which was cumbersome and required huge amounts of energy. The second generation of computers (1959–1964) introduced transistor technology, an improvement over vacuum tubes. Still the distance between transistors kept computers relatively large and, more importantly, relatively slow. Consequently, the third generation of computers introduced the integrated circuit, a wafer of silicon on which thousands of transistors have been connected with tiny wires.

Integrated-circuitry technology improved so much that even more transistors could be integrated on a chip through the process of large-scale integration. As this occurred, computers became physically smaller, but retained their power, becoming even faster data processors. This trend continues with very large-scale integration. As integrated circuitry becomes more sophisticated, computer power can be housed in smaller and smaller pieces of equipment. And as the size of computer hardware decreases, so does the purchase price of such equipment. That means that a greater number of people than ever before can afford to have computer power at their fingertips.

An important result of integrated-circuit technology has been a wide range of microprocessors that perform many types of functions. A microprocessor is a small computer that has been programmed to carry out a set of specific tasks. For example, microprocessors now control fuel intake of automobiles, monitor cooking in microwave ovens, and perform calculations for owners of pocket calculators or personal data assistants. Many traditional household appliances will depend on computer power in the homes of tomorrow, as we shall explore later.

The amount of power that a computer has is directly related to the amount of data and instructions that can be stored in its memory. The greater a computer's memory, the more powerful the computer. Computer scientists are continually in the process of researching alternate memory systems to store a maximal amount of information in a minimum of space.

Speech Synthesis and Recognition

Speech recognition refers to the computer's ability to recognize and interpret human speech (see Figures 15-1 and 15-2). Computers that recognize speech will possibly make keyboards unnecessary. A computer that recognizes speech and doesn't have a monitor uses the concept of a hologram to project text into space. This has a number of advantages.

For example, speech recognition just may make house keys obsolete and, at the same time, cut down on home burglaries. Imagine a computerized "lock" that opens doors only to those people whose voices it recognizes as members or guests of a household. Speech synthesis, on the other hand, refers to the computer's ability to duplicate sounds similar to the human voice. The speech synthesizers of today are rudimentary and often difficult to understand, but researchers are improving their quality constantly. Computer speech has the potential for great impact on the lives of people who are voice-impaired, and experiments are now being conducted with computers that speak for those who have no voice. Speech recognition capabilities continue to improve. Early speech recognition worked by the method of discrete speech. The user had to pause between words. Phone companies utilize this approach.

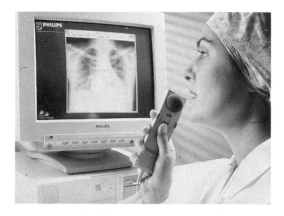

FIGURE 15-1   SpeechMagic—Phillips speech recognition engine. (*Courtesy of Philips*)

FIGURE 15-2   SpeechFlow—the PC-LAN–based digital dictation system. (*Courtesy of Philips*)

Continuous speech recognition is more sophisticated. A user can speak in a natural rhythm with close to normal speaking pace. Speech and voice recognition software usually allows the computer to be "trained" to recognize your individual voice patterns, rhythm, syntax, and vocabularies. The legal and medical professions actively utilize this software. Legal briefs, letters, patient charts, and data collection are applications in practice. In education, Kurzweil and Microsoft have developed voice recognition products (see the websites listed after the bibliography at the end of the chapter). The future of this emerging technology is unlimited. We will see this technology applied to cars, appliances, and software; it will especially have an impact on educational software. This software will engage the learner in conversations that provide unlimited educational potential. A newer technology, "digitized" speech, has an improved, humanlike quality.

Graphics

Yet another area of technological advancement is graphics. With the phenomenal popularity of video games, both at home and in game arcades, computer graphics is becoming a popular art form. Researchers are working to make computer graphics more sophisticated (see Figure 15-3). Graphics will display a wider range of colors and more realistic effects. This will also have a great impact on classroom computers; spectacular graphics displays attract children to the computer and hold their attention.

The computers of the future, then, will most likely be physically smaller and less expensive, have greater memory capacity, be able to recognize and produce speech, generate more sophisticated graphics displays as well as take advantage of other emerging technologies. As the price of computers decline, more and more people will take advantage of the seemingly infinite benefits of computer technology. But specifically how will tomorrow's computers be used?

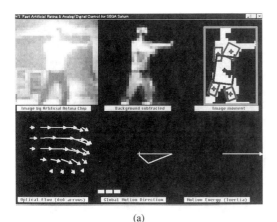
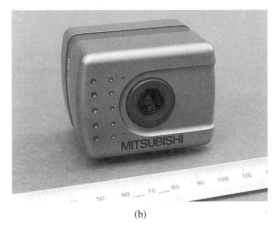

(a)   (b)

FIGURE 15-3   (a) Image processing steps of human-interface system. (b) Human-interface system. *(Courtesy of Mitsubishi)*

Applications of Tomorrow's Technology

We can see the roots of tomorrow's technology in the computers we use today (see Figure 15-4). For example, cities now use computers to monitor and control the flow of rush-hour traffic. This system cuts down on accidents and helps alleviate the frustration of bumper-to-bumper traffic congested areas. Such systems are likely to be more widespread in the future. Many experts predict that within 10 years, the use of autopilots in automobiles will be commonplace. Drivers will program their automobiles to deliver them safely to predetermined destinations. This will certainly decrease the number of deaths and injuries caused by traffic accidents in which human error is the culprit. Presently, computerized highway, road, and street maps are available for automobile dashboards.

Similarly, airplane pilots will be assisted by computer-controlled devices that regulate takeoffs and landings. Because most serious airplane accidents occur during either takeoff or landing, we can expect that these computer-controlled devices will save a substantial number of lives.

Health care is another area that will be greatly aided by computer power. Already hospitals use sophisticated computerized devices to monitor patients' vital signs. This allows health care professionals to be aware of unusual conditions that jeopardize human lives and to circumvent the devastating effects of such conditions. Research in this area will result in increasingly precise monitoring devices. Along with this, computers are being used to assist doctors in diagnosing illness. Given a set of symptoms and conditions, the computer draws from its memory of diseases an accurate diagnosis, prognosis, and treatment. Using state-of-the-art technology and telecommunications, doctors and surgeons are able to instruct, supervise, and direct sophisticated surgical procedures and diagnostic consultations from medical facilities thousands of miles away.

Law enforcement agencies will find it easier to locate and keep track of offenders. Complex monitoring devices will help police officers to detect violations of motor vehicle

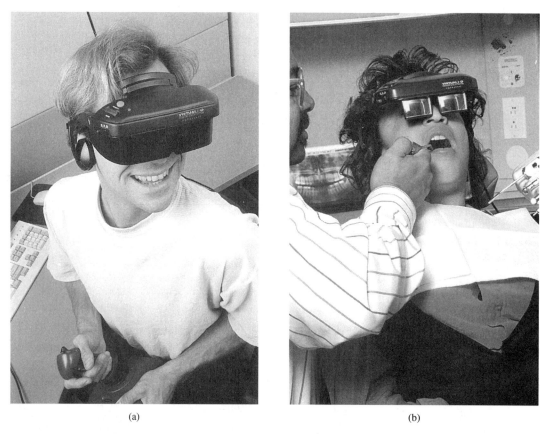

(a)   (b)

FIGURE 15-4 (a) Virtual reality headset. (*Courtesy of Virtual i-O Inc.*) (b) Virtual reality is often a pleasant distraction from reality itself. (*Courtesy of Virtual i-O Inc.*)

laws. Monitoring devices note speed limit violations, for example. In addition, centralized computers will keep track of records of law violations, and this will help law enforcement agencies to coordinate efforts in apprehending offenders who move from state to state to avoid prosecution.

Other government agencies will also rely on new and better computers. Employers will use computer terminals to record the earnings of their employees, and this information will be reported automatically to various tax authorities. This system will make tax evasion more difficult and tax reporting much easier.

Computers in the Schools

One of the most exciting and promising areas of technological advancements is in computer-aided instruction (CAI). As costs of computers decrease and the economic demand for computer-literate adults increases, school systems will install large numbers of microcomputers in traditional classrooms. Very young children will learn to use computers not only for the purpose of becoming computer literate, but also to study conventional academic areas such as mathematics, history, composition, science, and international languages (see Figure 15-5). Indeed, every subject that is taught in schools today can be adapted to computer learning. Curriculum content will be applied to the classroom with real issues and problems. Simulations as well as real community life–based activities will be designed to give teachers and students opportunities to problem solve and interact with other professionals outside of the school setting.

Widespread use of CAI will have a radical effect on education. Perhaps most importantly, it will make education available to virtually everyone. Special needs students who cannot attend regular classes, for example, will be able to "attend" class via the microcomputer. Students will be able to take courses offered at schools five miles or 5,000 miles from their homes without ever having to travel to the sites where these classes are taught. Imagine being able to study physics with a professor from the Massachusetts Institute of Technology and philosophy with a professor from the University of California at Berkeley in the same semester. This will be commonplace in the near future.

Programming activities, CAI, and functional software, such as text editing, will allow for more individualized instruction. Instead of gearing most activities toward the average student, teachers can challenge gifted students and provide remediation for students who require it. The computer is a patient teacher that allows students to determine their own pace for learning, thus freeing the teacher to work with students on a one-to-one basis. The computer serves as a kind of instant learning center, suitable for a myriad of purposes. And, freed from the necessity of conducting routine drills and performing many management duties, the teacher has more time to be the vital human link between student and knowledge. The computer does not supplant teachers; it supports them.

With authoring programs, students are able to create and write their own "stacks" of information. The use of multimedia and hypermedia within the classroom will continue to expand to further address multisensory learning channels and to introduce the global range of perspectives brought to bear on an issue, problem, or concept.

Although the classroom of tomorrow will most likely have a few microcomputers, it will probably not have a traditional library down the hall. The storage capacity of computers will make traditional libraries obsolete in the years ahead. Tomorrow's libraries will include

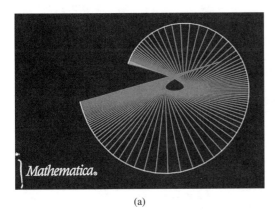

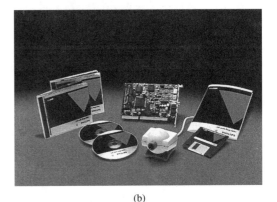

(a)   (b)

FIGURE 15-5   (a) Mathematica used to solve complex math problems. Here, as the string wrapped around the cubic is unwound, its end traces out an involute. (*Courtesy of Wolfram Research*) (b) EasyCam videoconferencing kit. (*Courtesy of Philips*)

fewer shelves of books and periodicals; instead there will be a number of computer terminals through which students can access the very latest information on whatever topics they are researching. This process of data storage and retrieval, or databases, will become vital links between information and the people who require that information.

The Future Student Computer

The future student computer "palmtop" will have Internet access, word processing, and many mathematical capabilities. All the graphing calculator capabilities will be available. Many of the technologies listed before will be available on the "palmtop" or be accessible via this computer and the Internet. So this future device will provide a calculator, graphing capabilities, spreadsheet, geometry construction tools, simulations, algebra systems, intelligent tutor capabilities, and it will be able to adapt to the user's interests and abilities, and may even talk to you. It is clear that future technologies will become more interactive promoting exploration, problem solving, communication, and higher-order thinking.

Databases in the Future

A natural consequence of the trend toward buying and using personal computers will make databases important in the future. Many databases exist today, serving the medical profession, the legal profession, and many other groups. These databases provide access through a computer terminal to vast amounts of information that would be too expensive and too bulky for most people to purchase and store. Databases have the additional benefit of being updated constantly so that the information they contain is the latest and best available. Consider, for example, how vital this is to a doctor who must treat an illness that is obscure or that is currently being researched. The doctor can access up-to-the-minute information about such an illness, and this information may mean the difference between life and death.

A number of general databases are in existence today. For example, many commercial vendors offer subscribers access to information on a wide range of subjects. For a monthly fee, subscribers can tap into the latest information on hobbies, health concerns, financial information, and an impressive number of other topics. All that the subscriber needs is a computer through which to receive this information.

As we have already mentioned, it is likely that libraries as we know them today will someday be obsolete. Rather than having to drive to a library, search through the stacks for the volumes we want, and then find that we may have to wait until those volumes are returned by another borrower, we will simply sit down at our home computer, type in a particular code, and then request the text we want to read. Should we desire to purchase a copy of that text for our home library, we will use a special printer to print a copy quickly and quietly.

Databases for special interests will develop rapidly in the future. Information of all kinds will be available at the touch of a finger. As society becomes more complex and more facets of our life are affected by technology, it will become essential that we have immediate access to accurate and constantly updated information. Databases will help us to stay fine-tuned to the world around us.

The emergence of a public networking system, the National Public Telecomputing Network, similar to the Public Broadcasting System, offers a broad range of information services and databases to schools, communities, and home microcomputer users. The Internet is an electronic superhighway allowing users access to universities and other large resource-sharing entities across the United States.

Data Communications

Another area destined for rapid and significant development in the future is data communications, or the transfer and reception of data by electronic means. Many large computer users already rely on data communications via telephone lines. This allows large corporate offices to keep in constant communication with branch offices. It allows for centralized record keeping and enables a corporation to coordinate the efforts of all its branches to best meet the needs of its customers. It is an effective means of keeping business healthy. This trend toward communicating over data networks will continue to grow, becoming faster and more reliable than it is today (see Figure 15-6).

Government will certainly work toward developing more effective means of data communication. It is important for governmental agencies to keep in contact with each other, for remote military bases to maintain communication, and even for nations to monitor each other's activities. More sophisticated means of data communications, such as fiber optics and microwave, will make communication fast and more effective in the future.

Artificial Intelligence

Along with databases and data communications, the field of artificial intelligence (AI) will undergo rapid changes and development. Artificial intelligence refers to devices capable of imitating human cognitive processes: thinking, remembering, learning, inferring, and so forth. For the past 25 years, researchers have been working to develop a "teachable" computer. Although today's computers process numerical data, the AI computers of the future are expected to process nonnumerical data with technology that is being developed all over the world.

In addition, future generations of computers with artificial intelligence are expected to be able to decode instructions given them in ordinary human language. They may be able to compile their own instructions to perform virtually any task they are asked (literally!) to perform. Researchers say that these computers will be available in the near future.

Much work that has been done by humans is now being performed by robots and this is expected to increase in the future. The term *robot* calls to most minds an image of a metal humanoid similar to the Tin Man in *The Wizard of Oz* or the two characters in the *Star Wars* series, R2D2 and C3PO. Yet robots are highly sophisticated machines capable of performing many tasks. They are particularly well-suited to jobs that are

FIGURE 15-6   PCtel modem.
(*Courtesy of PCtel*)

repetitious, dangerous, or difficult for humans to perform. Robots can be exposed to situations that might injure the health of human workers. In addition, they are capable of working 24 hours a day, seven days a week, with very little need for work stoppage. Although the initial purchase price of robots is high, robots are extremely cost-effective workers.

The advent of computerized robots in manufacturing raises an important issue. Many people fear computers because they believe that these technological wonders will make human workers obsolete. What will happen to the large percent of the labor force whose jobs are eventually automated? Actually, there will be plenty of employment opportunities available in the future, but the nature of those jobs will be different than the jobs today. This is why the retooling and retraining going on in business and industry are such enormous tasks.

According to the U.S. Bureau of Labor Statistics, the need for qualified people to work in computer-related careers will double in the next decade. Many experts say that that estimate is too moderate and predict that the demand for such workers will easily triple by the end of the century. It is logical to assume, then, that those workers who find themselves displaced by automation on the job will be retrained to assume computer-related positions. The robots cannot exist, after all, without human workers to design, manufacture, operate, and maintain them.

But robots in industry are merely one facet of the fascinating field of artificial intelligence. The impact of AI on computers in the schools will be momentous. Very young children will be able to operate computers without the need for typing skills or knowledge of programming languages. They will be able to "teach" the computer to carry out the activities they want done. Since AI computers function as intelligent aids to their users rather than as merely programmable machines, computers will become more effective teachers, listening to the students, responding according to information stored in memory, and then storing information away for later use. They will no longer rely on rigidly defined software.

Other Emerging Technologies

The Network Computer, Digital Video, Internet 2, DVD, personal digital assistants, handwriting recognition, and WWW communication are a few of the emerging technologies that will have an impact on education. The *Network Computer* (NC) is a fully functional, low-priced multimedia computer that accesses and uses internal and external networks. It works similar to a television or telephone. Every student would have their own NC. Each NC is an intelligent system connected to networks and gains all its power from the network. The unit cost is minimal and provides a means for web browsing, electronic mail, applications software, and educational software that is on the network. Students could do their assignments offline and download to the school network for teacher or peer review. Potentially, the NC can have a major impact on education. *Digital Versatile Disc* (DVD) is the next generation of optical media. Its impact is in multimedia, video games, music, consumer electronics and entertainment, and is now beginning to provide full-length movie availability. DVD is slowly expected to replace videotape because of its excellent video quality and its interactive potential. In essence, DVD is a digital storage technology that has a large data storage capacity that provides for high-quality playback of video, audio, images, and text (see Figure 15-7). For PCs, DVD allows for high rates of data transfer

FIGURE 15-7   Digital Versatile Disc (DVD) player. (*Courtesy of Panasonic*)

paving the way for the convergence of TV and the computer. Education will be able to combine the interactivity with high video and sound quality into sophisticated interactive learning programs.

Personal digital assistants (PDAs), or knowledge navigators, are becoming available to everyone. These represent smaller, more compact computers that function as message centers, personal secretaries, and passports to electronic networks to access and share information (see Figures 15-8, 15-9, 15-10, 15-11, 15-12).

Hand Writing Recognition is beginning to appear in personal digital assistants (PDAs), where the computer converts the handwriting to text (see Figures 15-13 and 15-14). The data entry is some sort of pressure-sensitive electronic writing surface and a pen. Although research in this activity began in the early 1950s, progress has been slow. Online handwriting potential for education appears unlimited with the potential of the writing table to enter the written information directly into the digital computer. Digital Video has the capability to provide full motion, full screen, and full color for desktop computers. Quick Time is a common video file format for computers. The emergence of digital video will play an important role in the delivery of video on the Internet. In education, Computer Based Instruction (CBI) and the World Wide Web (WWW) enable the integration, manipulation, and delivery of various media.

Internet 2 is a collaborative effort of the nation's leading universities, the private sector,

FIGURE 15-8   Sharp Personal Information Organizer. (*Courtesy of Sharp Electronics Corp.*)

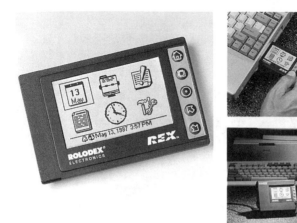

FIGURE 15-9 Personal Information Management Organizer. (*Courtesy of Franklin Electronic Publishers*)

FIGURE 15-10 E-mail and Internet-ready hand-held computer. (*Courtesy Geofax, Inc.*)

FIGURE 15-11 Cassiopeia—handheld computer. (*Courtesy of Casio, Inc.*)

and federal government to develop the next generation of Internet technology and applications. This development will enable schools to send and receive high-quality programs that are now limited due to transmission and delivery capabilities. For example, video will be delivered full screen in real time (see Figure 15-15). This potential is unlimited. Of course, these are only a few of the emerging technologies that will impact education.

FIGURE 15-12   Color personal digital assistant (PDA).
(*Courtesy of Brother*)

Computers in the Homes of Tomorrow

Some of the most significant changes that we in the Computer Age will witness will take place in our own homes. During the past several years, there has been a significant increase in the number of microcomputers being purchased for home use. No longer is computer power an advantage enjoyed by a few very large corporations. Indeed, the decreasing size and price of powerful microcomputers will result in microcomputers becoming standard household appliances by the dawn of the twenty-first century (see Figures 15-16, 15-17, and 15-18). How will this affect our daily lives?

Microcomputers are capable of performing any number of routine tasks now done by humans. Many microcomputer users now monitor budgets and bank accounts with their computer systems. Their computers are faster and more accurate than the users are. Tomorrow's homeowner will not need to keep account books, budgets, and voluminous files of papers to maintain a close watch on household matters; the microcomputer will assume these tasks.

When it is not busy balancing the checkbook, the home computer will keep an electronic "eye" on other household appliances. It will regulate the climatic conditions inside and outside the house in order to maintain a comfortable environment with the least amount of fuel. It may be used as a recipe file to store family favorites. The microcomputer may serve to turn on lights, turn off the microwave oven when dinner is fully cooked, and keep

FIGURE 15-13 Pen-based computing. (*Courtesy of Texas Microsystems, Inc.*)

FIGURE 15-14 Wireless personal digital assistant (PDA). (*Courtesy of Minstrel*)

FIGURE 15-15 Virtual reality for the Internet. (*Courtesy of NTT Soft*)

FIGURE 15-16 Philips Magnavox Internet TV terminal. (*Courtesy of Philips*)

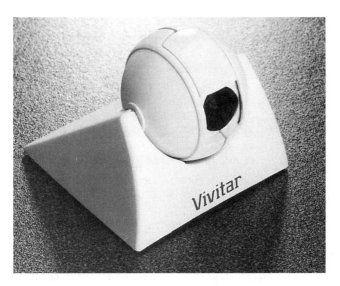

FIGURE 15-17 Plug-n-play Internet video camera. (*Courtesy of Vivitar*)

FIGURE 15-18 Forty-six-inch plasma wall hanging display for high-definition television (HDTV). (*Courtesy of Mitsubishi*)

an inventory of food items on the cupboard shelves, adding items to a grocery list as they are used.

Because much of our shopping will be done via computer, the microcomputer will report its grocery list to a computer at the grocery store. The necessary items will be ordered automatically. Microcomputers may even perform comparative shopping for users, compiling lists of prices from various stores and determining which store is most economical for the items needed.

After dinner is finished, children will use the microcomputer to do their homework. They will be able to use CAI software at home as well as in their classrooms. They can learn from mathematics tutorials, practice spelling, and even compose essays on their home computers. Schools and parents will communicate with each other via the Internet to a greater extent. Teachers will recommend software to be purchased, borrowed, downloaded, or rented that meets the individual needs of children and substitutes for some of the more traditional kinds of homework assignments. Family members may access the local public library via computer and the Internet/WWW, search through the collection for a specific book or a favorite author, reserve the materials or access an article electronically via the World Wide Web. Since the computer will be part of your television set or home entertainment unit, most, if not all, children will have home access to computers and the WWW. When the children are finished with their homework, parents and older sisters and brothers can take college courses via distance education. Even graduate and postgraduate courses will be available to microcomputer users. Best of all, students of any age can set their own pace for learning. The computer is both patient and challenging.

Because the computer will save its user many hours spent in dull household chores, personal computer owners will have more leisure time. Some of this time they may choose to spend enjoying the many fascinating and challenging activities available via the web. There will be many sorts of activities to enjoy. Again, the computer can challenge all ages and levels of ability. It can play "Go Fish" with a very small child and chess with an adult.

If the user is not in the mood for games, then he or she may use the microcomputer to create art of many types. For example, a visual artist can use the graphics capability to create stunning displays. A writer can use the word processing capability to compose the Great American Novel or to write a sonnet. Musicians can compose complex pieces of music and then hear their compositions performed immediately by computerized music synthesizers.

As more and more people purchase home computers and experiment with their capabilities, more applications of computers in the home will become apparent. Home life as we know it is destined to change in the future as computers relieve us from routine, often boring chores that we now perform. More than likely, we will find the microcomputer no more intimidating than an oven or a refrigerator.

Computers for People with Disabilities

One of the most promising areas of technological advancement to watch in the future is the research and development of devices to aid the disabled population (see Figure 15-19). Many such devices are under study today and will become more accessible as computer technology develops smaller and less expensive computers. Speech recognition is one of many future technological developments that will have a major impact on aiding the disabled population.

CAI has proven extremely effective in special education environments. Slow learners are comfortable using computers to learn academic subjects that have proven difficult for them in the past. Also, students who are paralyzed or suffer muscle impairment that prevents them from holding a pen are capable of writing essays and solving mathematical problems with a computer. Severely handicapped or special needs students can use CAI to learn in their homes if they are unable to attend classes (see Figure 15-20).

FIGURE 15-19   Bausch and Lomb PC Magni-Viewer™ magnifies on-screen information 175 percent. (*Courtesy of Bausch and Lomb*)

FIGURE 15-20   Voice mail with voice recognition to e-mail software. (*Courtesy of Wizzard Software*)

Computers also help people with disabilities in other ways. Voice synthesizers allow the speech-impaired to communicate their thoughts, perhaps for the first time. Still other devices help the vision-impaired to read and generate written texts. Because artificial-intelligence research promises to make computers more capable of imitating human activities, computer aids for the disabled are sure to be developed in the future (see Figure 15-21). This gives hope to many today.

Clearly, we are in the midst of a technological revolution. As we look around us daily, we often wonder whether we have accidentally stepped into a time machine that has carried

FIGURE 15-21   Foot-controlled mouse. (*Courtesy of Hunter Digital*)

us far into the future. The phenomenal advancements in technology that we have witnessed during the past 20 years are only the tip of the iceberg. What technological achievements lie in our future is anyone's guess! Because our technological society will have deep roots in math and science concepts, people of all ages will be expected to become both scientifically and technologically literate.

Summary

In the future, we may expect to see rapid technological advancements in computers. Research and development is geared toward five areas in particular: continued miniaturization, greater memory capacity, speech synthesis and recognition, artificial intelligence, and enhanced graphics displays. Greater amounts of computer power will be built into physically smaller units that will be more affordable and, hence, more accessible to the average person. These smaller computers will be made more powerful by new systems of memory that allow for greater storage. Speech synthesis and recognition will make computers easier to use because they will be able to communicate directly with humans. Finally, improved graphics capabilities will make computers more attractive to those who wish to generate visual displays.

The computers of tomorrow will be used in a great number of applications, both social and personal. They help regulate traffic flow, control airplane landings and takeoffs, and monitor the vital signs of hospital patients. They serve to diagnose illnesses and prescribe treatment. In addition, they play a more important role in the educational system as a greater number of schools implement curricula that employ CAI, WWW activities, and functional software, such as electronic messaging and databases.

We can also expect to see expanded use of databases by the general public. Databases give computer users access to up-to-the-minute information on a wide range of subjects. Not only are databases extremely useful to professionals such as doctors, lawyers, and law enforcement officers, but they also provide special-interest information on hobbies, first aid, and current events. Tomorrow's complex society will necessitate fast access to updated information.

Data communications, or the transfer and retrieval of data via electronic means, will develop to become an important way for large corporations to keep in constant contact with their branch offices. It will also be used more widely by government agencies and others who must maintain close contact with remote locations.

Yet another promising area of technological advancement is artificial intelligence. Future computers will be capable of imitating human cognitive activities such as thinking, remembering, and inferring. They will be able to compile their own instructions based on commands given them in ordinary human language, allowing more people to "program" computers without extensive knowledge of computer programming languages. Also, AI robots will continue to be used widely in industry, causing a significant shift of the labor force from industrial work to technically-oriented jobs.

Home computers will expedite the work of homeowners by keeping records, maintaining budgets, and regulating household inventories. They will also serve as important learning tools either to supplement education received in traditional classrooms or to serve as a medium of taking classes via distance education. This access will be able to provide many forms of entertainment. More people will use their microcomputers to work at home without the need for traveling to a work site. DVD will combine the TV and PC into one home entertainment unit combining excellent video and sound capabilities with interactivity that will revolutionize home entertainment. Education will utilize this technological impact with parent, school, and home communication and interactivity.

People with disabilities will enjoy numerous new computerized devices that will improve the quality of their lives. Speech synthesizers, for example, will allow the speech-impaired to communicate orally.

The future holds great promise of technological advancements that will change our lives for the better.

LEARNER ACTIVITIES

1. Interview a computer scientist about the future of technology and write a summary of the discussion.

2. Write your own scenario of the technology-based classroom of the future.

3. Research predictions of future technology by several computer experts. Include any research findings on the success or lack of success of emerging technologies. Report on your findings.

4. Consider how the development of artificial intelligence will affect computer-assisted instructions.

5. Develop a lesson plan in which students explore the future of technology.

6. Write a report reviewing the literature on the role of emerging technologies for special needs students.

7. Write a report on the potential impact of voice recognition on education.

8. Write a report on the impact that the Digital Versatile Disc (DVD) will have on the future of education.

9. Write a report on the implications of interactive multimedia via the WWW on business, industry, and education.

10. Design a hand-held student computer. Include a drawing, size specifications, and include capabilities and applications that this computer will possess.

BIBLIOGRAPHY

Artificial intelligence goes postal. (1997). *Science, 275,* 1073.

Austin, M. B. (1994). A comparison of three interactive media formats in an RTV/DVI computer-mediated lesson. *Computers and Education, 22,* 319–333.

Benedikt, M. (Ed.). (1991). *Cyberspace: First steps.* Cambridge, MA: The MIT Press.

Cheng, D., & Yan, H. (1997). Recognition of broken and noisy handwritten characters using statistical methods based on a broken-character-mending algorithm. *Optical Engineering, 36,* 1465–1479.

Collins, H. M. (1990). *Artificial experts—Social knowledge and intelligent machines.* Cambridge, MA: The MIT Press.

Decker, R., & Hirschfield, S. (1992). *The analytical engine: An introduction to computer science using Toolbook.* Belmont, CA: Wadsworth.

Devotee, C. (1997, September 15). Look ma, know hands! *Computer World, 93.*

D'Ignazio, F. (1990). Electronic highways and the classroom of the future. *The Computing Teacher, 17*(8), 2–24.

East, P. (1990). On the basics of education in the 21st century. *The Computing Teacher, 17*(6), 6–7.

Finkel, L., Rawitsch, D., & Brady, H. (1990). Memories: A ten-year retrospective. *Classroom Computer Learning, 10*(8), 14–15, 18–31.

Haugeland, J. (1986). *Artificial intelligence: The very idea.* Boston: The MIT Press.

Hofmeister, A. M. (1991). Expert systems and decision support in special education: Results and promise. *Educational Technology, 31*(10), 23–28.

Hughes, T. (1990). *American genius.* New York: Penguin.

Gader, P. D., Keller, J. M., Krishnapuram, R., Chiang, J.-H., & Mohamed, J. A. (1997). Neural and fuzzy methods in handwriting recognition. *Computer, 30,* 79–86.

Girard, K. and Dillon, N. (1997). Market grows for voice applications. *Computerworld 31*(32), 55–56.

Kim, G., & Govindaraju, V. (1997). A lexicon driven approach to handwritten work recognition for real-time applications. *IEEE Transactions on Pattern Analysis and Machine Intelligence, 19,* 366–379.

Kirkpatrick, S. N., & Biglan, B. (1990). AI in the elementary, middle, and secondary classroom. *The Computing Teacher, 17*(5), 14–19.

LaBarge, R. S. (1996). *DVD Today,* Vol. 1 [CD-ROM]. Crofton, MD: NB Digital Solutions.

Leedham, D. G., & Qiao, Y. (1992). High speed text input to computer using handwriting. *Instructional Science, 21,* 209–221.

McCullough, M., Mitchell, W. J., & Purcell, R. (Eds.). (1990). *The electronic design studio: Architectural knowledge and media in the computer era.* Cambridge, MA: The MIT Press.

National Foundation for the Improvement of Education. (1991). *Images of potential.* Washington, DC: Author.

Pearlman, R. (1989). Technology's role in restructuring schools. *Electronic Learning, 8*(8), 9, 12, 14–15, 56.

Roberts, G. I., & Samuels, M. T. (1993). Handwriting remediation: A comparison of computerbased and traditional approaches. *Journal of Educational Research, 87,* 118–125.

Scannel, E. (1997, September 8). ViaVoice's installation encourages users. *InfoWorld, 29.*

Schenkel, M. E. (1995). *Handwriting recognition using neural networks and hidden markov models.* Kontanz, Germany: Hartung-Gorre Verlag.

Sheingold, K. (1991). Restructuring for learning with technology: The potential for synergy. *Phi Delta Kappan, 73,* 17–27.

Shipside, S. (1997, May 22). If only they could talk: computers can order a pizza, but sarcasm goes over their heads. *The Guardian* [Online], 10.

Sin, B.-K., & Kim, J. H. (1997). Ligature modeling for on-line cursive script recognition. *IEEE Transactions on Pattern Analysis and Machine Intelligence, 19,* 623–633.

Solomon, G. (1990). Learning to use the tools of the future. *Electronic Learning, 9*(5), 14–15.

Szuprowicz, B. O. (1995). *Multimedia networking.* New York: McGraw-Hill.

Tamashiro, R., & Bechtelheimer, L. (1991). Expert systems in the elementary grades: Developing thinking skills and independent learning. *The Computing Teacher, 18*(5), 21–26.

Ubois, J. (1997). Betting the ranch. *Internet World,* 83–87.

VRML industry microcosms in the making. (1998). *New Media, 8*(3), 21–24.

Wildstrom, S. H. (1997, September 29). PC, take a letter to Mr. Jones. *Business Week,* 18.

Willis, W. (1998). Speech recognition: Instead of typing and clicking, talk and command. *T.H.E. Journal, 25*(6), 18–22.

Ziegler, Bart. (1998, January 29). New generation of hand held PC's inches closer to ideal. *Wall Street Journal,* p. B1.

WEBSITES

Calligrapher Features. (1997, February 28). *Paragraph International:*

Canon DV: DV Format. (1997): <www.canondv.com/shared/dvinfo/dvinfo3.html>

Cappuccio, D. (1997). Network computers—Panacea and Pandora's box. *Garter Research:* <gartner4.gartnerweb.com/public/static/consulting/tco/tv000032.html>

Communication Intelligence Corporation. (1997, July 21): <www.cic.com>

Corbato, S. (1997, February 10). Internet 2: Pragmatic views from higher education, University of Washington Computing & Communications: <www.academ.com/manog/fete1997/corbato/index.html>

Eggimann, F. (1995). Neural networks and their use in handwriting recognition. *Swiss Federal Institute of Technology:* <www-snf.unizh.ch/SPP-IF/results/5003-034449r.html>

Graves, W. H. (1996, October). Why we need Internet II. *Educom Review, 31*(5): <educom.edu/web/pubs/review/Articles/31528.html>

Handwriting Recognition for Windows. (1996, October 14): <www.papassoc.com/html/handwriting_recognition_for_windows.html>

Leiner, B. M., Cerf, V. G., Clark, D. D., Kahn, R. E., Kleinrock, L., Lynch, D. C., Postel, J., Roberts, L. G., & Wolff, S. (1997). A brief history of the Internet, <www.isoc.org/ internet-history/Internet2>. Project description, mission statement, and frequently asked questions: <www.internet2.edu/html>

Lexicus Handwriting Recognition Technologies. (1996). Motorola, Inc.: <www.mot.com/MIMS/lixicus/handwriting/index.html>.

National Science Foundation. (1996, August 16). Next generation commercial internet: <www.newswise.com/articles/INTERNET.NSF.html>

NB Digital Solutions Homepage: <www.nbdig.com>

The Open Group. (1997). *Network computer reference profile.* Document Number X975: <*www.rdg.opengroup.org/public/pubs/catalog/x975.htm*>

Panasonic DVD homepage: <www.panasonic.com/PCEC/dvd/indexdvd.html>

Perry, J. H. (1997, March/April). The coming of Internet 2: Can higher education reinvent the Internet? <www.napanet.net/~janetp/article/internet2.html>

Rawson, C. E. (1996, July 5). Breaking down the last document automation barriers! An overview of Natural Handwriting Recognition (NHR): <www.infotivity.com/hwr.htm>

RealMedia 5.0 Content Creation Guide. (1997): <205.158.7.51/docs/ccguide50.pdf/dvd/index.htm>

Sony DVD Homepage: <www2.sony.com/SEL/consumer>

SRI International. (1997). Handwriting recognition, signature verification and pen-input computers: <www-mpl.sri.com/topics/Pen-Input.html>

Srihari, S. N. (1997, August 5). Recent advances in off-line handwriting recognition at CEDAR. *Center of Excellence for Document Analysis and Recognition (CEDAR):* <www.cedar.buffalo.edu/Publications/TechReps/OLHWR/offlinehwr.html>

Srihari, S. N. (1995, June 14). Handwritten word recognition. *Center of Excellence for Document Analysis and Recognition (CEDAR):* <www.cedar.buffalo.edu/Linguistics/hwwr.html>

Srihari, S. N., & Kuebert, E. J. (1997, May 31). Integration of hand-written address interpretation technology into the United States Postal Service Remote Computer Reader System. *Center of Excellence for Document Analysis and Recognition (CEDAR):* <www.cedar.buffalo.edu/Publications/TechReps/HWAIPaper/integration_of_hwai-2.html>

Zakon, R. H. (1997, October). Hobbes' Internet timeline v3. 1: <info.isoc.org/guest/zakon/Internet/History/HIT.html>

Speech Recognition Sites

<www.hitl.washington.edu/publications/dissertations/Savage/home.html>

<www.dragonsys.com/marketing/comdex_awards.html>

<www.dragonsys.com/marketing/dragondictate.html>

<www.kurzweil.com/pcapps/vppro/>

<www.software.ibm.comlis/voicetype/>

Speech Commander
<www.voicecommander.com>

Personal Communication Attendent
<www.pcahome.com>

Speechviewer
<www.software.ibm.com>

Kurzweil Voice
<www.ihs.com>

Microsoft Diction
<www.research.microsoft.com/research/srg/>

APPENDIX A

Software Publisher Contact Information

ABC News Interactive
Order from Optical Data Corp.

A.D.A.M. Software
1600 RiverEdge Parkway, Suite 800
Atlanta, GA 30328
770-980-0888
800-755-2326
Fax: 770-955-3088
<http://www.adam.com>

Adobe Systems, Inc.
Contact Douglas Stewart for
reseller referrals
800-279-2795
Fax: 608-221-5217
<http://www.adobe.com>

Against All Odds
PO Box 1189
Sausalito, CA 94966
415-331-6300
<http://www.digiville.com>

**Aladdin Books/Children's Division
of Simon & Schuster**
1230 Avenue of the Americas
New York, NY 10020
800-223-2348
<http://www.simonsays.com>

Aladdin Systems, Inc.
165 Westridge Dr.
Watsonville, CA 95076
408-761-6200
Fax: 408-761-6206
<http://www.aladdinsys.com>

Alfred Publishing
Visit your local music store or
check their Web site
818-891-5999
800-625-3733
Fax: 818-892-9239
<http://www.alfredpub.com>

Allegiant Technologies, Inc.
PO Box 261209
San Diego, CA 92196-1209
619-587-0500
800-255-8258
Fax: 619-587-1314
<http://www.allegiant.com>

**Annenberg/CPB Math and Science
Collection, Dept. C-97**
PO Box 2345
S. Burlington, VT 05407-2345
800-965-7373
Fax: 802-864-9846
<http://www.learner.com>

Apple Computer, Inc.
20525 Mariani Ave.
Cupertino, CA 95014
408-996-1010
<http://www.apple.com>

Apple Education
408-987-3022
800-747-7483
Fax: 408-987-7105

Arch Publisher's Group
Order from Educorp

Arizona State University
Attn: Gary Bitter
Technology Based Learning
and Research
Tempe, AZ 85287-0111
602-965-3322
<http://tblv.ed.asu.edu>

ARS NOVA Software
PO Box 637
Kirkland, WA 98083
425-889-0927
800-445-4866
Fax: 425-889-8699
<http://www.ars-nova.com>

Astarte
1261 Guerrero St.
San Francisco, CA 94110
415-821-1788
Fax: 415-647-6633

Attica Cybernetics, Inc.
8936 Nestle Ave.
Northridge, CA 91325
818-882-9184
Fax: 818-882-9185

Aurbach & Assoc.
9378 Olive Street Rd., Suite 102
St. Louis, MO 63132-3222
314-432-7577
800-774-7239
Fax: 314-432-7072
<http://www.aurbach.com>

Autodesk, Inc.
Order from an authorized
distributor
<http://www.autodesk.com>

BareBones
PO Box 1048
Bedford, MA 01730
781-687-0700
Fax: 781-687-0711
<http://www.barebones.com>

Big Top Productions
548 4th St.
San Francisco, CA 94107
415-978-5363
800-900-7529
Fax: 415-978-5353
<http://www.bigtop.com>

BMG Interactive
Order from a national educational
software distributor
<http://www.bmg.com>

Bogas Productions
751 Laurel St., Suite 213
San Carlos, CA 94070
415-592-5129
Fax: 415-592-5196

Borland International
PO Box 66001
Scotts Valley, CA 95067-0001
408-431-1000
800-331-0877
Fax: 408-431-4358
<http://www.borland.com>

Boxer Math
100 2nd St. NW
Charlottesville, VA 22902
804-977-5900
800-736-2824
Fax: 804-977-6484
<http://www.boxer.com>

Broderbund Software
PO Box 6125
Novato, CA 94948-6125
415-382-4400
800-825-4420
Fax: 415-382-4419
<http://www.broderbund.com>

Brooks/Cole Publishing
511 Forest Lodge Rd.
Pacific Grove, CA 93950
408-373-0728
800-354-9706
Fax: 408-375-6414
<http://www.brookscole.com>

Bytes of Learning
c/o FFI 908 Niagara Falls Blvd.
#240
North Tonawanda, NY 14120-2060
416-495-9913
800-465-6428
Fax: 416-495-9548
<http://www.bytesoflearning.com>

Bytes of Learning
150 Consumers Rd., Suite 203
Willowdale, ON M2J 1P9
Canada
416-495-9913
800-465-6428
Fax: 416-495-9548
<http://www.bytesoflearning.com>

Caere Corp.
100 Cooper Ct.
Los Gatos, CA 95030
408-395-7000
800-535-7226
Fax: 408-395-1994
<http://www.caere.com>

Calliope Media
Order from Sumeria
<http://www.calliope.com>

Cambrix Publishing
9304 Deering Ave.
Chatsworth, CA 91311
818-993-4274
800-992-8781
Fax: 818-993-6201
<http://www.nowwhat.com>

Cascade International
Order from a national educational
software distributor or through their
Web site
<http://www.cascade-int.com>

CE Software
PO Box 65580
West Des Moines, IA 50265
515-221-1801
800-523-7638
Fax: 515-221-2258
<http://www.cesoft.com>

Cendant Software
PO Box 2961
Torrance, CA 90509
310-793-0600
800-545-7677
Fax: 310-793-0601
<http://www.education.com>

**Center for Image Processing
in Education**
PO Box 13750
Tucson, AZ 85732-3750
520-322-0118
800-322-9884
Fax: 520-327-0175
<http://www.cipe.com>

Chancery Software
2211 Rimland Dr., Suite 224
Bellingham, WA 98226
206-738-3211
Fax: 206-738-3255
<http://www.chancery.com>

Chancery Software
275-3001 Wayburne Dr.
Burnaby, BC V5G 4W1
Canada
604-294-1233
800-999-9931
Fax: 604-294-2225
<http://www.chancery.com>

Chariot Software Group
123 Camino De La Reina
San Diego, CA 92108
619-298-0202
800-242-7468
Fax: 800-800-4540
<http://www.chariot.com>

Coda Music Software
Order from a national educational
software distributor
<http://www.codamusic.com>

Cognitive Technologies Corporation
5009 Cloister Dr.
Rockville, MD 20852
301-581-9652
800-335-0781
<http://www.cogtech.com>

Corbis
Order from Forest Technologies
<http://www.corbis.com>

CORD Communications
PO Box 21206
Waco, TX 76702-1206
254-776-1822
800-231-3015

Coronet/MTI
PO Box 2646
Columbus, OH 43216
614-876-0371
800-777-8100
Fax: 614-771-7361

Creative Multimedia
PO Box 10845
Salinas, CA 93912-9894
503-241-4351
800-262-7668
Fax: 408-655-6071
<http://www.ledgemm.com>

Creative Wonders
Order from The Learning Company

Critical Thinking
PO Box 448
Pacific Grove, CA 93950-0448
408-393-2388
800-458-4849
Fax: 408-393-3277
<http://www.criticalthinking.com>

Cultural Resources
30 Iroquois Rd.
Cranford, NJ 07016
908-709-1574
Fax: 908-709-1590

CyberPuppy
Download from the Internet
<http://www.cyberpuppy.com>

Davidson & Associates
Order from Cendant Software

Delorme Mapping
PO Box 298
Yarmouth, ME 04096
207-846-7000
800-452-5931
Fax: 800-575-2244
<http://www.delorme.com>

DeltaPoint
22 Lower Ragsdale
Monterey, CA 93940
408-648-4000
800-446-6955 or 800-367-4334
Fax: 408-648-4020
<http://www.sitetech.com>

DEMCO, Inc.
4810 Forest Run Rd.
Madison, WI 53704
608-241-1201
800-831-0811
Fax: 608-241-1799
<http://www.demcomedia.com>

Deneba Software
7400 SW 87th Ave.
Miami, FL 33173
305-596-5644
Fax: 305-273-9069
<http://www.deneba.com>

Design Science, Inc.
4028 Broadway
Long Beach, CA 90803
310-433-0685
800-827-0685
Fax: 310-433-6969
<http://www.mathtype.com>

Discis
Order from Harmony Interactive

DK Multimedia
3817 Sharpsburg Dr.
Modesto, CA 95357-1562
209-529-0368
800-903-5040
Fax: 209-549-0464
<http://www.dkonline.com>

Don Johnston, Inc.
1000 N. Rand Rd., Bldg. 115
PO Box 639
Wauconda, IL 60084-0639
800-999-4660
Fax: 847-526-4177

Dragon Systems
320 Nevada St.
Newton, MA 02160
617-965-5200
800-825-5897
Fax: 617-527-0372
<http://www.naturalspeech.com>

Eastgate Systems
134 Main St.
Watertown, MA 02172
617-924-9044
800-562-1638
Fax: 617-924-9051
<http://www.eastgate.com>

Edmark
PO Box 97021
Redmond, WA 98073-9721
425-556-8400
800-426-0856 & 800-691-2986
Fax: 425-556-8430
<http://www.edmark.com>

Educational Activities
PO Box 392
Freeport, NY 11520
516-223-4666
800-645-3739
Fax: 516-623-9282

Educorp
12 B West Main St.
Elmsford, NY 10523
914-347-2464
800-843-9497
Fax: 914-347-0217
<http://www.educorp.com>

Electronic Bookshelf
5276 S. County Rd., 700 West
Frankfort, IN 46041
765-324-2182
800-327-7323 (EBS-READ)
Fax: 765-324-2183
<http://www.ebsread.com>

Emerging Technology Consultants, Inc.
2819 Hamline Ave. North
St. Paul, MN 55113
612-639-3973
Fax: 612-639-0110
<http://www.emergingtechnology.com>

Encyclopedia Britannica Ed. Corp.
310 S. Michigan Ave.
Chicago, IL 60604
312-347-6900
800-554-9862 & 800-668-1644 (Canada)
Fax: 312-347-7903
<http://www.ebec.com>

Equilibrium
475 Gate Five Rd., Suite 225
Sausalito, CA 94965
415-332-4343
800-524-8651
Fax: 415-332-4433
<http://www.equilibrium.com>

Fairfield Language Technologies
165 South Main St.
Harrisonburg, VA 22801
540-432-6166
800-788-0822
Fax: 540-432-0953
<http://www.trstone.com>

Falcon Software, Inc.
One Hollis St.
Wellesley, MA 02181
781-235-1767
Fax: 781-235-7026
<http://www.falconsoftware.com>

FileMaker, Inc.
5201 Patrick Henry Dr.
Santa Clara, CA 95052
408-987-7000
800-747-7483
Fax: 408-987-7563
<http://www.filemaker.com>

Follett Software Company
2233 West St.
River Grove, IL 60171-1895
708-583-2000
800-621-4345
Fax: 708-452-9347
<http://www.follett.com>

Forefront Group
Order from Forest Technologies

Forest Technologies
514 Market Loop, Suite 103
West Dundee, IL 60118
847-428-2184
800-544-3356
Fax: 847-428-1310
<http://www.foresttech.com>

Fractal Design
Order from Ray Dream, Inc.

FreeSoft Company
150 Hickory Dr.
Beaver Falls, PA 15010
412-846-2700
Fax: 412-847-4436

Gale Research
835 Penobscot Bldg.
645 Griswold St.
Detroit, MI 48226
800-877-4253
248-699-4253
Fax: 800-414-5043
<http://www.gale.com>

Gessler Publishing
10 East Church Ave.
Roanoke, VA 24011
540-456-5825
800-456-5825
Fax: 540-342-7172
<http://www.gessler.com>

Great Wave Software
5353 Scotts Valley Dr.
Scotts Valley, CA 95066
408-438-1990
800-423-1144
Fax: 408-438-7171
<http://www.greatwave.com>

Grolier Education
PO Box 1716
Danbury, CT 06816
203-797-3500
800-243-7256
Fax: 203-797-3197
<http://www.grolier.com>

Group Logic
1408 North Fillmore St., Suite 10
Arlington, VA 22201
703-528-1555
800-476-8781
Fax: 703-528-3296

Gryphon Software
7220 Trade St., Suite 120
San Diego, CA 92121
619-536-8815
800-795-0981
Fax: 619-536-8932

GT Interactive Software
212-726-6526
800-499-8386
Fax: 800-791-7128
<http://www.gtinteractive.com>

H.W. Wilson & Co.
950 University Ave.
Bronx, NY 10452
718-588-8400
800-367-6770
Fax: 718-590-1617

Harmony Interactive
4936 Yonge St., Suite 702
North York, ON M2N 6S3
Canada
416-225-6771
Fax: 416-221-8631
<http://www.harmonyinteractive.
com>

Harvard Associates Inc.
10 Holworthy St.
Cambridge, MA
617-492-4610
800-774-5646
Fax: 800-776-4616
<http://www.harvassoc.com>

Hasbro Interactive
50 Dunham Rd.
Beverly, MA 01915-1844
508-921-3700
Fax: 508-921-3704
<http://www.hasbro.com>

Hi Tech Expressions
1800 NW 65th Ave.
Plantation, FL 33313
800-447-6543

Hi Tech of Santa Cruz
Order from Forest Technologies
<http://www.teachertools.com>

Houghton Mifflin Interactive
120 Beacon St.
Somerville, MA 02143
617-351-5000
800-733-2828
Fax: 800-733-2099
<http://www.hmco.com>

Humanities Software
Order from Sunburst

Humongous Entertainment
Order from GT Interactive
<http://www.humongous.com>

IBM K–12 Education
<http://www.solutions.ibm.com/
k12/welcome.html>

Information Access
362 Lakeside Dr.
Foster City, CA 94404
415-378-5249
800-227-8431
Fax: 800-676-2345

Insignia Solutions, Inc.
41300 Christy St.
Fremont, CA 94538
510-360-3700
800-848-7677
Fax: 510-360-3701
<http://www.insignia.com>

Inspiration Software, Inc.
7412 SW Beaverton Hillsdale
Hwy., Suite 102
Portland, OR 97225-2167
503-297-3004
800-877-4292
Fax: 503-297-4676
<http://www.inspiration.com>

Intellimation
PO Box 1922
Santa Barbara, CA 93116
805-968-2291
800-346-8355
Fax: 805-968-9899
<http://www.abc-clio.com>

**International Thomson
Publishing**
5101 Madison Rd.
Cincinnati, OH 45227
513-527-6159 & 513-271-8811
Fax: 513-527-6951
<http://www.thomson.com>

Interplay Productions
16815 Von Karman Ave.
Irvine, CA 92606
714-553-6655
800-INTERPLAY
Fax: 714-252-2820
<http://www.interplay.com>

Intuit
PO Box 7850
Mountain View, CA 94039
415-944-6000
800-624-8742
Fax: 619-784-1070
  & 888-241-0502
<http://www.intuit.com>

IVI Publishing
7500 Flying Cloud Dr.
Minneapolis, MN 55344-3739
612-996-6000
800-785-7775
Fax: 612-996-6001
<http://www.ivi.com>

Jostens Home Learning
9920 Pacific Heights, Suite 500
San Diego, CA 92121
619-587-0087
800-247-1380
Fax: 619-622-7873

Jump! Music
201 San Antonio Circle,
  Suite 172
Mountain View, CA 94040
415-917-7460
800-289-5867
Fax: 415-917-7475

Key Curriculum Press, Inc.
PO Box 2304
Berkeley, CA 94702
510-548-2304
800-995-6284
Fax: 510-548-0755
  or 800-541-2446
<http://www.keypress.com>

Knowledge Adventure
Order from Cendant Software

Knowledge Revolution
66 Bovet Rd., Suite 200
San Mateo, CA 94402
650-574-7777
800-766-6615
Fax: 650-574-7541

Laureate Learning Systems, Inc.
110 East Spring St.
Winooski, VT 05404-1837
802-655-4755
800-562-6801
Fax: 802-655-4757
<http://www.llsys.com>

Lawrence Productions
PO Box 458, 1800 S. 35th St.
Galesburg, MI 49053
616-665-7075
800-421-4157
Fax: 616-665-7060
<http://www.lpi.com>

LCSI
PO Box 162
Highgate Springs, VT 05460
514-331-7090
800-321-5646
Fax: 514-331-1380
<http://www.lcsi.ca>

LCSI
3300 Cote Vertu Rd.,
  Suite 201
Montreal, QC H4R 2B7
Canada
514-331-7090
800-321-5646
Fax: 514-331-1380
<http://www.lcsi.ca>

Learn Technologies Interactive
361 Broadway, Suite 600
New York, NY 10013
212-334-2225
888-292-5584
Fax: 212-334-1211
<http://www.learntech.com>

Learning Company, The
One Athenaeum St.
Cambridge, MA 02142
617-494-1200
Fax: 617-494-1219
<http://www.learningco.com>

Learning in Motion
500 Seabright Ave., Suite 105
Santa Cruz, CA 95062-3481
408-457-5600
800-560-5670
Fax: 408-459-6876
<http://www.learn.motion.com>

Learning Inc.
10 Industrial Ave.
Mahwah, NJ 07430
201-236-9500
Fax: 201-236-0072

Legacy Software
8521 Reseda Blvd.
Northridge, CA 91324
818-885-5773
800-532-7692
Fax: 818-885-5779
<http://www.legacysoft.com>

LEGO DACTA
550 Taylor Rd.
Enfield, CT 06082
860-749-2291
800-527-8339
Fax: 860-763-2466

Lingo Fun
PO Box 486
Westerville, OH 43081-0486
614-882-8258
800-745-8258
Fax: 614-882-2390

Little Planet Publishing, Inc.
5045 Hillsboro Rd.
Nashville, TN 37215-3745
615-386-0058
888-974-2248
Fax: 615-385-9496

LivingSoft, Inc.
PO Box 970, 711-700 Pine Acre Rd.
Janesville, CA 96114-0970
916-253-2700
800-626-1262
Fax: 916-253-2703
<http://www.psln.com/livingsoft>

LOGAL Software Inc.
125 Cambridge Park Dr.
Cambridge, MA 02140
617-491-4440
800-564-2587
Fax: 617-491-5855
<http://www.logal.com>

Logos Research System, Inc.
2117 200th Ave. W
Oak Harbor, WA 98277
360-679-6575
800-875-6467
Fax: 360-675-8169
<http://www.logos.com>

Lotus Development Corporation
Order from a national educational
software distributor

Macmillan/McGraw-Hill
195 Scott Swamp Rd.
Farmington, CT 06032
860-678-1212
Fax: 860-677-5405
<http://www.mmhschool.com>

Macromedia, Inc.
Order from a national educational
software distributor

Maris Multimedia
4040 Civic Center Dr., Suite 200
San Rafael, CA 94903
415-492-2819
800-639-8717
Fax: 415-492-2867

Mark of the Unicorn
1280 Massachusetts Ave.
Cambridge, MA 02138
617-576-2760
Fax: 617-576-3609
<http://www.motu.com>

MathResource
5516 Spring Garden Rd.,
    Suite 203
Halifax, NS B3J 1G6
Canada
902-429-1323
800-720-1323
Fax: 902-492-7101
<http://www.mathresources.com>

Maxis
2121 N. California Blvd. #600
Walnut Creek, CA 94596
510-933-5630
800-336-2947
Fax: 510-927-3581
<http://ftp.maxis.com>

McGraw-Hill
195 Scott Swamp Rd.
Farmington, CT 06032
860-678-1212
Fax: 860-677-5405
<http://www.mmhschool.com>

MECC
Order from The Learning
Company
<http://www.mecc.com>

MediAlive
19160 Cozetti
Cupertino, CA 95014
408-863-4800
Fax: 408-863-4801
<http://www.cdtechnotogy.com>

Meridian Creative Group
5178 Station Rd.
Erie, PA 16510-4636
814-898-2612
800-695-9427
Fax: 800-530-9968
<http://www.meridiancg.com>

MetaTools
Order from a national educational
software distributor
<http://www.metacreations.com>

Microsoft Corporation
Order from a national educational
software distributor
<http://www.microsoft.com>

Microspot Software
Order from a national educational
software distributor

Mindplay
160 W. Fort Lowell Rd.
Tucson, AZ 85705
520-888-1800
800-221-7911
Fax: 520-888-7904
<http://www.mindplay.com>

Mindscape
88 Roland Way
Novato, CA 94945
415-897-9900
800-234-3088
Fax: 415-897-8286
<http://www.mindscape.com>

Miracle Software
13 Missouri Ave.
Pottsdam, NY 13676-1821
315-265-0930
Fax: 315-265-1162
<http://www.MiracleInc.com>

Misty City Software
13625 NE 126th Place #430
Kirkland, WA 98034
425-820-2219
800-795-0049
Fax: 425-820-4298
<http://www.mistycity.com>

**National Geographic
Educational Services**
PO Box 98018
Washington, DC 20090-8018
202-828-6605
800-368-2728
Fax: 301-921-1575

Netscape Communications
Download from Web site
<http://www.netscape.com>

New Media
PO Box 390
Pound Ridge, NY 10576-0390
914-764-4104
800-672-6002
Fax: 914-764-0104

Newsbank
58 Pine St.
New Canaan, CT 06840-5426
203-966-1100
Fax: 800-762-8182
<http://www.newsbank.com>

Nordic Software
PO Box 6007
Lincoln, NE 68506
402-488-5086
800-306-6502
Fax: 402-488-2914
<http://www.nordicsoftware.
    com>

Optical Data Corp.
512 Means St. NW, Suite 100
Atlanta, GA 30318
800-524-2481
Fax: 404-221-4520

Optimum Resources
18 Hunter Rd.
Hilton Head, SC 29926
803-689-8000
888-784-2592
Fax: 803-689-8008
<http://www.stickybear.com>

ORBIS Software
PO Box 73745
Puyallup, WA 98373
253-848-6899
Fax: 253-848-6505

Paramount
Order from a national educational
software distributor

PC Direct
800-426-7235
<http://www.pc.ibm.com>

Peter Norton Computing
Order from a national educational
software distributor

Physics Academic Software
Dept. of Physics
North Carolina State University
Raleigh, NC 27695-8202
919-515-2524
Fax: 919-515-2682

Pierian Spring Software
5200 SW Macadam Ave., Suite 570
Portland, OR 97201
503-222-2044
800-213-5054
Fax: 503-222-0771
<http://www.pierian.com>

Piranha Interactive Publishing
1839 West Drake Suite B
Tempe, AZ 85283
602-491-0500
Fax: 602-491-8990
<http://www.piranhainteractive.
com>

PowerLab Studios, Inc.
616 Ramona St., Suite 20
Palo Alto, CA 94301
415-614-0900
800-843-8769
Fax: 415-614-0909
<http://www.powerlab.com>

Qualcomm
6455 Lusk Blvd.
San Diego, CA 92121-2776
619-450-9681
<http://www.qualcomm.com>

Quark
307-772-7100
800-676-4575
Fax: 307-772-7123
<http://www.quark.com>

Queue
338 Commerce Dr.
Fairfield, CT 06432
203-335-0906
800-232-2224
Fax: 203-336-2481
<http://www.queueinc.com>

Quiltsoft
PO Box 19946
San Diego, CA 92159-0946
619-583-2970
Fax: 619-583-2682

Rand McNally
PO Box 1906
Skokie, IL 60076-9714
800-678-7263
Fax: 800-934-3479

Ray Dream, Inc.
Contact Douglas Stewart for
retailer referrals
800-279-2795
Fax: 608-221-5217

RES Software
Professional Plaza Suite 215,
3155 Route 10
Denville, NJ 07834
973-328-8088
800-969-9673
Fax: 973-328-2893
<http://www.wowwords.com>

Roger Wagner Publishing
1050 Pioneer Way, Suite P
El Cajon, CA 92020
619-442-0522
800-497-3778
Fax: 619-442-0525
<http://www.hyperstudio.
com>

**ROM Tech (Virtual
Reality Labs)**
3534 Empleo St. Unit A
San Luis Obispo, CA 93401
805-545-8515
800-829-8754
Fax: 805-781-2259

**Sanctuary Woods
Multimedia, Inc.**
Order from Theatrix
<http://www.theatrix.com>

Scantron Quality Computers
20200 Nine Mile Rd.,
PO Box 665
St. Clair Shores, MI 48080
810-774-7200
800-777-3642
Fax: 810-774-2698
<http://www.thelinq.net>

Scholastic New Media
PO Box 7502
Jefferson City, MO 65102
212-505-3130
800-541-5513
Fax: 314-635-5881
<http://www.scholastic.com>

School Zone Publishing Co.
1819 Industrial Dr.
Grand Haven, Ml 49417
616-846-5030
800-253-0564
<http://www.schoolzone.com>

Sierra On-Line, Inc.
Order from Cendant Software

Simon & Schuster
1230 Avenue of the Americas
New York, NY 10020
212-373-8500
800-223-2348
Fax: 212-373-8192
<http://www.simonsays.com>

SIRS, Inc.
PO Box 2348
Boca Raton, FL 33427-2348
561-994-0079
800-232-7477
Fax: 561-994-4704
<http://www.sirs.com>

SmartStuff Software
PO Box 82284
Portland, OR 97282
503-231-4300
800-671-3999
Fax: 503-231-4334
<http://www.smartstuff.com>

Softkey School
Order from The Learning Company
<http://www.mecc.com>

Soleil Software, Inc.
3853 Grove Court
Palo Alto, CA 94303
650-494-0114
800-501-0110
Fax: 650-493-6416
<http://www.soleil.com>

Steck-Vaughn Company
PO Box 690789
Orlando, FL 32819-9998
800-531-5015
<http://www.steck-vaughn.com>

Strata
Order from a national educational software distributor

Sumeria Inc.
329 Bryant St., Suite 3D
San Francisco, CA 94107
415-904-0800
Fax: 415-904-0888
<http://www.sumeria.com>

Sunburst Communications
101 Castleton St.
Pleasantville, NY 10570
914-747-3310
800-321-7511
Fax: 914-747-4109
<http://www.sunburstonline.com>

SurfWatch Software, Inc.
175 South San Antonio Rd.
Los Altos, CA 94022
650-948-9500
800-458-6600
Fax: 650-948-9577
<http://www.surfwatch.com>

Symantec Corporation
Order from a national educational software distributor
<http://www.symantec.com>

Tanager Software
1933 Davis St., Suite 208
San Leandro, CA 94577
510-430-0900
800-841-2020
Fax: 510-430-0917

Teacher Support Software
3542 NW 97th Blvd.
Gainesville, FL 32606
352-332-6404
800-228-2871
Fax: 352-332-6779
<http://www.tssoftware.com>

Tenth Planet
Order from Sunburst

Terrapin Software
Order from Harvard Associates
<http://www.harvassoc.com>

Texas Caviar
3933 Steck Ave., Suite B-115
Austin, TX 78759
512-346-7887
800-648-1719
Fax: 512-346-1393

Texas Instruments
7800 Banner Dr.
Dallas, TX 75251
800-TI-CARES

Texas School for the Deaf
PO Box 3538
Austin, TX 78764-3538
512-440-5420

Theatrix Interactive
1250 45th St., Suite 350
Emeryville, CA 94608-2924
510-658-2800
800-955-8749
Fax: 510-658-2827
<http://www.theatrix.com>

Thynx
141 New Rd.
Parsippany, NJ 07054
201-808-2700
Fax: 408-655-6071

Tom Snyder Productions
80 Coolidge Hill Rd.
Watertown, MA 02172-2817
617-926-6000
800-342-0236
Fax: 617-926-6222
<http://www.teachtsp.com>

True BASIC
12 Commerce Ave.
West Lebanon, NH 03784
603-298-5655
800-872-2742 or
800-436-2111
Fax: 603-298-7015
<http://www.truebasic.com>

Turner Educational Services, Inc.
One CNN Center,
  Box 105366
Atlanta, GA
404-827-3149
800-344-6219
Fax: 404-827-3954
<http://www.turner.com>

Turner Multimedia
105 Terry Dr., Suite 120
Newtown, PA 18940
800-344-6219 &
800-563-4422 (in Canada)
Fax: 215-579-8589
<http://learning.turner.com>

Ventura Educational Systems
910 Ramona Ave., Suite E
Grover City, CA 93433
805-473-7380
800-336-1022
Fax: 805-473-7382
<http://www.venturaES.com>

Vicarious Entertainment
3 Lagoon Dr., Suite 300
Redwood City, CA 94065
415-610-8300
800-465-6543
Fax: 415-610-8302
<http://www.vicarious.com>

Videodiscovery
Order from The Learning Company

Virgin Sound and Vision
122 South Robertson Blvd.
Los Angeles, CA 90048
310-246-4666
800-814-3530
Fax: 310-246-9999
<http://www.vsv.com>

Vividus Corp.
378 Cambridge Ave., Suite I
Palo Alto, CA 94306
415-321-2221
Fax: 415-321-2282

Voyager Company
Order from Learn Technologies
  Interactive
<http://www.learntech.com>

VR Didatech
720 Olive Way, Suite 930
Seattle, WA 98101-3874
<http://www.vrsystems.com>

VR Didatech
4250 Dawson St., Suite 200
Burnaby, BC V5C 4B1
Canada
604-299-4435
800-665-0667
Fax: 604-299-2428
<http://www.vrsystems.com>

Waterloo Maple Inc.
450 Phillip St.
Waterloo, ON N2L 5J2
Canada
519-747-2373
800-267-6583 (U.S. & Canada)
Fax: 519-747-5284
<http://www.maplesoft.com>

White Pine Software, Inc.
542 Amherst St.
Nashua, NH 03063
603-886-9050
800-241-7463
Fax: 603-886-9051
<http://www.cuseeme.com>

William K. Bradford
Publishing
16 Craig Rd.
Acton, MA 01720
508-263-6996
800-421-2009
Fax: 508-263-9375

Wolfram Research, Inc.
100 Trade Center Dr.
Champaign, IL 61820-7237
217-398-0700
Fax: 217-398-0747
<http://www.wolfram.com>

World Book Educational Products
Order from Edmark or PC Direct
<http://www.worldbook.com>

World Game Institute
3215 Race St.
Philadelphia, PA 19104-2597
215-387-0220
Fax: 215-387-3009

World Library, Inc.
2809 Main St.
Irvine, CA 92614
805-473-1770
800-443-0238

APPENDIX B

Designing Lesson Plans

Logo as a Learning Tool

As we have noted earlier, an important part of computer literacy is to familiarize students with the process of programming computers to perform specific functions. With the advent of languages such as Logo, programming skills can be taught to even the youngest of students. The use of computer programming need no longer be limited to specialized secondary courses.

Many people have found that they can learn a great deal about programming by simply typing into the computer a Logo program that has been written by another person. This technique can be quite effective in the classroom. The student gains a sense of control over the computer by entering a set of program instructions and then observing while the computer carries out the instructions. Students come to understand some of the fundamentals in this manner. They see, for example, that the computer can only do that which it has been programmed to do. They see the need for very accurate and concise instructions to avoid errors. They begin to understand that the computer can work for them once they learn to communicate with it.

For this reason, it is a good idea to begin exploring programming with languages that are user friendly such as Logo. Students need to see that the computer can understand commands in plain English, and that programming languages are not overwhelmingly complicated sets of numbers and esoteric symbols. The lesson plans in this appendix use Logo as the programming language because it is relatively accessible and understandable to students. Other options are Hypercard or Linkway.

A number of books have been published with public domain programs that students can key into the computer for practice. Some perform basic calculations to solve problems or track numerical data and others play games. The programs range from very simple to very complex, providing practice for students of all grade and skill levels. A word of caution is necessary, however. Not all the programs to be found have been debugged carefully. Students may be frustrated if they spend hours typing and correcting their typed instructions only to find that the program does not work as promised even when the instructions are typed correctly. Teachers who possess strong programming skills can help their students out of such difficulties. Teachers with less experience in this area may do well to read reviews of the materials before using them in the classroom.

Another good source of programs for students to use is popular Logo computer periodicals. Some of these periodicals feature program instructions (also called code) and documentation on a regular basis. Since many school libraries subscribe to these periodicals, the materials are often readily available to teachers and students.

The lesson plans presented in this appendix all focus on the area of mathematics. Gifted or highly motivated students can be encouraged to venture out on their own by tailoring the programs to perform other or additional functions as well. The lesson plans focus on using the computer as a tool for problem solving, since this is really the forte of the computer. The authors suggest that teachers can introduce programming early and in a non-threatening way by integrating programming skills into subject areas across the curriculum. Specifically, since the computer is an excellent mathematical tool, it makes good sense to integrate the use of Logo to teach and explore mathematics. Students can learn programming skills with relative ease while they are mastering mathematical concepts. This appendix presents lesson plans for teachers who want to introduce Logo to explore mathematics in their classrooms.

The lesson plans are organized according to grade level, with two lesson plans presented. Teachers should use their own judgment in adapting the lesson plans for use with their own students. How well students perform in programming depends on a number of factors, including previous experience, attitudes toward computers, and perceived value of programming skills. Class discussions conducted before these lesson plans are presented can aid the teacher in discovering and exploring these crucial factors.

As in Chapters 9 and 10, the lesson plans presented in this chapter are offered as guidelines for the teacher who wants to make better use of the computer in the classroom. The lesson plans can be introduced as appropriate topics throughout the school year. Teachers should feel free to tailor and adapt the lesson plans as they see fit and to use the lesson plans as a springboard for their own creativity in their unique classroom situations.

Lesson Plan 1: Turtle Graphics

Grade Level: K to 3

Objective: Students will use Logo to explore and create circles, triangles, squares, and rectangles.

Subject: Math—geometric shapes

Materials Needed: Turtle Graphics software, compatible hardware.

Preparation: Students should be familiar with the parts of a computer and with a computer disk. Teachers can choose from a number of Logo and Turtle Graphics packages on the market. Make sure that the software you purchase is compatible with your hardware. Also, determine which package will best meet the unique needs of your classroom. For example, some packages require more advanced typing skills than do others, and this should be taken into consideration.

Activity: First, demonstrate how the program is loaded into the computer. This is a good opportunity to discuss the steps involved in proper handling and care of software. Have the class make a poster showing the steps involved in booting the system. Introduce the basic commands involved in drawing shapes:

Left
Right
Home
Hide
Show

Have the students practice using these commands. Encourage students to spend time exploring what the turtle can do.

Evaluation: Can students use the commands effectively?

Follow-Up: Draw simple shapes on the board and have students copy them with the turtle.

Note: Teachers who use a Turtle Graphics package that uses single keystroke commands will need to modify the lesson plans accordingly.

Lesson Plan 2: Problem Solving with Logo

Grade Level: 4 to 6

Objective: The students will use Logo to solve mathematical and geometrical problems.

Subject: Math—symmetry

Materials Required: Computer, compatible Logo software, activity sheet, mirror.

Preparation: Students will benefit from some previous exposure to Logo, including the commands used to draw shapes. Duplicate enough copies of the activity sheet for all students. Draw some simple shapes on paper. Then using the mirror, introduce the students to the concept of mirror images.

Activity: Ask students to write a Logo program that will produce mirror images of the shapes displayed on the activity sheet. After students have written their programs, have them test the programs to see how well they run. Finally, assist the students in performing any debugging that may be required in order for the program to recreate the shapes accurately.

Evaluation: Do the students' programs draw mirror images of the shapes on the activity sheet? Have students been successful in locating and correcting errors in their programs?

Follow-Up: Another interesting experience would be to give students only one half of a shape so that the mirror image they create would complete the picture. Simple shapes such as houses or faces can be used effectively.

Summary

This appendix presented two lesson plans to assist teachers in using the computer to teach mathematical skills. As has been noted, even the youngest students can begin acquiring skills that are necessary in writing instructions for computers to follow.

The lesson plans can be adapted to other grade levels with minor modifications. All of the lesson plans are aimed at the subject of mathematics, but this is only one area in which teachers can begin to introduce Logo activities.

In fact, there are a number of excellent resources available to teachers of all subject areas who want to use Logo in their lesson plans. Students can learn a great deal about programming by typing into the computer the programs found in these resources and experimenting with them. Students also learn by modifying simple Logo programs to fit their own needs. Teachers should check their school media centers as well as local libraries for availability of computer periodicals that feature Logo activities.

Many of the lesson plans contain suggestions for additional or follow-up activities.

Logo programming activities often pave the way for class discussions or for further research. Students are also a valuable source of inspiration in the use of Logo. It is a good idea to encourage students to look for ways of enhancing programs or expanding applications of programs. After all, the more creative our future programmers are, the brighter the future is for all of us.

LEARNER ACTIVITIES

1. Interview a student taking a computer programming class in a local school and write a summary about his or her experiences and expectations.

2. Present one of the lesson plans in this chapter and report on the results to a class.

3. Locate a Logo tutorial and follow several lessons.

4. Create a poster showing common commands in Logo.

5. Adapt one of the lesson plans in this chapter to a higher or lower grade level.

6. Write one or more additional lesson plans suitable for your class. Follow the lesson plan format used in this chapter.

7. Locate a Logo programming lesson plan in a computer periodical. Write a review of the lesson plan outlining its strengths and weaknesses.

8. Select one lesson plan and modify to use either HyperCard (Apple) or Linkway (IBM).

9. Plan a sequence of lessons utilizing Logo to teach mathematical concepts correlated to the National Council of Teachers of Mathematics' standard on geometry.

10. Does Logo have a future use in education? Why or why not? Support your position with classroom scenarios.

BIBLIOGRAPHY

Kosko, T. (1985). Some projects for your programming classes. *The Computing Teacher, 12*(6), 24.

Maddux, C. D. (1985). *Logo in the schools.* New York: Haworth Press.

Maddux, C. D., & Johnson, D. L. (1988). *Logo: Methods and curriculum for teachers.* New York: Haworth Press.

Shimabukuro, G. (1989). A class act: Junior high students, Lego and Logo. *The Computing Teacher, 17*(5), 37–39.

Watt, D. (1989). Research on Logo learning as a path to professional teacher development. *Electronic Learning, 8*(5), 22–24.

Wiburg, K. M. (1989). Does programming deserve a place in the school curriculum? *The Computing Teacher, 17*(1), 8–11.

APPENDIX C

Word Processing

Advancements in the data-processing world appeared after the punched card was replaced by the display terminal. The ability to store information on a disk, store the disk for later use, and print the output stored on the disk at an even later date provided the basis for using the computer for textual material as well as mathematical calculations. Word processing has become an everyday function in classrooms and offices that handle large quantities of written text. **Word processing** refers to writing, manipulating, and storing textual material in a computerized medium.

Word Processing: Its History and Popularity

IBM introduced the Magnetic Tape/Selectric Typewriter (MT/ST) in 1964. Because MT/ST stored characters entered by the operator on magnetic tapes, this was the beginning of word processing. The tape was used to store manuscripts, portions of which could be corrected and reused. Another advance occurred in 1973 when IBM introduced the Magnetic Card Selectric Typewriter. Typed documents were stored on magnetic cards that could be revised more easily than could be done on previous machines. This system also contained an electronic main memory.

The first word processor for microcomputers was developed by Seymour Rubinstein and Bob Barnaby. Other early word processors were Electric Pencil, Scripsit, and WordStar. After the mid-1970s, the field of word processing blossomed as many different companies began to develop programs to suit various needs. During the 1980s, word processors became the most popular microcomputer software.

Word processing is popular because writing, editing, storing, and copying text can all be done much more efficiently by computer than by typewriter. Although text is usually entered via the keyboard (as with a typewriter), changes during entry can be made much more easily than with a typewriter, either before printing the document or after. (The user does not have to retype an entire document to accommodate changes. The printer simply prints out the new version.) The document can also be saved and retrieved later, simply with a few keystrokes. Once retrieved, the text can be edited if desired—changes, additions, and deletions can be made easily to the file; the file can then be printed out and saved for future use. The document or portions of it can be copied and printed as many times as the user likes and can be used in the original form or combined with other documents.

Obviously, the advantages over simple typing make word processing useful in almost every field. Business and government use word processing to prepare letters, reports, instructions, and advertisements. Educational uses include teacher preparation of written material for students; student preparation of reports, newspapers, and letters; and administrative paper work.

Word Processing in Education

Elementary and high school students can use word processing equipment to compose text. They can enter and edit essays before and after teachers have critiqued the material on paper; they can adjust prose or poetry on the screen and then reprint the text. Word processing activities may include the following:

Writing letters
Writing introductory sentences and paragraphs
Writing closing statements or paragraphs
Creating a group story
General writing
Describing a person, place, or thing
Writing a biography
Writing an autobiography
Writing a news article
Writing an essay
Writing a fantasy story
Writing an editorial
Writing a review
Writing a play
Writing a poem
Writing instructions for using a device
Editing an article or story

Word processors in the classroom can expand the horizons of learning in ways not possible before this technology was available. In writing, for example, students learn far more than just how to create text. As they create a document, the word processor prompts them to consider how the material will appear on the printed page. This includes choices about margins, spacing, and type style, to name a few.

Spelling and vocabulary are other areas where students can have instant feedback. By using the spell check feature now available with most word processors, students can tell if a word is spelled incorrectly; the word processor may even give them the correct spellings. This immediacy is especially advantageous: It promotes learning and prevents students from repeating their errors.

Another option now offered by many word processors is a thesaurus, which can expand students' vocabulary when properly used. Just as spell check offers a list of correctly spelled words, a **thesaurus** provides a list of words with similar meanings. Thus, students are able to write in a more diverse and interesting manner and learn new words at the same time.

Also available on many word processors is a **grammar check.** This feature examines sentences for grammatical correctness. The user can make the appropriate changes to avoid grammatical errors.

By using a word processor's many functions, students can produce better first drafts that are also eye-pleasing and easy for the teacher to read and grade. When revising and rewriting, students retrieve the original and make the necessary changes, without having to reproduce the whole text.

The teacher might prefer to evaluate the text on a screen display rather than from a printed copy, have the student make revisions on screen, and print a copy only after all desired changes have been made. The time saved for both student and teacher is one of the positive aspects of word processing.

Subjects other than creative writing benefit equally from the use of word processing in the classroom. For example, teachers can create interactive documents that require student response. History, social studies, English, foreign languages, science, and the arts are all adaptable to this kind of instruction. In addition, teachers can administer and grade exams and quizzes using a word processor.

In addition to its uses for teaching, word processing can help educators meet their scholarly and administrative needs. At the university level, word processors are used to write manuscripts, research reports, grant proposals, and public relations materials. Much of this information remains the same over an extended period of time and only changes need to be incorporated. On any level, teachers can prepare lesson plans, examinations, and other classroom material on the word processor. Again, the material can be updated from year to year as necessary without having to recreate the whole body of information.

Whatever the application and whoever the user may be, certain characteristics are common to most word processing systems. Generally, the user enters text on a typewriter-like keyboard. Instead of a sheet of typing paper inserted into a typewriter, a monitor displays each character (letter, numeral, or symbol) as it is typed. A **cursor**—a small marker of space—moves along the line of type, indicating the position at which the next character typed will be entered. In addition to common typewriter symbols, the keyboard includes directional arrows that, when pressed, move the cursor up and down, and to the left or right, at the discretion of the user. Other keys allow the user to insert or delete characters, spaces, or lines. Further adjustments to a text are possible by giving different commands to the system. Although these commands are given different names in different systems, the various word processors perform similar tasks.

In the following sections, some of the more frequently used terms and commands are discussed. Although different software packages do not use identical terms, teachers and students will soon become familiar with the terminology of their software. The following examples do not define commands for every application; rather they are approximations of terms to be found in most word processing packages.

Word Processing Terms

Word Wrap.   On a conventional typewriter, typists must press a carriage return key at the end of each line to return the carriage to the left margin of the next line. However, in most word processing systems, the cursor moves there automatically. This is often called **word wrap.**

Justify.   The word processor can easily produce text with equal, or **justified,** right and left margins. Before the advent of word processors, justified margins were only available for typeset material. (Electronic typewriters, with proportional spacing can produce justified margins also.)

Spacing.   Spacing refers to how many blank line spaces there are between lines of text. The usual options are single spacing and double spacing; however, many systems also offer the option of half-line spacing.

Margins.   The size of margins may be specified, left and right as well as top and bottom. On most word processors, margins may also be changed within the document.

Tab.   Similar to a typewriter tab, the cursor moves a predetermined number of spaces to the right each time the tab key is pressed. This is useful for typing tables or columns. Many programs also include tab left.

Column.   Student-produced newsletters and other desktop published items require a sophisticated procedure for setting up **columns** (vertical arrangement of printing), which allows two or more columns per page. Text or numbers in one column can be changed without affecting other columns of information.

Type Style.   Type style refers to the font and size. In word processing, **font** refers to the design of the characters. Word processors also allow you to choose from a variety of sizes, from 8 point to large custom sizes.

Header.   The **header** is the first few lines at the top of a page; this space can be used to create headings, page numbers, or any other text that the user wishes to have appear on every page or specified pages of a document.

Footer.   The footer is the last few lines at the bottom of a page and, like the header, may be programmed to appear on all or any number of specified pages. During pagination, footers are automatically numbered and placed at the bottom of the appropriate pages with a line inserted to separate them from the body of the document. If a document is revised, footers are automatically renumbered and repositioned as necessary.

Word Processing Commands

In addition to cursor movement and the editing features offered by the keyboard, word processors employ **commands,** which tell the program to perform various tasks. Commands such as the following are generally available from pull-down menus or buttons on a toolbar.

Bold.   An individual character, a word, or a block of text may be printed in **bold** type for emphasis.

Underline.   Characters, words, or blocks of text may be <u>underlined.</u> Sometimes the user can specify that underlining be either continuous (words and spaces) or separate (words only).

Copy.   The user can highlight and **copy** text already entered in one part of a document to another part of the document automatically without having to retype it.

Spell Check.   **Spell checking** features use a preloaded dictionary of common words. The size of the dictionary (the number of words it contains) varies with each program (the larger the dictionary, the more efficient the spell checker). When activated, the spell checker will highlight words that are spelled incorrectly or that it doesn't recognize; it may also supply a list of similar words. The user may then choose the correct word from the list and instruct the system to insert it in place of the misspelled one. If the correct word does not appear on the list, the user may type it in.

Thesaurus.   The **thesaurus** works much like the spell checker. The computer will, upon command, produce a list of words of similar meaning that may be substituted for a given word. If the iist contains a more appropriate word, the user may then instruct the computer to exchange one word for another.

Grammar Check.   The **Grammar Check** command finds grammatical mistakes in the word processed document. For instance, it can detect split infinitives, confusing language, incorrect punctuation, and jargon.

Find.   Given the **Find** command, the word processor will find and pause at every occurrence of a particular word, phrase, or number in a text. This allows changes in text to be made quickly and accurately throughout an entire document. Usually, the system offers both automatic and prompted changes. If a word or number is to be changed in some instances but not in others, the user selects the prompted option to decide each instance. With the Search feature, some programs count the number of times a given word appears in the text, thus allowing the writer to determine whether there has been too much repetition.

Merge.   Most word processors can **merge,** or combine, the contents of more than one document. For instance, when part of a letter must be placed in another letter, retyping is unnecessary—the appropriate texts can simply be merged with the Merge command.

Documents may also be created for the specific purpose of merging. For example, if an identical letter must be sent to different individuals or organizations, the document containing the letter can be combined with a document containing any number of names and addresses. The computer may then be instructed to print one letter for each addressee.

Center.   The word processor can speedily center titles and other text when given the **Center** command.

Save.   The **Save** command copies the document to a disk for storage. Documents can generally be saved in a variety of formats to be accessible in other word processing programs.

Print.   The **Print** command directs the computer to print an entire document or only a portion of it. The user may be able to select the number of copies desired; other print options may be available, depending on the program.

In addition to the preceding terms, which are basic to most word processors, there are numerous other functions and capabilities for the user to consider. The following section contains a list of these, which should help novices to determine what best fits their needs.

Columns and Tables

Often, it is desirable to present text and numbers in columns and in tables. Many word processors allow the user to design columns and tables to fit their data. Most systems offer two types of columns—tabular (or parallel) and text (or newspaper). Creating either involves three basic steps: (1) defining the columns, (2) activating the column feature, and (3) typing text and numeric data into each column.

Tables consist of parallel columns, which keep blocks of text next to (parallel to) each other on the same page. A history teacher could use parallel columns to display descriptions of historical events from different time periods. By placing these descriptions in columns side by side on a page, students can compare them more easily and efficiently. (If a parallel column continues from one page to another, the user must define a page break, or create a new set of columns for each page, depending on the software in use.)

Parallel columns would also be useful to display scientific formulas and other information. Such information displayed side by side for comparison and explanation makes it easier for the student to comprehend and simplifies the teacher's task of presenting the material.

As the name implies, newspaper columns are used for text (or numbers or both) that continues from one column to another on the same page, and can continue onto subsequent pages. Newspaper columns use the word wrap function to do this, keeping the text within the defined column width.

The creation and publishing of a class or school newspaper would be an excellent use for newspaper columns. Such a project offers students opportunities far beyond the lessons in journalism that are apparent in this application. For example, students might learn that communication between varied groups requires presenting different kinds of information in different ways. Publishing a newspaper, even with the limited scope of a single classroom, provides experiences that mirror the political, civic, and academic environments of the larger world.

For both parallel and newspaper columns, the number of columns is limited only by the width of the document itself. The document width, of course, is determined by setting the left and right margins. Column width may also vary. For example, the user may need a two-character column for a number and a forty-character column to contain a paragraph of text.

It's also possible to create columns for existing data. This procedure varies from one software program to another. Some allow users to create the columns with the data in place, whereas others instruct the user to create columns and then retrieve data into them. Usually, either way is simple and is explained by on-screen messages during the process.

Columns can be manipulated in much the same way as other text. They can be inserted, deleted, moved, and copied. When revising a document, each column is treated as a separate block of text and can be changed without affecting other columns. Printing enhancements such as boldface type and underlining can be used in columns.

Some word processors allow the user to set up reference areas, either at the top of a table of columns or at the left side. Reference areas identify what a column or row of data contains and are especially helpful when revising the contents. Top reference areas identify columns, and side reference areas (appearing at the left side of the screen and document) identify rows.

Merge

Many word processing software programs have a merge function that allows for two or more documents to be combined. One of the most common applications of the merge function is to create form letters that appear to be individualized. The basic form letter is typed once, with special codes inserted where data will differ for each letter. This is called the primary document.

A secondary document is then created that contains a page for each letter that is to be produced. Each page in turn contains the **variable** data for a particular letter. (Examples of variable data are name, address, phone number, salutation, account balance, and so on.)

When the two documents are merged, the system will print one letter for each page in the secondary document. Each letter will contain the variable data from the secondary document page plus the complete basic letter from the primary document. In this way, names, addresses, and salutations can be inserted at the beginning of a form letter, which then looks as if it were originally created only for the addressee.

The classroom teacher can use merge to create a form letter that, when printed, would appear to be a personalized letter addressed to the parents of each student. In addition to a different name, address, and salutation for each letter, other variable information can be inserted as desired. This function can save the teacher a great deal of time in communicating with parents without sacrificing the ability to make each letter pertinent to the individual student's situation.

The secondary document can also be used to print lists of names, addresses, or virtually any text contained within the document. It can be used to generate mailing labels. If there is a large amount of variable information, it can be contained in a database that can be merged with a word processed document in the same way.

Another way to create documents for merging is to type one paragraph per document page. During the merge process, the user can then specify which paragraphs are to be included in a particular document by specifying page numbers to be merged. Teachers can use this method for writing up objectives for individual students.

In addition, many word processors allow the user to type information at predetermined locations within the document. This eliminates the step of creating a secondary file. However, since it doesn't save the variable data for future use, it's most useful for one-time situations. For instance, teachers could create documents in which students insert the appropriate information, to teach or reinforce spelling, vocabulary, and grammar concepts.

Macro

A **macro** is a simple process of recording and saving a sequence of keystrokes in a file that can be recalled for future use. It is a shortcut for entering frequently used commands. Data, or a combination of data and commands, can also be entered in this way. Macros can range from short, simple entries to elaborate chains of commands. Obviously, the more complex the function, the more time is saved by creating and using a macro, if it is needed often enough to warrant it.

A macro is assigned a name that the user types in to implement the series of keystrokes or data that it represents. Instead of names, macros can be assigned to specific keys; this is sometimes called keystroke programming. To activate the macro, the user presses the specified key (or more often a combination of two keys) rather than typing in a macro name.

The macros just described are permanent and will remain on the disk on which they have been saved. Temporary macros may also be created for use during one word processing session and are deleted automatically when the session ends.

Macros may also be combined with merges. The possible combinations are numerous and differ greatly from one software program to another. With use, it will become apparent which of the available options and combinations of options will be of most benefit.

One of the concerns inherent in using microcomputers and word processing software in the classroom is the amount of time needed to implement the various functions. Using macros is an ideal way to decrease the time needed for all students to arrive at a particular point in the lesson. By pressing one or two keys instead of many, the time saved can be devoted to the lesson itself.

Disadvantages of Word Processing

Although word processing allows fast, accurate text editing, it has some potential disadvantages. Fluctuations in electrical current can damage disks or keep text that is being entered from going into memory. In this case, the text must be entered (retyped) again. Also, diskettes are fragile and easily damaged. If damage occurs, text will not be properly stored on the disk and must be retyped. Damage to hardware can result in text being removed unexpectedly from memory or disk.

To minimize the risk of data loss, the user can create backup disks. This is a simple matter of copying one or more files (or the entire contents) from the original disk to a new disk. Text stored on a computer's hard disk should always be backed up on diskettes as a safeguard in the event of power failure or system malfunction.

While creating a document of some length, it's a good practice to save the data after several pages are input. In this way, large amounts of data will not be lost in case of system failure.

Many software programs allow the user to save the document without leaving it; he or she can then continue to create or revise it. This helpful feature allows for quick and easy protection of data while the cursor remains at the same place in the document; the user can resume input immediately without having to exit and reenter the document.

Summary

Word processing refers to writing, manipulating, and storing text in a computerized medium. The use of computers to input and output text is one simple definition of word processing. Word processing allows text—such as essays or reports—to be entered by means of a keyboard similar to that of a typewriter. Further adjustments of a text are possible by giving different commands to the system.

Word processing began in 1964 when IBM introduced the Magnetic Tape/Selectric Typewriter, which stored characters entered by the operator on magnetic tapes. The first word processor for a microcomputer was developed by Seymour Rubinstein and Bob Barnaby. Word processing software has become the most popular use of the microcomputer. After the mid-1970s, the field of word processing blossomed as many different companies began developing programs to suit various needs.

School districts purchase word processing software for elementary and high school classrooms where students compose text. Universities purchase word processors for many uses, including the writing of manuscripts, research reports, grant proposals, and public relations materials.

Word processing is useful in teaching many subjects in addition to writing. Through the process of computer instruction, students also learn about how things work in the world beyond school. Teachers gain time to teach concepts, while letting the computer perform some of the more routine tasks that previously were part of their responsibilities.

This chapter provided an overview of word processing terms and commands. A checklist, covering document creation, editing, formatting, utilities, and special features, summarized the commands offered by popular word processing software packages. Teachers and administrators can use the checklist to help them choose a package that meets their needs.

More detailed descriptions of some of the highly sophisticated and valuable functions of word processing were also discussed. The columns and tables function allows users to create columns and tables to fit their data. Merge allows two or more documents to be combined. Common applications of the merge function are creating form letters that appear to be individualized and creating documents of paragraphs that can then be merged in any combination. Macros, which record and save a sequence of keystrokes in a file that can be recalled for future use, are a shortcut for entering frequently used commands.

While word processing allows fast, accurate text editing, it has several disadvantages. Fluctuations in electrical current can damage disks or keep text that is being entered from going into memory. Also, diskettes are fragile and easily damaged. Damage to hardware can result in text being removed unexpectedly from memory or disk.

To minimize the risk of data loss, the user can create backup disks. Text stored on a computer's hard disk should always be backed up on diskettes as a safeguard in the event of power failure or system malfunction.

A wide variety of hardware and software are available to classroom teachers who wish to incorporate word processing into their teaching. Many factors must be considered when choosing a word processor, such as the teacher, the student population, the curriculum, the school district, and the funds available and how they are allocated. However, once a decision is made and equipment is in place, both teachers and students will benefit greatly from this classroom tool.

APPENDIX D

Spreadsheets

One of the most widely used computer applications is the electronic spreadsheet. Perhaps the best way to describe an electronic spreadsheet is to visualize on the computer screen an accountant's ledger sheet with its array of horizontal rows and vertical columns. Each row and column contains information (which can be both letters and numbers) that may be organized in such a way as to be easily understandable to the viewer. The term spreadsheet itself implies material spread before the eye of the user for quick and easy reference.

Although the electronic spreadsheet performs exactly such a function, that is only the beginning of what it can do. Each piece of data entered into the spreadsheet is considered in its relationship to all the other data contained therein. In this way, any change made in one part can affect the whole spreadsheet. Information can be manipulated to reflect potential change in any or all sections of the spreadsheet.

The electronic spreadsheet can automatically recompute and change any data affected by an entry, almost instantaneously. It takes little imagination to recognize the time saved over doing the same task on a ledger sheet, with an eraser and calculator at hand. In addition, since computers do not make mistakes in calculations as humans are apt to do, the potential time saved in looking for errors is even more impressive. The spreadsheet has presented speedy solutions to many tasks. As it develops further, it continues to present ever more sophisticated capabilities.

Spreadsheets: Their History and Use

The electronic spreadsheet made its debut in 1979, a creation of two Harvard Business School graduate students, Daniel Bricklin and Robert Frankston. They named their program VisiCalc, and it became the prototype for many other software programs that formed the first generation of electronic spreadsheets.

The second generation came on the scene with the introduction of Lotus 1-2-3. This program was unique in that it was the first integrated software program. An integrated software program blends several different programs so that information can be presented in various forms. For example, a graphics option allows the user to create visual aids, such as line graphs, vertical and horizontal bar graphs, and pie-shaped charts. In this way, the figures from the spreadsheet can be converted to graphs that show at a glance what the user wishes to communicate about the financial picture.

Another option contained in Lotus 1-2-3 is database management. A database is an electronic filing system in which large volumes of data (information) can be stored and organized. For instance, names, addresses, phone numbers, and account numbers can be entered into a database. That information can then be sorted alphabetically, numerically, or in any other way that will be helpful to the user. In an integrated program, when any of the stored information is needed, it can be retrieved from the database and inserted into the spreadsheet. The time saved in locating and adding data to a spreadsheet made this new generation of software a welcome addition to the electronic spreadsheet family.

The most recent addition to this family, and the beginning of the third generation, is the integrated software program with extended capabilities, adding word processing, expanded spreadsheet size, and communications between computers. Word processing allows text to be added to the report. In this way, an explanation of the spreadsheet figures or the graphic pictures can complete a financial report.

Another improvement is the potential size of spreadsheets. Spreadsheet programs vary in the numbers of rows and columns available, but average size is much larger now than what was originally offered. Any number of these columns and rows may be used, depending on the needs of the user and the memory capacity of the computer. Although only a small portion of this total picture appears on the computer screen at one time, the user may move around within the spreadsheet to display any part of it.

The other improvement in this latest generation of spreadsheet programs is the ability of computers to communicate with each other. Through the new technology of telecommunications, computers in different locations can communicate by telephone lines and exchange data as needed. Examples of programs combining all of the preceding options are Appleworks and Microsoft Works.

With these enhancements and increased options available to the user, many more educational applications became apparent. The following is a discussion of some of those applications.

Spreadsheets in Education

One of the most obvious uses for spreadsheets in education is to teach education accounting, both principles and practical applications. Math and science also have a similar need to teach concepts and theories, as well as to manipulate vast amounts of numerical and statistical information. Additionally, math teachers find the spreadsheet helpful in teaching students to write and use mathematical formulas.

In a math class using spreadsheets, students can see displayed on a computer screen the logical relationship between numbers and mathematical operations. Other lessons are also enhanced by teaching math on spreadsheets. For example, the logic of transferring a problem written in text, usually called "story problems," to a spreadsheet sharpens students' cognitive skills.

By entering instructions in the form of formulas, students reinforce the learning of mathematical symbols and the standard order of precedence. Decimals, percentages, and the computation of simple and compound interest are other areas of math study that are expedited and explained more fully when displayed in spreadsheet format.

In addition to math, other subjects may also be better explained, as well as made more interesting, with the use of spreadsheets. The analysis of social studies data (such as population growth, income distribution, census information) and the results of scientific studies are only a few of the potential uses for spreadsheets in classroom teaching.

Spreadsheets can be used to maintain student records and specifically grade reports. To most effectively use the computer's ability to manipulate data, grades can be combined to compute their average, mean, median, and various ranges in a class, or group of classes. On the other hand, specific data can be isolated from the rest (e.g., to view an individual student's records). Virtually any piece of information desired is at the user's fingertips.

Schools, colleges, and universities are organizations with employees, income, and expenses just like any other business. Therefore, all uses of computer technology in general and spreadsheets in particular that apply to business and industry apply also to educational organizations. For example, employees' personnel and payroll records, the organizational budget, balance sheets for income and overhead, and reports supporting need for additional funding are only a few of the many administrative tasks for which the spreadsheet can be helpful. Various special interest groups and clubs also exist in the educational environment. They, too, have budgets, income, and expenses that can be managed through the use of spreadsheets.

Still another educational function for spreadsheets is the management of data by researchers. Large amounts of demographic and statistical information can be gathered through survey questionnaires and entered into a computer's database. Then the computer's spreadsheet compiles and analyzes the data in whatever way fits the purpose of the researcher.

Spreadsheets for Individuals

Although all of the preceding activities affect us as individuals, there are even more personal ways in which the electronic spreadsheet serves us. It can balance the checkbook, manage household expenses, organize and store income tax records, project interest income, and aid in budgeting and planning for the future.

Students will be working in the real world—in business and industry, education, or in government or nonprofit agencies. Spreadsheets will inevitably be a part of their world. For that reason students will benefit from hands-on classroom training with the spreadsheet.

Now that we know how helpful a spreadsheet can be, let's look at the practical application and fundamentals of electronic spreadsheets.

Fundamentals of Spreadsheets

The spreadsheet has three modes of operation: ready, entry, and command. It always begins in the ready mode, in which the user presses the directional, or arrow, keys to move around within the spreadsheet. When the user begins to enter data into the spreadsheet, the entry mode is activated automatically. The **command mode** is used to manipulate data for various purposes that we will explore later. The command mode is also invoked when the user is ready to perform calculations on the data entered. A third function of this mode is to instruct the computer what to do with the spreadsheet once it is completed.

In the past, the typical ledger sheets used by accountants and others who deal with figures were already laid out in a specific pattern and preprinted on paper. The electronic spreadsheet, on the other hand, is a blank computer screen that may be designed by the user to suit a particular need. The number and arrangement of columns and rows to accommodate the data to be entered are the first items to be considered. These considerations also determine the size of the finished spreadsheet.

Spreadsheet Size

The size of a spreadsheet is limited by the software program being used. Some spreadsheets are as small as 63 columns by 255 rows. One of the best-selling spreadsheet programs has 254 columns by 2,048 rows. Other programs have varying numbers of columns and rows. The size of the formatted spreadsheet is determined by the number of rows and columns needed to perform a specific task. Only a small portion of the entire spreadsheet is visible on the display screen at one time. However, the user can view any other portion of the spreadsheet by using the cursor keys to bring other areas into view.

Cursor Movement

Cursor keys are the ones with directional arrows that move the cursor to the left or right and up or down. Some programs allow the cursor to move more rapidly when the **Home, End, Page Up,** or **Page Down** keys are pressed. In addition, most programs allow the user to move directly to any specific area of the spreadsheet with a **Go To** command. The most common key used to activate the **Go To** command is the equal sign (=). After pressing the **Go To** key, the user must tell the computer where to go. This is accomplished by designating a cell location.

Cells

A cell is the point on the spreadsheet at which a row and column intersect. Most programs provide letter designations for columns, for example, A, B, C, . . . on to Z, then AA to AZ, BA to BZ, and so on for as many columns as the spreadsheet contains. Rows, on the other hand, are numbered beginning with 1. Thus, a cell location might be D3, meaning the intersection of column D and row 3.

There are some programs that use numbers for both rows and columns. In that case, the preceding cell location would be designated as C4 R3, again meaning the intersection of column number 4 and row number 3.

When the user activates the **Go To** command and enters a cell location, the program instantly moves the cursor to that position. The cell where the cursor is currently positioned is referred to by most programs as the **current,** or **active, cell.**

Two different kinds of entries are possible at the current cell position. Either text (letters) or numeric data (numbers) can be entered from the keyboard. Numeric data are used to make calculations. Text, of course, cannot be used in this way.

To ensure accuracy as entries are made, many programs provide a line, sometimes called a *data entry line,* where the information appears as it is typed. The data do not go directly into the cell, but remains on the entry data line until the **Enter,** or **Return,** key is pressed. If there are errors, they can be corrected on this line before the data are placed in the cell. When the **Enter** key is pressed, the computer transfers what appears on the entry line into the current cell.

After information is entered into cells, some programs move automatically to the next cell. If the program in use does not have this feature, the user must move to the next cell with one of the cursor keys.

In addition to number and arrangement of columns and rows, other decisions must be made by the user regarding headings, labels, values, formulas, and commands. We discuss these one at a time in the following sections.

Headings

Headings appear at the top of the spreadsheet. Headings are titles, names, or any identifying information that describes the contents of the spreadsheet. A heading should give an accurate picture of what the spreadsheet was created for and what it contains. The heading should be clear and concise, as shown in the following example, so that anyone who receives a copy of or works with the spreadsheet can easily see what it contains.

Example: EMC522 EVALUATION OF SOFTWARE

(INSTRUCTOR'S NAME)

SEMESTER GRADES FOR SPRING 1999

This heading makes it quite clear that this spreadsheet contains students' grades for the Spring 1999 semester in a specific course taught by the identified instructor. More detailed identification of the spreadsheet contents may be made by the use of *labels*.

Labels

Like headings, **labels** are titles, names, or other identifying information that describes the contents of rows or columns. They need to be descriptive, informing the viewer of exactly what is contained in each row and column. For example, in the spreadsheet for students' grades, the row labels might consist of students' names and the column labels would contain identifying names of what will be graded (tests, papers, class participation).

Labels may consist of both letters and numbers. However, if the label begins with a number, the user must make it clear to the computer that this is indeed a label. This is done by pressing a key defined by the software program to indicate that what follows is a label. The data are then typed and entered into the cell. The most common character used to designate a label is the quotation mark ("). If a distinction is not made in some manner for a label that begins with a number, the computer will confuse it with a *value*.

Values

Values are numbers entered into any cell. The computer always interprets numeric entries as values, unless indicated otherwise (as described before). Values are used to enter financial and statistical information into cells. It is crucial that only entries that are true representations of values be input as numerical data. It is also important that the values be entered accurately.

An aid for entering data correctly is the status line. The status line tells you where the cursor is located and what the cell contains. In addition, the status line of some programs indicates what kind of entry is being made. If numbers are being entered, the line will read "value," and if letters are typed, it will say "label" or "text."

Formulas

Once the columns and rows are labeled and the financial or statistical information is entered into cells, the user must tell the computer what is to be done with this data. This is accomplished by the use of **formulas.** The formulas used in spreadsheets are much like the mathematical formulas used elsewhere.

Most spreadsheets use the standard mathematical order of precedence. That is, mathematical functions are performed in the same order that they are done on paper. Higher orders of precedence are performed before the lower orders. For instance, multiplication and division are calculated before addition and subtraction. Also, whatever is enclosed in parentheses is always calculated first.

However, some spreadsheets do not use the order of precedence but calculate from left to right. It is necessary to determine how the spreadsheet program being used handles calculations. Formulas may then be written to perform calculations in the order desired. Consider the following equation:

$$2 + 8 * 9 = ?$$

The asterisk (*) is used by many programs to indicate multiplication. Therefore, the standard order of precedence is multiplication first, then addition, giving a total of 74 (8 times 9 = 72, plus 2 = 74). On the other hand, a left-to-right calculation results in a total of 90 (2 plus 8 = 10, times 9 = 90).

Since there is an obvious discrepancy in the two answers, it is easy to see the importance of knowing how your spreadsheet program performs calculations, in order to ensure accuracy. It is also necessary to know how your program designates specific math functions. Usually, the plus (+) sign is used for addition, the minus (–) sign for subtraction, the asterisk (*) for multiplication, and the slash (/) for division.

To make these procedures easier, most spreadsheets have preprogrammed formulas, called **functions,** which consist of those formulas that are most commonly used in spreadsheets. They are preprogrammed for convenience and speed. In addition, on many keyboards, there are special function keys, usually called **F** or **PF** keys and numbered from one to the maximum number the keyboard contains. By pressing one of these keys, its specified function is brought into play, thus eliminating the need to input formula information over and over.

The names of function keys are descriptive of the calculations that they perform. For instance, **Sum** adds numbers in a designated group of cells. **Count,** as its name implies, counts the number of entries in a specified group of cells. **Avg** performs two tasks: It will total the numbers in a group of cells and calculate the average.

Different spreadsheet programs have different names assigned to the various functions. These names are then reserved, or restricted, and may not be used for other purposes within that program. The user must become familiar with the names and functions unique to the spreadsheet program being used.

Formulas are entered into the cell where the result is to be displayed. Although the cell actually contains the formula, the user does not see it but its numeric result on the screen. Because the formula remains in the cell, whenever a value is changed in any of the cells that the formula uses, the resulting numerical value changes automatically. Let's consider a formula for simple addition.

Example: Column B contains 10 numbers in cells B2 through B11.

It is always a good idea to leave a blank row between the total and the column being added. A blank row separates the total from the other numbers and makes it more visible. Therefore, leave cell B12 blank, place the cursor on cell B13, and enter a formula. The formula tells the computer to add the numbers and display the total in cell B13. This may be done as follows:

SUM(B2+B3+B4+B5+B6+B7+B8+B9+B10+B11)

However, as in this instance, there may be lots of numbers to add and this method would be cumbersome. For that reason, the formula may be written in an easier and quicker way by defining a range of cells as follows:

SUM(B2 . . . B11)

The three periods (. . .), also called ellipses, are used by many programs to separate the first and last cell designations. The colon (:) or period (.) is also commonly used for this purpose.

After the formula is entered into the cell, the computer adds the numbers in cells B2 and B11 plus all the cells in between. It will then display the total in the cell containing the formula. As long as the formula remains in cell B13, if the value of any cell between B2 and B11 is changed, the total in cell B13 will automatically be changed and displayed.

Many spreadsheets use the "at" symbol (@) along with the function name to indicate a function or predefined formula. However, this is not true of all spreadsheet programs. The user must learn the language of the particular program in use in order to input words and symbols that the computer will understand.

Commands

Each spreadsheet program also has its own group of commands. Commands are an additional method of manipulating data within the spreadsheet to accomplish the user's purpose. Users will become familiar with the language and methods of their particular spreadsheet. Windows- or Macintosh-based spreadsheets offer these command options as bottons on a toolbar, generally found at the top of the screen. Now that we have a way of getting in and out of the command mode, let's look more closely at what the different commands do.

Format.   The **Format** command is used to define the arrangement and placement of data within the spreadsheet. The **Format** command does not change the data, only the way they appear on the spreadsheet.

You must define how much of the spreadsheet will be affected by the format settings, either the entire spreadsheet, designated columns, designated rows, or the current cell only.

One way to arrange data is to choose the width of columns. Column width can be adjusted to accommodate the data that the cells will contain. Obviously, some information requires more than the nine-character width commonly assigned to a column. By choosing a wider format for column width, the additional space can be added to one column, or to more than one, as needed.

Another reason for changing column width is to enable the user to view more columns at one time on the screen. If less than nine characters are needed for the values and labels in a column, it can be narrowed to the required number of characters, thus allowing extra columns to occupy the display area.

An additional format option is alignment of data. This is a method of arranging data by defining how and where the data are to be placed within the cell. The **Format** command can instruct that the text and numbers be centered. They can also be placed at the extreme left or the extreme right position in a cell, which is called justification. The data are then said to be right- or left-justified.

In addition to data alignment in each cell, the user can decide how the data will look once placed there. Numerical data, for instance, can contain commas to make long numbers more readable. They can begin with a dollar sign ($) to indicate money values. They can contain up to four decimals, to indicate dollars and cents, percentages, or highly accurate numbers. All these choices, as we have already learned, may be defined for the entire spreadsheet or for specified ranges (columns, rows, or cells) by using the **Format** command.

Edit.   Often, in addition to changes in the appearance of data, the user wishes to make changes (**edit**) in the data themselves. It is possible to simply retype the data in a particular cell and replace what is there. However, there is an easier way, and that is to change or modify what has already been entered. The **Edit** command is used for this purpose. The cursor may be placed on the cell to be changed, the **Edit** command entered, and characters inserted, deleted, or changed as necessary.

Insert.   Sometimes the user may wish to add (**insert**) an entire row or column. If data have already been entered, this can be done without disturbing what the spreadsheet already contains. The user can call up the **Insert** command, which allows you to insert an entire blank row or column. By placing the cursor at the point where the new row or column is desired, and by choosing Row or Column, the **Insert** command instantly places the user's choice at that location.

Delete.   On the other hand, perhaps the user wishes to remove (**delete**) a row or column. The **Delete** command works in the same way as **Insert.** A word of caution is necessary here. The entire row or column will be deleted, along with all the data contained in it. In most cases, once this information has been deleted, it is gone forever. There are some programs with an **Undo** command that retrieves the last block of information deleted, in case of error. However, since most programs do not, the **Delete** command should be used carefully.

Most spreadsheet programs contain an interesting automatic feature that is helpful when using the **Insert** and **Delete** commands. It automatically adjusts formulas that have been moved into different columns or rows as the result of an insert or delete. That is, the column letters or row numbers within the formula will be changed to those of the new position. This is a great time saver and eliminates much editing and possible errors.

Copy. Sometimes the user wants information to appear in the same form in more than one area of an electronic spreadsheet. The **Copy** command saves many hours of duplicating information in different areas. Copying is done in two ways: duplicating (or exact copying of data) and replicating (sometimes called relative copying).

Exact copying is self-explanatory. A block of data, which can be defined by cell, row, column, or a range of these, is copied exactly as it appears. In some programs, a space must be prepared before data can be copied there. This is done by inserting blank rows or columns where the information is to appear.

The other option, replication, applies to formulas and functions. Replicating adjusts the formula to reflect its new position. This process changes the column letters or row numbers so that, when performed, the calculation will operate on the data contained in the correct column or row. The term *relative copying,* then, refers to copying the data relative to its position after copying is complete.

Scroll. Scrolling is a term used for moving quickly through the spreadsheet. Most spreadsheets will be larger than a display screen can accommodate at one time. Display screens are usually 24 rows long and 80 characters wide. This allows for approximately 6 or 8 columns by 20 rows. The entire spreadsheet, including the part that is not displayed, may be thought of as a long and wide scroll. Scrolling then refers to moving the spreadsheet vertically or horizontally to display another portion.

Window. Occasionally, the user wants to view two separate portions of a spreadsheet at the same time for purposes of comparison. A window is a portion of the spreadsheet that is displayed on the screen at the same time that another portion appears. This may be done at the top or bottom of the screen, or side by side. This display is very similar to the split screen we are accustomed to seeing on our television sets. Many programs allow two or more windows at one time to display portions of a spreadsheet.

Save. Once the spreadsheet has been formatted, all the data entered, the calculations performed, and the desired results obtained, the user will want to save the entire project. This can be done in different ways. The **Save** command copies the spreadsheet to a specified disk drive. The spreadsheet can be placed on a hard disk, if the computer contains one. (A hard disk is a permanent part of the computer.) If the computer does not have a hard disk, the file can be saved on a floppy disk (which is removable). It is always wise to make a backup copy on floppy disk in any case. The disk copy can be stored in a safe place, and can be used on a different computer if necessary.

Print. The **Print** command causes a printed copy (often called a *hard copy*) to be made. Spreadsheets can be printed in two different versions. Display Print, a copy of the displayed data and calculation results, is the obviously useful option. It contains financial or statistical information that is meaningful to those involved with it.

Contents Print, the other option, prints precisely what appears in each cell, including formulas. This printout is especially useful for checking the accuracy of formulas for calculation. An error may have occurred during entry of a formula that causes calculations to be performed incorrectly. The user can also make sure that all the data were entered and that they were entered correctly.

The spreadsheet should always be saved before printing. This will avoid loss of data in the event of an electronic failure.

Template

Another helpful and very effective time saver is a **template,** which is a formatted spreadsheet that has not yet had data entered. If, for instance, a spreadsheet is being created for a report that is generated periodically, the same format will be needed again. The formatted spreadsheet can be saved and copied to a disk before any information is entered. Then, the next week, month, quarter, or year when the same report needs to be generated, a blank spreadsheet containing the basic format is available.

When saving the template and indeed any file, the user must assign a name to it. Its name identifies it and allows it to be retrieved as needed. As with all filenames, a descriptive name helps the user identify the file for retrieval.

After saving the template under one name, its blank spreadsheet can be used to enter data and perform calculations. This spreadsheet is then saved as well (under a different name).

Another use for the template is to generate reports that are similar but not identical. For example, a monthly report may be combined with two other monthly reports to generate a quarterly (three-month) report. The template saved from the monthly report format can be modified to satisfy the requirements for a quarterly report.

Analysis and Projection

Now that we know how spreadsheets are created and saved, let's explore how they are used. Spreadsheet information is essential in analyzing the financial condition of any organization. Spreadsheets also make analysis of statistical information more manageable and much faster. Analysis then, is one of the more important uses of electronic spreadsheets. A natural outcome of analysis is projection for the future. Let's look now at the value of spreadsheets in these two areas.

Analysis

In business and other organizations, analysis is the examination and evaluation of data to measure their impact on the particular organization for which it is being performed. Spreadsheets are an excellent way to compare data. To accomplish this, spreadsheets can be combined, both in part and in total. By defining a range of cells, rows, or columns, any part of a spreadsheet may be retrieved and made a part of others. In this way, very complicated data can be displayed for comparison. Windowing, discussed earlier, is most helpful for these operations.

Another way to analyze data is to use **modeling.** As its name implies, this technique —which employs what-if statements—creates a model of what might occur if certain conditions existed. Modeling may be likened to the actual building of a physical model, such as architects do when designing a building. A spreadsheet model is created and its figure displayed; the user then asks the computer "what if" a specific value were to be changed. The value can be a change in actual numbers or an increase or decrease by a specified percentage rate.

Again, it is easy to envision the time saved over hand calculations when the computer can display instantly how a change in one number affects all other numbers relating to it. The ways in which this is helpful to any organization and its decision makers are virtually endless.

Modeling is especially effective in education. Due to changes and shifts in population, it is important for educational institutions to assess their immediate future needs, as well as long-term ones. By asking what-if questions based on census information and other known statistics, school districts, colleges, and universities can be better prepared to offer quality education. In the classroom, probability situations can be modeled with a spreadsheet. By experimenting with various probabilities, students can examine the basic theories of probability.

As in education, planning for other public and social programs is dependent upon knowing what will happen if certain changes take place within society. Changes in the political climate, for instance, have an impact on almost every area of life. The educational community will obviously benefit quite as much as private business and industry by using the analytic properties of electronic spreadsheets.

By combining the information gained from analysis of a spreadsheet with expectations for the future, it is possible to project what may happen.

Projection

Projection is the predicting, or forecasting, of what may be logically expected to occur in the future based on what we know about the past. There are three basic types of planning for the future: *operational, tactical,* and *strategic.* There are also two basic areas where planning is necessary—expense and income.

In the area of expense, operational planning is the simplest and covers a period of only a few months at a time. It deals with day-to-day operations. Usually done by lower-level managers, this type of planning obviously is short-term and therefore requires less complex spreadsheet information than other types. An example of operational planning is the adjustment of teaching staff and classroom space.

Tactical planning is for an intermediate period, perhaps covering a time span of one to three years. This includes planned stages of development working toward long-term goals. An example of this type of planning is the revision of school budgets in response to projected increased enrollment.

Strategic planning occurs at the highest level of management and addresses the overall, long-range welfare of the organization. Examples of this level of planning are direction of growth, curriculum development, and expansion of school districts.

Future income also requires planning and projection on the part of school administrators. For instance, expected changes in income due to school bond issues can be included in planning.

For higher-level educational institutions, administrators must predict potential changes in student population and project income based on tuition and fees. For instance, funds allotted from other agencies may change from time to time. For this and other reasons, planning for the future is essential to a smooth operation.

Government agencies have a similar need to make projections based on changes in population, income, and societal needs. One of the most obvious areas of public service is transportation. How many freeways to build? What is the projected need for public transportation? This is only one of many services provided by local, state, and national government agencies that may be better analyzed through the use of electronic spreadsheets.

Summary

Computers have been used by business, education, government, and individuals to organize and analyze all kinds of information. The spreadsheet is a useful tool for managing financial and statistical information in this manner. Called an electronic spreadsheet when done by a computer, this technique has become one of the most effective time-savers of our new technology.

From the prototype created by two Harvard students in 1979, to the latest sophisticated integrated software packages, electronic spreadsheets have grown from a useful tool to an indispensable fact of life. All areas of daily existence have been influenced by this development.

In education, spreadsheets are used in various ways. Some of those ways are teaching (e.g., accounting, math, and science classes); maintaining student records; budgeting for both the entire school and various groups within it; and management of data by research groups.

Government agencies are also big users of electronic spreadsheets. They manage and manipulate vast amounts of data, analyze changes in all areas of society, and plan for the future needs of communities and the nation.

We as individuals benefit from this new tool as well. We use electronic spreadsheets for personal banking, household management, tax records, and budgeting.

Each of us is influenced in either direct or indirect ways by the widespread use of spreadsheets in the real world. For this reason, the practical application of spreadsheets has been stressed in this chapter. To implement a spreadsheet, a user must be familiar with the terms, modes, commands, formulas, and functions presented here.

Once a spreadsheet has been created and data entered, it may be used to analyze the data it contains, and to make projections for the future based on that data and other knowledge and expectations. What-if statements may be used to set up theoretical conditions; the spreadsheet then calculates the potential results. The instant answers given by this method save many hours of tedious labor, without mathematical error.

Spreadsheets serve us all in many ways. In some cases, we use them to make our individual tasks easier. In other instances, we benefit from their use in business, government, and education.

APPENDIX E

Databases

Before the advent of computer technology, organizations and individuals had no choice but to maintain their files manually. In a manual system, simple files are often kept on index cards stored alphabetically (or numerically) in a box or drawer. More complex files are maintained in file folders and stored in drawers of file cabinets.

A manual system requires much physical manipulation of the files themselves, since it is often necessary to add to, delete from, or modify them. A library card catalog, for example, is continuously updated as new acquisitions are added and outdated material is removed. Classroom teachers keep many different kinds of records pertaining to their students that require updating. Here again, the physical manipulation and revision of records take much time and energy.

When computers came on the scene, programs were developed that allowed people to store information electronically. For instance, a company might run inventory accounts using information originated and updated with each set of transactions. Another program might keep track of the company's sales (requiring the same information as the inventory program, but entered independently). Although these programs were an improvement to manual record keeping, the redundancy of their methods became obvious to programmers during the third generation of computers. At this time, the concept of databases—programs that tie the various files together—was developed.

With the creation of database programs, files can be manipulated by the computer, thus saving hours of physical labor in handling, updating, and moving them when changes are made. Database programs enable users to

- create new files
- add, delete, or change entries in files
- perform limited calculations using files
- sort files
- merge two or more files into one
- select records that have specific attributes for further use

A **file** is created when information such as identification numbers, names, social security numbers, grades, and other pieces of data are gathered. As with manual files, the file must be revised constantly to be useful. New information must be added; records that are no longer needed must be removed from the file. Name changes, statistical updates, and corrections of errors are just a few of the factors that require file updates.

After new records are added to a file, it is usually necessary to change the order of records in the file so that they are once again in correct sequence. The computer can perform a **sort** to accomplish this task—often in a matter of seconds. Sometimes it is necessary to **merge,** or **join,** two or more files into one. Usually, a **sort** is done while files are being merged to put the new files into proper sequence.

At times, it is helpful to **select** only certain records within a file for processing. For example, a principal may want to generate a mailing list of parents of a specified segment of the student population; however, the database files contain addresses of parents of all the students. The computer can be instructed to search for only the specified parents and to print out all relevant address information.

Databases in Education

The educational community has been one of the primary beneficiaries of the database's ability to compile, store, and manipulate huge amounts of demographic and statistical information. Student records, for example, once entered into a database can then be accessed by whatever criteria the user wishes and compiled to generate specific and individually designed reports. School districts and universities have built databases to handle student files, which can include currently enrolled students, classes, financial accounts, grades, and schedules.

Databases are also an invaluable new tool for the classroom teacher. A database can be created for members of an individual class and used to arrange information as the teacher requires. Curriculum enhancements are also available through the use of databases created by libraries and other sources of reference materials. By implementing a search in one of these databases for information relevant to the subject being taught, a teacher can locate many different sources of material in much less time than that required for a physical search.

In the early days, the only database programs available were database managers. These programs provided the format and computer power for creating a database, but required the user to gather and enter the information. This was a great deal of work, especially for busy classroom teachers. Then database programs were developed that contained data files as well. In education, these programs even included suggestions on how to implement them in specific teaching situations.

Now there are software programs that teach students how to use a database. These programs are self-contained: They have a built-in database manager, a database containing data, and tutorials that ask questions about the data and their implications. Whatever a teacher may want to convey to the students can be better presented and covered more comprehensively by the use of a database.

In teaching computer classes and many other disciplines, databases can save hours of routine and repetitious data entry into the computer. That time may be better used to teach the concepts and practical applications of the particular subject. In the case of quantitative subjects, such as math and science, much basic information can be contained in databases, in this way eliminating human error in transferring it to specific problems to be worked on.

The individual student can also benefit from the timesaving potential of a database. In writing research papers, for example, a database of references is very useful. Often blocks of written information pertaining to one subject also relate to other subjects; if retained in a database, they can be called up at will for reference or inclusion.

School administrators must deal with a great amount and variety of information. For instance, personal information about students and their families, courses completed and grades attained, class schedules, and financial information are just a few areas that generate large amounts of data. The computer's ability to store data as well as to manipulate it for various purposes serves to expedite and simplify these tasks.

Information about courses and class schedules, for instance, is needed to generate student and instructor schedules. With the ability to access a database containing thousands of pieces of information, much time is saved, with a resulting saving of both private and public monies.

Databases in Society

In addition to their uses in education, databases are widely used in other sectors of society. Government agencies, nonprofit organizations, businesses, and private individuals all use them.

Federal, state, and local governments make extensive use of databases. Vast bodies of information can be accessed easily for a number of purposes. For example, information collected and updated periodically by the U.S. Census Bureau is accessible to university scholars for research, to government officials who must determine allocations of grants, and to many others.

Law enforcement agencies rely on databases to help coordinate their efforts across the nation. Agencies on the East Coast have access to information on crimes committed on the West Coast by virtue of nationwide databases. This can help law enforcement in many ways, for instance, to capture criminals who cross state boundaries to avoid prosecution.

Databases also help us cope with several pressing social issues. For example, in recent years, databases with information on runaway adolescents have been established. Similarly, databases about children who have been abducted by parents who do not have legal custody have helped find these children, who are often taken out of state. Many families have been reunited, thanks to the advent of databases.

In business, databases have expedited many procedures, especially in the airline industry. Enormous databases are now shared by all the airlines; since each airline no longer has to input separate sets of information, records are not duplicated and computer processing time is reduced. This allows travel agents to determine fares, flight schedules, and connections for various airlines with lightning speed.

Although airlines are no doubt the largest passenger-carrying organizations to use databases, the same concept applies to ships, trains, and buses. Other carriers, such as those in the trucking industry, also benefit from database technology in moving goods from place to place and maintaining schedules and inventory.

All of the uses mentioned so far are advantageous to us as citizens and individual recipients of goods and services. However, the database can be used in a more personal manner.

For many years, large computers handled databases. However, with the advent of chips that can accommodate large amounts of data, databases on microcomputers have become a reality.

A home microcomputer and a database can help its owner to keep track of medical appointments, visits to the veterinarian, dinner engagements, upcoming cultural events, vacations, school conferences, birthdays, anniversaries, or other events that, if forgotten, could cause embarrassment or inconvenience. A database can also be used to store and update a personal mailing list and to keep track of personal finances.

Database Structures

Generally, all databases are organized into **records,** each of which contains categories, called **fields,** which hold **data items** (a data item is an individual unit of alphanumeric data that is entered into each field). For instance, a college application could translate into records for individual students: Each category on the application—student name, address, social security number, and so on—would become a field in the record; each completed application would result in responses that could be entered as data items in the appropriate fields.

A group of related records is called a **file.** One file, on admissions, for instance, may contain students' names and other pertinent information. Another file, for class enrollment, will show who is enrolled in which classes as well as other related facts. A third file for finances could hold students' payment records. All three files have at least one identical field (in this case, student name), which allows them to be organized into a database (a group of related files).

Although all databases share the preceding characteristics, there are several different methods of data access. These methods divide database programs into those that are hierarchical, network, or relational models.

Hierarchical Databases

The simplest database is the **hierarchical,** or tree-structured, **model.** By the nature of its organization, information is accessed from the top down. For example, a social security number may be used to identify a record. It would therefore be the first data item entered and would be placed at the top of the treelike structure. Following it might be a student's name and address, which would be placed on lower branches of the tree. Therefore, if the known item is a student's name, the system must follow the hierarchical path (starting from the top) to reach that particular item.

This method is said to be a parent-child relationship, that is, each item relates only to the one above and below it in the hierarchy. This procedure naturally suits many business management functions, such as organizational tables, charts of accounts, and personnel records.

However, the necessity to follow the hierarchical structure can be cumbersome and ill suited to other kinds of needs. For this reason, network models were developed.

Network Databases

To meet the needs of users who wanted more flexibility of access, the **network model** was devised, where multiple, explicit relationships exist. In other words, the relationships are numerous, not necessarily from top to bottom, and are explicit because a pointer is established to direct the computer from one item to another.

The network model differs from the hierarchical because the search structure is less rigid. Through the pointers, or links, set up within the system, the shortest distance to the required information is followed, rather than a top-to-bottom route, which is unchangeable. Although this is an improvement over the previous model, it is still cumbersome.

The complexity of the system makes modification also a complex procedure. When modifying data within such a system, great care must be taken to maintain all the pointers that join the relationships so that none of the links in the chain is lost. Since the relationships are explicit, the route from one relationship to another must be consistently maintained.

This model works well for standardized operations where transactions predictably follow a preconceived path. For instance, banking transactions, airline reservations systems, and inventory control are examples of transactions that remain the same for each occurrence. Therefore, defining an explicit relationship with pointers from one step to the next is a practical application.

When transactions are not so predictable, a less explicit path from one record to another is desirable. For that purpose, the relational model was developed.

Relational Databases

A **relational model** is set up in a table format. Thus, it is two-dimensional, with rows and columns. What was formerly referred to as a file is now a relation. A record is now a row; a field is now a column. In order to avoid confusion, we will continue to refer to files, records, and fields.

The relational database performs three basic functions:

1. Two files may be **merged** into one; this is called **joining.**
2. Fields may be extracted from various files to form a new file; this is called **projection.**
3. Various records may be chosen according to the user's own criteria; this is called **selection.**

A relational database is useful in situations such as our school records example. Student information, course information, class information, instructor information, and financial information can all be stored in a database, then managed according to the desired results. Schedules can be created and modified for a student, for an instructor, for a department, or for the whole institution. Grades can be maintained, averaged, compared, printed, and mailed to students.

Libraries are another area where relational databases are used with extreme effectiveness. Huge volumes of text, as well as scientific data, can be stored in a database and accessed according to the interest of the user.

One disadvantage of the relational model is that there is no practical way to link one field with many others that may relate to it. Its very flexibility in mixing and managing fields limits its ability to establish explicit links. Files can be created by the user using any number of fields, limited only by the contents of the database. However, the user must define and implement the creation of the files; it is not done by the system. For this reason, most database systems are not strictly relational.

There are advantages and disadvantages to the three models discussed. The user must choose the one that best meets his or her needs. There is no best way to do it, except as defined by the desired end result.

Creating a Database

After determining the structural model to be used, the next step is to actually create a database and enter data. The data can then be modified and managed to accomplish the user's objectives.

Because fields, records, and files are added, modified, joined, projected, and selected, an obvious question arises: What happens when a piece of data is changed, for instance, a name, an address, or telephone number? The database system manages this with a data dictionary. A data dictionary keeps track of the names of all fields and their widths, types, and file locations in the database. When a change is necessary, the change is made in the data dictionary. Since all other occurrences of the field are dependent on the dictionary, accuracy is maintained.

Database Commands

As with any program, users will become familiar with the language and methods of their particular database. To avoid confusion in distinguishing between database commands, it helps to remember that fields are equivalent to columns and records are the same as rows. In the relational mode, files are also called relations.

Enter.   When the user chooses the **Enter** command, the system displays the format established in the data dictionary, with spaces provided for entering the data. Each time the **Enter** command is activated and data entered, a new record is created and stored in the file. Most systems give the user an opportunity to correct any errors before the data are stored on disk. Once the user signals that the data are correct and complete, they become a permanent part of the file.

Edit.   The **Edit** command is used to change or modify data that are already part of the file. The system displays the entire record; any field can be altered as necessary. Entered changes replace the earlier entries.

Sort.   **Sort** can be used to arrange records in a specific order. It operates on any one field in each record of a file. For example, records can be arranged alphabetically according to students' names or numerically according to zip codes, for mailing purposes.

Sorting can be done in ascending or descending order. **Ascending order** is from lowest to highest (A to Z or 1 to 9). Descending order is from highest to lowest (Z to A or 9 to 1). Since the **Sort** command operates on only one field at a time, data are sorted by the field chosen. For instance, it may be necessary to have all students' names in alphabetical order or it may be more desirable to have them listed according to class standing. The choices are limited only by the number of fields designated when creating or modifying a database.

Select.   The **Select** command searches for and copies into a working file all the records (rows) containing the specified data. For instance, the user could select all students whose major is computer science and copy those records into a new file.

Print.   The **Print** command tells the computer to print the contents of a file. Each record is printed as a row; fields are printed in a series of columns.

Analysis and Testing

Once a database is created, it is necessary to analyze the system, its structure, and how it will work. An accepted practice is to construct a set of test data to be processed by the database. The primary purpose is to determine whether the database will do its job. In addition to providing information, the database should be capable of formatting the data for printing reports in precisely the manner requested.

In order to be a comprehensive test of the system's capabilities, the test should execute all functions, including input, processing, output, and storage. To assure the best results at this stage of the process, the user would have had to exercise analytical skills from the very beginning.

To create, test, and manage a successful database, it is necessary to have a thorough understanding of the data to be stored, the reason for their existence, and how they can be managed to provide the end product desired. Only then will the user have the full advantage of the many benefits provided by a database.

Social Implications of Database Access

We are living in the midst of an information explosion. It is incomprehensible how this vast amount of information might have been managed before the advent of computer technology. Since we are fortunate to have the technology, the availability of information changes life in ways not even imagined a few short years ago. Now we can access encyclopedias, airline reservations, and research data in a few minutes. Before databases, these activities were long, tedious processes. A look into the future would probably reveal a computer in every home with access to huge databases. In the meantime, there are other methods of access for groups and individuals.

Whereas many Americans naively believe that any computer-directed activity is good, without considering the possibility of adverse consequences, some people fear the misuse of databases. Consider the huge database that the Internal Revenue Service maintains on taxpayers. Might not a family's financial situation be of interest to businesses or other government agencies? Nowadays, corporations maintain databases on personnel, schools maintain databases for academic records, and credit bureaus maintain databases on financial status. Any of these databases accessed by an individual or group for purposes other than originally intended could endanger an individual's right to privacy and perhaps cause real harm. During the next decade, our legislators will be charged with the responsibility of determining the legal and illegal uses of databases based on their potential threat to the privacy of the individual.

Summary

The concept of databases has expanded computer capability, making it possible to store large amounts of data for repeated use in many different applications. Business and industry, educational institutions, and government agencies all use databases to expedite their many functions. This has resulted in reduced costs and eliminated tedious manual data management. Although organizations have probably benefited the most from databases, they are by no means the only recipients of the advantages. With the addition of databases to microcomputers, individual users have benefited as well.

The three most commonly used database models are hierarchical, network, and relational. Each model has advantages and disadvantages depending on the application for which it is intended.

All databases contain files that consist of individual records. The records contain fields of various types of information. This information can then be combined to create new files, revise existing files, perform limited calculations, and prepare reports in varied formats by organizing the data in different ways.

Data are stored in a data dictionary created within the database. All information is stored there; therefore, when changes are necessary, they are made in the data dictionary. This allows accuracy to be maintained, since all other files are dependent on the dictionary for information.

The use of databases can be controversial. The benefits are obvious. However, there is apprehension on the part of some that large amounts of personal and confidential information centrally maintained and easily accessible may bring with it a temptation for its misuse.

Lawmakers are being asked to anticipate potential problems with database use. They must pass legislation to prevent the abuse of this technology while preserving its benefits for society.

APPENDIX F

Only the Best
Software Instructions

ASCD's Only the Best: The Annual Guide to Educational Software and Multimedia is a fully searchable database of programs which have met stringent criteria for excellence (see evaluators link on the opening screen). To peruse the database, click on the "search" button. This will take you to a screen which will allow you to search for programs using nine different fields.

Search Fields

Publisher.   Clicking on the button to the right of the publisher field will bring up a listing of publishers whose programs are available on this demo disk. Select a publisher using your mouse. If you are not using any more search parameters, you can then click on the "OK" button at the bottom of your screen. This will bring up a listing of titles by the publisher that you selected.

Title.   If you know the name of the program you are trying to research, simply fill in this information in the title field. You can search by full or partial name (i.e., typing in either "Castle" or "Castle Explorer" will bring you the same results), but you must spell out at least one word in its entirety.

Grade.   Entering a grade by number will pull all of the records associated with that grade. For example entering the number 5 will identify all the records that are geared toward fifth-graders. It is important to keep in mind, however, that many of the programs listed span multiple grades and some are even K–12 titles.

Copyright.   Entering a copyright year will identify all of the programs which were produced in a given year. For example, entering 1994 will only identify those records with a 1994 copyright date and not those before or after. To broaden your search, you may insert the word "or" in between two years (1994 OR 1995) and the results will include programs from both years.

Subject.   To search by subject, click on the button to the right of the subject field. This will activate the term field. From this page, select and move a topic to the search area by double-clicking on the word or by selecting "add." This will add a content area to your search parameters. You may use the key in the lower right hand corner to place an "and" or an "or" in your search parameters. You may add as many terms as you like and you can remove them by simply highlighting the term and then clicking "remove." Once you have highlighted the terms that you wish to use, click on "OK" to continue your search.

Cost.   To utilize the cost field, you will need to know the exact price of a product (including cents). Enter that amount in the cost field and click on "OK." You will be presented with a listing of programs that are equal to the cost field.

Keywords.   As the name implies, this field is where you enter terms that are relevant to your search. For instance, typing in "King" would return records which mention Martin Luther King or the King of England.

Platform.   In the platform field, simply click on the button to the right and then select a platform that meets your needs. Move this term into your search box by either double-clicking on the term or highlighting it and clicking on "add." You can delete a section by clicking on "remove."

Format.   To activate format, click on the button to the right of the field. Here you will be presented with two choices—diskette or CD-ROM. Move this term into your search box by either double-clicking on the term or highlighting it and clicking on "Add."

Summary

You can use from one to nine of the above listed search fields to sort through the records of *Only the Best.* Using more than one search field will refine your search. However, using too many of the search fields at once may cause you to eliminate more records than you desired.

Hardware Requirements

Macintosh.   Requires 680X0 Macintosh or PowerMac System 7.0 or higher, 16MB RAM, 7.5MB free disk space, 2X CD-ROM drive (4X recommended), color monitor.

Windows   Requires at least a 33MHz 486DX, 8MB RAM, 6MB free disk space, 2X CD-ROM drive (4X recommended), color monitor.

Note: *Only the Best* features a demo clip from a commercial software program. To view the clip, simply call up the record "Eyewitness History of the World" in the search field, click on "OK," and then select "Eyewitness History of the World." You will notice that when this record appears, a small movie icon appears in the top right-hand corner of your screen. Double-click on this icon to watch the film clip. Once the clip has been played, simply click the "x" in the box to close screen.

INDEX

Credits

Screen Image Credits: 63, 75, 76, 77, 80, 147, 148, 152, Copyright © 1998 Netscape Communications Corp. Used with permission. All Rights Reserved. This electronic file or page may not be reprinted or copied without the express written permission of Netscape. Netscape Communications Corporation has not authorized, sponsored, or endorsed, or approved this publication and is not responsible for its content. Netscape and the Netscape Communications Corporate Logos are trademarks and trade names of Netscape Communications Corporation. All other product names and/or logos are trademarks of their respective owners.; 63, reprinted courtesy of University of Washington; 66, reprinted courtesy of Liszt; 80, reproduced with the permission of Digital Equipment Corporation. Digital, Alta Vista, and the Alta Vista logo are trademarks or service marks of Digital Equipment Corporation. Used with permission.; 81, reprinted courtesy of WS-FTP; 82, reprinted courtesy of Fetch; 113, reprinted with permission from SuperKids Educational software Review, http://www.superkids.com; 113, reprinted with permission from the University of Connecticut. The Way Cool Software Reviews Project is sponsored by the A. J. Pappanikou Center: A UAP, at the University of Connecticut; 127, reprinted courtesy of the U.S. Department of Education; 128, reprinted with permission from Concourse C, Inc. Education World and the Education World logo © are registered trademarks of Concourse C, Inc. All Rights Reserved.; 129, reprinted with permission from InSITE: Information Network of the Society for Technology and Teacher Education; 130, reprinted with permission from Nancy Casey. Copyright © 1992 Nancy Casey; 131, reprinted with permission from the University of North Dakota; 131, reprinted with permission from the Arizona Mars K-12 Education Program; 132, reprinted with permission from Capitol Advantage, McLean, VA; 132, reprinted with permission from the American Civil War Homepage; 133, reprinted with permission from the John F. Kennedy Center for the Performing Arts; 134, reprinted with permission from the Children's Music Workshop; 135, reprinted with permission from Global Online Adventure Learning Site (GOALS); 135, reprinted with permission from the Educational Resources Information Center (ERIC); 136, reprinted courtesy of the Library of Congress; 137, reprinted with permission from The Kidlink Network; 187, 197, 220, 222, 225, reprinted by permission from Microsoft Corporation; 224, Hyperstudio® is a registered trademark of Roger Wagner Publishing, Inc. This Hyperstudio screen image is used with the permission of Roger Wagner Publishing, Inc.

Photo Credits: 14, 15, 249, courtesy of Wolfram Research; 16, 17, courtesy of New York Public Library; 20, courtesy of Texas Instruments; 20, courtesy of Hewlett-Packard; 21, 22, courtesy of Apple Computer, Inc.; 23, courtesy of Cray Research, a Silicon Graphics Company; 25, courtesy of Toshiba; 25, courtesy of Compaq; 27, courtesy of Interlink Electronics; 28, courtesy of IBM; 30, 253, courtesy of Panasonic; 30, 31, 32, 221, courtesy of Samsung Electronics America, Inc.; 31, courtesy of Plustek; 32, courtesy of SMILE International, Inc.; 33, courtesy of Sharp Electronics Corp.; 34, courtesy of Fargo Electronics, Inc.; 34, courtesy of Mita; 36, courtesy of FTG Data Systems; 37, courtesy of TDK Systems; 37, 247, 257, courtesy of Mitsubishi; 50, 54, courtesy of Thomas M. Schaefges/Omegatype Typography, Inc.; 89, 95, courtesy of Compton; 92, courtesy of Davidson & Associates; 94, 98, courtesy of MECC; 95, courtesy of Virgin Sound and Vision; 96, courtesy of DK Multimedia; 100, courtesy of Sunburst Communications, Inc.; 104, courtesy of Voyetra Technologies; 206, courtesy of Curtis Computer Products; 221, 257, courtesy of Vivitar; 221, 254, courtesy of Casio, Inc.; 222, courtesy of Digital Vision, Inc.; 246, 249, 256, courtesy of Philips; 248, courtesy of Virtual i-O Inc.; 251, courtesy of PCtel; 254, courtesy of Franklin Electronic Publishers; 254, courtesy of Geofax, Inc.; 255, courtesy of Brother; 256, courtesy of Texas Microsystems, Inc.; 256, courtesy of Minstrel; 256, courtesy of NTT Soft; 259, courtesy of Bausch and Lomb; 259, courtesy of Wizzard Software; 259, courtesy of Hunter Digital.